Reclaiming Sodom

Reclaiming Sodom

EDITED BY JONATHAN GOLDBERG

ROUTLEDGE
NEW YORK   LONDON

Published in 1994 by

Routledge
29 West 35 Street
New York, NY 10001

Published in Great Britain by

Routledge
11 New Fetter Lane
London EC4P 4EE

Library of Congress Cataloging-in-Publication Data

Reclaiming Sodom / edited by Jonathan Goldberg.
    p. cm.
  Includes bibliographical references.
  ISBN 0-415-90754-3 (hb)—ISBN 0-415-90755-1 (pbk)
    1. Homosexuality—History. 2. Sodomy—History. 3. Sexology—
Philosophy. I. Goldberg, Jonathan.
HQ76.R39 1994
906.76'6'09—dc20   93-43680
                                         CIP

British Library Cataloguing-in-Publication Data also available.

Table of Contents

II   Pleasures and Dangers

Acknowledgments

I'm grateful to Bruce Russell for a number of brainstorming sessions, and for putting the resources of the Kalos collection at my disposal; to Alan Bray, Judith Butler, Albert Liu, Karen Newman and Michael Warner for advice at various stages of this project; to T. Sean Holland for his superb research skills; to Michael Moon for his support and suggestions. And above all to Bill Germano for putting me up to this.

The editor gratefully acknowledges permission to republish these essays.

Robert Alter, "Sodom as Nexus: The Web of Design in Biblical Narrative," from *The Book and the Text,* ed. Regina Schwartz (Oxford, Blackwell Publishers, 1990), pp. 146–60, used with permission of Blackwell Publishers Ltd.; Jonathan Ned Katz, selections from "Introduction: The Age of Sodomitical Sin, 1607–1740," from his *Gay/Lesbian Almanac* (New York: Harper & Row, 1983), pp. 31–65, used with permission of the author; Marc Daniel, selections from "Arab Civilization and Male Love," from *Gay Roots: Twenty Years of Gay Love,* ed. Winston Leyland (San Francisco: Gay Sunshine Press, 1991), pp. 38–42, used with permission of the editor; Gerald W. Creed, "Sexual Subordination: Institutionalized Homosexuality and Social Control in Melanesia," from the journal *Ethnography* #23 (Pittsburgh: Department of Anthropology, University of Pittsburgh, 1984), pp. 157–76, used with permission of the author and publisher; Makeda Silvera, "Man Royals and Sodomites: Some Thoughts on the Invisibility of Afro-Caribbean Lesbians," from *Coming Out,* ed. Stephen Lokosky (New York: Pantheon, 1992), pp. 87–97, used with permission of the author; Cindy Patton, selections from "Inventing 'African AIDS'," from *Inventing AIDS* (New York and London: Routledge, 1990), pp. 87–97; David Shannon, "Out in the City," from *The Montreal Mirror,* August 20–27, 1992, pg. 24; Janet E. Halley, "The Politics of the Closet: Towards Equal Protection for Gay, Lesbian and Bisexual Identity," originally published in 36 *UCLA Law Review* pp. 915–76, copyright 1989, The Regents of the University of California, all rights reserved; Marquis de Sade, from *Justine, Philosophy in the Bedroom and Other Writing,* translated by Richard Seaver and Austryn Wainhouse, copyright © 1965 by Richard Seaver and Austryn Wainhouse, pp. 230–32, 247, 273–78, 326–29, used with the permission of Grove/Atlantic, Inc.; Dorothy Allison, "Her Body, Mine, and His," from *Leatherfolk,* ed. Mark Thompson (Boston: Alyson Publications, 1991), pp. 44–48; Pierre Klossowski, *Sade My Neighbor,* trans. Alphonso Lingis (Evanston, Il.: Northwestern University Press, 1991), pp. 22–32, 34–38, used with permission of the publisher; Guy Hocquenghem, "Aux pederastes incomprehensible," from *La Derive Sexuelle,* trans. Chris Fox, as *Towards an Irrecuperable Pederasty* (Paris: Delarge, 1977), by permission of the publisher; Rocky O'Donovan, "Reclaiming Sodom," reprinted from *QFM* (Salt Lake City, Utah); Leo Bersani, "Is the Rectum a Grave?" reprinted from *October* 23, by permission of the MIT Press, Cambridge, Massachusetts, copyright 1987; Lee Edelman, "Seeing Things: Representation, the Scene of Surveillance, and the Spectacle of Gay Male Sex," from *inside/out,* ed. Diana Fuss (New York: Routledge, 1991), pp. 93–116; Neil Bartlett, "Who Was That Man?" © Neil Bartlett, 1988, published by Serpent's tail, 4 Blackstock Mews, London N4 2BT.

Introduction

Jonathan Goldberg

"Sodomy—that utterly confused category": Michel Foucault's memorable phrase sums up the fortunes of sodomy as a juridical category, the paramount role it has played in the West.[1] But it also suggests the *productive* role that sodomy has played and can play as a site of pleasures that are also refusals of normative categories. It suggests thereby an impetus for reclaiming Sodom rather than assuming that the weight of tradition is entirely and monolithically a site of oppression.

Consider, for example, this fantasy (not, as will quickly become clear, exactly, properly, my own):[2] First, some text: "I had always had this fantasy about fucking a man with a strap-on dildo . . . after years of searching I found someone who wanted the same! Sooo—we went to my place. I strapped on my dildo and . . ." The text stops, but already some of the productive confusions have been articulated, even in the resistance first voiced, the "years of searching" and the ultimate discovery of a man who has "the same" fantasy as the speaker. Whatever the source of the resistance—the social regulation of gender, which is part of the work of sodomy with its imposition of a highly straitened form of procreative heteronormativity, seems most likely—it is not so much overcome as worked through in a sequence of images that now replaces the text (here my prose must substitute for them—I am describing a strip from *Tits and Clits Comix*).

First shot: both of them seen from the rear—the possibility of desiring "the same" has to do with the fact that men and women both have anuses, can locate their desires there (hence, the woman's fantasy about penetrating a man also lights on the anatomical place both genders share as a sexual site). The first frame exposes the male's behind, while the woman's is clothed; "the same" is thereby also differentiated, but in terms of the diacritical difference, naked/clothed, that more usually marks—within the heterosexual pornographic, but also within the ordinary conventions of

1

Western art—the difference between female and male. (Think of Manet's *Déjeuner sur l'herbe* for a spectacularly familiar deployment of the trope.) The frames that follow now show her frontally, her strap-on greeted at first with dismay; then she fills the frame, coming forward, her hair turning into a mane, her face registering animal desire. What do we see here? a figure that passes beyond the bounds of gender—her breasts are as insistently registered as is the erect penis/dildo (you can't tell them apart in a picture)—and beyond the human. One of the confusions around sodomy—that it is also bestiality—is mobilized here as a locus of fearful pleasures. Heterosexual difference, gender difference, the borders between human and animal behavior, are being dissolved, not, it should be added, in some entirely comfortable or comforting way. Having the same fantasy and enacting it is not something equally shared; if it is his view of her that transforms her into an animal, it may be too her view of what it would mean to go beyond her gender, to have the privilege and power associated with having a penis—privileges that also are dismantled by the fact that this penis is declared from the first to be a strap-on and incapable of being fully naturalized.[3]

Now she is behind him, his face cut by the frame, but looking less perturbed. Then the scene of penetration, close up. Finally, some more text: "having rolled him on his soft underbelly . . . cracked his ass and given him the best fuck of his life, . . . " and a parting shot: he sucks her off. The transformative energies of sodomy are best represented in these acts. Is this "the best fuck of his life" because he has never been on the receiving end before? Or is it "the best" because of the fantasy being fulfilled, one that involves giving up certain prerogatives of hetero gender assignments on both parts? (We never see his penis, for instance.) And what is to be made of the final frame—beyond, that is, its inclusion of fellatio under the rubric of sodomy? A worship of the artificial penis as a true site of pleasure? A sign that this relationship with her is homosexual? Indeed, what sexuality is involved in this fantasy? What does it mean for a woman to want to wear a strap-on, and to use it with a man? What, moreover, if the fantasy addresses itself to a presumptive lesbian readership? Is it not to call into question the regulatory apparatuses both of heterosexual and of lesbian desire, especially when the latter claims for itself as its proper site a woman-identification? (The reader will encounter, further on, Dorothy Allison raising similar questions around "extreme" sexual practices.) But is not the masculinity of the man involved also questioned, and thereby his sexuality, but, if so, to pose problems to the too-easy collapse of male homosexuality into effeminacy?

These questions do not exhaust the meanings of the cartoon I have been describing; nor, by posing them would I want to undercut the pleasure I take in this scenario, in its knowing play with so many conventions, and in its celebration of "wrong" desire. The point to make here, however, is a simple one—at any rate it is one hypothesis governing the choice of selections that follows: that the act of sodomy enables the productive confusions and rigorous questioning of a range of presumptions and conventions governing gender, sexuality and the relations of fantasy and acts. That's why I want to put this scene first, before thinking about the regulatory apparatuses that subtend it, and with which it seeks to break, for it is by such a reversal of priorities that one can, I think, prepare to engage the texts that follow in this collection. The agenda involves questioning of the sort announced by Guy Hocquenghem in the essay included here, a refusal to allow the apparatuses of the law, the narratives that flow from the story of Sodom in Genesis (the urtext reread in a number of these essays) to govern what may be said about sodomy, what it can mean or has meant. That sodomy is "utterly confused" even in its founding documents is something which must be grasped, not to deny the work that the category has done, the ways in which it has been used to bear down upon bodies and behaviors, but in order not to lose sight of the pleasures—and dangers— that this first example suggests. And it is more than an aside to note too that in choosing to being with this fantasy—one, as I've mentioned, but it's worth stressing, that derives from *Tits and Clits Comix,* I want to counter the prevailing tradition that has seen sodomy solely as a practice that males engage in with each other. This has been the case as much in the regulatory apparatuses as it has been in much of the literature that refuses those controls, and it is therefore important to note the powerful interventions of sex-positive lesbians who have, for many years now, been challenging the suppressions and regulations around women's desires. As Hocquenghem points out in his account of the origins of gay liberation in France, it would not have been possible without the women's movement. So, too, in seeking the most expansive frame for a consideration of sodomy, this collection is inspired by the work of such people as Dorothy Allison, Susie Bright, Pat Califia, Joan Nestle, Cherríe Moraga, Cindy Patton and Gayle Rubin.[4]

"Sodomy—that utterly confused category": Foucault has in mind the juridical apparatuses in which sodomy flourished in the West as the name for every form of sexual behavior besides married, heterosexual, procreatively aimed sex. Sodomy could include sex between men or between women, sex between men and women not sanctioned by marriage or bent on frustrating reproduction, sex between humans of whatever gender and animals (a fundamental confusion in the category is its failure to distinguish between human sex and human/animal sex, the collapse of sodomy, buggery and bestiality that can be found in the laws and in learned discussions). Not the least of these confusions lies in the fact that the laws were variously applied, that they hardly provided—or provide now, since they remain on the books in many places—a uniform codification of acts; developed over centuries, they are indices of local differences, of varying sites of control (the state, the church).[5] One understands therefore why John Boswell, in *Christianity, Social Tolerance, and Homosexuality: Gay People in Western Europe from the Beginning of the Christian Era to the Fourteenth Century*, sought to eschew the term; "wherever possible," he notes, "the term 'sodomy' (*sodomia*) has been excluded from this study, since it is so vague and ambiguous as to be virtually useless in a text of this sort," and he continues by listing some of the confusions to which I have just alluded.[6] The "uselessness" of sodomy, from Boswell's point of view, lies in its inability to be referential—it designates neither a specific act nor actors. What this has meant, on the one hand, is that virtually any sexual act could somewhere at some time fall under its aegis. Within most legal codes, the consequence was death—a penalty still in force in England until the mid-nineteenth century.[7] On the other hand, perusal of medieval penitentials provides a host of far less stringent exactions, and begins to suggest that sodomy—however defined—was recognized as far more common and perhaps as far less heinous in the same-sex communities (monasteries, nunneries) for which the penitentials were initially intended.[8] And perhaps where this leads is to the counterfact produced by the "vagueness" of sodomy as a term, that it also functioned as a site of tacit permission precisely because it did not claim definitional clarity. At once, then, in the hands of the most repressive institutions, a site of massively annihilative energies, and always a menace; but, on the other hand, an inefficient device of regulation. This is, in a word, to suggest, *contra* Boswell, the immense usefulness of the term.

It is also, following Foucault's memorable summary sentence in *The History of Sexuality*, in which he divides the regimes of sexual identity along the axis of sodomy—"the sodomite had been a temporary aberration; the homosexual was now a species" (43)—a reminder that sodomy as a designation for acts does not thereby designate persons; a sodomite is anyone who performs the acts involved. The supposed definitional clarity that separates persons according to sexual orientations or sexual identities is not something the term delivers, neither in the codes nor, as our first example has suggested, in contemporary imaginings of the act. (This poses a question to Foucault's breathtaking schema that is also raised by the continued existence of sodomy laws beyond the advent of "the homosexual.") What this must mean, then, is that although sodomy designates a set of sexual acts, it is not exactly a sexual crime, for it cannot be explained in terms of the sexuality of the persons performing the act. It is this fact about sodomy that explains some aspects of the vagaries of the application of the law: for those apprehended as sodomites were always otherwise suspect. Or so Alan Bray argues in his indispensible *Homosexuality in Renaissance England*,[9] as he explores the meaning of sodomy. His point is that the term cannot be collapsed into a synonym for homosexuality, rather that it is mobilized in the face of threats to the social order—those, in England, represented by papists, traitors and the like. Bray's point can be extended to other contexts, where heretics or foreigners—in short, whatever a culture wishes to see as dangerously other—were the most likely sodomites. That is, the accusation of sexual misbehavior is seen to follow from the violation of the social order. As Bray suggests, the consequence of this way of thinking is that sodomy is unnameable, invisible, so long as it occurs within socially sanctioned relations, where the sexual acts that regularly accompanied relations of friendship or patronage went unnoticed.[10] Sodomy, from its earliest codifications, has been the crime not to be named among Christians[11]—on the one hand, because it seems to be nothing short of world-destroying; but, on the other, because not to name it is a way to allow it.

What this implies, in short, is that sodomy is a sociopolitical designation. And it is so from the start. The biblical story in Genesis describes a community destroyed, and the conflagration of Sodom and Gomorrah, as Robert Alter suggests in the essay included here, serves as a "great monitory model." Yet what the crime was of the cities on the plain has caused much debate; the confusions around "sodomy" in the codes that harken back to this monitory moment echo the confusions in the biblical text, its failure to name specifically what was involved. Fundamentalist readers of the text have no doubt that homosexuality is the crime that brought Sodom down; such readers, however, assume a transhistorical homosexuality available anywhere any time and always to be abominated.[12] Readers seeking to save the biblical story from such a reading—notably Derrick Sherwin Bailey and those, including Boswell, who have subscribed to his arguments[13]—have offered instead that the crime against the angelic visitors to Sodom was inhospitality. While there is something to this claim—insofar as it registers that a social violation is at the root of the narrative—such readings have attempted to efface sexual matters entirely, and this is difficult to do, since, even if the Sodomites had not unambiguously sought sexual relations with the angels, Lot's offer of his daughters as a substitute is a far less equivocal act. It may be that women's bodies were more easily traded than men's, and that social mores were not violated so doing, but that also suggests continuities, rather than an absolute distinction between the sexual and the social in this founding text for the sodomitical imaginary.[14] Alter's approach recognizes that the narrative is embedded in the story of the founding of the nation; it thus makes a particularly salutary point (even if he too easily assumes that nationhood and same-sex relations are mutually incompatible). "As the biblical imagination conceives it," he writes, choosing a verb that participates in this imaginary, "neither national existence nor the physical act of propagation itself can be taken for granted," and Sodom is the warning posted about the precariousness of these two regimes. What this means, arguably, is that neither nation nor procreation are natural facts, that the designation of so-called "unnatural" acts through the monitory counternation of Sodom serves therefore to "naturalize" (in a word, to ideologize) nation-founding by linking it to procreation.

So much is suggested, too, by Jonathan Ned Katz's "Introduction" to his *Gay/Lesbian Almanac*, in a section prefacing documents from "The Age of Sodomitical Sin, 1607–1740," which is excerpted in this volume. As Katz argues, following the Foucauldian schema that has been alluded to, sodomy cannot be equated with homosexuality; rather, it must be read along the diacritical axis of procreative/nonprocreative sex, with its ramifying connections to sociopolitical arrangements. For the colonists, as perhaps too for the tribes whose history is told in Genesis, nation-founding was inseparable from procreation, and the particular economic, social and patriarchal gender arrangements in the colonies was subtended by the crime of sodomy. Sodomy was, as Katz suggests, a crime against the family and the state, "political sodomy," in short. These are arguments that have been furthered, most notably in a remarkable series of essays by Michael Warner, which suggest how fundamental to the U.S. national imaginary sodomy has been.[15] Moreover, as Warner argues (and as I do too in *Sodometries*[16]), the desire to treat sodomy as anithetical to the nation is everywhere belied by the fearful spectre of its complicity with the nation. In a society that was male-dominated, that regarded male-male relations as the privileged site not only for political but also for the most valued emotional ties (links that could be regarded as forming a spiritual community), sodomy (mis)names the normative effusion of spirit that joins men to each other. As Warner suggests, pursuing the lines from the colonial imaginary to the modern liberal state, the abjection of and stigmatization of male-male relations can never quite be separated from male privilege; the blindness of a certain heteronormativity to its complicity with what it seeks to suppress is everywhere evident, though always to be rethought under the various sociopolitical situations that distribute power and privilege.[17] Thus, in colonial America, sodomites were more often than not lower-class servants, and the shoring up of patriarchal power was imbricated in nascent class divisions. One has only to look to other colonial situations of the time to see that that was not the only way the category of sodomy was being mobilized; the Spaniards, for instance, prone to see sodomites among the Moors in Spain, saw native cultures as hotbeds of irregular sexual practices.[18] But perhaps because so many of the *conquistadors* were themselves men of insecure social backgrounds making a way for themselves as conquerors, the apparatuses of sodomy were far less likely to be used against other Spaniards, far more likely to be used against the Indians.[19] A protoracial imaginary thus accompanies sodomy in colonizing practices and discourses that the English were far more likely to participate in when dealing with the East than in their encounters with the "newfoundland" of America.[20]

Once again, then, sodomy can hardly be reduced to either a simple or a singular sexual crime, and its uses within a national imaginary are similarly differentially mobilized. This can be seen even by comparing the various laws against sodomy, as well as the enforcement of these laws, in the U.S. colonies, for once again there are vast differences, the Southern colonies keeping closer to English law than the New England statutes.[21] In the South, execution for sodomy was practiced far more than in the North, although that was the penalty in both locales; in New England, those accused of having sex with animals commonly received the death penalty. Again, explaining such discrepancies is no easy task, but such differences serve as a salutary reminder when one reads the majority decision in *Bowers v. Hardwick*, the 1986 U.S. Supreme Court decision which ruled that consensual "homosexual sodomy" (as the court termed it) was not guaranteed by the Constitution of the U.S.

This decision was reached in part by appeals to the biblical tradition, to commentators like Aquinas, to the history of sodomy trials through the Middle Ages and beyond (Blackstone, the eighteenth-century jurist, is quoted with relish by Chief Justice Burger) and especially by an insistence on a national commitment to the suppression of sodomy to be found from the very start of U.S. history. This account has received devastating commentary, most recently in a painstaking essay by Janet E. Halley that reveals that the 1968 Georgia statute in question in the decision, as well as the history of sodomy in Georgia, can hardly be reduced to the singular account that Justice Byron White and his colleagues offered.[22] Halley has been one of the most notable commentators on the Supreme Court decision, and the piece reprinted here is painfully necessary reading, since it suggests the ways in which guarantees for homosexuals cannot be made to rest on the kinds of privatizing claims for the rights of individuals that formed the basis of Michael Hardwick's appeal to the court, as well as the dissenting views of the minority.[23]

Bowers v. Hardwick was a narrow decision, narrowly reached, and only barely. The admonition of Daniel C. Richman—at the time one of the clerks to the justices—that, in construing the case as solely about homosexual sodomy, the justices were ignoring the fact that the acts they were proscribing for homosexuals are regularly performed by heterosexuals, is tellingly to the point of Halley's arguments.[24] For the judges were dealing with a Georgia law that, true to the history of sodomy, did not use the act of sodomy to distinguish the sexuality of those performing it—anyone, hetero or homo, under the Georgia statute, could be a sodomite. The justices, instead, took sodomy to be an act that meant differently when performed by differently-gendered as opposed to same-gendered couples. In effect, the distinction between (potentially) procreative and nonprocreative acts was the diacritical marking, between acts performed by marriageable and nonmarriageable couples. (As one commentator has suggested, following a remark by Justice Blackmun, the decision thus also harkens back to the enforcement of miscegenation laws, which the Supreme Court ruled unconstitutional only in 1967.[25]) In seeking to argue that future attempts to overturn sodomy laws must be based on Fourteenth Amendment guarantees to equal protection rather than on rights to privacy, Halley insists that sodomy is thus not merely a matter of private consensual sexual behavior. Her argument, that is, stresses the fact that sexual identity is not necessarily an immutable category, but rather, a socially constructed one; that therefore what *anyone* needs to be protected from is the wielding of categories of sexual identity in discriminatory ways; in sum, that homosexual identity is not a matter of private sexual acts but a public, socially formed identity. The Fourteenth Amendment, a guarantee most often applied in cases of racial discrimination, offers a real analogy: for what constitutes racial identity is a fully manipulable category, and how it is wielded can be highly discriminatory (just think of the ways various codifications of the amount of "black blood" have constituted persons as being Black[26]); so too for sexual identity. Sodomy cannot be sutured to homosexuality in part because the act is one that anyone can perform; but more, because homosexuality itself is a highly contestable category. The cordoning off of homosexuality to a limited number of persons, to specific acts, to sexual behavior, all too conveniently ignores the fact that many persons perform the same acts, that public assumptions about who is or is not a homosexual

often count more than what people do. This, for example, has been particularly clear since Bill Clinton became President of the U.S. in 1993, and
sought to lift the ban on gays in the military. Everyone knows that there
have always been gay men and lesbians in the armed forces, but what
everyone seems now to want is for gays not to announce publicly that they
are there. So long as the fiction obtained that everyone in the military was
straight, anyone could do anything sexual with a fellow soldier without
having to be thought of or to consider him or herself gay. Halley's arguments
bring to bear these recognitions of the ways in which the enforcement of
the closet work, and why, therefore, a call for privatized individual rights
for homosexuals to perform sodomy is not the way to make the case.[27]

It should be remarked, too, that the act involved in *Bowers v. Hardwick*
was not anal sex; a blow job was interrupted by the arrival of a policeman
in Michael Hardwick's bedroom. At least one commentator has maintained
that nineteenth-century American courts tended to construe sodomy as anal
sex, and tended also to claim that fellatio was not the same thing as
sodomy.[28] Once again, the confusions of the category are mobilized, and
the "unconfusing" of the category in the Supreme Court's collapsing definition (the assumption that any acts performed by members of the same sex
are sodomy—and that such acts prove the actors to be homosexuals) is
put into the service of the state and its abilities to wield Alice-in-Wonder-
land-like definitional leverage. But what the court ignores, in its ignorant
rehearsal of family and national values and their enduring tradition from
the Bible, English law, and the like, is another confusion briefly and
tellingly registered in David Shannon's column from the *Montreal Mirror*,
reprinted in this volume; that just north of the border, in Canada, a country
with much the same heritage as the U.S., sodomy laws are no longer the
law of the land (Shannon adds a witty twist to this fact). What might also
be noted is that the protonational imaginary in Canada, at least as offered
in the Jesuit accounts from its early years of colonization, was more prone
than the English to discover sodomites among the natives; though the mixed
English and French heritage of Canada also allowed sodomy to be seen
among those Whites of lower status who were thought to be in some way
socially disruptive.[29] The fact that present-day North America and colonial
North America were and are still hardly monolithic in their views of sodomy
is worth noting, therefore. But perhaps, too, because it furthers a point
already suggested, but which requires some more discussion: sodomy not
only participates in a colonial imaginaire, it cannot—and not solely because
of the "contaminatory" effects worked by Western discursive categories
on native practices—be confined to the Judeo-Christian tradition.

So much is suggested by recalling that the Koran also knows the story of Sodom, and that in Islamic legal formulations the crime of sodomy is known as *liwāṭ* and takes its name from Lot.[30] As Marc Daniel suggests, in his discussion of Arabic poems celebrating the love of boys, from which an excerpt on Arab customs and the Koran is included in this volume, male-male sexual practices can be found throughout the Mediterranean world, and although the Koran takes a dim view of the sin of Lot, it also does not share the Judeo-Christian emphasis on procreation as the only proper aim of sex. In effect, as Daniel argues, this means that a far wider range of sexual practices is valued in Islamic tradition, and the law goes out of its way to make condemnations of *liwāṭ* exceptionally difficult, requiring four unimpeachable witnesses (which in Islamic culture means freeborn Islamic males) for a conviction. Or, to put it another way, what seems to be subject to the law is public sex between men. Commentators on the Islamic tradition writing after the heady days of gay liberation which mark Daniel's text (it appeared originally in *Arcadie* in 1975 to 76), have raised doubts about the "liberality" of Islamic sodomy, but often from a point of view that needs to be questioned.[31] One of the "confusions" of sodomy lies in the fact that, since everyone has an anus, the act can be performed interchangeably. This, as Hocquenghem remarks, is perhaps the democratic, utopian ideal of the practice; sodomizer and sodomized can shift parts (in the case of women, by exchanging the strap-on). But that ideal is not all that often realized, as Hocquenghem goes on to say. Those who have found that Islamic mode of sex less than ideal have done so because it does not readily accommodate itself to the utopian vision. Rather, sexual relations are hierarchized and stratified, and everywhere imbricated in the power differentials that shape Islamic society. The one who is fucked is thought to be in a female position, and Islamic society is highly gender-stratified. While this certainly poses a real limit to regarding sodomy as *eo ipso* a revolutionary act or always utopian in its aims, it nonetheless reminds us of something that Foucault's work, in the more theoretical introductory volume to his *History of Sexuality* and in his examination of sexual practices in the ancient world in the subsequent volumes, insists upon: the inextricable relationship of sexuality and power; indeed, to go further, the insistence that part of what makes sex sexy lies in differences (which is not to say, of course, that these must take the form of brutalizations that repeat social oppressions).[32] It's hard not to sense in the summary reproach to Islamic culture for feminizing those who get fucked a latent misogyny and erotophobia.

Projections of sodomy Western-style have often taken place, both in colonial situations and in the disciplines that grow from those encounters, and nowhere more so than in anthropology. Gerald Creed suggests as much reviewing the deplorable absence of consideration of male-male sexual practices in the anthropological literature, and the tendency to label them, when seen, as sodomy, and therefore as condemnable. But he also goes on, valuably, to explore the more recent—and, of course, important—work done by gay-affirmative anthropologists (Gilbert Herdt most notably[33]), and to call into question the ways in which a positive valuation of the societies that institutionalize homosexual practices (for example, in Melanesia the passing of semen among males by way either of oral or anal sex) has tended to divorce these institutionalized practices from the wider social contexts in which they arise. The Melanesians, to speak broadly, operate the procreative/nonprocreative divide in terms of gender difference; women are "naturally" linked to procreative processes, and therefore are innately, biologically their gender. Men, on the other hand, have to be made, and the transmission of semen is how this is accomplished. Such a view nicely calls into question the status of the Phallus, and could be accommodated to Lacanian and post-Lacanian debunkings of its value. But, as Creed points out, the transmission of semen is hardly a utopian scheme; not only are the roles in the act anything but immediately reversible (they are governed by age difference), but the act itself repeats patterns of hierarchy and subordination that inform social life through and through. Once the differences between boys and men is read through the relations of men and women; once it is recognized that sexuality and sexual practices cannot be regarded as if unrelated to gender; once, moreover, sex and gender are recognized as sociopolitical, as marked by economies of difference, then one begins to have the analytic tools necessary to take stock of the "positive" value that male-male sexual practices have in societies outside the Judeo-Christian tradition.[34]

Creed's piece makes one other powerful intervention. For while it seeks a fuller social understanding of sex, it also wishes not to reduce sex simply to its institutionalized place. "Institutionalized homosexuality is still sex," Creed writes, "and it may still serve a pleasureable function. Analyses that neglect this fact are incomplete."[35] Pleasure may not be always politically correct, but it is also not rendered unreal just because certain acts are permitted rather than regarded as illicit. Which is to say that the prohibitions that have marked sodomy in the West are not the only source of its pleasures.

Indeed, it is in exploring the pleasures of her identification with "strong women," and measuring that against the monitory language of Sodom, that Makeda Silvera writes about her experiences as an Afro-Caribbean lesbian growing up in Jamaica, as well as about her present life in Canada. In her childhood, the word for the women she admired was "man royal" or "sodomite," and Silvera writes powerfully about the ways in which a sexual imaginary coincided with a colonial one in which the function of women was to serve for procreation and nothing else. Equally strongly, she interrogates the ways in which the First World (that is, White) feminist and gay movements have responded problematically to the existence of lesbians of color. Silvera seeks to reclaim the Jamaican "sodomite" and to give visibility to her, both in Silvera's past and her present (in perhaps something of the way in which Dorothy Allison returns the taunt of "faggot" by demanding recognition as a lesbian). The axes of race, gender, sexuality and nationality are nowhere more fraught than in the situations Silvera describes, in which various degrees of invisibility and visibility are at play, and in which axes of oppression cross. They have been only heightened as the sodomitical imaginary has become imbricated with the pandemic of AIDS.

This is suggested by Cindy Patton's work on the supposed African origin of AIDS, a piece of which is here excerpted from her exemplary study, *Inventing AIDS*. As Patton stunningly argues, racist imaginings of anal sex have been at work in the language describing unsafe practices, producing "a metaphoric cross-inscription" in which "U.S. (White) homosexuals were said to have made of their bodies something of the order of the sewerage system of a Third World country." These have been constellated in the imputation of African origins of AIDS, and especially in the weird ways in which the anuses of African women have been supposed capable of doing what White male anuses are supposed not to do: transmit the disease. Patton shows how the transportation of Western categories of homo/hetero-sexuality have been misapplied in non-Western situations,[36] and especially how the practice of anal sex, when viewed through the lens of sodomy, has become a site in which African heterosexual practices display something the West would deny about its own (the majority of the justices in the *Bowers v. Hardwick* decision provide an example of this too). In effect, this has been to homosexualize/sodomize Africa, and to make it therefore ripe for the kinds of "scientific" observations and practices that Patton so devastatingly details (for instance, treating Africans as a population that can be tested in the ways reserved in the West only for animals—a further sodomitical projection).

That sodomy as pleasure, as practice, as theorized, as imagined, need not succumb entirely to these complicities can be seen in what might be called a Sadean tradition in which the *Tits and Clits* comic participates, and to which the selections in this volume, following the pages from *Philosophy in the Bedroom*, could be said to contribute. As Pierre Klossow-ski points out in the excerpt from *The Philosopher-Villain* reprinted here, sodomy in Sade functions as the central case, the epitome and root of all perversion. In contrast to the tradition which has been reviewed above, in which sodomy is opposed to reproductive practices, and is seen as sterile (a belief countered by the Melanesian man-making rituals of sperm transference, of course), Sade, as Klossowski unfolds the category of the perverse in his texts, sponsors sodomy as a monstrous form of reproduction, one that insures neither the species nor the individual, however. Profoundly antihuman and antihumanist, the monstrosity of sodomy has to do precisely with the fact that it is a practice which refuses the hetero distinctions of gender (something suggested as well by Dorothy Allison and Geoff Mains, who form an alliance to see who can take more carrots up their asses); likewise, it disputes the primacy of sexuality as an expression of the human in its urge to reproduce itself. Sodomy is reproductive insofar as it sets up a mimetism without limits, a parody of reproduction which also gives the lie to the normative function of reproduction and the institutions that promote it.[37] In this, Sade can be read against the control of populations that Foucault argued was one of the major deployments of sexuality in the eighteenth century.

The mimetic and exchangeable function of sodomy is perhaps best exemplified in pages from *Philosophy in the Bedroom* not reprinted in this volume, in the amazing daisychains in which the men and women participate. In the dialogues, Eugénie is introduced to all sorts of debauchery by Madame de Saint-Ange, her brother and Dolmancé, the major spokesman in the dialogue. Dolmancé prefers above all anal sex with boys, but in no way excludes women from anal pleasures. Indeed, Eugénie comes to prefer them, and to be convinced by the arguments that Dolmancé advances, in which atheism, sadism and the like, are seen as necessary consequences of the act. Moreover, stunningly overturning the centuries-long discourse in which sodomy is declared unnatural, Dolmancé opines that if Nature only wanted people to have sex in order to procreate, then Nature would have arranged for that to be the only sexual possibility. Rather, as he goes on to say, Nature seems bent on every form of sexual pleasure other than reproduction, and Nature is utterly indifferent to the survival of the species or of nations—or to the institutions of state and nature that seem to guarantee the individual (in the final pages of *Philosophy of the Bedroom*, these arguments are brutally realized on the body of Eugénie's mother). In a move that anticipates the rhetoric of the Front Homosexuel d'Action Révolutionnaire, whose doctrines Guy Hocquenghem presents and critiques, Sade insists on a political sodomy: in the very exchanges, in its perverse powers of mimetism and substitution, Sade sees in sodomy nothing less than republican values, and Dolmancé traces a history of sodomy to make the point.

The kinds of issues raised by notions of reciprocity in the act of sodomy, which were occasioned by the "brutality" of Islamic practices, also are addressed by Hocquenghem, as well as by Leo Bersani in the pages from *Is the Rectum a Grave?* reprinted in this volume. (Bersani's title comes from Simon Watney's important book on AIDS, *Policing Desire*,[38] and Bersani's inquiry into anal pleasures and perils is inspired in part by the erotophobia that AIDS has unleashed). Both Hocquenghem and Bersani relentlessly critique a too-easy gay politics of liberation, the sort perhaps represented best in Charles Shiveley's still thrilling and utopic pieces that appeared in *Fag Rag* in the 1970s on perverse sexual practices as revolutionary acts.[39] Hocquenghem argues for an "irrecuperable pederasty," that is, for a homosexual movement that is not merely an instance of weak deconstruction, of an overturning of heteronormativity for a homonormativity. He seeks to expand the revolutionary goals of gay liberation by going beyond identity categories and beyond political pieties. At the heart of his arguments here, and even more so in the full development of them in *Homosexual Desire*,[40] sodomy is taken as the telling instance of homosexual desire. In the essay reprinted here, Hocquenghem offers an autocritique of this colleagues on the Left as well as his fellow members of FHAR for not going far enough; the anus is unassimilable to normativizing politics (whether capitalist or Marxist) as well as to a naturalizing of heterosexuality, which Hocquenghem suggests distorts the impulses of Freud's own texts on questions of sexuality. Bersani's essay, as with much of his work, is invested in teasing out unassimilable aspects of psychoanalytic theory. A similar point is pursued stunningly in Edelman's essay, in which *Nachträglichkeit*, the inevitable retro movement that characterizes all acts of consciousness, is reread as a "(be)hindsight," always attempting to glimpse, as the urmoment of the sexual unconscious, nothing less than a primal scene of sodomitical sex.

The decisively unsentimental insistence on the value of the devalued anus that marks Leo Bersani's foray into an endorsement of an adverseness in sex, and especially in the so-called "passive" and "female" position of the one getting fucked (the position reclaimed as a site of extraordinary male pleasure in the cartoon from *Tits and Clits*) has parallels to the antihumanist rhetoric in Hocquenghem, and to its embrace of the sites of humiliation of which Sodom is the first great example. Hocquenghem's essay begins by recalling the moment early in Proust's *Cities of the Plain*, in which a homosexual movement that reclaimed Sodom (Proust draws an analogy with the Zionist movement) is declared impossible: the territory of shame and humiliation and abjection cannot be embraced.[41] Hocquenghem argues against this, but without denying the negativity that might be embraced along with the declaration that one is proud to be gay. Rocky

O'Donovon does this, too, in his piece from *Queer Fuckers Monthly* in which he reclaims Sodom, and in so doing insists on redrawing the national map, a move by way of Sodom that makes it the capital of a queer nation. O'Donovan's Sodom almost could be the center of what Michael Warner has recently advocated, a queer planet rather than simply a queer nation, one which would not have the sotadic/sodomitic zones whose boundaries Burton traced in his "Terminal Essay" to *The Arabian Nights*; rather, a remapping that would recognize the entire globe as an erogenous zone.[42]

The point, then, might be the one that Neil Bartlett arrives at in his discussion of the 1870 sodomy case of Boulton and Park, whose flagrant public behavior served as evidence that they could not be what they appeared to be. So long as alternative sexualities and sexual practices are assumed to exist only in the dark, so long as they are treated merely as private affairs, the very publicity of Boulton and Park served only to prove that they could not be what they were. For as Bartlett brilliantly writes, to see them as sodomites "would involve an admission that they lived in the same city" as those who were passing judgment, the admission that the U.S. Supreme Court shirked when it divided hetero from homosexual sodomy. This might also be to the point of the scene of spying male-male sodomy in *Fanny Hill*, with which Edelman starts his discussion of behindsight. What Fanny sees and wishes to stop (she calls for the police) is an entrancing and infecting vision, the making public of sodomy. As Edelman argues, when the crime not to be mentioned or seen is seen and decried, even the attempt to stop it leads inevitably backwards and forwards, ramifying in every direction, challenging even the promiscuity of Fanny Hill, which rests still on certain hetero norms of the perverse.[43] But anal sex challenges homonormativities too, lesbian and gay ones, and raises the stakes—political and representational—for claims on public space and recognition. By way of Sodom and sodomy, as Janet Halley argued, a claim can be made under the law for that which challenges and yet is coextensive with the guarantees of the law.

Bartlett's discussion of the case of Boulton and Park serves as a prelude to his main theme, the case of Oscar Wilde, notoriously accused of posing as a "somdomite" (in the ignorant spelling of the Marquess of Queensberry) but who received two years of hard labor, not as a sodomite, but under the Labouchere Amendment to the 1885 Criminal Law Amendment Act.[44] That amendment for the first time made private as well as public sex between men a matter of public notice—it labelled it not sodomy but gross indecency. In making no distinction between public and private, the amendment effectively denied that homosex is a private matter. This is as true for heterosex, whose state sanction is marriage. Reproduction (as the debates on abortion suggest) is a matter of public interest; but so, too, is the "nonreproductive." From the initial biblical story on, sodomy has been not merely one sexual act among others, but a paramount challenge to heteronormativity. Tied to political and national interests, it has, to give Lee Edelman the final word, "widespread and uncontrollable implications."

Notes

1. Michel Foucault, *The History of Sexuality: An Introduction*, trans. Robert Hurley (New York: Pantheon Books, 1978), p. 101. Further citations appear in my text.

2. I quote and describe here a fantasy that is not exactly my own; rather, my source is *Tits and Clits Comix*, a 1977 strip drawn by C♀RY, which I have unfortunately not been able to reproduce here. The comic strip seems to me a graphic demonstration of the role of sex-positive lesbian thinkers in reclaiming Sodom, a point to which I will return below.

3. For a theoretical view compatible with the ways in which the privilege of the phallus and its "natural" suturing to bodies is dismantled in the cartoon, see Judith Butler, "The Lesbian Phallus and the Morphological Imaginary," *differences* 4.1 (1992), pp. 133–71, reprinted in her *Bodies That Matter* (New York, Routledge, 1993).

4. Work by most of these writers can be found in the collection of papers from the 1982 Barnard College Conference, *Pleasure and Danger*, ed. Carol Vance (Boston: Routledge and Kegan Paul, 1984), in the SAMOIS collection, *Coming to Power* (Boston: Alyson, 1982), and in *The Persistent Desire*, ed. Joan Nestle (Boston: Alyson, 1992). In addition, see Susie Bright, *Susie Sexpert's Lesbian Sex World* (Pittsburgh: Cleis, 1990), especially the chapter "Ass Forward," and *Susie Bright's Sexual Reality* (Pittsburgh: Cleis: 1992); Joan Nestle, *A Restricted Country* (Ithaca, NY: Firebrand Books, 1987); among Cindy Patton's essays on pornography, see "Hegemony and Orgasm—Or the Instability of Heterosexual Pornography," *Screen* 30 (1989), pp. 100–12, and "Safe Sex in The Pornographic Vernacular," in *How Do I Look?*, ed. Bad Object Choices (Seattle: Bay Press, 1991).

5. For some surveys of the early modern period, see the essays collected in Kent Gerard and Gert Hekma, *The Pursuit of Sodomy: Male Homosexuality in Renaissance and Enlightenment Europe* (New York: Harrington Press, 1989), and Robert Purks MacCubbin, ed., *'Tis Nature's Fault: Unauthorized Sexuality During the Enlightenment* (Cambridge: Cambridge University Press, 1987). On relations between state and church, see, especially, Mary Elizabeth Perry, *Gender and Disorder in Early Modern Seville* (Princeton: Princeton University Press, 1990) and William Monter, *Frontiers of Heresy* (Cambridge, Cambridge University Press, 1990). For differences among Italian Renaissance states, see Guido Ruggiero, *The Boundaries of Eros* (Oxford: Oxford University Press, 1985), for Venice, and Michael J. Roche, "Il controllo dell'omosessualità a Firenze nel XV secolo: gli *ufficiali di notte*," *Quaderni storici* 66 (1987), pp. 706–23, for Florence. For eighteenth-century France, see Claude Courouve, *Les gens de la manchette* (Paris, 1978).

    The question of the relationship of sodomy laws to female sexuality is, if anything, even more complicated than their relationship to men. Louis Crompton attempts to disabuse his readers about "The Myth of Lesbian Impunity: Capital Laws from 1270 to 1791," *Journal of Homosexuality* 6 (1980/81), pp. 11–26, and trial records for 1721 are provided by Brigitte Erickson on pp. 27–40 in the same volume. The fullest account of judicial procedures (the investigation of a convent) in which "lesbianism" figures is provided by Judith Brown, *Immodest Acts* (Oxford: Oxford University Press, 1986), while the most sophisticated survey of the terminology of lesbian desire and the instances of its coincidence with discourses of sodomy in the period is offered by Valerie Traub, "The (In)significance of 'Lesbian' Desire in Early Modern England," in Susan Zimmerman, ed., *Erotic Politics* (NY: Routledge, 1992), reprinted in Jonathan Goldberg, ed., *Queering the Renaissance* (Durham: Duke University Press, 1994).

6. John Boswell, *Christianity, Social Tolerance, and Homosexuality* (Chicago: University of Chicago Press, 1980), p. 93 n. 2. The terrains of sodomy in the medieval period have been mapped in Michael Goodich, *The Unmentionable Vice* (Santa Barbara, CA: Ross-Erikson, 1979) and more fully in James A. Brundage, *Law, Sex, and Christian Society in Medieval Europe* (Chicago: University of Chicago Press, 1987). Still useful, too, is John T. Noonan, *Contraception: A History of Its Treatment by the Catholic Theologians and Canonists* (Cambridge, MA: Harvard University Press, 1966), which takes up sodomy often in the context of acts meant to frustrate the procreative aims of marriage, a point more recently pursued in R. J. Cormier & H. J. Kuster, "Old Views and New Trends: Observations on the Problem of Homosexuality in the Middle Ages," *Studi Medievali* 25 (1984), pp. 587–610. The impossibility of collapsing sodomy into homosexuality in the period is argued by Vern L. Bullough, "The Sin Against Nature and Homosexuality," in Bullough and James Brundage, ed., *Sexual Practices and the Medieval Church* (Buffalo: Prometheus Books, 1982).

7. The first sodomy statute in England was passed by Parliament in 1533. The text reads:

> For asmoche as there is not yett sufficient and condigne punyshment appoynted and lymytted by the due course of the lawes of this Realme for the detestable and abhomynable vice of buggery commyttid with mankynde or beaste; It may therfore please the Kynges Hyghnes with the assent of his Lordes spirituall and temporall and the Commyns of this present parliament assembled, that it may be enacted by auctorytie of the same, that the same offence be from hensforth adjuged felonye, and such order & forme of proces therin to be used ayenst the offendours as in cases of felonye at the commen lawe; and that the offenders being herof convicte by verdicte confession or outlarye shall suffer suche peynes of dethe and losses and penalties of theire goods catallis Dettes londes tenements and hereditaments as felons byn accustomed to doo accordyng to the order of the commen lawes of this Realme, and no person offendyng in any such offence shabbe admyttid to his clergie . . . . (25 Henry VIII c. 6)

The law was renewed in 1536, 1539 and 1541; it was repealed and then reenacted in slightly less stringent terms by Edward VI in 1548, repealed by Mary, reenacted in its original terms by Elizabeth I (5 Eliz. c. 17). For further details of this history, see Bruce R. Smith, *Homosexual Desire in Shakespeare's England* (Chicago: University of Chicago Press, 1991), pp. 41–53. The death penalty was not removed until the 1861 Offenses Against the Person Act (24 & 25 Vict. c. 100). For a factually rich account, see A. D. Harvey, "Prosecutions for Sodomy in England at the Beginning of the Nineteenth Century," *Historical Journal* 21 (1978), pp. 939–48. For a consideration of the subsequent fortunes of sodomy laws in England, see Ed Cohen, "Legislating the

Norm: From Sodomy to Gross Indecency," in Ronald R. Butters, John M. Clum and Michael Moon, ed., *Displacing Homophobia* (Durham: Duke University Press, 1989) and F. E. Frenkel's wide-ranging "Social History of Sex Crime," *JHI* 25 (1964), pp. 333–52, which usefully notes that the Wolfenden Commission left sodomy on the books. A general survey of legal history is offered by H. Montgomery Hyde, *The Other Love* (London: Mayflower Books, 1972).

8. For a discussion of this subject, see Pierre J. Payer, *Sex and the Penitentials* (Toronto: University of Toronto Press, 1984), pp. 40–47, 135–39. For a virulent attack inspired in part by the laxness of the penitentials, see Peter Damian, *Book of Gomorrah*, trans. Pierre J. Payer (Waterloo: Wilfrid Laurier University Press, 1982).

    A similar point might be made by way of Dante: it is well known that in the *Inferno*, and in his encounter with his former teacher, Brunetto Latini, Dante meets a band of sodomites and usurers; less frequently noted is that there is also a group of sodomites in *Purgatorio* XXVI, and it includes Dante's precursor, Guido Guinicelli; the sin does not necessarily entail eternal damnation, and in fact seems intimately related to Dante's work as a writer. For a consideration of the relationships between sodomy in the *Inferno* and humanist pedagogic/pederastic relations, see Leonard Barkan, *Transuming Passion* (Stanford: Stanford University Press, 1991). For a reading of the passage in the *Inferno* in terms of Alan de Lille's notions of the relations between sodomy and grammar in *The Complaint of Nature*, see John Ahern, "*Nudi Grammantes*: The Grammar and Rhetoric of Deviation in *Inferno XV*," *Romanic Review* 82 (1990), pp. 466–86.

9. Alan Bray, *Homosexuality in Renaissance England* (London: Gay Men's Press, 1982). This is the fullest and best historical treatment of sexuality in the early modern period; its initial chapter explores the lexicon of "sodomy" and the integuments suggested in my discussion below.

10. This is the argument of chapter three of *Homosexuality in Renaissance England*, extended in Bray's "Homosexuality and the Signs of Male Friendship in Elizabethan England," *History Workshop Journal* 19 (1990), pp. 1–19; reprinted in *Queering the Renaissance*.

11. See, on this, Jacques Chiffoleau, "Dire l'indicible: rémarques sur la categorie du *nefandum* du XIIe au XVe siècles," *Annales* 45 (1990), pp. 289–384.

12. For a recent example, see James B. De Young, "The Contributions of the Septuagint to Biblical Sanctions Against Homosexuality," *Journal of the Evangelical Theological Society* 34 (1991), pp. 157–77.

13. Derrick Sherwin Bailey, *Homosexuality and the Western Christian Tradition* (London: Longmans, Green & Co., 1955). Bailey argues that the biblical text is about inhospitality, that only later texts make Sodom a site for what comes to be called sodomy. So far as he can, Bailey wants to argue that the Bible is not opposed to homosexuals—just to homosexual acts—a position that he affirms as well. Bailey's way of saving the Bible for homosexuals has to do with denying the links between acts and persons, and by "unconfusing" the categorical confusions of the texts he considers. So doing, a proper "homosexuality" emerges unscathed by the Bible, and its exactions are against acts that ought not to be performed, in Bailey's view. Paradoxically, it is because historically there was no category of *the homosexual* that Bailey can find that the Christian tradition does not condemn homosexuals. A recent similarly "liberal" view can be found in Frederick J. Gaiser, "Homosexuality and the Old Testament," *Word and World* 10 (1990), pp. 161–65.

14. A word about the term "imaginary." Its provenance is Lacanian, describing the psychic formations of undifferentiated identification that exist before the advent of the law (what Lacan calls the symbolic—the law is the oedipal formulation, its diacritical marker is castration, and with it the sexes are divided). In using this term, I mean not to suggest some primordial, virtually atemporal atavism or infantilism. Rather, I depend upon those who have argued that the work of ideology is to suture the identities of subjects—political subjects—to the law, the state, various apparatuses like schools and churches, in ways that produce identifications with and naturalizations of the law so that they come to feel innate, embodied. (See, on this point, the fundamental essay by Louis Althusser, "Ideology and Ideological State Apparatuses," in *Lenin and Philosophy*, trans. Ben Brewster (London: New Left Books, 1971), as well as Fredric Jameson's early and important "Imaginary and Symbolic in Lacan: Marxism, Psychoanalytic Criticism, and the Problem of the Subject," *Yale French Studies* 55/56 (1977), pp. 338–95.) The kinds of historical and sociopolitical mobilizations that I want to convey in this shorthand usage of the term can be compared to the arguments in Benedict Anderson, *Imagined Communities* (London: Verso, 1983), who argues for a range of fictive unities that found the nation/state; national identities (their supposed origins, for example) are lived fictions. Imaginary relations do not exist solely in the imagination.

15. See Michael Warner, "New English Sodom," *American Literature* 64 (1992), pp. 19–47, reprinted in *Queering the Renaissance, "Walden's* Erotic Economy," in *Comparative American Identities*, ed. Hortense Spillers (New York: Routledge, 1991), "Thoreau's Bottom," *Raritan* 11 (1992), pp. 53–79. For a survey of New England views, see Roger Thompson, "Attitudes Towards Homosexuality in the Seventeenth-Century New England Colonies," *Journal of American Studies* 23 (1989), 27–40.

16. Jonathan Goldberg, *Sodometries: Renaissance Texts, Modern Sexualities* (Stanford: Stanford University Press, 1992); see, especially, Part 3 on the New World.

17. For a theoretical essay of Warner's that argues this point, see "Homo-Narcissism; or Heterosexuality," in *Engendering Men*, ed. Joseph Boone and Michael Cadden (New York: Routledge, 1990).

18. Besides *Sodometries*, see, on this point, Walter L. Williams, *The Spirit and the Flesh* (Boston: Beacon, 1986), and João S. Trevisan, *Perverts in Paradise* (London: Gay Mens Press, 1986).

19. An anthology of Spanish texts on the New World that depicts native cultures as sodomitical can be found in Francesco Guerra, *The Pre-Columbian Mind* (London: Seminar, 1971).

20. There are, of course, traditions of same-sex sexualities in Asia that are not represented in this collection. On this subject, see Bret Hinsch, *Passions of the Cut Sleeve* (Berkeley: University of California Press, 1990), for China; and Ihara Saikaku, *The Great Mirror of Male Love*, trans. and ed. Paul Schalow (Stanford: Stanford University Press, 1990), for Japan.

21. Laws and cases are usefully compiled by Jonathan Ned Katz in *Gay American History* (New York: Thomas Y. Crowell, 1976), and in his *Gay/Lesbian Almanac* (New York: Harper & Row, 1983). For further discussion, see, in addition to *Sodometries*, Louis Crompton, "Homosexuals and the Death Penalty in Colonial America," *Journal of Homosexuality* 1 (1976), pp. 277–93; Robert Oaks, " 'Things Fearful to Name': Sodomy and Buggery in Seventeenth-Century New England," *Journal of Social History* 12

(1978), pp. 268–81; Oaks, "Defining Sodomy in Seventeenth-Century Massachusetts," *Journal of Homosexuality* 5 (1980/81), pp. 79–83.

22. Janet E. Halley, "*Bowers v. Hardwick* in the Renaissance," in *Queering the Renaissance*. See also Anne B. Goldstein, "History, Homosexuality, and Political Values: Searching for the Hidden Determinants of *Bowers v. Hardwick*," *Yale Law Journal* 97 (1988), pp. 1073–1103.

23. On this see also Halley's "Misreading Sodomy: A Critique of the Classification of 'Homosexuals' in Federal Equal Protection Law," in *Body Guards*, eds. Julia Epstein and Kristina Straub (New York: Routledge, 1991). For an equally hard-hitting piece, see Kendall Thomas, "Beyond the Privacy Principle," *Columbia Law Review* 92 (1992), pp. 1431–1516. Thomas argues for a complicity between sodomy laws and violence against gays and lesbians; rather than appeals to privacy, he argues that the Eighth Amendment, guaranteeing U.S. citizens freedom from "cruel and unusual punishment," needs to be the basis for overthrowing sodomy laws. In his terms, before gays can enjoy privacy (rather than experiencing it as a realm of privation, secrecy and hiding from state-sanctioned violence), they must share with heterosexuals a right to physical security that constitutes full membership in the body politic. For Thomas, sodomy laws do not so much seek to regulate private pleasures as to sanction political power. "The criminalization of homosexual sodomy *legitimizes* homophobic violence," he writes (p. 1486 n. 194).

24. In capital letters, Richman wrote: "THIS IS NOT A CASE ABOUT ONLY HOMOSEXUALS. ALL SORTS OF PEOPLE DO THIS KIND OF THING." As cited in the *New York Times* (May 25, 1993), p. A16, in a piece on the revelations about *Bowers v. Hardwick* in the papers of Thurgood Marshall; as these notes reveal, the court might easily have gone the other way; as he himself admitted after his retirement from the court in 1990, the swing vote in the case was that of Justice Lewis F. Powell, who came to regret that he joined the majority in what he continued to believe was basically a "trivial" case.

25. See Andrew Koppelman, "The Miscegenation Analogy: Sodomy Law as Sex Discrimination," *Yale Law Review* 98 (1988), pp. 145–64, and the discussion of *Bowers v. Hardwick* in *Sodometries*, pp. 6–18.

26. For this point, see Eva Saks, "Representing Miscegenation Law," *Raritan* 8 (1988), pp. 39–69; on p. 54 Saks notes parallels between miscegenation and sodomy laws.

27. Halley depends on the brilliant analysis offered by Eve Kosofsky Sedgwick, *Epistemology of the Closet* (Berkeley: University of California Press, 1990).

28. See Lawrence R. Murphy, "Defining the Crime Against Nature: Sodomy in the United States Appeals Courts, 1810–1940," *Journal of Homosexuality* 19 (1990), pp. 49–66. The vernacular sense of sodomy as anal sex seems to have become commonplace in the eighteenth century; the notion of a difference between homo and hetero sodomy (often effacing the existence of the latter) seems the product of the much more modern aegis that presumes an absolute homo/hetero distinction.

29. On this history, see Gary Kinsman, *The Regulation of Desire* (Montreal: Black Rose Books, 1987), and Paul-François Sylvestre, *Bougerie en Nouvelle-France* (Hull: Asticon, 1983), which also includes some documents of a 1691 case that seems to have involved the kinds of divisions among the French Canadians of the sort Katz suggests were at work in the U.S. As Sylvestre points out (p. 31), it was the Jesuits who saw buggery as a native vice, and who intervened in a 1648 case to save a White man accused of sodomy from being executed.

30. On the vocabulary of male-male sexual relations, see Arno Schmitt, "Different Approaches to Male-Male Sexuality/Eroticism From Morocco to Usbekistan," Jehoeda Sofer, "Sodomy in the Law of Muslim States," and Charles Pellat, "Liwāṭ," in *Sexuality and Eroticism Among Males in Moslem Societies*, eds. Arno Schmitt and Jehoeda Sofer (New York: Harrington Park Press, 1992).

31. For representative samples, see the discussions of sexual practice gathered in *Sexuality and Eroticism Among Males in Moslem Societies*. Even more to be questioned, of course, are the views of "traditional" scholars who seek to deny or to denigrate male-male sexual practices; see, for example, the essays in *Society and the Sexes in Medieval Islam*, ed. Afaf Lutfi al-Sayyid-Marsot (Malibu, CA.: Udena, 1979) and the rejoinder to such work in Everett K. Rowson, "The Categorization of Gender and Sexual Irregularity in Medieval Arabic Vice Lists," in *Body Guards*.

32. These issues are worried at by, for example, Jonathan Drake, " 'Le Vice' in Turkey," *International Journal of Greek Love* 1 (1966), pp. 13–27, who wishes to adjudiate the question of whether man-boy relations in Turkey were platonic or exploitative (they must be a bit of both, Drake concludes, still hoping to find "deep reciprocal affection" [24] as the true basis of Turkish practices), and by Minoo S. Southgate, "Men, Women, and Boys: Love and Sex in the Work of Sa'di," *Iranian Studies* 17 (1984), pp. 413–52, who notes the interchangeability of men and women as desired objects in late thirteenth-century Iranian poetry, but also the deplorable treatment of women; like Drake, he seems happiest with poems that transform sex into more acceptable practices, in his case, those that are eroticized spiritual ones.

33. See *Guardians of the Flute* (New York: McGraw-Hill, 1981), and the two important anthologies edited by Herdt, *Rituals of Manhood: Male Initiation in Papua New Guinea* (Berkeley: University of California Press, 1982) and *Ritualized Homosexuality in Melanesia* (Berkeley: University of California Press, 1984), the latter of which contains the essay by Shirley Lindenbaum, "Variations on a Sociosexual Theme in Melanesia," to which Creed refers in his essay. For a broad survey, see Part I ("Before Homosexuality") in David F. Greenberg, *The Construction of Homosexuality* (Chicago: University of Chicago Press, 1988).

34. This needs to be distinguished, I think, from the position that simply collapses male-male relations into male-female ones, often by way of a "third sex" model; see, for example, Unni Wikan's discussion of the Xanith as a "third gender role" in *Behind the Veil in Arabia* (Baltimore: Johns Hopkins University Press, 1982), or Serena Nanda, "The Hijras of India: Cultural and Individual Dimensions of an Institutionalized Third Gender Role," *Journal of Homosexuality* 11 (1985), pp. 35–54.

35. For a similar evaluation of *Rituals of Manhood*, see the review by Bruce M. Knauft in *American Ethnologist* 4 (1987), pp. 401–14.

36. For a related argument, see Ana Maria Alonso and Maria Teresa Koreck, "Silences: 'Hispanics,' AIDS, and Sexual Practices," *differences* 1.1 (1989), pp. 101–24.

37. Rather than supporting the modern regimes of sexual orientation, it thus leads to recognitions of sexual *disorientation*, to borrow a term that organizes the recent work of Michael Moon; see, e.g., "A Small Boy and Others: Sexual Disorientation in Henry James, Kenneth Anger, and David Lynch," in *Comparative American Identities*.

38. Minneapolis: University of Minnesota Press, 1987.

39. See, e.g., Charles Shiveley, "Cocksucking as a Revolutionary Act," *Fag Rag* 3 (1972); "Assholes: Rimming as an Act of Revolution," *Fag Rag* 7/8 (1974).

40. Guy Hocquenghem, *Homosexual Desire*, trans. Daniella Dangoor (Durham: Duke University Press, 1993).

41. For a brilliant discussion of this analogy, see Eve Kosofsky Sedgwick, *Epistemology of the Closet*, ch. 5. In current work-in-progress, Sedgwick is importantly exploring the territories of shame in ways that bear upon the discussion here. For Sedgwick's advocacy of anal pleasures, see "A Poem is Being Written," *Representations* 17 (1987), pp. 110–43, reprinted in her *Tendencies* (Durham: Duke University Press, 1993).

42. See Michael Warner, "Introduction" to *Fear of a Queer Planet*, ed. Michael Warner (Minneapolis: University of Minnesota Press, 1993).

43. For another reading of this scene, see Kevin Kopelson: "Seeing Sodomy: *Fanny Hill*'s Blinding Vision," in *Homosexuality in Renaissance and Enlightenment England*, ed. Claude J. Summers (New York: Harrington Park Press, 1992). In an important, as-yet-unpublished essay, Forrest Tyler Stevens has situated *Fanny Hill* within the context of eighteenth-century libel laws.

44. The text reads:

> Any male person who, in public or private, commits or is party to the commission of, or procures the commission by any male person of, any act of gross indecency with another male person, shall be guilty of a misdemeanor, and being convicted thereof shall be liable at the discretion of the court to be imprisoned for any term not exceeding two years with or without hard labour.

This is, as Ed Cohen puts it in "Legislating the Norm: From Sodomy to Gross Indecency," in *Displacing Homophobia*, "the first legal classification of a sexual relation (as opposed to a sexual act) between men" (p. 191, from which the amendment is also cited). For further considerations of the law, see Jeffrey Weeks, "Inverts, Perverts, and Mary-Annes: Male Prostitution and the Regulation of Homosexuality in England in the Nineteenth and Early Twentieth Centuries," *Journal of Homosexuality* 6 (1980/81), pp. 113–34, reprinted in Weeks, *Against Nature* (London: Rivers Oram Press, 1991), and in *Hidden from History*, ed. Martin Duberman, Martha Vicinus and George Chauncey, Jr. (New York: Meridian, 1989).

Besides Bartlett's *Who Was That Man?* for further contextualization see Ed Cohen, *Talk on the Wilde Side* (New York: Routledge, 1993); for a reading of a Wilde text in the context of his notoriety, see Christopher Craft, "Alias Bunbury: Desire and Temination in *The Importance of Being Earnest*," *Representations* 31 (1990), pp. 19–46.

I

Laws of Desire

Genesis 19

And there came two angels to Sodom at even; and Lot sat in the gate of Sodom: and Lot seeing them rose up to meet them; and he bowed himself with his face toward the ground;

2 And he said, Behold now, my lords, turn in, I pray you, into your servant's house, and tarry all night, and wash your feet, and ye shall rise up early, and go on your ways. And they said, Nay; but we will abide in the street all night.

3 And he pressed upon them greatly; and they turned in unto him, and entered into his house; and he made them a feast and did bake unleavened bread, and they did eat.

4 But before they lay down, the men of the city, even the men of Sodom, compassed the house round, both old and young, all the people from every quarter:

5 And they called unto Lot, and said unto him, Where are the men which came in to thee this night? bring them out unto us, that we may know them.

6 And Lot went out at the door unto them, and shut the door after him,

7 And said, I pray you, brethren, do not so wickedly.

8 Behold now, I have two daughters which have not known man; let me, I pray you, being them out unto you, and do ye to them as is good in your eyes: only unto these men do nothing; for therefore came they under the shadow of my roof.

9 And they said, Stand back. And they said again, This one fellow came in to sojourn, and he will needs be a judge: now will we deal worse with thee, than with them. And they pressed sore upon the man, even Lot, and came near to break the door.

10 But the men put forth their hand, and pulled Lot into the house to them, and shut to the door.

11 And they smote the men that were at the door of the house with blindness, both small and great; so that they wearied themselves to find the door.

12 And the men said unto Lot, Hast thou here any besides? son in law, and thy sons, and thy daughters, and whatsoever thou hast in the city, bring them out of this place;

13 For we will destroy this place, because the cry of them is waxen great before the face of the Lord; and the Lord hath sent us to destroy it.

14 And Lot went out, and spake unto his sons in law, which married his daughters, and said, Up, get you out of this place; for the Lord will destroy this city. But he seemed as one that mocked unto his sons in law.

15 And when the morning arose, then the angels hastened Lot, saying, Arise, take thy wife, and thy two daughters, which are here; lest thou be consumed in the iniquity of the city.

16 And while he lingered, the men laid hold upon his hand, and upon the hand of his wife, and upon the hand of his two daughters; the Lord being merciful unto him: and they brought him forth, and set him without the city.

17 And it came to pass, when they had brought them forth abroad, that he said, Escape for thy life; look not behind thee, neither stay thou in all the plain; escape to the mountain, lest thou be consumed.

18 And Lot said unto them, Oh, not so, my Lord:

19 Behold now, thy servant hath found grace in thy sight, and thou hast magnified thy mercy, which thou hast shewed unto me in saving my life; and I cannot escape to the mountain, lest some evil take me, and I die:

20 Behold now, this city is near to flee unto, and it is a little one: Oh, let me escape thither (is it not a little one?) and my soul shall live.

21 And he said unto him, See, I have accepted thee concerning this thing also, that I will not overthrow this city, for the which thou hast spoken.

22 Haste thee, escape thither; for I cannot do any thing till thou be come thither. Therefore the name of the city was called Zoar.

23 The sun was risen upon the earth when Lot entered into Zoar.

24 Then the Lord rained upon Sodom and upon Gomorrah brimstone and fire from the Lord out of heaven;

25 And he overthrew those cities, and all the plain, and all the inhabitants of the cities, and that which grew upon the ground.

26 But his wife looked back from behind him, and she became a pillar of salt.

27 And Abraham gat up early in the morning to the place where he stood before the Lord;

28 And he looked toward Sodom and Gomorrah, and toward all the land of the plain, and beheld, and, lo, the smoke of the country went up as the smoke of a furnace.

29 And it came to pass, when God destroyed the cities of the plain, that God remembered Abraham, and sent Lot out of the midst of the overthrow, when he overthrew the cities in the which Lot dwelt.

30 And Lot went up out of Zoar, and dwelt in the mountain, and his two daughters with him; for he feared to dwell in Zoar: and he dwelt in a cave, he and his two daughters.

31 And the firstborn said unto the younger, Our father is old, and there is not a man in the earth to come in unto us after the manner of all the earth:

32 Come, let us make our father drink wine, and we will lie with him, that we may preserve seed of our father.

33 And they made their father drink wine that night: and the firstborn went in, and lay with her father; and he perceived not when she lay down, nor when she arose.

34 And it came to pass on the morrow, that the firstborn said unto the younger, Behold, I lay yesternight with my father: let us make him drink wine this night also; and go thou in, and lie with him, that we may preserve seed of our father.

35 And they made their father drink wine that night also; and the younger arose, and lay with him; and he perceived not when she lay down, nor when she arose.

36 Thus were both the daughters of Lot with child by their father.

37 And the firstborn bare a son, and called his name Moab: the same is the father of the Moabites unto this day.

38 And the younger, she also bare a son, and called his name Benamml: the same is the father of the children of Ammon unto this day.

Sodom as Nexus: The Web of Design in Biblical Narrative

Robert Alter

The very terms we habitually use to designate the sundry biblical narratives reflect an uncertainty as to whether the stories taken in sequence have something that could be called a structure, and as to what sort of larger configurations they might form. The first eleven chapters of Genesis are usually called the Primeval History, as though they constituted a continuous historical narrative, despite the repeated scholarly arguments that they are in fact an uneven stitching-together of the most heterogeneous materials. On the other hand, we often speak of the Patriarchal Tales or the Wilderness Tales, a designation that suggests something vaguely anthological. Or again, it is common practice to invoke with a certain ring of academic authority the Abraham cycle, the Jacob cycle, the Elijah cycle; but if that term has a precise application for Norse sagas or Wagnerian opera, it seems chiefly an evasion in the case of biblical narrative. We do, of course, talk about the Joseph story and the David story, but this is only because these are rare exceptions in which the ancient Hebrew writers have given us a relatively lengthy, continuous narrative—apart from a few seeming interpolations—that follows the chronological movement of a central figure's life.

If one's standard of unitary narrative is drawn from self-consciously artful novels like *Madame Bovary*, Ford Madox Ford's *The Good Soldier*, or even, on a more ambitiously panoramic scale, *Anna Karenina*, it goes without saying that biblical narrative is far from unitary. Scholarly opinion has by and large jumped to the conclusion that if biblical narrative is not unitary, it must be episodic. Episodic structure, as Aristotle first observed, means no necessary sequence among the incidents told. In the case of a single author, episodic structure may be quite intentional, and often expresses a rejection of hierarchies, an enchantment with the teeming heterogenity of experience, as in *Don Quixote*, Lesage's *Gil Blas* or *Huckleberry*

Finn. By contrast, the episodic character of biblical narrative, as it is usually represented in scholarly analysis, is the result of editorial inadvertence rather than authorial intention: the anonymous redactors, working under the constraints of authoritative ancient traditions in ways we can no longer gauge, are imagined patching together swatches of very different materials, sometimes splicing two or more versions of the same story, sometimes inserting extraneous stories that originated in radically different contexts.

It may be helpful in trying to think about the larger configurations of biblical narrative to keep in mind that only a minority of long narratives anywhere, whether prenovelistic or novelistic, are consistently unitary. Dickens, for example, often used the devices of tightly sustained suspense of the detective-novel plot, and modern criticism has celebrated the symmetries of his symbolic structures, yet the typical Dickens novel is studded with anecdotal digressions and, in the earlier phase of his career, with interpolated tales. Fielding is justly praised as one of the most architectonic of English novelists—Coleridge rated the plot of *Tom Jones*, along with that of *Oedipus Rex* and Ben Jonson's *The Alchemist*, as one of the three most perfect in world literature—yet both *Tom Jones* and *Joseph Andrews* include long, interpolated tales that are different from the surrounding narrative in style, tone, genre and personages. The instance of Fielding is particularly instructive because it suggests that even a writer so supremely conscious of unified artifice—in *Tom Jones* one might mention the structural symmetry of six books in the country, six on the road, six in town, or the tonal unity conferred by the ubiquitous ironic narrator—might for his own good reasons introduce materials whose chief connection with the main narrative was a matter of shared theme or mere analogy.

Let me propose that something quite similar repeatedly occurs in biblical narrative in the juxtaposition of disparate materials that are purposefully linked by motif, theme, analogy and, sometimes, by a character who serves as a bridge between two different narrative blocks otherwise separated in regard to plot and often in regard to style and perspective or even genre. Obviously, in the Bible the proportion of such insertions is quite unlike what one finds in Fielding, who makes only occasional use of them. Indeed, it may be inaccurate to speak at all of "insertions" in the case of the Bible, for the artful juxtaposition of seemingly disparate episodes is more like a basic structuring procedure, a feature especially evident in Numbers, Joshua, Kings and, above all, in the Book of Judges, but also discernible elsewhere. This would appear to be the expression of an activity that in recent years has come to be called redactional art, but in what follows I shall speak of the writer rather than the redactor in the interests of accuracy as well as of simplicity, for we need to remind ourselves that the redactor, however enshrined in modern biblical scholarship, remains a conjectural entity, and the more one scrutinizes his supposed work, the more the line between redactor and writer blurs.

Rather than try to describe the overarching design of a whole book or sequence of books, a project that would require a great deal of space for persuasive execution, I would like to demonstrate the general principle by following the biblical text at a point where there seems to be a break in narrative continuity. In fact, the example I have chosen involves what looks like a triple break from the surrounding narrative, but I shall try to show that all three stages of the break are firmly linked together and locked into both the immediate narrative context and the larger thematic design of Genesis and subsequent books in a way that complicates the thread of meaning.

In Genesis 17, God appears before the ninety-nine-year-old Abram, changes his name to Abraham and Sarai's to Sarah as an affirmation of the covenant, and resonantly announces a future of progeny through Sarah—a promise so improbable that it causes Abraham to laugh in disbelief. In the first half of the next chapter, we have the story of the three mysterious visitors who come to Abraham (from what one can make out, they are God himself and two of his messengers), one of whom brings the good tidings that within the year Sarah will bear a son. This time, it is she, overhearing the promise from the tent opening, who laughs in disbelief, perhaps even sarcastically. Documentary critics have been quick to identify these two sequenced stories as a duplication from two different sources, P and then J. Whether in fact scholarly analysis has succeeded in "unscrambling the omelette" here, to borrow a telling phrase from Sir Edmund Leach, is something I shall not presume to judge. More essential to our purposes is that the writer wants a double version of the promise of progeny, partly for the sheer effect of grand emphasis, but also because he needs first a patriarchal version and then a matriarchal one. In chapter 17, Abraham alone is present before God; the plight of the ninety-year-old barren Sarah is mentioned only in passing and in secondary syntactic position after Abraham (verse 17); and male biology is very much at issue in the stress on the newly enjoined commandment of circumcision (though Abraham undertakes it for himself and all his future sons, its placement in the narrative sequence makes it look like a precondition to the begetting of the son, as, analogously, in Exodus 4, the tale of the Bridegroom of the Blood, the circumcision of the son is the necessary means for his survival). In the first half of chapter 18, we encounter the inaugural instance of the annunciation-type-scene. As a conventional tale, it is preeminently matriarchal, for the good news always comes to the wife, often in the absence of the husband. Here, however, perhaps because of the force of the idea of Abraham as founding father, there is a partial displacement from matriarchal to patriarchal emphasis, the angel speaking to Abraham while Sarah eavesdrops on her own annunciation. In any case, it is she who laughs, and it is her biology—the twice-stated fact of her postmenopausal condition—that is at issue. The shift, even if it is a somewhat qualified one, from patriarch to matriarch in the second version of the promise is crucial, for in what follows women and sexuality, women and propagation, will be central.

Now, in all other occurrences of the annunciation type-scene,[1] the first two motifs of the conventional sequence—(a) the woman's condition of barrenness; (b) the annunciation—are immediately followed by the third motif of fulfillment, (c) the birth of the son (*cf.* Gen. 25:19–25; Judg. 13; I Sam. 1; II Kings 4:8–17). Here, however, there is a long interruption before the birth of Isaac at the beginning of Genesis 21. First, God announces to Abraham his intention to destroy Sodom and Gomorrah, and Abraham launches upon his memorable effort to bargain with God over the survival of the doomed cities, starting with the possibility of fifty righteous souls therein and working down to ten (18:17–33). The first half of chapter 19 tells the story of the destruction of Sodom, concluding with what looks like an etiological tale (to explain a geological oddity in the Dead Sea region) about Lot's wife turning into a pillar of salt. The second half of the chapter is a very different kind of etiological tale, accounting for the origins of two trans-Jordanian peoples, the Moabites and the Ammonites, in the incestuous copulation of Lot and his daughters. The whole of chapter 20 is then taken up with the second of three versions of the sister-wife story; the patriarch in a southern kingdom (here, Abraham in Gerar) who proclaims that his wife is his sister, in consequence almost loses her to the local potentate, but in the end departs with wife intact and heaped with riches by the would-be interloper. Since nowhere else are there such interruptions of the annunciation's fulfillment, we are surely entitled to ask what all this has to do with the promise of seed to Abraham. Let me suggest that in the view of the biblical writer, progeny for the first father of the future Israelites involved a whole tangle of far-reaching complications, for the adumbration of which these three intervening episodes were necessary, and that Sodom, far from being an interruption of the saga of the seed of Abraham, is a major thematic nexus of the larger story.[2]

We should observe, to begin with, that the dialogue between Abraham and God in the second half of Genesis 18 sets up a connection between the convenantal promise and the story of Sodom by adding a new essential theme to the covenantal idea. The two previous enunciations of the convenant, which take up all of chapters 15 and 17, are ringing promises of progeny and little more: your seed, God assures the doubting Abraham, will be as innumerable as the stars in the heavens. The only condition hinted at is that Abraham remain a faithful party to the convenant, but remarkably, no *content* is given to this faithfulness. It looks almost as if a trap were set for the audience, encouraging them at first to think that the divine promise was a free gift, entered into through a solemn ritual (the sacrificial animal parts of chapter 15) and perpetually confirmed by still another ritual (the circumcision of chapter 17). Now, however, when God reaffirms the language of blessing and the future of nationhood in chapter 18, he adds this stipulation about Abraham and his posterity: "For I have singled him out so that he might instruct his sons and his family after him, that they should keep the way of the Lord *to do righteousness and justice*" (Genesis 18:19, my emphasis). Survival and propagation, then, depend on the creation of a just society. This idea is immediately picked up as God goes on to warn Abraham of his intention to destroy the Cities of the Plain because of their pervasive wickedness. Abraham, aghast at the possibility that the righteous might be wiped out with the wicked, tosses back the very phrase God has just used about human ethical obligations: "Will the judge of all the earth not *do justice*?" (18:25). The echo of *shofet*, judge, and *mishpat*, justice, will then sound loudly in a jibe about Lot made by the citizens of Sodom, whom he has implored to desist from their violent intentions: 'This fellow came to sojourn, and now he presumes to judge, yes, to judge' (19:9). The verb *shofet* also means "to rule," which may be its primary sense here, but the play with "doing justice" of the previous chapter is quite pointed: Sodom is a society without judge or justice, and a latecomer resident alien will hardly be allowed to act as *shofet* in any sense of the word.

As many commentators have noted, the hospitality scene between Abraham and the divine visitors at the beginning of Genesis 18 is paralleled by the hospitality scene between Lot and the two angels at the beginning of Genesis 19—paralleled with a nuance of difference, for Lot's language to the angels is more urgent, in a string of imperative verbs, less deferentially ceremonious than Abraham's language, and here the narrator gives us nothing like the details of the menu and the flurry of preparations for the feast that we are offered in the pastoral setting of the previous chapter. Lot's rather breathless hospitality—is he already scared by what could happen to strangers in his town?—is, of course, the single exception to the rule in Sodom. The story of the doomed city is crucial not only to Genesis but to the moral thematics of the Bible as a whole (compare the use of Sodom in Isaiah I and Judges 19) because it is the biblical version of anti-civilization, rather like Homer's islands of the Cyclops monsters where the inhabitants eat strangers instead of welcoming them. If we wondered momentarily what God had in mind when he told Abraham that the outrages of Sodom—literally, its "crying out"—were so great that they reached the very heavens, we now see all the male inhabitants of Sodom, from adolescent to dodderer, banging on Lot's door and demanding the right to gang-rape the two strangers. The narrator offers no comment on the homosexual aspect of the threatened act of violence, though it is safe to assume he expects us to consider that, too, abhorrent, but in regard to this episode's place in the larger story of progeny for Abraham, it is surely important that homosexuality is a necessarily sterile form of sexual intercourse, as though the proclivities of the Sodomites answered biologically to their utter indifference to the moral prerequisites for survival.

At this ominous point, in one of the most scandalous statements uttered by any character in ancient literature, Lot's daughters, not previously mentioned, are brought into the story. "Look," Lot tells the assailants, 'I have two daughters who have not known a man. Let me bring them out to you, and do to them whatever you want. But to these men do nothing, for they have come under the shadow of my roof-beam" (19:7). Some have sought to naturalize this outrageous offer by contending that in the ancient Near East the host-guest bond (someone coming under the shadow of your roof-beam) was sacred, conferring obligations that exceeded those of a man to his virgin daughters. The impassive narrator, as is his wont, offers no guidance on this question, but the unfolding of the story, and its contrastive connections with the surrounding narrative, cast doubt on this proposition that Lot was simply playing the perfect ancient Near Eastern host in rather trying circumstances. It is important for what happens at the end of the chapter that the two girls should be virgins, and Lot clearly imagines he is offering the rapists a special treat in proclaiming their virginity. What we are not told, in a shrewd maneuver of delayed exposition, is that both the girls are betrothed. This information is not divulged until verse 14, when Lot, at the angels' insistence, entreats his prospective sons-in-law to save themselves from the imminent destruction. Their response is to think Lot must be joking, *metsaheq*, the same verb of laughter that designates Abraham's and Sarah's response to the promise of progeny, and that here, in polar contrast, becomes a mechanism of skepticism that seals the doom of the two men. Now, at least according to later biblical law, the rape of a betrothed woman is a crime punishable by death (cf. Deut. 22:23–27), and it is reasonable to infer that Lot evinces a disquieting readiness here to serve as accomplice in the multiple enactment of a capital crime directed against his own daughters. The implicit judgment against Lot is then confirmed in the incest at the end of the chapter, to which we shall turn momentarily.

Let me first add a brief comment on the motif of sight and blindness, which helps structure the story thematically and also links it with the surrounding narrative. The transition to Sodom was first signalled visually when Abraham escorted the two visitors out on their way and they "looked down" on Sodom, far below in the Dead Sea plain (18:16). The conclusion of the destruction is symmetrically marked at 19:28 when the next morning Abraham, in the equivalent of a cinematic long shot, "looks down" (the same verb) on the Cities of the Plain and is able to discern columns of smoke rising from the distant ruins. In the Sodom story proper, the angels smite the assailants with blindness so that they are unable to find the door of Lot's house. Then, before carrying out the terrible devastation, the angels warn Lot not to look back; and, most famously, when his wife does just that, she is turned to a pillar of salt. I don't pretend to know precisely what this taboo—also attested to elsewhere—of looking back, or looking on the destruction, meant in the imagination of the ancient folk. I would observe, however, that the taboo against seeing has regular sexual associations, in the Bible (as, of course, it also does in psychoanalytic terms). To "see the nakedness" of someone is the standard biblical euphemism for incest. Genesis 19 does not use that idiom, but this rampant mob struck with blindness at a closed door is, after all, seeking forbidden sexual congress, and the story ends with a tale of incest.

That episode (19:29–38) is presented in an unsettling manner of impassive factuality, the narrator providing no indication whether the double incest should in any way be condemned. It would sadly reduce the story to think of it simply as a satiric representation of the dubious origins of two enemy peoples, the Moabites and the Ammonites, for its more important function is to tie together several thematically significant connections with the immediate and larger context of biblical narrative. Lot, we recall, has fled with his two daughters to the city of Zoar, which, as a special dispensation for his sake, has alone been saved from destruction among the Cities of the Plain. But Lot is afraid to stay in Zoar, whether because he fears still another wave of cataclysm or Sodom-like behavior on the part of the Zoarites, and so he flees once more with his daughters, this time to the rocky hill-country above the Dead Sea plain, where they take refuge in a cave. The despairing daughters—who, we should remember, enjoyed prenuptial status when we first encountered them—conclude that the whole country, or rather the whole earth ('erets), has been laid waste, and that there is no man left to lie with them. On two successive nights, then, they get their father drunk, and, the firstborn going first, each takes a turn in bed with him and is impregnated by him. Twice we are told that "he knew not when she lay down and got up," a wry play on the sexual meaning of the verb, for he knows his daughters well enough in the other sense, knows them without "seeing" them. Thus the man who precipitously offered his betrothed daughters to gang-rape now is tricked into deflowering them himself.

This strange story alludes to the aftermath of the Deluge, and that connection in turn may help us see why it is placed precisely here in the Abraham narrative. The destruction of the Cities of the Plain is a second Deluge: there, iniquitous humanity was destroyed by water; here, by fire. A concrete link between the two is probably suggested by the writer's choice of a graphic verb, "The Lord *rained down* on Sodom and Gomorrah brimstone and fire from the Lord, from the heavens" (19:24). The framing of the sentence by repeating "the Lord" at both ends, and the odd syntactic obtrusion of "from the heavens" at the very end, reinforce this sense of cataclysm showering from heaven to earth (no earthquake this), like the earlier devastation when the floodgates of the heavens were flung open. After the Deluge, Noah plants a vineyard and forthwith gets drunk. It is precisely in his state of inebriation that Ham his son "see his nakedness" (the idiom implicit in the alluding text is explicit in the text alluded to) and incurs his father's curse when Noah wakes from his drunken stupor and discovers what has happened. (There is a long tradition of exegetical opinion, whether right or wrong, that more than mere seeing has happened: many say, a sexual act, and in the opinion of some medieval exegetes, castration, which readily reminds us of analogues in Greek myth.) Interestingly, Ham's two brothers then cover their naked father with a cloak by walking backwards with it into the tent, taking care never to look behind them, in symmetrical contrast to the unfortunate Mrs. Lot (see Gen. 9:20–27).

The Noah-Lot conjunction brings us back to the notion of the physical survival of group or species made conditional on moral performance. Abraham, the man who has in this very sequence demonstrated his sense of justice by daring to call God himself to the standard of justice, has one son, by his concubine, and will soon have a second son by his legitimate wife. Against these, Lot has two daughters, who as daughters figure, alas, in ancient Near Eastern imagination more as conduits for male seed than as the true progeny itself. Beginning with the son to be born within the year, from Abraham's loins a great people will spring, destined to be a blessing, as God has repeatedly promised, to all the nations of the earth. Lot's daughters, imagining that a second cataclysm has laid waste all the earth, desperately conclude that the only way to "keep the seed alive" (19:32, 34) is by turning back to him who begot them. The propagation is carried out, but the two peoples that derive from it will carry the shadow of their incestuous origins in the (folk-) etymology of their names, Moab, from-the-father, and Benei Ammon, sons-of-kin; and perhaps we are encouraged to infer that in their historical destiny these peoples will be somehow trapped in their own inward circuit, a curse and not a blessing to the nations of the earth, in consonance with their first begetting.

At this point, it might seem logical for the narrative to revert to the fulfillment of the promise of offspring to Abraham. Instead, still another episode, taking up a whole chapter, intervenes. For the second time, Abraham goes to a southern kingdom, in this case Gerar in the Negev rather than Egypt and, as before, having announced that Sarah is his sister, finds she is taken into the harem of the local ruler. Now, it seems to me a piece of modern simple-mindedness to say, as is conventionally done, that since Abraham would appear to have learned nothing from the previous near-disaster in Egypt (Gen. 12:10–20), we must conclude that this is a duplication of sources, and a particularly clumsy one, at that. I do not think the biblical writers were concerned with consistent narrative verisimilitude in quite this way, or in any case such concerns could be overridden by the requirements of what I shall call compositional logic. Let me stress that I am not addressing myself to the issue of whether this thrice-told tale originated in different sources, but rather to the compositional effect the writer achieves in retelling it as he does. (I will set the third occurrence of the story in the Isaac narrative, Genesis 26, as beyond the scope of the present discussion.) For our purposes, it is important to note that the story of Abraham and Sarah in Gerar is strikingly different from the story of Abraham and Sarah in Egypt in regard to both details and expositional strategy. Most of these differences, as we shall see, flow directly from the placement of the Gerar story directly after the destruction of Sodom and before the birth of Isaac.

In Genesis 20 no mention is made of a famine as the reason for the patriarch's temporary sojourn in the south. And, indeed, a famine at this point, just after Abraham has been promised the imminent birth of a son, and after the destruction of the Cities of the Plain, would throw the narrative out of balance, introducing still another catastrophe at the moment before the great fulfillment. Sarah's beauty, much stressed in Genesis 12 in conjunction with the clearly implied concupiscence of the Egyptians, is not referred to here. Perhaps that may be because of her advanced age at this point in the narrative, though I'm not sure this is a consideration that troubled the writer. In any case, there seem to be a desire to shift the emphasis from Sarah's sexual attractiveness to the mere fact that the future mother of Isaac is evidently appropriate to take into a harem. In this version, Abraham offers no explanation at the beginning for his odd strategem of passing Sarah off as his sister ("lest they kill me for my wife"); that comes only at a late point in the story in his nervous attempt at self-exculpation to the offended Abimelech. Abimelech, in turn, is assigned a much more elaborate role than Pharaoh in the earlier version, and the terms of that role have a great deal to do, I think, with the immediately preceding story of Sodom.

When God appears to Abimelech in a dream to threaten him with death for taking a married woman (this, too, a contrast to Pharaoh, whose only communication from the Lord is through physical affliction), the Gerarite king responds in moral indignation: 'Will you slay even innocent people?' (20:4) The Hebrew here is a little peculiar, for strategic reasons having to do with the two previous chapters. The word for innocent, *tsadiq*, also means righteous, and is the very term Abraham used when he challenged God: "Far be it from you to do such a thing, to put to death the righteous with the wicked so that the righteous would be like the wicked. Far be it from you. Will not the judge of all the earth do justice?" (18:25) It is for this reason that death is threatened to Abimelech but not to Pharaoh, so that Abimelech can be made, in a brilliant ironic turn, to take up Abraham's own recently stated moral theme. Abimelech cries out against the possibility that God might slay a righteous "people" (*goy*), apparently referring to himself. As an idiom, this is anomalous enough in biblical Hebrew to have encouraged emendations of the text, but it is a word-choice that makes perfect sense against the backdrop of Sodom, where an entirely wicked people was destroyed. The Gerar story presents an initial parallel with the Sodom story that immediately swerves into sharp contrast. Here also, two strangers come into a town, and one of them is promptly seized for the purpose of sexual enjoyment—but then she has been passed off as an unmarried woman. The moment Abimelech discovers Sarah's actual status, he speaks as a model of conscience, and he scrupulously avoids touching her. God identifies Abraham as a "prophet" with powers of intercession, which seems appropriate just after Abraham has made his great effort to intercede on behalf of Sodom. The punctilious Abimelech nevertheless feels, with some justice, that Abraham has behaved badly: "Things that should not be done you have done to me" (20:9). When Abraham finally responds (to the king's first challenge he remains silent, as though at a loss for words), he spells out his fears in the following language: "For I thought, surely there is no fear of God in this place, and they will kill me for my wife" (20:11). Abraham, in other words, assumes that Gerar is another Sodom, while Abimelech's behavior demonstrates that the contrary is true. The issue of judge and justice first raised in chapter 18 is here seen to involve a shifting interplay of peoples and performance, with by no means all instances of justice set up on the side of Abraham and his seed. For this reason, the livestock and slaves that Abraham acquires in Egypt seem to accrue to him almost without an agency except the divine one (Gen. 12:16), whereas here we witness Abimelech both performing and announcing acts of munificence, and adding, to boot, a thousand pieces of silver to the livestock and slaves.

There is one final way in which the Gerar story diverges from the Egypt story that most vividly illustrates how carefully the latter episode has been placed in the surrounding narrative configuration. Of Pharaoh we are told that the Lord afflicted him and his household with "great plagues" (*nega'im*). The nature of these plagues is not specified, but surely the term is used to heighten the effect of foreshadowing in Genesis 12, which looks forward far more directly than does Genesis 20 to a time when Abraham's descendants, once more threatened with starvation, will sojourn in Egypt and will need God to heap plagues on Pharaoh and his people in order to obtain their release from enslavement. In Gerar, on the other hand, we are first told not of plagues but only of a death-threat by God—significantly, a threat not only to Abimelech but to his entire household, or perhaps his entire people—which, as I have indicated, aligns the story with the destruction of Sodom. Then, at the very end of the episode, it is revealed that Abimelech and his whole palace have in fact also been suffering from an affliction ever since Sarah entered the harem, an affliction of a specified character: "For the Lord had closed fast every womb in the household of Abimelech because of Sarah, Abraham's wife" (20:18). The very next words in the text—we should keep in mind that in the ancient scroll there would have been no indication of the chapter break introduced by a much later tradition—are, "and the Lord remembered Sarah as he had promised." Indeed, given the perfect tense of the verb and the reversal of the usual predicate-subject order, the actual implication of the statement, within the paratactic constraints of biblical Hebrew, is something like: But in contrast, God remembered Sarah as he had promised.

Propagation appears at the beginning of Genesis as a divinely ordained imperative for humanity. But as the moral plot of human history rapidly thickens into the most terrible twists of violence and perversion, it becomes progressively clear that propagation and survival are precarious matters, conditional, in the view of the Hebrew writers, on moral behavior. This idea is first manifested on a global scale in the Deluge story, and we have seen why the writer feels it is important to invoke the Deluge in his representation of the aftermath of Sodom. Precisely because of the biblical writer's sense of history as an arena fraught with danger, it would be too simple, too smooth, for the narrative of the founding father to proceed uninterrupted from divine promise to the initiation of the covenanted people through the birth of a son. Unusual shadows must be cast over the way to fulfillment. The first of these is biological: the extreme old age of the patriarch, and, especially, of the matriarch, which has no equivalent in any of the other annunciation type-scenes. Beyond that, the three intervening episodes of the destruction of Sodom, the act of incest between Lot and his daughters, and the sojourn in Gerar convey to us an urgent new sense of perilous history which is the thematically needed prelude to the birth of Abraham's son. As the biblical imagination conceives it, neither national existence nor the physical act of propagation itself can be taken for granted. A society that rejects the moral bonds of civilization for the instant gratification of dark urges can be swept away in a moment; the elemental desire for survival in a seemingly desolate world may drive people to desperate means, to a kind of grim parody of the primeval command to be fruitful and multiply; the very danger of illicit sexuality may blight a kingdom with sterility, until the favored man intercedes, the near violation of the stranger woman is transformed into princely reparation, and the innocent intentions of the afflicted man are publicly recognized. The historical scene Isaac is about to enter is indeed a checkered one, and he and his offspring will have troubles enough of their own, in regard to both moral performance and physical survival.

As to the larger unfolding design of biblical literature, Sodom, firmly lodged between the enunciation of the covenantal promise and its fulfillment, becomes the great monitory model, the myth of a terrible collective destiny antithetical to Israel's. The biblical writers will rarely lose sight of the ghastly possibility that Israel can turn itself into Sodom. When Isaiah, having begun his prophecy by mordantly referring to Israel as "sons" who have betrayed their father, goes on to liken the people to Sodom and Gomorrah, we are meant, I think, to recall the full tension of interplay between Genesis 19 and Genesis 17–18. Still more shockingly, when the author of Judges 19 wants to represent in the Benjaminites at Gibeah a wholly depraved society, he adopts a strategy of elaborate allusion, borrowing not only the narrative predicament of two strangers taken in by the only hospitable inhabitant of a violently hostile town but also reproducing nearly verbatim whole sequences of narratorial phrases and dialogue from Genesis 19. Here the host has but one virgin daughter to offer to the mob in place of the demanded male visitor, and so he makes up the tally of two proffered women by adding the visitor's concubine. This being a version of Sodom without divine intervention, the denouement is grimmer. The visitor is no angel in any sense of the term, and instead of striking the assailants with blindness, he thrusts his concubine out into the street where she is gang-raped all night long. At daybreak he finds her expiring on the threshold, and compounding the real act of mayhem with a symbolic one, he hacks her body into twelve pieces, which he send to the tribes of Israel in order to rally them against Benjamin. As we might expect, the writer has drawn from the Sodom story not only the grisly plot but also its principal thematic ramifications. The Gibeah story, like that of Sodom[3] is prefaced by two hospitality episodes; the lavish and finally importunate hospitality of the concubine's father to the estranged couple, and then the ill-fated hospitality of the old man—like Lot, not a native of the place but a resident alien—at Gibeah. The depravity of the town results in its destruction, not through supernatural means but in a bloody civil war (Judg. 20). And here, too, what is finally at issue is the survival of the group. Thus we have the peculiar story in Judges 21 of the tribes of Israel taking a vow not to give their daughters in marriage to the Benjaminites, which places the latter in the male equivalent of the plight of Lot's daughters, who fear "there is no man on earth to lie with us." The tribes then regret their vow, fearing that "a tribe of Israel will be cut off," and so they are compelled to devise two rather bizarre stratagems, the first a violent one, for providing the Benjaminites brides. One is not sure whether the very end of the Lot story, in which taboo copulation produces ambiguous offspring, is meant to be part of the pattern of allusion. In any case, this extraordinary instance of Sodom *redux*, where pervasive viciousness triggers an upheaval that calls a people's futurity into question, provides a fitting conclusion to the Book of Judges as an account of the chaotic period when "there was no king in Israel, each man did what was right in his own eyes."

What may be inferred from the example of Sodom about the way the various pieces, small and large, of biblical narrative fit together? The tendency of more than a century of scholarly analysis has been powerfully atomistic, encouraging us to imagine the Bible as a grand jumble of the most disparate and often contradictory materials. In strictly literary terms, this is a conclusion that simply does not hold up under a close inspection of the sundry texts and their interconnections. There are, of course, elements of overlap and incongruity between different texts; but one should not mistake every allusion or recurrence of a convention for a stammer of ancient transmission, and what is often called a "contradiction" may prove to be either the imposition of provincially modern norms of consistency or, as in the case of the sister-bride story, may be an inconsistency deemed secondary by the writer to the primary concern of thematic composition.

In the foregoing discussion, I have edged away from the term "structure" because it may suggest an architectural solidity and symmetry not entirely characteristic of biblical narrative. *Tom Jones* is a book that preeminently has a structure; I doubt if one could say the same of the Book of Genesis, not to speak of the larger narrative sequence that runs from Genesis to the end of Kings. Nevertheless, the way the Sodom episode reaches back multifariously into the Abraham narrative, and further still to the Deluge and ultimately the creation story, and forward to the future history of Israel, suggests that there is elaborate if irregular design in this large complex of stories. It might be better to think of it less as structure than as finely patterned texture, in which seemingly disparate pieces are woven together, with juxtaposed segments producing among them a pattern that will be repeated elsewhere with complicated variations.

Perhaps it could not have been otherwise for the Hebrew writers. Historical and moral reality was in their sense of it too untidy, too quirky, too precipitously changeable, to lend itself to the schematism of a highly defined structure. At the same time, there was nothing purely fortuitous, nothing intrinsically episodic, in reality: everything, however perplexing, was ultimately linked to everything else in the large movement of God's purpose through the difficult medium of history. Let me suggest that this tension between the baffling untidiness of the surface and deep design is worked out formally in the very texture of biblical narrative in the way each of its seemingly discrete units is tied in to what goes before and after. It is easy enough to admire the artistry of biblical narrative within the limits of an episode, and much keen analysis in recent years has been devoted to just that task. But it is equally important to see how the episode is purposefully woven into larger patterns of motif, symbols and themes, keywords, key phrases and plots, for otherwise we are likely to underread the individual episodes and grasp at best imperfectly the broader horizon of meaning towards which the biblical writers mean to lead us.

Summary: The Sodom Nexus in Genesis

Chapter 17   Covenantal promise of seed to Abraham (patriarchal).
Abraham laughs.
Commandment of circumcision.

Chapter 18   (a) Annunciation type-scene–promise of seed (matriarchal).
Sarah laughs.
Sarah after menopause.

bridge: "looking down" on Sodom.

(b) Covenantal promise to Abraham with moral stipulation ("to do what is right and just").

(c) Abraham bargains over Sodom and Gomorrah, expecting God to "do what is just."

Chapter 19 (a) The destruction of the Cities of the Plain.

closure: Abraham "looks down" on Sodom.

(b) Incest between Lot and his daughters.

Chapter 20 Abraham and Sarah in Gerar.

Chapter 21:1–7 The birth of Isaac.

Notes

1. I have followed out this particular type-scene in "How Convention Helps Us Read: The Case of the Bible's Annunciation Type-Scene," *Prooftexts*, 3/2 (May 1983), pp. 115–30. I first proposed the concept of type-scenes as a component of biblical narrative in *The Art of Biblical Narrative* (New York: Basic Books, 1981), ch. 3.

2. J. P. Fokkelman provides an excellent discussion on progeny and survival as organizing themes of Genesis in his article on that book in *The Harvard Literary Guide to the Bible*, eds. Robert Alter and Frank Kermode (Cambridge, MA: Harvard University Press, 1987).

3. I was first alerted to the fact that the hospitality episode of Genesis 18 is part of the pattern of allusion through an astute seminar paper by Nitza Kreichman.

The Age of Sodomitical Sin, 1607–1740

Jonathan Ned Katz

Terms, Concepts, Sodomy, Society and Time

The language and ideas of the early English colonists provide clues to their responses to licit and illicit intercourse. Analyzing the early colonists' terms and concepts provides a way into their heads, hearts and lives—a way out of our own time-bound minds. The colonists' language and modes of thought are analyzed here as tools with which they named, organized and produced their social world. Their words and ideas are seen, not simply as reflections of a particular sociohistorical structure, but as material and conceptual means by which they shaped it. Analysis reveals links between early colonial modes of speech, the thought behind the speech, and that society's organization of procreation, pleasure and desire, of production, religious salvation, and legal control.

Sin Against the "Family and Posterity": Crime Against the State

A number of early colonial documents speak of sodomy as a sin specifically against marriage, the family and procreation. In 1642, the Reverend John Rayner of Plymouth declared that sodomy should be punished by death even though it might not involve quite the same "degree of sinning against the family and posterity" as some other "capital sins of uncleanness." As a sin against the "family and posterity," sodomy was quite serious enough to warrant death. Describing the execution of William Plaine in the New Haven Colony in 1646, John Winthrop explained that Plaine, though "a married man," was guilty of sodomy in England, as well as of inciting the youth of Guilford, Connecticut, to "masturbations." Plaine's crime was "dreadful" because it "tended to the frustrating of the ordinance of marriage and the hindering the generation of mankind." In

1674, the Reverend Danforth condemned sodomy and other carnal transgressions as violations of the marriage ordinance, an institution decreed by God to quench "boiling and burning lusts."

As a sin against marriage and posterity, sodomy, in the early colonies, violated the legally established and strictly enforced social organization of procreation and family life—institutions with significantly different social functions, meanings, value and legal status from those in American in the 1980s. Understanding that marriage, family and procreation were the major productive institutions of early colonial society, we can see why sodomy, considered a threat to those institutions, was made a mortal sin and capital crime, and why that death penalty was enforced.

As a sin against marriage and the family, sodomy was also a sin against the household. The households of married couples were often the legally established places of residence for all persons, providing living space for both single and married. At least three New England colonies, Massachusetts Bay, Plymouth and Connecticut, passed laws requiring unmarried people to live in "well ordered" families, as servants or boarders. But even before such laws were passed, town officials acted to discourage persons from living outside the household of a married couple. . . .

The household of a married couple not only provided the approved abode for all, but this living arrangement was consciously intended as a means of supervising and controlling behavior. The legal enforcement of familial living suggests the difficulties facing two persons of the same sex who might have wished to set up a household. Two men were certainly discouraged from living together; two women doing so was even more unfeasible.

As a sin against the family household, sodomy was also a sin against the major unit of production. As historian John Demos summed it up in his study of the Plymouth Colony, the colonial family was "an absolutely central agency of economic production and exchange." Each family household served as the primary productive unit, and as school, place of vocational and religious training, house of correction and welfare institution. As a threat to the family and sin against production, sodomy was subversive to the economy.

As a sin against marriage and posterity, sodomy was also a sin against the legally established and enforced social organizations of procreation. Sodomy, and other forms of nonprocreative sex, were seen as fundamental threats to the reproduction and increase of the colonial population, in particular, the reproduction of badly needed new laborers. In this primitive economy, the manufacture of offspring was a major, essential branch of production, analogous to farming, which, with hunting, fishing and trading, were the dominant kinds of work.

Procreation was at this time informed by an agricultural metaphor: Sperm was "seed," a female was a "ripe" or "unripe vessel." Procreative activity was thought of as a kind of "planting," and children as a valuable crop of future producers, a particularly useful and perishable "fruit." A man's seed was spoken of as if it were scarce, limited and precious, like grain; for a man to "spill," "spend" or "waste" his seed in any form of nonreproductive sex was, in this necessarily frugal economy, analogous to wasting or destroying the grain from which new crops would grow and on which survival depended. In this agricultural economy, a "husband" was not only the partner of a wife, but also usually a "husbandman" or farmer, as well as one who husbanded his resources, spermatic as well as productive. A recent study indicates that in the colonies, human sexual activity resulting in conception (as measured by the recorded months of birth) followed an agricultural cycle. The "planting" of the early settlements on the shores of America involved the implanting of sperm, the fertilization of females and the procreation of new planters, as much as it did the planting of crops.

This was a period of extreme labor scarcity and of primitive technology; new producers were valued for their labor, labor power and as a basic means of production. The manufacture of a large number of offspring was encouraged to supply the labor-intensive economy, and the colonial American birth rate was soon higher than any in Europe. The high birth rate of the early American colonists is often mentioned by historians. But this fecundity is not often linked to a specific sociohistorical mode of procreation, a particular, institutional organization of intensive baby-making, a social system with strict negative sanctions against nonprocreative sex. Maximized procreation in the early colonies was connected closely with survival—in a way that baby production is not in present-day America.

. . .

The legally enforced institutions of marriage and family were also the means by which male owners of private property in land, houses, implements and agricultural product transferred this property to their children. Sodomy, as an act against marriage and the family, was also an act against the system of property inheritance. The function of colonial marriage and family as a means of property transfer is strikingly different from the function of these institutions in present-day America. Now, if anything is passed from parents to children, it is usually property in consumption goods and money, not in the basic means of work. In the early colonies, that inheritance passed from fathers to their children was usually land, the major means of economic production necessary for family existence. Sodomy, as a sin against family and marriage, was a sin against the basic institution of private property. . . .

"Buggery" in England

The first English civil statute to criminalize "buggery" drew on French law and English popular use of the word "buggery" for the act clerics usually called "sodomy." The English word "buggery" derived from the French words *bougre* and *bougrerie*, referring, respectively, to heretics and heresy and, it seems, usurers and usury. In the 1200s, it was said the French then called usurers *bougres*.

English popular sexual folklore also associated sodomy with usury and, specifically, with Italians from Lombardy. As early as 1376, the English Parliament, expressing old complaints of London traders against these Italians, requested that

> all the Lombards who practice no profession than that of Moneychanger quit this land as soon as possible; given that wicked Usury and all underhanded strategems are devised and maintained by them. . . . [These Lombard moneychangers] are of no use except to do evil: given that some among them who are considered Lombards are Jews, Saracens [Moslems], and private Spies; and have lately practiced in this land a very horrible vice which should not be named. By which the Kingdom cannot fail shortly to be destroyed, if stiff punishment be not speedily ordained for it. . . .

That early association between Lombards and unnameable "vice" became part of English sexual folklore; it was repeated 157 years later in the English "buggery" law of 1533.

That English law was the first civil statute of the country to make a secular crime of an act which, up to then, had been only an infraction of church law. The "buggery" law of 1533 was passed as one legal step in that Reformation by which Henry VIII, as head of the English state, expropriated the Roman Catholic Church's large landholdings, and the Italian Church's monopoly of the means of moral judgment and spiritual salvation.

In 1529, Henry, with the Crown's economic needs in mind, was already contemplating the expropriation of the Roman Catholic Church's monasteries in England. In 1531, he declared himself the head of the Catholic Church in England, an act of religious devotion ensuring that large revenues no longer needed to be paid to the Roman pope. The "buggery" law of 1533 was one of the first in a series of Reformation acts cutting the English Church off from the Italian. Three years later, Henry VIII's investigators accused some of the Catholic monasteries in England of being centers of "manifest sin, vicious carnal, and abominable living." Henry used these charges to convince Parliament to allow him to actually expropriate these monasteries. Part of the church land confiscated was later redistributed to a new class of landowners and commercial farmers, who thus owed title to their property, and their allegiance to the king.

Until 1533 in England, "sodomy" was a sin, judged and punished by ecclesiastical authorities. Only in 1533 did "buggery" become a crime, to be punished by civil courts—by death and loss of property, with, significantly, no exception made for "clergy."

The first English "buggery" law stated that as there was no adequately severe punishment provided in civil statute "for the detestable and abominable Vice of Buggery committed with mankind or beast," it might therefore please the king, his spiritual and temporal Lords and the Parliamentary Commons, to make the offense a "felony"—a crime graver than a "misdemeanor." Offenders under the new law were to suffer death and such "losses and penalties of their goods, chattels, debts, lands, tenements," and other transferable property, as felons were accustomed to under common law. The convicted party was to suffer the dispossession of estate and death, with no appeal to that ritual called "benefit of clergy," by which persons in holy orders were exempted from the usual penalties of the criminal law, and were subjected to less harsh church proceedings.

Henry VIII's "buggery" law thus originated in the political and economic struggles of church and state. The terminological change in England from "sodomy" as sin to "buggery" as crime expressed an increasing secularization of power and control. The word "sodomy" evoked Sodom and Gomorrah, the Bible, theology, and God's earthly representatives. "Buggery" was a term adopted by the Crown from the language of the people, a popular, secular word, distinguished from "sodomy," the word of God as retailed by the clergy. The terminological change from "sodomy" to "buggery" thus expressed a change in the balance of political and economic power between church and state. The conceptual change from sin to sin-crime similarly expressed, in the realm of ideas, a change in the property relations of Roman pope and English king.

In all the early American colonies, as in England, the sin of sodomy was made one of the highest crimes, penalized by death. The Massachusetts Bay code (1641) for example, provided death for heresy, witchcraft, blasphemy, three varieties of murder, bestiality, man lying with man as with a woman, adultery, male "carnal copulation" with a "woman-child" under ten years, male rape of a married or engaged female, male rape of a single female over ten, the stealing of a servant, false witness with intent to take a life, and treason. Other laws provided death for such crimes as idolatry, kidnapping, arson, robbery, and children over sixteen cursing, smiting or rebelling against their parents. The unique New Haven law of 1656 provided death for male-female anal intercourse, incitement to masturbation, and undefined acts of women "against nature."

The moral-theological-legal concept of sodomy as a sin-crime was openly expressed in early colonial laws in the frequent use of evaluative terms, usually of biblical origin. A "detestable and abominable Vice" was the phrase characterizing "buggery" in the English law operative in the southern colonies. Sodomy was explicitly called an "unnatural sin" in the Pennsylvania law of 1683; sodomy was among the "Offenses against God" in the East New Jersey law of the same year.

Early colonial statutes overtly expressed religious judgments made covert in the laws of later, ostensibly secular periods. This early expression in civil law of religious morality, and the universal death penalty for sodomy operative in all the colonies, and several times carried out, reflected clerics' monopoly of otherworld connections, their this-world power. But the ministers' power was not unlimited.

In practice, colonial ministers defined sodomy more broadly than colonial magistrates; the ministers included a greater variety of acts under the nomenclature of "sodomy." And the ministers' more inclusive definition was not enacted into law by the magistrates. A conflict over the definition of sodomy existed in the early colonies between religious and civil authorities. But even the magistrates' narrower, operative definition was derived directly, often even word for word, from the Old Testament. Though ministers could not be magistrates, and the opinions of the two groups might differ, close working relations generally existed between them; churchmen were asked to help define legal categories and penalties. Men of God were the chief ideologists, religion the dominant ideology. This all-pervasive sway of God contrasts with America of the late 1800s, in which medical men and "science" competed for influence with legal authorities and their ideas.

The sin of sodomy was occasionally spoken of as having the ability to "infect." Referring to an outbreak of sodomy, bestiality, adultery and fornication in 1642, William Bradford warned that "one wicked person may infect the many." In 1677, a witness in the sodomy trial of Nicholas Sension reported being worried about Sension's attempted sodomy "infecting the rising generation." Although the word "infect" did already refer to physical disease, it also referred to a metaphorical, moral contagion, and it is not clear in the documents cited whether the term was used in one or the other (or both) senses. In any case, the idea of sodomy and other "sexual perversions" as actual diseases became the dominant concept only with the rise to power of professional physicians of the mind in the late 1800s, and the publicity given their medical definition of "homosexuality" in the 1920s and thirties.

Colonial sodomy was not a disease, and no one thought of consulting a doctor about it. (The Reverend Wigglesworth did, however, consult a doctor about an imagined venereal ailment seemingly inspired by sodomitical guilt). In the early colonies, as sin and crime, sodomy might be prosecuted, charged, confessed, admitted, denied, judged, proved, punished, repented or affirmed; it was not "treated" or "cured." As sin, sodomy was an act "committed" or not "committed," an act (and inclination) for which one was "guilty" or "not guilty," ashamed or unashamed. As sin, the act of sodomy might be taught by "bad" example, but no one thought (as did late-Victorian doctors) of distinguishing between "acquired" sodomy and "congenital." A sodomitical impulse was an inherent potential of all fallen male descendants of Eve and Adam. Only in the twentieth century would the doctors' allegedly objective and scientific concept of "homosexuality" hide the negative value judgment explicit in the colonial concept of sodomy as sin.

In the early colonies, sodomy included feeling as well as act. But sodomy was not essentially psychological; it was not a "psychosexual disturbance," "mental illness," "fixation of emotional development" nor the symptom of such, as "homosexuality" was perceived in the twentieth century. Colonial sodomy had no individual psychological "etiology." As sin, sodomy was said to originate in the unfortunate propensity of all human beings to follow the tempting immoral example. Since sodomitical and other lustful inclinations were universal, it was not their subjective "cause," but the objective stimulus to action that was of prime concern. "Sodomy," said Edward Coke, was "brought into" England by corrupt Italians. "Sodomy," suggested William Bradford, was brought into New England by "untoward servants." Sodomy, testified a witness at a Connecticut trial of 1677, was a "trade" which a sodomitical colonist had "taken up"—at school. Colonial sodomy, an inborn impulse and an act one learned, was like other nasty habits.

Only with the institutionalization of Enlightenment ideas after the American Revolution did the earlier, direct, moral-theological condemnation of sodomy begin to give way to the legal condemnation of sodomy as "crime against nature," a "nature" alleged to determine sodomy's objective and moral character. Only in the late 1700s would the term "sodomy" be superseded by the phrase "crime against nature." That secularization of thought in the late 1700s—the competition of a new legal philosophy of "natural rights" with the old theological morality of natural sin—reflected the relative loss of power of the clergy, the relative gain in power of lawyers. By the late 1700s, men of the bar were replacing men of the cloth as the major ideologists of a more fully developed commercial society. In the late 1700s, the institutionalizing of a new legal ideology ("constitutionalism") and a new interpretation of "natural law" ("natural rights" and the "crime against nature"), were linked to the rise of lawyers and a powerful commercial class.

Although the dominant early colonial ideology was theological, several kinds of evidence disprove the operation of a biblical or ecclesiastical determinism. A biblical death penalty does not "explain" the legal enactment of that penalty, or its enforcement. The usual failure of New England legislators to enact St. Paul's death penalty for women who changed the "natural use" (Romans 1:26: ". . . God gave them up unto vile affections: for even their women did change the natural use into that which is against nature") is one example of the colonists' selectivity in regard to New Testament injunction. The lawmakers' inclusion in their sodomy statutes of clauses concerning force and age were also colonial emendations of the absolute Old Testament mandate of death for both men who lay with each other as they lay with women (Leviticus 20:13). The colonists' usual failure to carry out the statutory death penalty for "adultery" is another example of their failure to practice Old Testament precept. And the usual early colonial death penalty for rape also had only ambiguous biblical sanction.

Speakable Sodomy

In this period, among these Christians, sodomy was not a secret, not unspoken, not unnamed. Sodomy, raised to capital status, was also raised to a relatively high degree of public consciousness. From almost the first years of English settlement on this continent, sodomy was publicly named as one of the major crimes against the state, one of the few infractions meriting death, one of those acts most meriting public naming. This is stressed because of our present tendency to attribute to seventeenth-century Puritans ideas and values specific to nineteenth-century Victorians—those who did make sodomy "unspeakable."

Political Sodomy

There was no question in the early colonies that sodomy, and other forms of nonreproductive and reproductive copulation were of pressing civil concern. The association of procreation with social survival made it a clear matter of political interest, legislative enactment and judicial judgment. However, though sodomy, bestiality, rape and adultery might often be placed next to each other on early colonial lists of capital crimes, there was usually no explicit emphasis on their carnal character; they were not called lust crimes. There was no category of legal infractions known as "sex crimes." In only one law (that of Rhode Island, 1647) were sodomy, bestiality, rape, adultery and fornication grouped together in a legal provision "Touching Whoremongers." The early colonists believed that a pervasive lust needed to be strictly regulated; but "sexuality" was not yet isolated as a separate entity, an individual problem. Sodomy was not a "sexual" as opposed to a "social" infraction; as carnal, sodomy was a social offense, one of many.

In contrast, the mid-twentieth-century medical concept of "homosexuality" made "sexuality" essential. "Homosexuality" was "sexual" not "social"; "personal" not "political"; "private" not "public"; an "individual problem," not a "social issue." Those modern medical oppositions did not inform the early colonists' concept of sodomy; they would not have understood the shock caused in 1969 by the link proclaimed in the title of Kate Millett's *Sexual Politics*. A colonial politics of lust was assumed.

Sodom and Sodomy

In his sermon, the "Cry of Sodom," published in 1674, the Reverend Samuel Danforth drew an explicit parallel between the city of Sodom and the settlements of New England. Danforth warned New Englanders that their failure to punish by death such sins as sodomy and bestiality would bring God's vengeance on everyone. The early colonists lived with an ever-present fear that an angry God would punish their entire society for the sins of some inhabitants. All colonists were thought of as mutually dependent, not as autonomous individuals. The behavior of one affected the fate of all. Rooting out sin was a means of self-preservation, maintained William Bradford in his analysis of an outbreak, in 1642, of sodomy, and other such "wickedness."

In the early colonies, the term and concept "sodomy" had connotations that they do not generally have for present-day Americans. For the colonists struggling to survive in the wilderness, the word "sodomy," no doubt, evoked the destruction of Sodom and Gomorrah, as much or more than illicit sex. For those early settlers perched precariously on the edge of a hostile continent, the term "sodomy" provoked thoughts of Sodom, that archetypal settlement destroyed for sin. Living from day to day with the threat of social dissolution, the early colonists no doubt felt a special kinship with that particular ancient city.

The early colonists found themselves at the mercy of natural, life-threatening forces which, personified as "God," seemed angry, vengeful and punishing. The biblical Sodom and Gomorrah story likewise reflected an era of social development in which natural disasters were seen as God's punishment for human moral error. Inhabited by a vindictive God, the early Puritan universe also included an active, malicious Devil, an often-evoked hell, and occasional malevolent witches. Early colonial lists of capital crimes included both sodomy and witchcraft. Only as colonial society became more secure, the survival and reproduction of the colonial labor force more assured, did sodomy gradually lose its previous, direct association with Sodom and social cataclysm. . . .

"Sodomy" or "Sodomite"; Act or Person

Not until the 1890s do American documents mention a person called "a homosexual" or "a lesbian." Not until the 1920s does "a homosexual" or "a lesbian" person become fairly common in American literature.

Though in the early colonies there was much mention of an act called "sodomy," rarely do we read in that era's documents of a person called a "sodomite," an individual named after the act. The term "Sodomites" was used in the early colonies to refer to Sodom's sinful citizens and their whole array of vices, but rarely to refer to persons guilty specifically and only of sodomy.

The early English settlers, following the Bible, did refer to "men lying with men as with a woman" and to women changing the "natural use" into that which is "against nature." But such persons' acts were not spoken of as transforming them into "a man-who-lies-with-men," or "a woman-who-changes-the-natural-use." Similarly, though American documents of this early period often referred to the act of "buggery" (meaning, usually, bestiality, and, sometimes, sodomy), no American reference has been found to a person called a "buggerer."

In early New England, sodomitical sinners were not thought of as differing in their essential natures from Puritan saints. All persons' "cursed Natures" inclined them to every variety of wickedness—the "holiest man hath as vile and filthy a Nature, as the Sodomites," said Reverend Danforth in 1674. Even the most outwardly respectable Puritan might be inwardly guilty of "heart sodomy" or "heart buggery"—as well as "heart whoredom," "heart blasphemy" and "heart drunkenness"—warned Reverend Shepard in 1641. No Puritan was perfectly pure. Only a deep faith in God distinguished the saved from the damned; both were equally corrupted by "original sin," both were potential committers of sodomy—and other sins. In today's terms, original sin was "normal," not "deviant."

The Puritans did not punish sodomitical sinners because they were "deviant," "different," "abnormal" or a "minority." As sinners, committers of sodomy belonged to the Puritan majority. Those graced by faith and salvation were the minority. Given this social situation, the idea of a "sodomitical minority" would have made no sense to the early settlers. In a society in which an elite few were the "elect," and the many were the damned, no democratic political ideology had yet influenced the social response to carnal intercourse. For the Puritans the numbers of persons who performed certain numbers of acts had no bearing on those acts' "naturalness" or "unnaturalness." An absolute, qualitative, procreative standard determined what was considered "natural," not a quantitative norm. It is anachronistic to speak of a "gay," "homosexual," or even a "sodomitical minority" as if it existed for the early colonists. Projecting modern concepts on the past prevents us from understanding those settlers' responses to copulation.

The detestable committer of sodomy was not thought of as a unique, distinct character type, a sodomitical being. The enactor of sodomy was perceived as kissing cousin of, and partner in sin to, those other major colonial malefactors—the committers of treason, murder, witchcraft, arson, idolatry, blasphemy, rape, bestiality, adultery, those who stole indentured servants, and those who smote their parents—those most abominable of sinners, penalized by death.

In the early colonies, one's work was of the essence, not some essential character trait, not one's "person." While good works definitely did not determine a Puritan's preordained salvation, such works were the earthly evidence, a present, reassuring sign, of an individual's future place in heaven. The political economy of the early colonies was not composed of "rugged individuals," "single entrepreneurs," or "self-made men." Nor was a prominent virtue "self-reliance" or a prominent activity "self-help." Self-annihilation, not self-aggrandizement, was the Puritan ideal. The family, not the individual, was the primary productive unit. This society was composed of a community-conscious population whose shared, precarious condition of life in the wilderness produced the sure knowledge that the survival of each depended on the effort of all, a population knowing in their bones that social survival was a communal work. Under such primitive conditions of economic cooperation no great emphasis was placed on the "individual." The focus was not on the "sodomite," but on "sodomy," and other sinful acts.

Sinful Feelings, Sinful Acts

The documents of the early colonial era, especially those of Puritan origin, vividly evoke a biblically defined universe of sinful emotions and sinful acts. These documents refer to "burning lusts, set on fire of hell," "boiling lusts," "unnatural lusts," "carnal lusts," "filthy lusts" and "infamous passions." To be sure, colonial laws and legal cases document the penalty for, and punishment of, only those caught in overt acts. But that was no doubt due to the technical difficulty of capturing, jailing, prosecuting, proving and executing illicit lust. Such wayward desire was not reported to the authorities. It might, however, be secretly confessed to one's diary—in code—as proof to God, and to oneself, of one's private self-chastisement, moral struggle and atonement. The Reverend Michael Wigglesworth's journal, written partly in code in the 1650s, recorded that "too much doting affection" for his male pupils (at Harvard) stimulated him to "filthy lust." But the possession of such immoderate affection, such dirty emotional secrets, made him not a "sodomite," but simply a "sinner."

Neither Wigglesworth nor any other known early colonial writer referred to "sodomitical lust," an emotion specific to sodomy. There was no sodom-eroticism. In the early colonies there was "sensual lust." But no special sodomitical desire opposed an "other," "different" or "opposite" lust. No "homoerotic" feeling for a "same sex" opposed a "heteroerotic" feeling for a "different sex," no "homosexual" emotion opposed a "heterosexual." "Filthy lusts" and "infamous passions" included a variety of feelings associated with fornication, adultery and a variety of other sins, not just sodomy, and not just sexual. The "lust" of early evangelical Puritans did not refer just to the erotic; they condemned all forms of lusting, desiring, willing and wanting, all self-assertion, playfulness and enjoyment. Thomas Shepard, for example, recalled his youthful sins of "lust and pride and gaming and bowling and drinking." Cotton Mather sought to "become a Man dead unto this World; crucified unto all Worldly Enjoyments." Michael Wigglesworth referred to his "carnal lusts," thus implicitly distinguishing between fleshly and other lusts. Wigglesworth prayed to God for "power over my still prevailing lusts, principally pride and sensuality, want of love to thee and fervent desires after communion with thee."

Lusts for the early Puritans were multiple and various. Sensual lust was only one variety of those passions and appetites condemned as sinful; only in renouncing human desire, in doing "God's will" and "God's work" was one demonstrating one's faith and pursuing a relatively sinless path. Lusting was a particularly intense form of desiring, and carnal lust was a variety of desiring requiring special legal controls. But the Puritans' condemnation of carnal lust was secondary to their condemnation of desire in general. Sodomy was punished primarily as socially destructive, only secondarily as a specifically carnal crime.

The original Puritans did not focus repressively on the carnal in the same single-minded way as late-Victorian doctors, for example, focused on "sexuality." Lust was not equated with "sexuality," a thing cordoned off, a secret underworld of acts, a secret unconscious world of the mind. Carnal lusts and carnal acts existed in the everyday, ordinary Puritan universe; concupiscence was not relegated to a hidden erotic, exotic ghetto. The term and concept "sexuality," an entity which is sex, was a Victorian, not a Puritan, invention. Our contemporary use of "Puritanism" to refer to a specifically sexual repression was an invention of the anti-Victorians of the early twentieth century.

The Puritans' focus on desiring and doing, on subjective feeling and objective act, reflected a society in which mental and manual activity was not completely divided, and organized in essentially different ways. Even the major colonial producer of ideas, the minister, worked at all those tasks necessary for survival, tasks as much manual as mental. Inner feeling was not radically alienated from overt act; no greater reality and value were assigned to act; feeling was as important and "real" as act. (Both act and feeling, however, alienated from the human, were experienced as God's doing.) Human activity was not yet divided and organized into waged acts called "labor," nonwaged acts called "feeling."

Man with Man, Woman with Woman

. . . Compared to the Victorians, the early colonists placed relatively little explicit emphasis on the idea of sexual "sameness" and "difference." The late-Victorian concepts of "homo-" and "heterosexuality," stressing a "same-sex"/"different-sex" eroticism, were foreign to the early settlers.

As we have seen, the basic distinction between the early colonial concept of sodomy and of licit copulation was that between procreative and nonprocreative. That distinction did not refer primarily to the anatomical similarity and dissimilarity of sexual actors; it applied equally to acts of females with males. Under that procreative standard, it was not the physiological "sameness" of actors that made sodomy seem like such a threat; sodomy was not punished because it violated boundaries of sexual "difference," standards of "masculinity" and "femininity."

Anal intercourse of males with males or males with females, like masturbation, the intercourse of women or men with animals, and adult males with prepubescent girls, were sins because they were nonreproductive. Sexual intercourse of human males with female beasts was condemned as not properly procreative; such relations were thought to result, possibly, in the birth of deformed, part human, part bestial creatures. The "adultery" of a male, either married *or single*, with a married or engaged female, as well as the rape of a female by a male were sins because, as violations of the legally established and strictly enforced social mode of procreation, they were seen as socially disruptive and threats to colonial survival. . . .

Early Colonial Patriarchy

The early colonists did sometimes make emphatic distinctions between those activities appropriate exclusively for women or men. In the spheres of church and state, preaching, legislating, judging and voting were exclusively men's work. Within those spheres a sharp sexual division of activity existed, a strict distinction between acts proper for women or men. Anne Hutchinson's attempt to preach is the most famous example of the harsh response to women's violation of men's control of ministerial activity. . . .

Although males dominated the religious and political spheres of early colonial patriarchy, within those spheres differences did exist in the activities, property and power of men. Although religious, political, legislative and judicial posts were limited to men, those positions were effectively limited to a few males. Though property distribution varied widely in different colonies, its distribution was such that those men with the most wealth had the most power. A division between classes intersected that between women and men, so that certain religious and political activities then closed to women were also effectively closed to most men. In the context of early colonial agricultural production, that activity prohibited to women and allowed to some men, was of relatively little importance compared to the necessary work of both sexes.

Within the sphere of domestic agricultural production, the male was spoken of as "head" of the household and family, the husband as "governor" of the wife, and the "patriarchs" of the Old Testament might be cited as the models for males in a society which was, in its own time, called "patriarchal." But the functional importance of the productive and procreative work of women undermined, to some degree, the sexual division of power favoring men. The essential, valued activity of women in production and procreation modified the character of early colonial patriarchy. Within the basic unit of production, the family household, women and men cooperated in similarly organized and essential work. There did exist a sexual division of work, legal power and social status within the family and out. But no distinction then existed between wage-work and nonwaged housework, between the basic organization of women's work and men's work. The cooperative mode of early colonial work resulted in much less stress on male-female difference than was later typical of middle-class Victorians, with their separate and differently organized male and female spheres. . . .

The Present Usefulness of the Early Colonial Past

In America in the 1980s, a Bible-based morality is often invoked as the right-wing rationale for a mean-spirited antihomosexuality. Yet that present antihomosexuality is determined, I think, not by an old text or value system, but by those objective economic changes transforming traditional relationships between women and men, parents and children. Concern about the effect on "the family" and children of a more "tolerant" social response to "homosexuality" informs present legal decisions and expressions of anxiety. But those modern consumers, "children," and that modern consumer unit, "the family," are qualitatively different from their early colonial counterparts. Present concern about "the family" has different social origins and implications from the early colonists' concern to preserve their "family." The "sodomy" laws remaining on the books in the 1980s, and the harrassment, arrests, trials and imprisonments based upon them, may have a certain ambiguous continuity with the earliest colonial American sodomy laws and cases. Yet those colonial statutes and prosecutions do not explain the present existence of sodomy laws and prosecutions. Today's legislators who allow old sodomy laws to exist, and those officials who prosecute homosexuals, reproduce a version of the past in the present. Unless we believe that past conditions act to reproduce themselves, unless we in the present are mechanically determined by the past, we need to explain present conditions by the group interests now served by the selective reproduction of the past.

The early colonists' response to sodomy as mortal sin and high crime differs greatly from twentieth-century Americans' response to "homosexuality" as either an individual "disease" to be "cured," a "problem" to be "pitied," a "life-style" to be "purchased," or as simply one way of feeling, acting and being human. To be sure, homosexuals are still sometimes physically beaten, even put to death (murdered, not executed). Homosexuals are now sometimes provoked to murderous hate, the destruction of self or others. Homosexuals are still encouraged to acts of public self-denial, each a little death. Fear and hatred of homosexuals, active, institutionalized antihomosexuality are, of course, still with us. But present historical forms of antihomosexuality are not explained by early colonial antisodomy. Present antihomosexuality is not causally linked to that colonial call for death.

Despite the much-touted, greatly exaggerated "sexual revolution," many of us today still struggle against a lingering "puritanism." But our contemporary "puritanism" differs basically from that original "Puritanism" documented here. It seems doubtful if any direct connections can be discovered between the early Puritan era and our own. Why then research and analyze that old, essentially superseded historical form of sex? If each form of sexuality is historically specific, what can the old forms tell us about our own society and lives?

One lesson of this history, I think, is precisely that the distant past has only a negative, contrasting relation to the present; our own contemporary social organization of sex is as historically specific as past social-sexual forms. Studying the past, seeing the essential differences between past and present social forms of sex, we may gain a fresh perspective on our own sex as socially made, not naturally given. Comparing past and present, we are usefully distanced from that sexuality whose specific social forms many of us, until recently, took for granted as "psychological," "biological," "natural" or "unnatural." Perceiving our own sex and affection as a historical, socially constructed form we better understand the possibility of reconstructing it. Understanding the different ways sodomy and other forms of sex were socially organized in the early colonies can help us question our own quite different historical organization of eroticism and intimacy.

Arab Civilization and Male Love

Marc Daniel,
Translated by Winston Leyland

Arab Customs Before Muhammad

The Arab tribes of Muhammad's time cut a sorry figure in comparison with the ancient and brilliant civilizations of the Near East, Egypt, Persia, India and the solid cultural traditions of Latinized northern Africa and Spain. Apart from a few commercial centers, such as Mecca and Medina, the Arabian peninsula was populated only with Bedouin nomads who lived by seasonal pastures, by raids and pillage, and whose cultural level was very rudimentary. There existed no major religion, comparable to the Syrian and Mesopotamian cults, which could at least cement a moral unity. The tribes were opposed to each other by ancestral feuds; they raided each other and kept the country in a permanent state of anarchy.

However, Arab poetry and folklore had existed from a very remote period, and has been transmitted to the present day partly by means of much later traditions.

What information do we possess on homosexuality in primitive Arabia? There is no doubt that boy-love and sexual inversion were known to the Arabs well before Muhammad. But from what we can ascertain, this particular form of love had no literary expression, and did not hold a position of importance in the erotic conceptualizations of the tribes. As for homosexuality, far from being honored as a divine manifestation, as it was in ancient Mesopotamia and in many other civilizations, it was rather considered a subject for ridicule.

In proof of this let me cite the following proverbs which were used by the different tribes to taunt each other. They have been handed down to us by classical Arab writers:

I swear, the seas and the deserts are smaller than the asses of the
Benū Laqīt! [a Bedouin tribe—TR.]. They are the most infamous of all
horsemen, the vilest of those who walk on foot.[1]

And a second one:

If a native of Kinda, this queer with curled hair, dresses for the occasion,
he does so with rich fabric, fancy shoes, a cloak or a necklace.[2]

The Quraysh tribe, to which Muhammad belonged, included many passive homosexuals—so numerous that they were proverbial.[3] At Mecca
"debauchery was flaunted with great impudence under the tent. Everything
encouraged it: the crowds of strangers and slaves, the frequent travels of
the merchants."[4] Moreover, the allusions of Muhammad himself in the
Qurʾān (often spelt "Koran") prove that homosexuality was well known
among the Arabs of his time.

As I mentioned earlier, pre-Muslim Arab literature, insofar as it is known
to us, makes no mention of this kind of love. The *muʿallakat*—those
"jewels" of Arab desert poetry—as well as the writings of the great pre-
Islamic poet Imruʾad-Qays (died circa 550) and those of his contemporaries,
deal mostly with three themes in which the sclerotic future is already being
prophesied: (1) evocations of abandoned desert encampments and of the
woman who has granted her favors to the poet; (2) accounts of travel,
hunts and wars; (3) eulogies and satires on people living or dead. Such
are the limits of the *qasīda*, a traditional form of Arab poetry, which,
much later, will evoke the sarcasms of "avant-garde" poets at the court of
Baghdad. An erotic element was certainly present, but it was heterosexual
only and was expressed in a very stereotyped form which encouraged
prosodic acrobatics more than sincerity of inspiration.[5]

The Qurʾān and Homosexuality

What nothing up to that time had succeeded in creating—the religious,
political and moral unity of the Arab tribes—the preaching of Muhammad
accomplished in twenty-two years, from 610 to 632, the year of his death.
Such a task could only be accomplished at the price of extreme tension in
all the moral resources of the country. It is therefore particularly important
for this study to determine what role homosexuality played in the message
of the Prophet and in subsequent Islamic tradition.

The Qurʾān, "the uncreated word of an uncreated God," is not a methodical treatise or a code of law in the modern sense of those terms. It includes all that, and many other things besides. The teachings of Muhammad on all kinds of subjects are mixed together, sometimes almost in contradiction to one another, and centuries of glosses and commentaries have not always succeeded in clearing up all the difficulties.

Muhammad shared the contempt of his countrymen towards homosexuals, thought of as "women" and consequently inferior. Moreover, he had been introduced to Jewish teachings by the Jews of Medina and knew the story of Sodom, as the Bible and the Talmud tell it, with the divine condemnation of homosexuality that is traditionally implied. This is the reason why Muhammad recounts the story several times in his teachings,[6] recalling that it was a shame for a man "to take advantage of men in place of women to assuage his carnal appetites."

However, this condemnation of homosexuality by Muhammad in no way parallels the precision and vehemence of the Bible or the Fathers of the Christian Church. One also cannot help pointing out that the presence of young boys alongside the beautiful, eternally seductive *houris* (maidens) in the Paradise promised to believers, implies, at the very least, a certain concession to the listeners of the Prophet.[7] It was undoubtedly only a minor problem in the eyes of the Prophet, since at no time did he cite homosexual practices in the list of grave sins which offend God. Muslim commentators later took advantage of the relative indifference of Muhammad on this point.[8]

Once in contact with societies more favorable to boy-love, Islam lost no time in finding theologians skillful at getting around the obstacles presented by the Qur'ān's condemnation. Orthodox traditionalists (the Sunnites) certainly remained obedient to the Qur'ān's condemnation, and even "improved" on it. The fourteenth-century writer an-Nuwairī, in his famous collection titled *Nihāyat al-Arab*, cited a great many texts with such an interpretation.[9] Among these figures especially a *hadīth* (a proverb attributed to Muhammad) according to which "God pays no attention to a man who has slept with a man, nor to a woman who has slept with a woman." To be sure, the commentator mentions that when the indignant angels went to God to ask that he annihilate these accursed ones (homosexuals), He answered them: "I am just and nothing escapes me." According to a Muslim tradition that an-Nuwairī also recounts, "sodomites" will be punished in hell by a truly Dantesque torture: they will be locked up in chests pierced by enormous iron nails reddened with fire. Another, less ferocious version forbids Paradise for a thousand years to those who have embraced a boy, and for five thousand years to those who have slept with him.

As for the fate of Sodom and Gomorrah, it is better not to joke about it: one day as two homosexuals were passing near the Dead Sea, one of them said to the other, "The town of our brethren stood here"; immediately a huge wave arose and swallowed both of them. One might wonder if a similar tragic fate was reserved for the character in the *Thousand and One Nights* who recited this irreverent poem:

> The present age recalls the good old days
> when Lot, the ancestor of Abraham lived.
> In his town of Sodom he lodged angels
> and gave to the crowd his daughters in exchange.
> His wife hindered him. God got rid of her
> By changing her suddenly into a big block of salt.[10]

As a general rule these theological opinions did not extend so far as to require bodily punishments for homosexuals. But there exists a *hadīth*, related by Assem ben Amr, recommending that "those who practice passive as well as active sodomy" be stoned. But the actual influence of this *hadīth* was negligible.[11]

If one is to believe the chronicle, shortly after the death of the Prophet, Caliph Abu Bakr, father-in-law and first successor of Muhammad, caused to be burned alive a certain Chuyā ben Warka al-Assadī, guilty of "having used his anus like the sexual organ of a woman."[12] But according to several historians, punishment by fire was not traditional in Islam and they place the authenticity of the anecdote in doubt.

Despite all this, the weight of pre-Islamic traditions counted much more than the Qurʾān's condemnation. From the tenth century on they began to find "accommodations with heaven" in order to legitimate homosexual love: namely, authorization for sexual intercourse with non-Muslim males and with slaves, a comparison of boy-love with love of God. . . .[13] In the tenth century it was openly admitted that this was not a crime deserving of a definite punishment, and that the *qādī* (judge) should be able to judge it freely.[14] Theologians thought that homosexuality did not deserve any bodily punishment, by reason of the following *hadīth*: "Muslim blood can only be shed legally because of adultery (*zinā*), denial of faith (*kufr*) or homocide."[15]

The true reason for this indulgent attitude is that in reality the "crime" or "sin" of homosexuality did not fit into the mental categories of Islam. Its condemnation by Judaism and Christianity is explained by the fact that these two religions, faced with manifestations of the sexual instinct in their midst, adopted a restrictive and hostile approach, which finally resulted in that puritanism not monopolized by seventeenth- and nineteenth-century

England. There was nothing quite similar in the Muslim world. The Qurʾān itself is quite open to the idea of sexual pleasure and tradition accentuated this tendency even more: "Each time that you make love, you perform a meritorious act before God" says a famous *hadīth*.[16]

In Muslim teaching the lawfulness of sexual pleasure was never connected with procreation, as it was by the Christians. On the contrary, sexual pleasure was viewed as a precursor of the joys of Paradise, since it is explicitly stated by the Prophet that believers will be able to make love throughout eternity.[17] Logical reasons for forbidding homosexuality on moral grounds are therefore absent. It's easy to understand why Muslim theologians are never in agreement among themselves whether or not to include homosexuality as part of their definition of the sin called *zinā*—adultery in the Muslim sense of the word.[18]

All of this explains why Muslim penal proceedings are especially mild regarding infractions of sexual morality. Rather than punishing the guilty, the law prefers protecting the innocent against wrong accusations, and totally surrounds condemnation with a thicket of conditions very difficult to meet: four witnesses are required, all Muslim, of male sex, freemen, adult and responsible, who themselves saw the illicit act and can certify that with their own eyes they saw the male organ inside the female organ "like a brush in a jar of liquid makeup."[19] Any perjury exposes the bearer to the gravest penalties, and the benefit of doubt is always in favor of the accused. This is a far cry from the "civilized" procedure of eighteenth-century France, during which period the jurist Jousse thought that for sodomy "even the attempt must be punished by death" and that for punishment it is not necessary for the *corpus delicti* to be "established by experts."[20]

In short, all of classical Arab civilization was immersed in an atmosphere of eroticism which would have rendered useless serious attempts at preventing any form of sexual pleasure. Whatever the theoretical condemnation (and even *that* was little emphasized) leveled against homosexuality by the Qurʾān, the force of events soon caused in the Arab world a vast flowering of homosexual love under all its forms.

Nonetheless—and this fact is important for the historian of sexual customs—the Qurʾān's prohibition of homosexuality definitely made it impossible in Muslim countries to resurrect the homoerotic cults of the Ancient World. Syria or Mesopotamia would never again see homosexual priests, sacred prostitutes, ritual transvestites—at least as an official cult. It was no longer possible to make an open defense of boy-love, as had been done previously in Athens and Ionia. Such a fact could not fail to profoundly affect, up to the present day, the physiognomy of homosexuality in Muslim countries.

With regard to the topic (boy-love) that I am dealing with in this article, perhaps more than in any other, allowance must be made for the gap which existed between "theoretical" morality—that which follows from treatises and theological commentaries—and "real" morality—that which was actually practiced. Nowhere did these two moralities exactly coincide. Even in the strictest Trappist or Carmelite monastery moral behavior is less austere than the ideal of the Rule. In the classical Muslim world this gap took on the proportions of a veritable gulf (less, perhaps, than in the Christian West during the Middle Ages).[21]

It is therefore foolish to deny the reality of homosexuality in the Arab world by quoting theological texts, as certain modern Arab scholars imbued with "European" prejudices have done, with a naïveté paralleled by insincerity. Alongside the principal condemnation of homosexuality by the Qur'ān and Sunnite commentators, the proofs of actual and frequently practiced homosexuality abound in texts celebrating boy-love.

Notes

1. Mas'ūdī, *Les prairies d'or* (after the French translation of Barbier de Montault, VI, p. 144).

2. *Id.*, p. 145.

3. Ahmād al-Tifāshī, *Les délices des coeurs*, trans. René R. Khawam, p. 255. (An English edition of *The Delight of Hearts* was published by Gay Sunshine Press, 1988.)

4. H. Lemmens, *Le berceau de l'Islam: l'Arabie occidentale à la veille de l'Hegire* (Paris, 1914), I, p. 283; see also L. Massignon, *La passion d'Al-Hosayn ibn-Mansour al-Hallāj* . . . , (Paris, 1922), II, p. 797, no. 2

5. On pre-Islamic Arab poetry, see R. Blachère's *Histoire de la littérature arabe des origines à la fin du XV siècle*, fasc. 1 and 2 (Paris 1952–1964), and M. Wiet's *Introduction à la littérature arabe* (Paris, 1966).

6. *Qur'ān* 7:78–79; II:80–84, etc.

7. *Qur'ān* 56:17 ff.

8. Let me add to these, verse 20 of Sūra 10 which took aim at those "who commit an infamous act." Numerous commentators took this to mean "sodomites." The prescribed punishment was indeterminate but very light, and pardon was prescribed if the guilty person repented. We are far removed from the hysterical condemnations ordered by Judaism and medieval Christianity.

9. An-Nuwairī, *Nihāyat al-Arab fi funūn al-adab* (Cairo, 1923), pp. 189–96.

10. *Histoire de Kamaralzaman et de la princesse Boudour* (translation by Mardrus). For quotes from Arab poems I have adopted a formula which doubtless will not please Arab scholars, but which, I hope, will make its reading easy for nonspecialists. It is not possible to translate into French the rhythms and the sonorities of Arabic which constitute the essence of poetry in this language. Rather than use a word-for-word translation, often clumsy and even laborious to read, I have preferred to keep the

essential meaning of the poems and to transpose them into nonrhymed French verse, which in default of literary pretensions, has at least the essential advantage of not translating verse by means of prose. [In translating the poems in this article from French into English I have adopted a similar principle—Winston Leyland.]

11. L. Bercher, *Les délits et les peines de droit commun prévues par le Coran*. Tunis, 1926, p. 95.

12. Ibn Hazm, *Le Collier de la Colombe*, trans. L. Bercher (Algiers, 1949), p. 367.

13. Massignon, *La passion*, II, p. 797, n. 2.

14. Mez, *El renacimiento*, p. 427.

15. Bercher, *Les délits*, p. 95.

16. G. H. Bousquet, *La morale de l'Islam et son éthique sexuelle* (Paris and Algiers, 1953), p. 36.

17. *Id.*

18. *Ibid.* p. 45.

19. *Id.*

20. Marc Daniel, "Histoire de la legislation pénale française concernant l'homosexualité," *Arcadie*, No. 96 (December 1961), p. 261.

21. G. H. Bousquet has rightly emphasized this essential point (*La morale de l'Islam*, p. 25).

Sexual Subordination: Institutionalized Homosexuality and Social Control in Melanesia

Gerald W. Creed

Like food and shelter, sex is a basic human need that different societies satisfy in manifold ways. Compared with other topics, however, anthropologists have provided relatively few studies of sexuality. Even holistic ethnographies skim over or ignore sexual behavior, and are not admonished for it. Anthropologists assume that all other dimensions of social behavior are socially constructed but, for whatever reasons, they disregard the social construction of sexuality and exclude it from social analysis. The roots of this bias are deep. As Malinowski's (1929) study of Trobriand sexual customs aptly demonstrates, early British ethnographers treated sexuality as an independent issue divorced from its broader political context. Influenced by the colonial administration's concern with tribal politics, British ethnographers conceptually divided the world into separate public and private spheres (for example, Fortes and Evans-Pritchard 1940). They located the political issues which concerned them in the public sphere and cloistered away sexual behavior in the private realm where it could be justifiably ignored.

If anthropologists have had difficulty treating sexuality in general, dealing with the sexual practices they were taught to abhor (such as homosexuality) was almost impossible. Although the tenet of cultural relativism entreats us to perceive our subject matter objectively, there is something about sexual issues, particularly those Western culture regards as "deviant," that prohibits us from putting aside our own feelings and inhibitions. Anthropologists deal with this problem in two ways. First, one may throw relativism to the wind and accept the moralistic values of one's own society. For example, Williams (1936:158) refers to "sodomy" among the Keraki as an "unnatural practice" and a "perversion." Second, and potentially more damaging to scholarship, is to maintain a relativistic stance but ignore sexual practices that pose a threat. Thus, Evans-Pritchard hesitated to report homosexual activity among the Azande. Even though he published several articles and books on the Azande, he only recently (Evans-Pritchard 1970) discussed their homosexual proclivities. Another version of this avoidance is manifested earlier in the research process when fieldworkers simply avoid investigating sensitive issues such as homosexuality, or do not pursue them as extensively as they would other issues. Kenneth Read (1980:184), reflecting on his own fieldwork among the Gahuku-Gama, admits that a more insistent investigation might have uncovered homosexual activity. That researchers are now admitting such omissions and oversights is a reflection of changing attitudes in our own society.

In order to grasp the broader political and social importance of sexuality we must reject the old public/private dichotomy, and realize that the private is political. Cohen (1969) took a giant step in this direction when he suggested that developing states used sexual regulations to gain political control of their citizenry, and since them many studies (Rowbotham 1973; Zaretzky 1976; Ortner 1978) have pursued the connection between sexuality and politics. Cohen (1969:664) suggested that "there is 'something' about sexuality that renders people vulnerable to control through it." This "something" may include the radically individualistic view of sexuality; the perception of sexuality as something so private and so personal means that controlling sexuality is virtually synonymous with controlling the individual. Furthermore, if we assume that every sex act contains an element of domination and subordination, then by controlling the occurrence of sex— by structuring who can have sex with whom and how—the inherent individual qualities of dominance and subordination can be generalized and assigned to particular groups of a population. Thus, we might view the insistence on heterosexuality as a way of ensuring male social and economic hegemony. Similarly, where homosexuality is a socially prescribed institution, we might look for a pattern of domination and subordination between those involved. I view ritualized/institutionalized homosexuality in New Guinea as a mechanism of social control that operates to perpetuate a system of inequality based on sex and age. New Guinea ethnographers (Kelly 1976; Herdt 1981; Van Baal 1966) have suggested similar ideas but they have not pursued or supported these suggestions. I will attempt to specify some of the ways in which ritualized homosexuality actually subordinates and controls women and young men.

Institutionalized Homosexuality in Melanesia

"Ritualized homosexual practices, usually introduced in male initiation, are virtually universal throughout the Papuan Gulf, extending from Anga groups (e.g., Menya, Sambia, Baruya) and the Fly headwaters west to Prince Hendrik Island and including fringe areas such as the Papuan Plateau (e.g., Etoro, Kalule) and Nomad River" (Herdt and Poole 1981:8). As the above quotation suggests, the practice of homosexuality in New Guinea is widespread, highly structured and culturally regulated. The particulars of this practice may vary from society to society, but there is a general skeleton of beliefs and actions that characterize the institution across Melanesia. Here, I will describe the anatomy of this common skeleton and then flesh out the particulars of several cases.

Institutionalized homosexuality is rooted in a belief that the attributes of masculinity are not innate in male biology but acquired through strict adherence to a ritualized regimen. This is in contradistinction to femininity, which is acquired naturally by women without such effort. Taking some liberties with old anthropological terminology, we might say that femaleness is an ascribed characteristic while maleness is an achieved one. The essence and focus of this maleness invariably is semen. Once this premise is accepted, the logical conclusion is clear; males must acquire semen in order to become real men. Basically, this is what ritualized homosexuality is all about; promoting masculine development by transferring semen from the haves to the have-nots.

This is always accomplished through a highly structured process. It usually takes place in the context of initiation rites, so that we must examine ritualized homosexuality in tandem with other aspects of male initiation. Even the sexual act itself is highly structured; there are restrictions on who may have sex with whom, and what role an individual may play in sexual encounters. Kinship and age factors structure the phenomenon, such that certain categories of kin are prohibited from having homosexual relations while other categories of male relatives may be prescribed. The younger partner in a homosexual episode must always receive the semen from the older male, but as a boy ages he graduates to the role of inseminator and eventually moves into a period of heterosexuality, marriage and child rearing.

Malekula

Although this paper focuses on New Guinea, it behooves us to first examine Malekula, an island in Eastern Melanesia, since there is documentation of homosexual activity there from a relatively early period, and the pattern is similar to that described above. Layard's (1942) monograph and the posthumous edition of Deacon's (1934) field notes together give a basic account of homosexual practices in the northern area of Malekula known as the Big Nambas. This area was not the primary fieldwork site of either ethnographer; Layard's work was concerned with the small northeastern island of Voa, and Deacon spent most of his time in the southwest of the island, making only a brief visit to the Big Nambas (Deacon 1934:xxii).

Both accounts suggest that the Malekula pattern of homosexual activity conforms in several ways to that found in New Guinea. Deacon (1934:262, 267) writes that up until the time a boy assumes his bark belt, which is the badge of the adult male, he is a "boy lover" to some older man. Once he assumes his belt this bond is terminated and he takes a "boy lover" himself. Neither Deacon nor Layard indicate the ages of boys at the time of their initial homosexual initiation, nor the age at which they receive the bark belt and graduate to homosexual dominants. Both authors are also unclear about how long men continue in the role of dominant inseminator, although some passages suggest that such involvements continue throughout adult life (Deacon 1934:260–262). Furthermore, neither ethnographer is clear about the ideology surrounding homosexual activities. Deacon (1934:262) relates that homosexual practices are believed to cause the boy's "male organ" to grow strong and large, and he assumes that this "male organ" is the penis. Recent work in New Guinea, however, has revealed a belief in an internal "semen organ" which swells up as semen acquired in homosexual intercourse accumulates there (Herdt 1981:217). The possibility exists that a similar mythical anatomical structure is the referent of the Malekulan "male organ." If so, this would make the connection between homosexuality and the transfer of semen which neither Deacon nor Layard makes explicit. Layard (1942:489) does say that ritualized homosexual practices constitute "a transmission of male power by physical means" but he does not say that semen is the vehicle of this transmission.

Two characteristics distinguish the Big Nambas case from the general pattern described above: the close, often monogamous relationship between a boy and his adult inseminator; and the existence of what appears to be hereditary chiefs. Unfortunately, neither author gives much information on the basis of chiefly authority or the benefits of chiefly privilege. Deacon (1934:49–50) superficially notes that chiefs owe their influence and power to their opportunities for acquiring greater wealth, but he does not elaborate on how they come into these opportunities. Chiefly status is important to an understanding of homosexuality because chiefs may take on many boy lovers, just as they may acquire many wives. Deacon does not investigate this interface of high status, wealth and sexual access. Furthermore, he (Deacon 1934:170) does not tell us whether the quality of the homosexual relationships between a chief and his boy lovers is any different from that experienced by the rest of the population, whose homosexual involvements appear to be monogamous.

Deacon's description of the quality of the average homosexual relationship is the strong point of his analysis. After the decision to hold circumcision rites, the father of a candidate will seek out someone to act as guardian to his son. After these arrangements have been made the guardian has exclusive sexual rights over his ward. He becomes the boy's "husband," and their relationship is very close. The boy accompanies his guardian everywhere, and if one of the two should die the survivor would mourn him deeply (Deacon 1934:261). Layard's description of homosexuality is primarily quoted from Deacon's account.

The Trans-Fly

Reports from the Trans-Fly area of Papua New Guinea suggest that the intimate monogamous dimension found in the Big Nambas is absent. The primary sources on this area are Williams (1936) and Landtman (1927). The latter is disappointing with regard to homosexuality—the author (Landtman 1927:237) merely mentions that "sodomy" is practiced within the context of initiation as a means to make youth strong and tall. Even this statement is confounded by the fact that initiation is not a single event among the Kiwai. Youths are initiated separately into each of the great secret ceremonies as they occur, none of which has exclusive reference to the initiates (Landtman 1927:237).

Williams's account of the Keraki is much more informative with regard to homosexuality. Although he uses derogatory expressions such as "unnatural practice" and "perversion," he gives an informed account of the institution. He (Williams 1936:158) relates that sodomy was fully sanctioned by male society, universally practiced, and that homosexuality was actually regarded as essential to a boy's bodily growth. Boys are initiated at the bull-roarer ceremony at about the age of thirteen. On the night of the ceremony the initiate is turned over to a youth of the previous group of initiates, who introduces the boy to homosexual intercourse. In all cases noted by Williams (1936:188), the older youth was the mother's brother's son or the father's sister's son of the new initiate. After this the boy is available to fellow villagers or visitors of the opposite moiety who wish to have homosexual relations with him. During this time the initiates live together in a seclusion hut for several months, during which they are supposed to grow rapidly with the aid of homosexual activities. At the end of the seclusion the youth becomes a "bachelor." He associates more freely with the elders and shows an increased interest in hunting, but he continues to play the passive role in homosexual relations for a year or so.

Near the end of this period the initiates go through a ceremony of lime eating. Lime is poured down their throats and the severe burns that result are thought to neutralize the effects of homosexual intercourse; that is, to ensure that the young men do not become pregnant. After this, a youth's compulsory service as a passive homosexual partner comes to an end. He is then entitled to adopt the opposite role when the next batch of boys is initiated into the bull-roarer (Williams 1936:200–203). "It is commonly asserted that the early practice of sodomy does nothing to inhibit a man's natural desires when later on he marries; and it is a fact that while the older men are not debarred from indulging, and actually do so at the bull-roarer ceremony, sodomy is virtually restricted as a habit to the *setiriva* [bachelors]" (Williams 1936:159).

Like Deacon and Layard, Williams emphasized the role of homosexuality in growth and development without explicitly connecting this function to the transfer of semen. On the other hand, no alternative explanation connecting homosexuality and growth is offered. Williams (1936:204) suggests that "the real motive is presumably self-gratification and although the idea of promoting growth is actually present . . . we may be sure that sodomy could get on very well without it." While this conclusion is perhaps a bit extreme, it directs our attention to the actual physical and erotic aspects of homosexuality, which are often overlooked when it is treated as institutionalized behavior. Institutionalized homosexuality is still sex, and it may still serve a pleasurable function. Analyses that neglect this fact are incomplete.

Marind-Anim

To the west of the Keraki are the Marind-anim, a coastal group studied by Van Baal (1966). The Marind occupy a vast territory extending along the entire southeastern coast of Irian Jaya. They are the epitome of what Wagner (1972:19) calls the "flamboyant coastal cultures." Homosexuality is prescribed for an extended period of about six years with boys engaging in anal intercourse. According to Van Baal's (1966:147) description this period probably begins when the boy is between seven and fourteen years old. Van Baal suggests that boys are subjected to both the sexual desires of their appointed mentors, usually their mother's brother, as well as the desires of the age-grade of youths above them. Thus, Marind custom seems to combine generalized sexual access with the idea of a single homosexual partner.

Actually, Van Baal's descriptions are not explicit about the details of homosexuality. He does not pay any attention to the distinction between active and passive roles within homosexual relations and, consequently, he does not document the transition from one role to another. Certain statements do suggest such a transition, however, when examined in the context of the male life cycle. A boy is given a mentor at the onset of puberty and "the relationship between the boy and his mentor is a homosexual one, the *binahorevai* [mentor] having the right to use him" (Van Baal 1966:118). At about the same time the boy moves into the *gotad*—a ritual seclusion hut. The boy spends his days here but joins his mentor in the men's house at night, where they sleep next to one another. When the boy's hair is long enough to be plaited into an elaborate hairdo, which is the pride of the Marind male, he is promoted to the age-grade of *wokraved*, where he stays for the next two or three years. According to Van Baal (1966:147) "the *wokraved* is called a girl, a qualification apparently referring to his role in the homosexual relationship with his *binahor*-father (and possibly with his older mates in the *gotad*)." This suggests that the *wokraved* plays the passive role in anal intercourse. It is confirmed by Van Baal's (1966:495) statement that the mother's brother might be seen as a mother substitute who promotes the boy's growth by depositing semen in his body.

Following the stage of *wokraved*, the adolescent young man becomes *ewati*. He remains in this age-grade for about three more years or until just before marriage, whereupon he leaves the *gotad*. "The promotion to *ewati* is a big event in the boy's life. It implies an important change in status. . . . The *ewati* is, to all intents and purposes, a man . . . and he need no longer obey his *binahorevai*. However, he is in no hurry to marry as he finds much gratification in his status as *ewati*." (Van Baal 1966:151–152). Based upon the pattern of the other societies examined, we might suspect that the termination of the youth's obedience to his mentor spells the end of their homosexual relationship as well. It is also likely that the *ewati*'s reluctance to marry and leave the *gotad* is due to the fact that some of the "gratification" he finds in his status is his new role as the dominant inseminator to a new group of *wokraved*. This suggestion, however, is not obvious from Van Baal's description.

Van Baal (1966:166) is explicit about the general transition to heterosexuality. Eventually the *ewati* arranges for marriage, becomes an adult man, and leaves the *gotad*. "To be married is the wish of every man; in Marind-anim opinion the unmarried male is a poor wretch." Thus, the Marind conform to the general cycle from homosexuality to heterosexuality, though it seems that Marind men may continue to engage in homosexual sodomy throughout their life. The ideological underpinnings of homosexuality among the Marind also conform to our general pattern. Like the residents of the Big Nambas and the Trans-Fly, the Marind believe homosexual relations promote the growth and development of boys. Unlike Layard's and Williams's descriptions, however, Van Baal's account states explicitly that this growth is attributed to the transfer of semen. Recent studies of the Papuan Plateau are even more insistent about semen being the pivotal issue of the homosexual cult.

The Papuan Plateau

Our knowledge of homosexuality on the Plateau comes to us from the work of Kelly (1976, 1977) and Schieffelin (1976) who conducted fieldwork among the Etoro and Kaluli, respectively. Homosexuality is also practiced by the Onabasalu and Bendamini but the researchers of these areas have not yet published any account of homosexuality there. The homosexual activities of the Onabasalu are known to us through a reference to them in Kelly's description of the Etoro. Based on personal communication with the fieldworker, Ernst, Kelly (1977:16) relates that Onabasalu initiation is focused on masturbation and the smearing of semen over the initiates' bodies. According to Ernst, the Onabasalu formerly practiced oral intercourse, and some Onabasalu boys were actually initiated at Etoro seclusion houses.

Schieffelin's (1976) description of the Kaluli is organized around an eloquent analysis of the *Gisaro* ceremony. The *Gisaro* is an exotic ritual drama in which dancers/singers from one longhouse community visit another community where they sing songs recalling some painful and depressing memory of their hosts. In a successful *Gisaro*, someone in the audience will be moved to such grief and sorrow that he will grab a torch and burn the dancer. Schieffelin treats the ceremony as a celebration of social reciprocity, and believes that the theme of reciprocity is the basic current flowing through all of Kaluli society.

Unfortunately, Schieffelin does not pursue the theme of reciprocity when dealing with homosexuality. He simply explains homosexuality as an extreme expression of maleness within a context of male-female opposition. On the other hand, Schieffelin (1976:123) claims that relationships between Kaluli men and women are unusual, by New Guinea standards, for their lack of hostility and for their affection. Why then, do we not find this extreme expression of maleness in New Guinea societies with greater sexual antagonism, such as those in the Highlands proper? Schieffelin is not concerned with such questions.

The characteristics of Kaluli maleness are concentrated in semen. Semen has a magical quality that promotes physical growth and mental understanding. Boys must, therefore, acquire semen in order to grow and develop masculine qualities. "When a boy is eleven or twelve years old he is engaged for several months in homosexual intercourse with a healthy older man chosen by his father. . . . Men point to the rapid growth of adolescent youths, the appearance of peachfuzz beards, and so on as the favorable results of this child-rearing practice" (Schieffelin 1976:124). Schieffelin does not tell us how much older this "older man" is or what criteria guide his selection, but he (Schieffelin 1976:126) does reveal that during periods of seclusion in the ceremonial hunting lodge, "homosexual intercourse was practiced between the older bachelors and the younger boys to make them grow, some boys and men developing specific liaisons for the time." Is this in addition to the homosexual relationship arranged by the boy's father? If so, how does it articulate with that relationship? Again, Schieffelin does not discuss the details.

Actually, Schieffelin says little beyond a basic statement of the relationship between homosexuality and adolescent development but, lest we criticize him for this, we should recall that his analysis is concerned with *Gisaro*, not with ritualized homosexuality, and his limited attention to homosexual practices makes sense in this context. At the end of the book, Schieffelin (1976:222) makes a connection between the generative role of homosexual intercourse in this world and the vitalizing, regenerative role that the *Gisaro* ritual plays in the "unseen world." In a report devoted to examining the *Gisaro*, Schieffelin tells the reader only enough about homosexuality to ensure that the symbolic connection between the two is grasped.

Kelly's (1976) descriptions of Etoro homosexuality are also circumscribed by his particular interests. He examines Etoro society from a structural perspective and his investigation of homosexuality provides another clue in his search for the underlying structural characteristics of Etoro social structure. In his well-known article on witchcraft and sexual relations, Kelly treats homosexual and heterosexual activities together, since they both represent a transfer of "life force" from one individual to another. In the case of homosexual intercourse, the passive boy is the beneficiary of the life force transferred to him in semen. In the case of heterosexual intercourse the unborn child is the recipient of this life force, since the Etoro believe that the semen deposited in the womb combines with the female's blood to form the child. Kelly (1976:41) suggests that witchcraft and sexual relations occupy analogous structural positions within the Etoro conceptual system, since they both constitute modes of interaction through which life force is transmitted from one human being to another.

Kelly (1976:52) stresses the role of homosexual intercourse in supplying boys with adequate life force/semen to ensure their proper growth and maturity. To this end, a boy is inseminated through oral intercourse by a single inseminator from about the age of ten until he is fully mature and has a manly beard, usually around his early to mid-twenties. Initiation appears to take place during the later portion of this period. Kelly (1976:47) states that "youths are initiated into manhood in their late teens or early twenties when they are physically mature (although not fully bearded)." About every three years, all young men who have reached this stage of development go to a seclusion lodge and cannot be seen by women. The previous group of initiates, who are now completely mature, also reside at the lodge, but Kelly does not say whether they engage in sexual relations with the neophytes. He (Kelly 1976:47) does say that a "generalized insemination of the youths by older men takes place at the seclusion lodge," but the reader is unsure if the previous group of initiates are part of this group of "older men." Kelly is also not specific regarding how long the seclusion lasts, but upon reaching maturity the Etoro initiate will become the inseminator of a new young neophyte, preferably his wife's (or his wife-to-be's) brother.

In his study of Etoro social structure, Kelly (1977) has more to say about the preference for the wife's brother as a homosexual partner. Here Kelly (1977:2) attempts to demonstrate that the principle of siblingship is as important as the principle of descent, and that Etoro social structure can be viewed as the outcome of managing these two contradictory principles. Kelly's discussion of homosexuality in this book is minimal, and submerged under detailed description of the kinship system. Regarding homosexuality, he focuses primarily on the preference for the sister's husband as her brother's inseminator. If this ideal is achieved, then a married sister and her younger brother have equivalent relationships of sexual partnership to the same man. The relationship between the sister's husband and her unmarried brother is "exceptionally strong" and sexual relations between the two continue until the younger marries and starts inseminating his own wife's brother (Kelly 1977:183). Kelly (1977:270) uses the Etoro organization of homosexuality as an example of the principle of siblingship, in this case, as it is mediated by an affine.

The Sambia

Herdt's (1981) analysis of the Sambia—occupants of the narrow river valleys in the remote Eastern Highlands—is the only full-length study of a New Guinea society concerned primarily with institutionalized homosexuality. Ironically, this narrow focus gives the impression that institutionalized homosexuality is a system unto itself, concerned only with the construction of gender identity—a suggestion that flies in the face of the anthropological tenet that culture is integrated. We would be better informed of the importance of homosexuality if we were given more information about its connection to kinship, politics, economics and so on. The only connection that Herdt really stresses is the role of homosexuality in reproducing a warriorhood—a warriorhood that is reproduced sufficiently in other New Guinea societies without the aid of homosexual activities (Meggitt 1977).

The narrow focus of Herdt's analysis is the product of two factors. First, his definition of culture as "the cognitive system of values, norms, and rules influencing perception and behavior" is mentalistic, and allows him (Herdt 1981:12) to give short shrift to material connections. Second, Herdt's goal is to discover the subjective experience of homosexuality for individuals by focusing on verbal behavior, especially idioms. His (Herdt 1981:11) primary concern is with intimate communication; what particular men in particular circumstances said to him in particular. Putting aside the question of whether or not one person can actually understand another's "subjective experience," there is still the question of the value of such an exercise. As a rule, anthropologists are not interested in individual idiosyncrasies but in social generalities.

Herdt discusses Sambia homosexuality in terms of stages of "masculinization." The Sambia believe that masculine attributes develop when young men acquire sufficient semen. By this point in the paper it should come as no surprise that the Sambia think that semen must be acquired by ingesting it in homosexual oral intercourse. Around the age of seven to ten years old, a boy is separated from his mother and subjected to painful and traumatic rituals directed toward purging the initiates of female contamination. Once purged, the initiates embark upon a period of consuming semen intended to provide them with the requisite for masculine development. Fellatio becomes a way of life, and elders reiterate that boys should ingest semen every night (Herdt 1981:235). Boys must consume a lot of semen in order to build a reservoir of maleness and strength that will last a lifetime.

The appearance of male physical traits around the age of fourteen to sixteen is taken as proof that the boy has ingested enough semen. He is promoted to the status of bachelor and required to serve as the dominant inseminator for a new group of initiates. This period leads into marriage, usually to a premenarche girl. The young wife may practice fellatio on her husband, but the new couple cannot engage in vaginal intercourse. During a period of about a year or two, then, a man can be truly bisexual, continuing to have oral sex with young initiates as well as his wife. Once the wife's menarche occurs, however, they begin coitus and homosexual activities should cease (Herdt 1981:252).

As the bachelor approaches coitus and fatherhood, which is the peak of manhood, his ritual practices are shifted to defend and maintain the manliness already acquired. For example, men begin drinking white "milk" sap after each occasion of heterosexual intercourse as a means of replacing ejaculated semen (Herdt 1981:251). But one wonders why milk sap is not used as the original source of semen for initiates. This enigma should have prompted Herdt to look for other possible functions of the homosexual relationship which could not be replaced by milk sap consumption, such as the subordinate-dominant relationship between homosexual partners, which is affirmed in the sexual exchange.

Herdt (1981:320) views homosexual contacts as powerful personal experiences that inculcate masculinity and further the unfinished process of male "separation-individuation." "Ritualized homosexuality reinforces the rigidity of the masculine ethic, it allows for no exceptions in the race for acquiring maleness" (Herdt 1981:322). In Herdt's (1981:305) terms, ritualization homosexuality is a process of "radical resocialization," a kind of "ritualized gender surgery" that replaces the gender identity a boy acquires at the hands of his mother with the appropriate masculine gender identity. Herdt does not say why homosexuality is the means of "radical resocialization," nor how other societies, which have to deal with the same problem, manage without it.

Homosexuality and Social Control

Herdt's suggestion follows Burton and Whiting's (1961) explanation of male initiation as "psychological brainwashing." They (Burton and Whiting 1961:90–91) suggest that puberty rites replace the feminine identity acquired by boys during the intense period of mothering with the appropriate masculine identity. Male initiation in general, and ritualized homosexuality in particular, are obviously connected to the formation of masculine gender identity, but restricting the role of homosexuality to this one function is a mistake. In fact, what Herdt (1981) calls the "radical resocialization" of boys may not be as necessary as he thinks. While the first several years of a boy's life are dominated by his mother, during this time he is continually confronted with the gender polarization around him. Despite the closeness of his mother, he could not be oblivious to the sexual divisions that define his environment. Furthermore, he is probably continually indoctrinated in the correct behavior for the different sexes—a mother surely reminds her young son of his sex and the behavior appropriate to it.

Ritualized homosexuality doubtless cements and guarantees the correct gender identity, but here I suggest a broader function of homosexual initiation—that it is a powerful component in a system of social control. This notion actually encompasses the former argument, since indoctrination of the acceptable gender identity is the first line of attack in keeping individuals within the boundaries delineated and accepted by society. A closer examination, however, reveals that ritualized homosexuality may serve to control more than individual psychology. Institutionalized homosexuality is a mechanism of control that operates to perpetuate a system of inequality based on sex and age. It supports the status and position of older men over and against women and young men. Kelly (1976:51) made a similar suggestion about the structural role of sexual relations and witchcraft in producing an elementary system of inequality based on sex and age, but he does not explain how the actual practice of homosexuality contributes to such a system. Herdt (1981:13) also suggests that initiation separates women and children as a class and reproduces the social order but, as mentioned above, his analysis is restricted to an examination of gender identity, and he does not specify any of the actual connections between homosexual practices and the oppression of young men and women.

Male homosexuality may seem completely removed from anything having to do with women, but, paradoxically, this separation and isolation are related to the control and subordination of women in several ways. First, the secrecy which in most cases surrounds the male homosexual cult (the Marind-anim seem to be the only exception) keeps women ignorant of male activities. This ignorance itself is a powerful controlling mechanism. Men state that women have no idea of male ritual activities, and in most of the societies discussed above initiates are instructed not to reveal any of the secrets they learn. Williams (1936:185) states that young Keraki initiates were threatened with execution if they revealed any ritual secrets. Furthermore, the seclusion of small boys in initiation huts and their reappearance after the period of rapid adolescent development is intended to impress upon women the power of the male cult. Schieffelin's (1977:126) account of the Kaluli, for example, states that young men were strictly secluded from women for periods of up to fifteen months. "The young men emerged from seclusion decked in their brightest finery, so handsome and so much grown, it is said, that their own relatives didn't recognize them." A more explicit example of the manipulation of ignorance revolves around the use of the bull-roarer, a noise-maker used by some societies in the context of male initiation and ritualized homosexuality. The bull-roarer makes a strange noise which can be heard by women and children. They know that it is connected with men's activities but they have no idea of its source (Williams 1936:192). Such ignorance of male ritual activity is easily turned into fear of its apparent power, and this fear ensures female submission.

Practitioners themselves actually view homosexual activity as a statement of male superiority over females. Van Baal (1966:489) says that Marind male pride and superiority find their fullest expression in homosexual rites. These rites stress the absolute superiority of the male sex. This expression, however, is a fiction that men are determined to maintain. Men are well aware that they depend upon women, not only for their substantial contribution to subsistence, but, more importantly, for their reproductive power. Among the Kaluli a man can develop the connections and influence that render him fully effective in his life only through a relationship with a woman (Schieffelin 1977:128). Similarly, among the Sambia only the birth of a child confirms complete manhood, and one's success in fathering children is an important gauge of one's prestige and social status (Herdt 1981:52). Thus, as Van Baal (1966:949) points out, the venerated power of men is not all it is pretended to be. "These self-sufficient males need the females and they know it; only they do not care to admit it." The conflict between the fiction of all-powerful masculinity and the reality of female reproductive power gives rise to masculine ritual and dogma that reinforces the former in face of the latter. Ritualized homosexuality is the critical element of the male defense system—they use it to deny their dependence upon women. Among the Sambia this is taken so far as the elaboration of a myth of male parthenogenesis which asserts that the female sex itself was the product of male homosexual intercourse (Herdt 1981). By denying the power of women, men are able to justify and assert their own authority and control. Men may try to demonstrate in many ways their ability to live without women, but male homosexuality is particularly effective in this regard since it denies the need for women in the area where women are most powerful—sexuality.

The contradiction between the myth of all-powerful masculinity and the reality of female reproductive power is paralleled within the male sex itself in terms of age. The social status and influence that come with age are well documented in the New Guinea literature. Van Baal (1966:115), for example, states that "relative age is important in Marind society. It finds expression in the somewhat exalted position of elderly people and in the system of age grades among adolescents." Herdt (1981:35) also confirms that age is a fundamental principle of hamlet organization among the

Sambia, as well as one of the primary sources of power and prestige. On the other hand, older men are not blind to the energy, vitality and determination possessed by youth. In fact, they may formally recognize it. In Marind society, for example, the important position of elders is juxtaposed to a special emphasis on youth: "what counts is youth and life" (Van Baal 1966:171). Similarly, Schieffelin (1977:125) points out that the Kaluli recognize that virgin youths and unmarried young men are the best hunters, not only because of their greater speed, stamina and sharpness of eye, but also because animals may be more likely to appear before them. If we accept the suggestion that homosexuality affirms masculine supremacy in the face of female power, we must also investigate the possibility that it operates in the parallel contradiction between the ideal of adult supremacy and the reality of youthful vitality.

The ways in which male initiation in general may help ensure adult ascendancy over younger males are numerous, and intermittently intertwined with the control of females. The same strategy of enforced ignorance used against women is also employed against youth. Very young boys are as ignorant of male cult secrets as their mothers are. Even as they grow and begin to learn the secrets of manhood, they are in no position to challenge the accumulated wisdom and knowledge of older adult men. As Meillassoux (1960:49) suggests regarding African elders, the authority of the elders rests on withholding knowledge, and it is this which supports and justifies the control of youth's labor products. Herdt's (1981:45) account supports this suggestion. He points out that the distinguished position of Sambia elders is based on their accumulated knowledge; they hold ritual secrets that younger men have not learned, and this knowledge gives them enormous power to constrain the actions of young men. Keraki adults also restrict the knowledge of younger men. According to Williams (1936) young boys learn some of the myths of the male cult in the context of initiation, but they may remain ignorant of other myths until much later in their life. Williams (1936:199) offers a poignant example of how knowledge is regulated. Bamboo pipes are revealed to initiates as the source of a mysterious, unknown sound they heard as children. After demonstrating the use of the pipes, adults give the initiates their own pipes and tell them to blow, but the boys may blow until they pass out without producing a sound, since they have been given a plain tube without the almost invisible splint responsible for the noise. Thus, this step in initiation removes some of the ignorance which boys share with their mothers, but not necessarily all of it.

As young boys become more aware of male ritual secrets through the process of initiation, new and additional mechanisms of control must be found to replace ignorance. In the societies examined here the very process of enlightenment—initiation into the homosexual cult—contains the new means of control. Initiation reveals to boys the powerful secret of male homosexuality, but the ideological underpinnings of this institution perpetuate their subordination. Ideologically locating "strength" in semen means that boys, like women, lack strength and are, therefore, weak and inferior. Furthermore, by denying that semen is acquired naturally and insisting that it is a limited good which can only be acquired from someone already possessing it, adult males make boys not only completely inferior to their seniors, but also absolutely dependent upon them for status mobility. In such a situation, as Herdt (1981:51) realizes, strength, maleness and manliness become virtually synonymous with conformity to the ritual routine. "Boys and youths alike must conform: either that, which rewards manhood, or else oblivion by weakness, female contamination, or death" (Herdt 1981:242).

Equating semen with strength and other masculine qualities is an economical controlling ideology since, at the same time that it affirms the ascendancy of males over females, it also denies boys the chance to capitalize automatically on the favorable position of their sex. They can acquire the prerequisite for domination only by subordinating themselves to those who already have semen and following their ritual dictates. These dictates may include painful purging rites, since the dogma of institutionalized homosexuality not only denies boys strength but also maintains that they are full of female weakness. A boy could not come from his mother's womb and go through an intense period of mothering without being infected by female pollution. Therefore, boys must be separated from this debilitating female influence, and may have to go through purging rites, such as nose-bleeding, to remove existing female contamination.

While the removal of feminine influence may be the stated purpose of the early stages of initiation, ritualized homosexuality may actually be a mechanism to maintain the feminine quality of youth as a way of perpetuating their inferiority. This suggestion challenges the established anthropological interpretations of initiation rituals as simply rites of passage which make boys into men (for instance, Van Gennep 1960, Turner 1967). While this is the recognized emic purpose of ritualized homosexuality, descriptions of the phenomenon suggest that it may be a means of maintaining control of growing boys and maturing young men by emphasizing their femininity and forcing them to play a role in homosexual intercourse analogous to that of women in heterosexual activity.[1] In so doing, adult men support their own superior position against the potential challenge or psychological threat of a new generation. Dundes (1976:232) points out that homosexual initiatory practices actually feminize the initiates, but he seems unaware that initiates are already feminized to a certain extent by their association with their mothers. More accurately, enforced homosexuality capitalizes on the existing femininity of initiates, and maintains it through homosexual intercourse in order to subordinate and control younger men and boys. Dundes is interested in psychological identity, and while he insightfully recognizes the component of feminization involved in ritualized homosexuality, he does not make the connection between feminization and subordination and control.

This feminine quality of the passive partner in homosexual initiation is also suggested by Etoro kinship terminology, which refers by the same kin term to a brother and a sister, who are equally appropriate sexual partners for an older male (Kelly 1977:182). Van Baal (1966:147) offers more explicit evidence. Marind mockingly call young initiates "girls" in reference to their role in homosexual relationships. In sexually polarized societies the association of young males with females must have extensive ramifications.

The anthropological interpretation of homosexual rituals as rites of passage simplifies the complex and gradual process of masculine development. By looking at initiation ceremonies as signalling the transition from boyhood to manhood, investigators may overlook the continuing age and status differentials which separate men throughout the life cycle. Becoming a "man"/adult in New Guinea societies is only one step in the larger process of achieving status, prestige and a prominent position in society. Ritualized homosexuality, then, is not just a rite of passage, but an integrated segment in the lifelong process that takes young boys from childhood, through a period as semen recipients, then through a period as semen providers, to a time of heterosexual marriage and fathering children. Concomitantly, ritualized homosexuality assures the authority and superiority of those at the end of this cycle by subordinating those at the beginning, and ensuring that they remain differentiated with no pretensions of status before their time.

The transition from semen recipient to semen donor, which is a general characteristic of institutionalized homosexuality, is also intelligible when viewed as part of a system of social control. The ideology of ritualized homosexuality describes semen as a limited good which boys acquire and then dissipate during the remainder of their lives. Logically then, those who have just acquired their store of semen through a period of homosexuality must have the most semen, and, by extension, the most strength. Switching to the role of dominant inseminator for an extended period depletes a young man of much of this newly acquired treasure, and perhaps undermines any ambitions he might have as a consequence of his new-found maturity. The institutionalized transition to semen provider forces those who have the most semen/strength to dissipate it for the benefit of the next group of initiates. In exchange they are able to dominate the prepubescent initiates who are dependent upon them for semen. Ideally, this subordinate relationship should continue after the initiates reach maturity, but as an added safety measure they will be forced to deplete their store of semen/strength for the next age-grade, thereby ensuring their continued subordination to their seniors and the perpetuation of the system. The system thus creates and maintains a structured hierarchy in which each age-grade is subordinate to the next oldest age-grade.

Psychologically this arrangement also provides an emotional outlet for energetic teenagers who, according to Herdt (1981:323), "feel their growing strength and want to test their power." No doubt they also feel anger and resentment about the abuse they suffered during initiation at the hands of their seniors. The transition to the dominant position in homosexual activities is a way of directing this dangerous combination of strength and anger away from their seniors toward those who are younger. According to Herdt (1981:56). Sambia elders actually assert that young initiates must become "strong" and "angry" because of what has been done to them, then "they can do something equally laden with power: they are encouraged to channel that anger and relax their tight penises by serving as dominant fellateds (for the first time) of younger initiates."

This quotation also suggests that anger and strength are not the only feelings being orchestrated by ritualized homosexuality. The suggestion that boys "relax their tight penises" represents a recognition of the developing libido of maturing boys. By requiring that these urges be satisfied in homosexual relations, older men defend their own monopoly over women and thereby assure their own ascendancy in a system that emphasizes marriage and fatherhood as important measures of social status. The importance of wives in New Guinea is well documented in the literature. For our purposes it is sufficient to note that wives are a valuable resource. Marriage extends a man's network of social relations and provides him with a productive laborer and childbearer. Older men can maximize their own access to this resource by prohibiting younger men from having heterosexual relations and directing their developing sex drive toward young boys. As Herdt (1981:322) points out, "all sexual contact is regulated . . . ritualized homosexual contacts cordon bachelors directing their erotic impulses."

If this is an objective of institutionalized homosexuality, then the early stage of the institution may be seen not so much as a way of masculinizing the new initiates, but as a way of using new initiates to satisfy and pacify the next older age-grade, and thereby keep them under control. This suggestion is further supported by the general improvement in living conditions that accompanies the transition to inseminator. As initiates graduate to this stage of their life they are usually released from many of the obligations and abuses they endured during the stage of passive homosexual service. For example, among the Marind the *ewati* has an enjoyable, gratifying role and is in no hurry to marry (Van Baal 1966;151–152). The relative ease of the *ewati*'s life, combined with the sexual gratification he receives from the new group of initiates, may temporarily obviate the *ewati*'s desire for a wife or female sexual partner. Consequently, young females are available to older men.

If this is true we would expect to find a marriage pattern in which very young girls marry older men. This is what Kelly (1977) found historically for the Etoro; girls were traditionally married at about two to twelve years old to men approximately ten years their senior. Kelly (1977:169) explains this age differential as a consequence of an imbalanced sex ratio. The sex ratio is obviously important, but Kelly would do well to also investigate the connection between this marriage pattern and the organization of ritualized homosexuality. I am not suggesting that ritualized homosexuality necessarily causes a certain marriage pattern, only that there may be a connection between the two that is worth examining. Western researchers have overlooked such connections because they see homosexual activities and heterosexual practices such as marriage as diametrical opposites rather than integrated components of a larger system. As Lindenbaum (1984) points out, this problem is further aggravated by "a method of analysis that proceeds to some degree with one sex at a time, when . . . gender is the mutual product of men and women acting in concert."

The arguments made so far regarding homosexuality revolve around the issue of controlling or influencing behavior. This same issue has been discussed more extensively with regard to initiation practices in general, and the role of initiation in socializing and disciplining initiates is well known. Burton and Whiting (1961:85) state that "regardless of the relative strength of infantile dependance, there remains a need for initiation to exercise authority over boys." Similarly, Williams (1936:247) suggests that Keraki initiation rites serve an expressly disciplinary function: "while he [the new initiate] is elevated, he must be humbled. He enters at the bottom of the class and must be taught to know his place." According to Van Baal's (1966:142) description of the Marind, a first disciplining begins as soon as boys become initiates in the seclusion hut. "Living in a kind of gang, the boys drill each other on the basis of the rule that the juniors are at the beck and call of their seniors, and have to win complete acceptance by living up to the rules." Ritualized homosexuality fits nicely into this general initiatory objective. Thus, Van Baal (1966:149) concludes "that the elements of disciplining and of being subservient to others, also in homosexual relationships prevail." Herdt is even more explicit. He says (Herdt 1981:56) that "the act of ritualized fellatio confirms the respective statuses of bachelor and initiate alike, and it establishes a definite pattern of eroticism, dominance, and subordination in their interactions for years to come."

Obedience and conformity are not necessarily the only socially desirable results of homosexual practices. Older adults also accrue political and economic benefits. We have already noted how institutionalized homosexuality reserves the economic contribution of women for older men, but there may be other economic benefits as well. In societies where older adults act as inseminators there are benefits that accompany this dominant role. Among the Big Nambas, for example, from the time a father selects a "husband" for his son until the time the boy takes on the status of an adult male, his mentor has absolute sexual rights over him, and would be extremely jealous of any other man having intercourse with the boy. In fact, Deacon (1934:261) claims that the older man will hardly let the boy out of his sight. However, a man may sell his rights to his boy-lover for a short period of time. This suggests a situation of privatized sexual rights which can be sold, or more accurately, rented out by a boy's "husband" for the "husband's" economic benefit.

Not surprisingly, these sexual rights go hand in hand with other service obligations, the most significant of which is the requirement that the boy work in his "husband's" garden. Deacon does not discuss the extent of this garden labor, but he (Deacon 1934:261) does say that this labor contribution is the reason chiefs acquire many boy-lovers, which suggests that the work is significant. Finally, a boy's mentor also receives compensation directly from his boy-lover and the boy's father. At some point after the seclusion period the boy must purchase his bark belt (the badge of adulthood) from his mentor with coconuts and tobacco. The homosexual relationship between the two continues until this payment is made (Deacon 1934:267). In addition, at the conclusion of the period of seclusion, the father of the initiate gives his son's mentor "a very considerable payment of pigs" (Deacon 1934:262).

Van Baal notes similar benefits which accrue to the dominant inseminator. He says (Van Baal 1966:845) that the guardian enjoys many privileges, and the lavish provisions he must make for the feasts given in honor of his wards are well balanced by the services they render him. "It is the boy's duty to assist his *bihahor*-father [his homosexual guardian] in gardening and hunting, to fetch coconuts for him and to render him various small services" (Van Baal 1966:148). The initiate's servitude is guaranteed by the fact that the transition to the next age-grade, which terminates his sexual and economic service to his guardian, requires the cooperation of his guardian in arranging the relevant feasts. As Van Baal (1966:161) succinctly puts it, "whether he likes it or not, he has to conform to the prescribed patterns of behavior." The economic dimension of this arrangement is even more obvious in cases where the guardian is childless. A man in this situation may prefer to have the boy as a helper for as long as possible, and may therefore delay the necessary feasts (Van Baal 1966:149).

Among the Keraki the primary inseminators are not older adults but the next older age-grade of youths. However, the services required of initiates by their homosexual partners appear to establish a pattern of servitude that extends into adulthood. Williams (1936:189) states that all the functionaries at an initiation ceremony, one of which is an initiate's primary inseminator, have special relationships to the initiate and continue to have claims on his services. The initiate is never supposed to refuse their requests. In this sense, semen and manhood may be seen as gifts which place the recipient in a situation of almost permanent indebtedness to the giver. Such indebtedness establishes a relationship of subordination and obligation which may last a lifetime. The only compensation for this predicament is the opportunity they have to balance their own indebtedness by subordinating a younger group of initiates in the same manner.

The subordination of those who are younger as compensation for one's own subordination points to one of the most efficient characteristics of homosexuality as a social control mechanism—it is self-perpetuating. The major investments are required of boys at a young age. By the time young men are at an age to offer resistance they are vested in the system, some of the benefits are already beginning to flow their way, and they need only wait for time to take them to the most favored positions. This progression undercuts any identification with women, who are forever destined to a subordinate position. Were young men to grow impatient, the rules and relationships indoctrinated via ritualized homosexuality provide a continued restraint.

The suggestion that institutionalized homosexuality is primarily a social control mechanism is essentially a functional explanation; as such it suffers from the usual problems and failings of functionalist theory. Perhaps the greatest pitfall of functional explanations is that they do not explain why a certain cultural phenomenon, in this instance homosexuality, is the means utilized to achieve a particular effect, in this case the control of women and youth, and the perpetuation of a social hierarchy based on sex and age. In other words, if we accept the suggestion that homosexuality is a mechanism of social control, we still do not know why it is used in some societies and not in others.

Lindenbaum (1984) offers some enlightening suggestions in this regard. She sees a connection between sister exchange and ritualized homosexuality, and suggests that the latter is a sort of bride service. According to Lindenbaum, a striking aspect of societies with ritualized homosexuality is that the pattern of marriage is sister exchange with no payment of bride-price. In such a situation semen is a kind of covenant that keeps the sister exchange system intact. Lindenbaum's discussion points out the important role of material valuables and ceremonial exchange in bride-price societies. In the Highlands proper, not semen exchange but the ceremonial exchange of shells, feathers, pigs, and so on is the center of attention. Marriage arrangements are cemented with bride-price valuables, and ritual is directed toward the making of men of status rather than the formation of masculine men.

This suggests that the relative paucity or absence of material wealth may be an important variable in accounting for the occurrence of institutionalized homosexuality. Where substantial amounts of material valuables and wealth are available, social ascendancy and control can be ensured by monopolizing that wealth. Where such wealth is absent, other means of control must be found and monopolized, and naturally occurring bodily substances are readily available alternatives. Semen is particularly well suited for the task since it naturally excludes women and children. In support of this suggestion, the societies with ritualized homosexual practices examined here do not appear to have vast amounts or numerous types of material wealth, nor do they seem overly concerned about such issues. Herdt (1981:52) actually states that the Sambia "have few material means of gaining control." Furthermore, as Lindenbaum (1984) points out, when such items do become available, they are utilized for bride-price payments, and sister exchange as a marriage pattern and ritualized homosexuality begin to break down in tandem. This argument still does not tell us why homosexuality developed nor why it was institutionalized into the male cult. These are historical questions that require and deserve more extensive research. However, the focus on material wealth points out one variable that may figure substantially in the answers to these questions.

Lindenbaum's (1984) analysis is also instrumental in showing the explanatory potential of comparisons with New Guinea societies which do not exhibit a ritualized homosexual complex. Generally, researchers interested in homosexuality treat it as a single type of behavior, and compare it cross-culturally (for example, Broude and Greene 1976; Carrier 1980). In response to this approach Whitehead (1981:81) claims that many cases of homosexuality (the modern United States, the berdache, the New Guinea examples and so on) are very different "animals" and not really comparable. While such comparisons are not worthless, we can learn more about the New Guinea cases by comparing them instead with nonhomosexual New Guinea societies. As Lindenbaum's paper demonstrates, our best clues to understanding homosexuality in New Guinea may be the other differences that distinguish homosexual and nonhomosexual societies within this culture area. More comparisons of this type must be attempted.

Discussion

The intention of this paper is not to answer all the perplexing questions surrounding ritualized/institutionalized homosexuality in New Guinea, but to examine existing accounts of the phenomenon, and to demonstrate that its role as a social control mechanism has been underestimated, or at least underinvestigated. In this attempt I have shown that institutionalized homosexuality is not an independent phenomenon that can be understood or explained in isolation. It is an aspect of culture integrated with the position of women, the ideology of pollution, the stratification of males by age, as well as the economic organization of the society. Obviously, these are not the only connections between homosexuality and the rest of social life. As a conclusion I will mention a few of the questions and issues that must be pursued if a complete or holistic understanding of ritualized homosexuality is to be achieved.

First and foremost, more reliable and comparable ethnographic descriptions must be compiled. Much of the existing literature is old and, due to the divergent interests of the ethnographers, the extent of their concern with homosexuality is highly variable. When they do discuss the phenomenon, their descriptions focus on different aspects or issues, and therefore undermine comparative and generalizing endeavors. The usual problems encountered when working with other people's data are even more troublesome when such time differences and such variation of focus are prominent. In addition, older accounts are often unclear about the source of their information, and whether or not they are referring to extant customs.

Only when we have a larger, more uniform ethnographic base will we be able to make generalizations about homosexuality in New Guinea or, conversely, make any suggestions about the variations in the practice within New Guinea. Just because several societies have institutionalized homosexuality does not mean that it serves the same role or function in each. The variations we have noted in the practice of homosexuality, such as the length of time a boy is subjected to it (from several months among the Kaluli to several years among the Etoro), or the differences between the "monogamous"-type arrangement between a boy and an adult inseminator and the situation where one or more youths from the next older age-grade act as inseminators, may be related to other sociocultural differences.

Even contemporary research does not adequately address certain issues, such as the articulation of institutionalized homosexuality with the kinship system. We have seen repeatedly that kinship relations are important concerns in establishing homosexual involvements. Kelly (1976) pointed out that the Etoro preference for the wife's brother as a homosexual partner is an example of the principle of siblingship, and there are probably other kinship connections worth examining. In sexually polarized societies such as the ones we are dealing with here, each "pole" must socially reproduce itself. We have already discussed how the organization of institutionalized homosexuality helps ensure the continuity of a male cult, but homosexual relations may also act to maintain and perpetuate an ideology of relatedness or "kinship" between generations within the male cult. In this way semen and homosexuality are to the male cult what blood and fatherhood are to the lineage—the means of descent.

Interesting in this regard is the fact that among the Etoro, the personal characteristics which a youth develops as he matures are believed to correspond to those of his primary inseminator. "If a man is strong, vigorous in his advanced years, a proficient hunter and trapper, and/or courageous warrior, then his protege will possess identical qualities and abilities upon attaining manhood" (Kelly 1976:46). According to Layard's (1942) description of the Big Nambas, this kind of connection may transcend several generations. He believes (Layard 1942:489) that the act of homosexuality represents a transmission of male power by physical means; this power does not come simply from the active partner but from the ancestors in direct succession through each generation. Indeed, since semen is a limited good passed down the generations, the semen men have now is the same semen possessed by their male ancestors. Elsewhere, Layard (1959:111) states that homosexual anal intercourse among the Big Nambas symbolizes "continuity with the ancestoral ghosts in the male line."

Alternatively, one might view homosexual relationships as crosscutting ties that bind together various kin groups. For example, among the Sambia all kin are taboo with regard to fellatio. As a rule, fellatio is permissible only with males from "outside one's security circle," that is with "unrelated, potentially hostile males" (Herdt 1981:238). Similarly, Kelly (1977:91) states that a boy gets his life-giving force in semen from individuals outside his lineage. Thus, homosexuality can be interpreted as somewhat analogous to the institution of marriage as explained by alliance theory—homosexual connections may ally potentially hostile groups. Unfortunately, the existing ethnographies do not discuss the role of homosexual relationships/connections in conflict or conflict resolution, but neither do they deny such a connection. The more general point is that, in societies where kin relations are crucial to social organization, the connections between kinship and institutionalized homosexuality have not been adequately investigated.

Another issue that needs attention is the issue of cultural change. As Lindenbaum (1984) points out, "the systematic interconnectedness of the various aspects of culture [is] best illuminated at moments of transformation." Apart from her paper, however, most studies treat homosexuality statically as an unchanging institution. In some societies rituals of homosexuality are disappearing (Godelier 1976); others are experiencing increasing exposure to societies and traditions that do not condone homosexuality and may even be hostile to such behavior. These dynamics obviously contribute to the current situation regarding homosexuality.

Change and contact are not merely recent developments. Deacon's (1934:22) early account of Malekula discusses the massive depopulation of whole districts caused by labor migration to large plantations. Such processes have become even more important and extensive in recent years. Kelly (1976:53) mentions in a footnote that young Etoro men were anxious for him to arrange work for them as contract laborers on the coast. Even among the more isolated Sambia, Herdt (1981:179) notes that young men have been leaving their hamlets for temporary work on coastal plantations since the 1960s. He estimates that twenty percent of unmarried males currently journey to the coast and remain for two to four years. Anthropologists have noted how the unusual circumstances of labor migration give rise to temporary periods of homosexuality (for example, Hogbin 1946:205–206, Mead 1930:193–199; Malinowski 1929:472) but the effect of such movements on those who carry a belief in ritualized homosexuality with them has not been investigated.

Labor migration is both a symptom and a cause of increasing involvement in a cash economy, yet the general impact of cash on homosexuality has not been addressed. The introduction of wage labor is a major metamorphosis that may put economic power in the hands of young workers. The effect of cash is, therefore, an important area to investigate in regard to the suggestion that homosexuality is a mechanism for controlling youth by denying them power. How does this new economic resource effect the youth's role in homosexual relations and his social status in general? Herdt (1981:46) mentions that the introduction of a cash economy and coffee production among the Sambia have led to the acceptance of the entreprenurial big man, but he does not mention the effect of this on the practice or ideology of homosexuality.

Labor migration and participation in a cash economy are manifestations of the broader issue of colonial and foreign intervention. Another major manifestation is pacification. The recreation of a warriorhood is referred to repeatedly in attempts to account for ritualized homosexuality, especially in Van Baal and Herdt. Van Baal (1966:160) asserts that the creation of a "warlike spirit" is one of the primary objectives of male initiation. Herdt (1981:315) repeatedly suggests that the crux of ritualized homosexuality, and the male cult in general, is the creation of warriors. He (Herdt 1981:50) also acknowledges, however, that Australian officials succeeded in completely pacifying the Sambia in 1968 and that fighting among the Sambia and their neighbors came to an end at that time. If homosexuality and warfare are as intertwined as Herdt and Van Baal suggest, it is inconceivable that pacification did not affect the practice or ideology of homosexuality. If there was no effect, then that fact in itself needs explanation.

The impact of colonial administration is not limited to warfare and migration. Kelly (1977:169) notes that the colonial government prohibited "child marriages" among the Etoro in 1966. As a result the average age at marriage for both men and girls increased about six years. Since marriage is a general point when homosexual activities are curtailed, one might expect that this legislation led to a prolonged period of homosexuality, but Kelly does not mention it.

The creation of tribal councils is another change that might influence the practice of homosexuality. Like wage labor, the creation of tribal councils opens up new avenues of power and influence for young men. Consequently, it might affect existing power relations between the generations. Herdt (1981:46) tells us that such councils were set up among the Sambia, but he does not discuss any ramifications for intergenerational relations or homosexuality.

Finally, the problem of missionary activity should be investigated. Needless to say, Christian missionaries do not look favorably on homosexuality. The impact of their moralizing and evangelizing might provide enlightening information about the nature and importance of ritualized homosexuality. For example, we might look for a relationship between the presence of missionaries and the degree of secrecy that shrouds homosexual practices.

In order to address these questions we surely must do more research on the topic, but we must go beyond static studies, narrowly focused on homosexuality. Institutionalized homosexuality, like all sexuality everywhere, is embedded in other social arenas, and changes as these other dimensions of society change. As Ross and Rapp (1981:54) point out, "sexuality both generates wider social relations and is refracted through the prism of society. As such, sexual feelings and activities express all the contradictions of power relations—of gender, class and race." This paper has concentrated specifically on the interaction of homosexual activities with the power relations between the sexes and between the generations. These are still only a few strands in the web of connections between homosexuality and other aspects of culture. If we hope to grasp the complexity of this web we must broaden our scope, and look at the multitude of interrelations between sex and society. Simultaneously, we must extend our time frame and adopt a processual view that can accommodate change.

Ross and Rapp, drawing upon Geertz's onion imagery, eloquently summarize these issues. They (Ross and Rapp 1981:54) state that "in sexuality as in culture, as we peel off each layer (economics, politics, families and so on) we may think that we are approaching the kernel, but we eventually discover that the whole is the only 'essence' there is. Sexuality cannot be abstracted from its surrounding social layers." Only when we succeed in connecting ritualized homosexuality to all the surrounding social layers of New Guinea society will we come close to understanding its "essence."

Notes

I am grateful to Professor Mervyn Meggitt for comments on an earlier version of this paper, and to Professor Shirley Lindenbaum for providing me with a copy of her paper, published in a collection of essays devoted to ritualized homosexuality in Melanesia edited by G. Herdt. At the time of my research I did not have access to the other papers included in that volume.

1. The attribution of feminine and despicable qualities to only the passive partner in a homosexual encounter is also found in nonhomosexual New Guinea societies (e.g., Whiting 1941:51), and in other culture areas such as the Mediterranean (e.g., Brandes 1981:232–233).

Bibliography

Brandes, S. 1981. "Like Wounded Stags: Male Sexual Ideology in an Andalusian Town." *Sexual Meanings: The Cultural Construction of Gender and Sexuality*, eds. S. Ortner and H. Whitehead, Cambridge, pp. 216–239.

Broude, G. J. & S. J. Greene. 1976. "Cross-cultural Codes on Twenty Sexual Attitudes and Practices." *Ethnology* 15:409–429.

Burton, R. V. and J. W. M. Whiting. 1961. "The Absent Father and Cross-Sex Identity. *Merrill-Palmer Quarterly of Behavior and Development* 7:85–95.

Carrier, J. M. 1980. "Homosexual Behavior in Cross-Cultural Perspective." *Homosexual Behavior: A Modern Reappraisal*, ed. J. Marmor, New York, pp. 100–122.

Cohen, Y. A. 1969. "Ends and Means in Political Control: State Organization and the Punishment of Adultery, Incest, and the Violation of Celibacy." *American Anthropologist* 71:658–687.

Deacon, B. A. 1934. *Malekula: A Vanishing People in the New Hebrides*. London.

Dundes, A. 1976. "A Psychoanalytic Study of the Bullroarer." *Man* 11:220–238.

Evans-Pritchard, E. E. 1970. "Sexual Inversion Among the Azande." *American Anthropologist* 72:1428–1434.

Fortes, M. and E. E. Evans-Pritchard. 1940. "Introduction. *African Political Systems*. eds. M. Fortes and E. E. Evans-Pritchard, Oxford, pp. 1–23.

Godelier, M. 1976. "Le sexe comme fondement ultime de l'ordre social et cosmique chez les Baruya de Nouvelle-Guinee." *Sexualité et pouvoir*, ed. A. Verdiglione, Paris, pp. 268–306.

Herdt, G. 1981. *Guardians of the Flutes*. New York.

Herdt, G. and F. J. P. Poole. 1981. "Sexual Antagonism: The Intellectual History of a Concept in the Anthropology of Melanesia." Paper presented at the annual meeting of the American Anthropological Association, Los Angeles.

Hogbin, H. I. 1946. "Puberty to Marriage: A Study of the Sexual Life of the Natives of Wogeo, New Guinea." *Oceania* 16:185–209.

Kelly, R. C. 1976. "Witchcraft and Sexual Relations: An Exploration in the Social and Semantic Implications of the Structure of Belief." *Man and Woman in the New Guinea Highlands*, eds. P. Brown and G. Buchbinder, Special publication of the American Anthropological Association, pp. 36–53.

———— 1977. *Etoro Social Structure: A Study in Structural Contradiction*. Ann Arbor

Landtman, G. 1927. *The Kiwai Papuans of British New Guinea*. London.

Layard, J. 1942. *Stone Men of Malekula*. London.

———— 1959 "Homo-eroticism in Primitive Society as a Function of the Self." *Journal of Analytic Psychology* 4:101–115.

Lindenbaum, S. 1984. "Socio-Sexual Forms in Transition in Melanesia: An Overview." *Ritualized Homosexuality in Melanesia*, ed. G. Herdt. Berkeley: University of California.

Malinowski, B. 1929. *The Sexual Life of Savages in North-Western Melanesia*. New York.

Mead, M. 1930. *Growing Up in New Guinea*. New York.

Meggitt, M. J. 1977 *Blood is Their Argument*. Palo Alto.

Meillassoux, C. 1960. *Essai d'interpretation de phénomène economique dans les sociétés traditionelles d'auto-subsistance*. Cahiers d'Etudes Africaines, 1:38–67.

Ortner, S. 1978. "The Virgin and The State." *Feminist Studies* 4:37–62.

Read, K. E. 1980 *Other Voices*. Novato, California.

Ross, E. and R. Rapp. 1981. "Sex and Society: A Research Note from Social History and Anthropology." *Comparative Studies in Society and History* 23:51–72.

Rowbotham, S. 1973. *Woman's Consciousness, Man's World*. New York.

Schieffelin, E. 1976. *The Sorrow of the Lonely and the Burning of the Dancers*. New York.

Turner, V. W. 1967. "Betwixt and Between: The Liminal Period in Rites de Passage." *The Forest of Symbols*, ed. V. Turner, pp. 93–111, Ithaca.

Van Baal, J. 1966. *Dema*. The Hague.

Van Gennep, A. 1960 (1909). *The Rites of Passage*, trans. M. K. Vizedom and G. L., Gaffee. Chicago.

Wagner, R. 1972. *Habu: The Innovation of Meaning in Daribi Religion*. Chicago.

Whitehead, H. 1981. "The Bow and the Burden Strap: A New Look at Institutionalized Homosexuality in Native North America." *Sexual Meanings: The Cultural Construction of Gender and Sexuality*, eds. S. Ortner and H. Whitehead, pp. 80–115. Cambridge.

Whiting, J. W. M. 1941. *Becoming a Kwoma*. New Haven.

Williams, F. E. 1936. *Papuans of the Trans-Fly*. Oxford.

Zaretsky, E. 1976. *Capitalism, the Family and Personal Life*. New York.

Man Royals and Sodomites: Some Thoughts on the Invisibility of Afro-Caribbean Lesbians

Makeda Silvera

I will begin with some personal images and voices about woman-loving. These have provided a ground for my search for cultural reflections of my identity as a Black woman artist within the Afro-Caribbean community of Toronto. Although I focus here on my own experience (specifically, Jamaican), I am aware of similarities with the experience of other Third World women of color whose history and culture has been subjected to colonization and imperialism.

I spent the first thirteen years of my life in Jamaica among strong women. My great-grandmother, my grandmother and grandaunts were major influences in my life. There are also men whom I remember with fondness—my grandmother's "man friend" G., my Uncle Bertie, his friend Paul, Mr. Minott, Uncle B. and Uncle Freddy. And there were men like Mr. Eden, who terrified me because of stories about his "walking" fingers and his liking for girls under the age of fourteen.

I lived in a four-bedroomed house with my grandmother, Uncle Bertie and two female tenants. On the same piece of land, my grandmother had other tenants, mostly women and lots and lots of children. The big veranda of our house played a vital role in the social life of this community. It was on that veranda that I received my first education on "Black women's strength"—not only from their strength, but also from the daily humiliations they bore at work and in relationships. European experience coined the term "feminism," but the term "Black women's strength" reaches beyond Eurocentric definitions to describe what is the cultural continuity of my own struggles.

The veranda. My grandmother sat on the veranda in the evenings after all the chores were done to read the newspaper. People—mostly women—gathered there to discuss "life." Life covered every conceivable topic—

economic, local, political, social and sexual: the high price of salt fish, the scarcity of flour, the nice piece of yellow yam bought at Coronation market, Mr. Lam, the shopkeeper who was taking "liberty" with Miss Inez, the fights women had with their menfolk, work, suspicions of Miss Iris and Punsie carrying on something between them, the cost of school books. . . .

My grandmother usually had lots of advice to pass on to the women on the veranda, all grounded in the Bible. Granny believed in Jesus, in good and evil and in repentance. She was also a practical and sociable woman. Her faith didn't interfere with her perception of what it meant to be a poor Black woman; neither did it interfere with our Friday night visits to my Aunt Marie's bar. I remember sitting outside on the piazza with my grandmother, two grandaunts and three or four of their women friends. I liked their flashy smiles, and I was fascinated by their independence, ease and their laughter. I loved their names—Cherry Rose, Blossom, Jonesie, Poinsettia, Ivory, Pearl, Iris, Bloom, Dahlia, Babes. Whenever the conversation came around to some "big 'oman talk"— who was sleeping with whom or whose daughter just got "fallen"—I was sent off to get a glass of water for an adult, or a bottle of Kola champagne. Every Friday night I drank as much as half a dozen bottles of Kola champagne, but I still managed to hear snippets of words, tail ends of conversations about women together.

In Jamaica, the words used to describe many of these women would be "Man Royal" and/or "Sodomite." Dread words. So dread that women dare not use these words to name themselves. They were names given to women by men to describe aspects of our lives that men neither understood nor approved.

I heard "sodomite" whispered a lot during my primary school years, and tales of women secretly having sex, joining at the genitals, and being taken to the hospital to be "cut" apart were told in the schoolyard. Invariably, one of the women would die. Every five to ten years the same story would surface. At times it would even be published in the newspapers. Such stories always generated much talking and speculation from "Bwoy dem kinda gal nasti sah!" to some wise old woman saying, "But dis caan happen, after two shutpan caan join"—meaning identical objects cannot go into the other. The act of loving someone of the same sex was sinful, abnormal—something to hide. Even today, it isn't unusual or uncommon to be asked, "So now do two 'omen do it? . . . what unoo use for a penis? . . who is the man and who is the 'oman?" It's inconceivable that women can have intimate relationships that are whole, that are not lacking because of the absence of a man. It's assumed that women in such relationships must be imitating men.

The word "sodomite" derives from the Old Testament. Its common use to describe lesbians (or any strong, independent woman) is peculiar to Jamaica—a culture historically and strongly grounded in the Bible. Although Christian values have dominated the world, their effect in slave colonies is particular. Our foreparents gained access to literacy through the Bible when they were being indoctrinated by missionaries. It provided powerful and ancient stories of strength, endurance and hope which reflected their own fight against oppression. This book has been so powerful that it continues to bind our lives with its racism and misogyny. Thus the importance the Bible plays in Afro-Caribbean culture must be recognized in order to understand the historical and political context for the invisibility of lesbians. The wrath of God "rained down burning sulfur on Sodom and Gomorrah" (Genesis 19:23). How could a Caribbean women claim the name?

When, thousands of miles away and fifteen years after my school days, my grandmother was confronted with my love for a woman, her reaction was determined by her Christian faith and by this dread word "sodomite"— its meaning, it implication, its history.

And when, Bible in hand, my grandmother responded to my love by sitting me down, at the age of twenty-seven, to quote Genesis, it was within the context of this tradition, this politic. When she pointed out that "this was a white people ting," or "a ting only people with mixed blood was involved in" (to explain or include my love with a woman of mixed blood), it was a strong denial of many ordinary Black working-class women she knew.

It was finally through my conversations with my grandmother, my mother and my mother's friend five years later that I began to realize the scope of this denial, which was intended to dissuade and protect me. She knew too well that any woman who took a woman lover was attempting to walk on fire—entering a "no-man's land." I began to see how commonplace the act of loving women really was, particularly in working-class communities. I realized, too, just how heavily shame and silence weighed down this act.

A conversation with a friend of my mother:

> Well, when I was growing up we didn't hear much 'bout woman and woman. They weren't "suspect." There was much more talk about "batty man businesses" when I was a teenager in the 1950s.
>
> I remember one story about a man who was "suspect" and that every night when he was coming home, a group of guys use to lay wait for him and stone him so viciously that he had to run for his life. Dem time, he was safe only in the day.

Now with women, nobody really suspected. I grew up in the country and grew up seeing women holding hands, hugging up, sleeping together in one bed, and there was no question. Some of this was based purely on emotional friendship, but I also knew of cases where the women were dealing but no one really suspected. Close people around knew, but not everyone. It wasn't a thing you would go out and broadcast. It would be something just between the two people.

Also one important thing is that the women who were involved carried on with life just the same, no big political statements were made. These women still went to church, still got baptized, still went on pilgrimage, and I am thinking about one particular woman named Aunt Vie, a very strong woman, strong-willed and everything, they use to call her "man royal" behind her back, but no one ever dare to meddle with her.

Things are different now in Jamaica. Now all you have to do is not respond to a man's call to you and dem call you sodomite or lesbian. I guess it was different back then forty years ago because it was harder for anybody to really conceive of two women sleeping and being sexual. But I do remember when you were "suspect," people would talk about you. You were definitely classed as "different," "not normal," a bit of a "crazy." But women never really got stoned like the men.

What I remember is that if you were a single woman alone or two single women living together and a few people suspected this . . . and when I say a few people I mean like a few guys, sometimes other crimes were committed against the women. Some very violent, some very subtle. Battery was common, especially in Kingston. A group of men would suspect a woman or have it out for her because she was a "sodomite" or because she act "man royal" and so the man would organize and gang-rape whichever woman was "suspect." Sometimes it was reported in the newspaper, other times it wasn't—but when you live in a little community, you don't need a newspaper to tell what's going on. You know by word of mouth, and those stories were frequent. Sometimes you also knew the men who did the battery.

Other subtle forms of this was "scorning" the woman. Meaning that you didn't eat anything from them, especially a cooked meal. It was almost as if those accused of being "man royal" or "sodomite" could contaminate.

A conversation with my grandmother.

I am only telling you this so that you can understand that this is not a profession to be proud of and to get involved in. Everybody should be curious, and I know you born with that, ever since you growing up as a child, and I can't fight against that, because that is how everybody get to know what's in the world. I am only telling you this because when you were a teenager, you always say you want to experience everything and make up your mind on your own. You didn't like people telling you what was wrong and right. That always use to scare me.

Experience is good, yes. But it have to be balanced, you have to know when you have too much experience in one area. I am telling you this because I think you have enough experience in this to decide now to go back to the normal way. You have two children. Do you want them to grow up knowing this is the life you have taken? But this is for you to decide. . . .

Yes, there was a lot of women involved with women in Jamaica. I knew a lot of them when I was growing up in the country in the 1920s. I didn't really associate with them. Mind you, I was not rude to them. My mother wouldn't stand any rudeness from any of her children to adults.

I remember a woman we use to call Miss Bibi. She lived next to us—her husband was a fisherman, I think he drowned before I was born. She had a little wooden house that back onto the sea, the same as our house. She was quiet, always reading. That I remember about her because she used to go to the little public library at least four days out of the week. And she could talk. Anything you want to know, just ask Miss Bibi, and she could tell you. She was mulatto woman, but poor. Anytime I had any school work that I didn't understand, I use to ask her. The one thing I remember, though, we wasn't allowed in her house by my mother, so I used to talk to her outside, but she didn't seem to mind that. Some people use to think she was mad because she spent so much time alone. But I didn't think that because anything she help me with, I got a good mark on it in school.

She was colorful in her own way, but quiet, always alone, except when her friend come and visit her once a year for two weeks. Them times I didn't see Miss Bibi much because my mother told me I couldn't go and visit her. Sometimes I would see her in the market exchanging and bartering fresh fish for vegetables and fruits. I used to see her friend, too. She was a jet Black woman, always had her hair tied in bright-colored cloth, and she always had on big gold earrings. People use to say she lived on the other side of the island with her husband and children and she came to Port Maria once a year to visit Miss Bibi.

My mother and father were great storytellers and I learnt that from them, but is from Miss Bibi that I think I learnt to love reading so much as a child. It wasn't until I moved to Kingston that I notice other women like Miss Bibi. . . .

Let me tell you about Jonesie. Do you remember her? Well, she was the woman who lived the next yard over from us. She is the one who really turn me against people like that and why I fear so much for you to be involved in this ting. She was very loud. Very show-off. Always dressed in pants and man-shirt that she borrowed from her husband.

Sometimes she use to invite me over to her house, but I didn't go. She always had her hair in a bob cut, always barefoot and tending to her garden and her fruit trees. She tried to get me involved in that kind of life, but I said no. At the time I remember I needed some money to borrow and she lent me, later she told me I didn't have to pay her back, but come over to her house and see the thing she had that was sweeter than what any man could offer me. I told her no and eventually paid her back the money.

We still continued to talk. It was hard not to like Jonesie—that's what everybody called her. She was open and easy to talk to. But still there was fear in me about her. To me it seem like she was in a dead end nowhere to go. I don't want that for you.

I left my grandmother's house that day feeling anger and sadness for Miss Jones—maybe for myself, who knows? I was feeling boxed in. I had said nothing, I only listened quietly.

In bed that night, I thought about Miss Jones. I cried for her (for me) silently. I remember her, a mannish-looking Indian woman, with flashy gold teeth, a Craven cigarette always between them. She was always nice to me as a child. She had the sweetest, juiciest Julie, Bombay, and East Indian mangoes on the street. She always gave me mangoes over the fence. I remember the dogs in her yard and the sign on her gate. "Beware of bad dogs." I never went into her house, though I was always curious.

I vaguely remember her pants and shirts, though I never thought anything of them until my grandmother pointed them out. Neither did I recall that dreaded word being used to describe her, although everyone on the street knew about her.

A conversation with my mother:

Yes, I remember Miss Jones. She smoke a lot, drank a lot. In fact, she was an alcoholic. When I was in my teens she use to come over to our house—always on the veranda. I can't remember her sitting down—seems she was always standing up, smoking, drinking and reminiscing. She constantly talked about the past, about her life. And it was always women, the fun they had together and how good she could make love to a woman. She would say to whoever was listening on the veranda, "Dem girls I used to have sex with was shapely. You shoulda know me when I was younger, pretty and shapely just like the 'oman dem I use to have as my 'oman."

People used to tease her on the street, but not about being a lesbian or calling her sodomite. People use to tease her when she was drunk, because she would leave the rum shop and stagger down the avenue to her house.

I remember the women she use to carry home, usually in the daytime. A lot of women from downtown, higglers and fishwomen. She use to boast about knowing all kinds of women from Coronation market and her familiarity with them. She had a husband who lived with her, and that served as her greatest protection against other men taking steps with her. Not that anybody could easily take advantage of Miss Jones, she could stand up for herself. But having a husband did help. He was very quiet, insular man. He didn't talk to anyone in the street. He had no friends, so it wasn't easy for anyone to come up to him and gossip about his wife.

No one could go to her house without being invited, but I wouldn't say she was a private person. She was a loner. She went to the rum shops alone, she drank alone, she staggered home alone. The only times I ever saw her with somebody were the times when she went off to the Coronation market or some other place downtown to find a woman and bring her home. The only times I remember her engaging in conversation with anybody was when she came over on the veranda to talk about her women and what they did in bed. That was all she let out about herself. There was nothing about how she was feeling, whether she was sad or depressed, lonely, happy. Nothing. She seemed to cover up all of that with her loudness and her vulgarness and her constant threat—which was all it was—to beat up anybody who troubled her or teased her when she was coming home from the rum shop.

Now, Cherry Rose—do you remember her? She was a good friend of Aunt Marie and of Mama's. She was also a sodomite. She was loud, too, but different from Miss Jones. She was much more outgoing. She was a barmaid and had lots of friends—both men and women. She also had the kind of personality that attracted people—very vivacious, always laughing, talking and touching. She didn't have any children, but Gem did.

Do you remember Miss Gem? Well, she had children and she was also a barmaid. She also had lots of friends. She also had a man friend named Mickey, but that didn't matter because some women had their men and still had women they carried on with. The men usually didn't know what was going on, and seeing as these men just come and go and usually on their own time, they weren't around every day and night.

Miss Pearl was another one that was in that kind of thing. She was a dressmaker, she used to sew really good. Where Gem was light complexion, she was a very Black woman with deep dimples. Where Gem was a bit plump, Pearl was slim, but with big breasts and a big bottom. They were both pretty women.

I don't remember hearing that word "sodomite" a lot about them. It was whispered sometimes behind their backs, but never in front of them. And they were so alive and talkative that people were always around them.

The one woman I almost forgot was Miss Opal, a very quiet woman. She used to be friends with Miss Oliver and was always out of her bar sitting down. I can't remember much about her except she didn't drink like Miss Jones and she wasn't vulgar. She was soft-spoken, a half-Chinese woman. Her mother was born in Hong Kong and her father was a Black man. She could really bake. She use to supply shops with cakes and other pastries.

So there were many of those kind of women around. But it wasn't broadcast.

I remembered them. Not as lesbians or sodomites or man royals, but as women that I liked. Women whom I admired. Strong women, some colorful, some quiet.

I loved Cherry Rose's style. I loved her loudness, the way she challenged men in arguments, the bold way she laughed in their faces, the jingle of her gold bracelets. Her colorful and stylish way of dressing. She was full of wit; words came alive in her mouth.

Miss Gem: I remember her big double iron bed. That was where Paula and Lorraine (her daughters, my own age) and I spent a whole week together when we had chicken pox. My grandmother took me there to stay for the company. It was fun. Miss Gem lived right above her bar and so at any time we could look through the windows and onto the piazza and street, which was bursting with energy and life. She was a very warm woman, patient and caring. Every day she would make soup for us and tell us stories. Later on in the evening she would bring us Kola champagne.

Miss Pearl sewed dresses for me. She hardly ever used her tape measure—she could just take one look at you and make you a dress fit for a queen. What is she doing now? I asked myself. And Miss Opal, with her calm and quiet, where is she—still baking?

What stories could these lesbians have told us? I, an Afro-Caribbean woman living in Canada, come with this baggage—their silenced stories. My grandmother and mother know the truth, but silence still surrounds us. The truth remains a secret to the rest of the family and friends, and I must decide whether to continue to sew this cloth of denial or break free, creating and becoming the artist that I am, bringing alive the voices and images of Cherry Rose, Miss Gem, Miss Jones, Opal, Pearl and others.
. . .

There is more at risk for us than for White women. Through three hundred years of history we have carried memories and the scars of racism and violence with us. We are the sisters, daughters, mothers of a people enslaved by colonialists and imperialists.

Under slavery, production and reproduction were inextricably linked.

Reproduction served not only to increase the labor force of slave owners but also, by "domesticating" the enslaved, facilitated the process of social control. Simultaneously, the enslaved responded to dehumanizing conditions by focusing on those aspects of life in which they could express their own desires. Sex was an area in which to articulate one's humanity but, because it was tied to attempts "to define oneself as human," gender roles, as well as the act of sex, became badges of status. To be male was to be the stud, the procreator; to be female was to be fecund, and one's femininity was measured by the ability to attract and hold a man and to bear children. In this way, slavery and the postemancipated colonial orders defined the structures of patriarchy and heterosexuality as necessary for social mobility and acceptance.

Socioeconomic conditions and the quest for a better life have seen steady migration from Jamaica and the rest of the Caribbean to the United States, Britain and Canada. Upon my arrival, I became part of the so-called visible minorities encompassing Blacks, Asians and Native North Americans in Canada. I lived with a legacy of continued racism and prejudice. We confront this daily, both as individuals and as organized political groups. Yet for those of us who are lesbians, there is another struggle; the struggle for acceptance and positive self-definition within our own communities. Too often we have had to sacrifice our love for women in political meetings that have been dominated by the "we are the world" attitude of heterosexual ideology. We have had to hide too often that part of our identity which contributes profoundly to make up the whole.

Many lesbians have worked, like me, in the struggles of Black people since the 1960s. We have been on marches every time one of us gets murdered by the police. We have been at sit-ins and vigils. We have flyered, postered, we have cooked and baked for the struggle. We have tended to the youths. And we have all at one time or another given support to men in our community, all the time painfully holding on to, obscuring, our secret lives. When we do walk out of the closet (or are thrown out), the "ideologues" of the Black community say, "Yes, she was a radical sistren but I don't know what happen, she just went the wrong way." What is implicit in this is that one cannot be a lesbian and continue to do political work, and, not surprisingly, it follows that a Black lesbian/artist cannot create using the art forms of our culture. For example, when a heterosexual male friend came to my house, I put on a dub poetry tape. He asked, "Are you sure that sistren is a lesbian?"

"Why?" I ask.

"Because this poem sound wicked; it have lots of rhythm; it sounds cultural."

Another time, another man commented on my work, "That book you wrote on domestic workers is really a fine piece of work. I didn't know you were that informed about the economic politics of the Caribbean and Canada." What are we to assume from this? That Afro-Caribbean lesbians have no Caribbean culture? That they lose their community politics when they sleep with women? Or that Afro-Caribbean culture is a heterosexual commodity?

The presence of an "out" Afro-Caribbean lesbian in our community is dealt with by suspicion and fear from both men and our heterosexual Black sisters. It brings into question the assumption of heterosexuality as the only "normal" way. It forces them to acknowledge something that has always been covered up. It forces them to look at women differently and brings into question the traditional Black female role. Negative response from our heterosexual Black sisters, though more painful, is, to a certain extent, understandable because we have no race privilege and very, very few of us have class privilege. The one privilege within our group is heterosexual. We all suffered at the hands of this racist system at one time or another, and to many heterosexual Black women it is inconceivable, almost frightening, that one could turn her back on credibility in our community and the society at large by being lesbian. These women are also afraid that they will be labeled "lesbian" by association. It is that fear, that homophobia, which keeps Black women isolated.

The Toronto Black community has not dealt with sexism. It has not been pushed to do so. Neither has it given a thought to its heterosexism. In 1988, my grandmother's fear is very real, very alive. One takes a chance when one writes about being an Afro-Caribbean lesbian. There is the fear that one might not live to write more. There is the danger of being physically "disciplined" for speaking as a woman-identified woman.

And what of our White lesbian sisters and their community? They have learnt well from the civil rights movement about organizing, and with race and some class privilege, they built a predominantly White lesbian (and gay) movement—a precondition for a significant body of work by a writer or artist. They have demanded and received recognition from politicians (no matter how little). But this recognition has not been extended to Third World lesbians of color—neither from politicians nor from White lesbian (and gay) organizations. The White lesbian organizations/groups have barely (some not at all) begun to deal with or acknowledge their own racism, prejudice and biases—all learned from a system that feeds on their ignorance and grows stronger from its institutionalized racism. Too often White women focus only on their oppression as lesbians, ignoring the more complex oppression of non-White women who are also lesbians. We remain outsiders in these groups, without images or political voices that echo our own. We know too clearly that, as non-White lesbians in this country, we are politically and socially at the very bottom of the heap. Denial of such differences robs us of true visibility. We must identify and define these differences, and challenge the movements and groups that are not accessible to non-Whites—challenge groups that are not accountable.

But where does this leave us as Afro-Caribbean lesbians, as part of this "visible minority" community? As Afro-Caribbean women we are still at the stage where we have to imagine and discover our existence, past and present. As lesbians, we are even more marginalized, less visible. The absence of a national Black lesbian and gay movement through which to begin to name ourselves is disheartening. We have no political organization to support us and through which we could demand respect from our communities. We need such an organization to represent our interests, both in coalition-building with other lesbian/gay organizations, and in the struggles that shape our future—through which we hope to transform the social, political and economic systems of oppression as they affect all peoples.

Though not yet on a large scale, lesbians and gays of Caribbean descent are beginning to seek each other out—are slowly organizing. Younger lesbians and gays of color are beginning to challenge and force their parents and the Black community to deal with their sexuality. They have formed groups, "Zami for Black and Caribbean Gays and Lesbians" and "Lesbians of Color," to name two.

The need to make connections with other Caribbean and Third World people of color who are lesbian and gay is urgent. This is where we can begin to build that other half of our community, to create wholeness through our art. This is where we will find the support and strength to struggle, to share our histories, and to record these histories in books, documentaries, film, sound and art. We will create a rhythm that is uniquely ours—proud, powerful and gay. Being invisible is no longer. Naming ourselves and taking our space within the larger history of Afro-Caribbean peoples is a dream to be realized, a dream to act upon.

Black Bodies/White Trials

Cindy Patton

The HIV/AIDS vaccine trials set for Africa differ in significant ways from those slated for Britain and those already underway in the U.S., where in some cases noble researchers try the vaccine on themselves. The trials in England and in the bodies of the researchers are Phase One and Two trials, designed to determine whether the person taking the vaccine experiences any side effects (Phase One) and what the exact dose and administration schedule should be (Phase Two). It is improbable that these vaccines will produce HIV-related immune suppression, though there is a possibility that anyone who has been erroneously tested as free of HIV infection could become sick as a result of the response of the body to the vaccine. Because of the risk that the varying doses of vaccine administered in Phase One and Two might be not be effective, and indeed that they might make it impossible for subjects to respond to a future, more effective vaccine, the small number of subjects in these trials is chosen from among people least likely to contract HIV in order to insure that they will never subsequently be exposed to HIV. There is, however, concern expressed that these noble, low-risk people might be falsely branded as "carriers" should their blood be tested and found antibody positive as a result of the vaccine rather than as a result of infection proper. Subjects will thus be issued identification cards stating that their antibodies have come from vaccination.

The trials slated for Africa, by contrast, are Phase Three trials, designed to determine whether the vaccine actually works as a deterrent to HIV infection. In other words, under current plans the trials in England and the U.S. will determine whether the vaccine is harmful to British and American bodies. In Phase Three, African subjects will discover whether they have received enough vaccine to stay uninfected. Clearly, this scheduling of trials in Africa tests on two assumptions which reveal the complicity of science in actually making AIDS in Africa worse:

(1) Vaccine trails are based on the assumption that Africans will continue to be exposed to HIV in large numbers—you can't test a vaccine's effectiveness unless people are subsequently exposed to the agent. Barring mass inoculation of trial subjects with HIV, vaccine trials must assume that "Africans won't use condoms," and that risk campaigns are destined to fail.

The October 1988 *Scientific American* special issue on AIDS contained an ad for Repligen, one of the companies working on a vaccine. The advertisement demonstrates the symbolic leakage between scientific process and lived experience. It read, "To develop an AIDS vaccine, you must choose your partners carefully." "Choice of partners" unconsciously reconstructs the multiple relations of power and the need to gain the cooperation of subjects which constitute AIDS research. Indeed, whatever its pretenses to objectivity, science would not exist without at least some docile object-bodies.

(2) The high risk involved in Phase Three vaccine trials is obscured by the colonial unconscious of ethical evaluations. There is a widely promoted image that Africa and Africans are already lost to the HIV epidemic; this is combined with the controversial new ethical concept of catastrophic rights, according to which trials which do not quite pass ethical muster should be allowed as "compassionate." While this concept has been important in opening up the complex political economy of drug trials (chiefly by letting drug companies off the hook for liability for the harms of "compassionately released" drugs), Africa is *already* considered a catastrophe, in the context of which Western colonialists are released from liability. If the notion of catastrophic rights is introduced into Africa, it seems likely that it will designate the "right" of Westerners to exploit the catastrophe they helped create, instead of giving those affected by HIV the right to receive a benefit that would otherwise have been withheld.

Even beyond the mental gymnastics required to imagine that "catastrophic rights" would entail "enhanced right to therapeutic self-determination" for anyone in Africa, there are several more basic questions. First, existing epidemiological data certainly does not suggest that HIV is more rampant in any African locale than in, say, San Francisco, Newark, Paris, or Amsterdam. Second, if all of Africa is dying of AIDS, as Western news reports suggest, who is left to serve as trial subjects? Third, if preventive measures *can* be successful, as some African governments claim (and here, ethicists must explain where and why prevention works—if it works in the Sodom of San Francisco, why not the Eden of Dar es Salaam?), then who benefits from the risks of the vaccine trials? Fourth, if some important number of the HIV cases in African cities are attributable to poor blood screening resulting from the low efficacy and high cost of the Western-developed tests, are we funding vaccine trials instead of improved screening? Is the moderately high (and unavoidable) risk of receiving an HIV-infected blood transfusion to be another route of exposure for potential vaccine trial subjects? Finally, what provisions ensure that Africans, and African societies as wholes, will actually be first to receive the vaccine, once developed? Here, the precise arguments about the problems in rural clinical practice—"They can't properly diagnose AIDS in Africa"—come into play as alibis for not distributing the vaccine.

The contradictory nature of the racist perceptions which construct the idea of Africa renders them all the more insidious. On one hand, researchers who want to run Phase Three trials in Africa argue that "AIDS" in Africa and "AIDS" in the West are the same. On the other hand, epidemiologists argue that "African AIDS" is something altogether different, with different modes of transmission having to do with dramatic differences in Western and African sexual practices. The desire for a radical and incommensurable racial difference runs rampant here. Miscegenation fears, oddly enough, seem to lead some epidemiologists to argue in support of White homosexuality; Alan Whiteside, a researcher in South Africa who analyzes demographic and economic trends in South African mines, has argued that because male-male relations in the migrant work force are "patron relationships" which, unlike White homosexuality, do not involve "anal intercourse," the Chamber of Mines need only worry about anti-discrimination education. What is in play here is not only the desire that Black and White blood should not mix in the issue of heterosexual union, but also that Black and White homosexuality be different and not a possible source of sexual congress. Whiteside described the country's "risk" demographics in terms of "White homosexuals" and "foreigners [meaning migrants from Botswana, Lesotho, Malawi, Mozambique, Swaziland, Zimbabwe and Zambia] and heterosexuals who are Black." "Ironically," he says, "political isolation and apartheid may have slowed the spread of AIDS." In fact, Whiteside is one of the few researchers who acknowledges the existence of male-male practices at all. Although there are no seroprevalence studies of Black males by work groups, many commentators claim that truck drivers, not miners, and heterosexual behavior, not male-male relationships, account for the movement of HIV. Infected miners, Whitehead suggests, brought HIV infections from home but did not acquire them in South African mining camps.

The irony, of course, is that there are gay-identified Black South Africans, and numerous forms of male-male sexuality in the Southern African cultural traditions, some existing before colonial regimes and continuing in the countryside, and some existing in the townships, reformed or created in resistance to colonialism. Indeed, Moody argues that the degree of male-male, cross-age relationships (with the younger or novice miners taking on the role of "mine wives") helped create the economic base for buying homesteads in countries of origin and for resisting the "proletarianization" which occurred when the miners became involved in town life. He suggests that, like the formation of gay communities in Europe and North America, accompanying proletarianization, some migrants chose to stay in or move to the townships in order to maintain their "gay life." The forms of wifery in the mines may not have dominantly involved "anal intercourse," as Whiteside suggests; however, the complex social transitions occurring before the 1970s (even the numbers of mine wives have declined since the 1970s due to shifts in the host countries and the general increase in permanent migration to cities) have to some degree sharpened the distinctions between lifelong "gay" relationships and economic/social male-male relationships circumscribed by migrancy and integrated into cross-gender, procreative economic relations. To reduce Southern African male-male sexuality to mine relationships ignores both historical and contemporary shifts in sexual patterns which are directly related to colonialism and apartheid. To locate all "homosexual" HIV transmission in the mines ignores Black gay men outside the mines. To overrate the possibilities of HIV transmission among men in the mines results in crackdowns on male-male practices (crackdowns which have occurred throughout mine history in the twentieth century, especially under the influence of Christianity), and destroys important social bonds which enable Blacks to resist cultural destruction. Ironically then, Black male-male relationships are invisible, and "homosexuality" is illegal under laws governing *White* conduct. White male-male relations are unlawful and Black male-male relations invisible in the eyes of the South African government. Two entirely different television campaigns (similar in strategy to campaigns in the U.S. though the "White" campaign actually represented "homosexual men") were produced; the White campaign was aimed at reducing homosexual practice, the Black campaign promoted monogamy and the closing of family ranks against outsiders, a cover *apologia* suggesting that apartheid and monogamy, both products of White colonialism, might protect Blacks from AIDS.

The efforts of Westerners, meanwhile, are focused on explaining the reasons for the apparent dominance of "heterosexual transmission" in the sub-Saharan continent overall (called Pattern Two by World Health Organization officials, but African AIDS by numerous researchers), versus the apparent homosexual (Pattern One) and injecting drug transmission in Northern Europe and North America. (Southern Europe claims transmission patterns more like those in Africa.) The attribution of transmission routes, of course, depends on self-reports of homosexual behavior, a social construction which varies, not surprisingly, according to these very same geographical clusters.

Ironically, the concern of Western researchers about possible heterosexual transmission among U.S. citizens came from looking at early African data at a time when U.S. data was particularly skimpy. The possibility of large-scale heterosexual transmission in the U.S. was initially dismissed (in 1984) because, scientists alleged, anal intercourse was the sole route of sexual spread, and unlike African heterosexuals, Euro-American heterosexuals were not believed to engage in this "primitive form of birth control." No data was ever offered in support of this belief and no one mentioned that anal sex might actually be a pleasure indulged in by heterosexuals worldwide. Thus when cases of apparent "heterosexual transmission" were identified in the U.S., the first explanation combined stereotypes about prostitutes with anxieties about anal sex—doctors alleged that men (mostly those under study by the Army's Walter Reed hospital) had been infected with HIV through anal sex with prostitutes. One researcher told me that men had anal sex with prostitutes because their wives "wouldn't do it."

In the early years of the epidemic, then, "Black"/"heterosexual" AIDS and "White"/"homosexual" AIDS were banished to an imaginary space, "Africa," and linked together, not through intimations of cross-racial/cross-preferential pairings, but through a metaphoric cross-inscription of bodies. U.S. (White) homosexuals were said to have made of their bodies something of the order of the sewerage system of a Third World country—free running waste comprising a prominent Western image of underdevelopment. African (Black) heterosexuals were homosexualized through their allegedly greater practice of anal sex—anality being a chief Western symbol of homosexuality.

The attempt here on the part of researchers was clearly to reconcile cultural anxieties and stereotypes with certain curiosities in their own data. Their efforts were directed toward explaining how in the West, and among Whites, active homosexuals passed the virus to passive homosexuals, while in Africa and among prostitutes and people of color in the U.S., women engaging in anal intercourse passed the virus to heterosexual men. The collision of homophobia and racism provided the anus with a curious but pivotal gender: the female anus was thought capable of doing what the male anus was not.

HIV prevalence and sexual practice studies in the mid-1980s quickly showed, however, that rates of anal intercourse among heterosexuals varied little around the world, not so much because Africans engaged in less than expected but because Euro-American heterosexuals engaged in more. (In general, African sex lives were disappointingly ordinary, squashing both the hopes of scientific explanations of epidemiological differences and Western racists' fantasies of exotic sexual otherness.) That theory was put forward in an attempt to explain why in Africa male-to-female seroprevalence ratios ranged from 2:1 to 1:1, while in Northern and Central Europe and North America, the ratios were between 7:1 and 9:1. This was taken to be evidence that in Europe and North America, AIDS is a "gay disease" while in Africa it is "heterosexual." This is a perplexing form of "new math" in the age of sophisticated computer modelling. Paradoxically, of course, the African ratio of 1:1 suggested that Africans were more prone to Victorian heterosexual bonding, while the ratio of 7:1 among Europeans not only suggested promiscuity, but somehow intimated that the female "1" was always the hapless victim of male homosexual forays into heterosexual intercourse. The mediating factor of injection drug paraphernalia-sharing— which was in fact occurring both within homosexual and heterosexual relationship systems, and in groups where both sharing and pairing were not rigorously governed by sexual labels—was politely ignored (especially in African contexts) as was the continuing inability of some African countries to screen blood to Western standards, and to gauge the range of people infected with HIV. Furthermore, African medical practice, in general, frequently transfuses women and children, and the subsequent higher levels of seroprevalence of these two groups is the "evidence" for Western researchers' view of "heterosexual AIDS."

In fact, the research on heterosexual AIDS in Africa was trying to explain away the wrong question; the insistent denial of homosexual routes and erasing of transfusion-related cases only confirmed the long-standing stereotype that prostitutes must be "spreading AIDS." Heterosexual AIDS in Africa (and soon in the U.S.) meant men who claimed to be heterosexual who "caught" HIV from prostitutes. In most African cities there is a wide variety of male-female quasicommercial relations as well as traditional polygamy and postcolonial modifications of formal polygamy, and it is not unusual for one man to support, in part or whole, several women. They may be wives, periodic partners or occasional "prostitutes." In addition, most women who Westerners identify as "prostitutes" are entrepreneurs who use "prostitution" to acquire capital. There are certainly some migrant women who strike economic bargains with men, but these men are likely to be locally understood as temporary husbands. (These patterns also hold in the U.S. and worldwide—the construction of the role "prostitute" has much more to do with laws designed to constrain women within narrow sexual contracts than they have to do with the self-identity of women themselves.) Nevertheless, the hyperheterosexualization of African AIDS aims at tracking the spread of HIV from prostitutes, not the other way around. But this actually flies in the face of both epidemiology and genitourinary clinical data. Even with the hypothesized greater transmission of HIV from women to men if men have genital ulcers, the probability of transmission cannot, and in the epidemiology does not, become equal. If prostitution were the chief explanation of AIDS in Africa, even if each "prostitute" "infected" several men, each of those men could in turn be expected to infect several other women (his wives and other prostitutes), since the odds of male-to-female (or male-to-male—it is the receptive partner who is át increased risk) infection are still greater. Combined with the increased infection of women due to blood transfusions, we should have *more* women than men, not the same number. Clearly, developing a coherent understanding of male and female cases internationally requires much more extensive analysis of the exact routes via which men versus women are subject to infection.

One thoroughly unethical study among "prostitutes" in Nairobi demonstrates both the real frequency of women becoming infected during intercourse, and the callousness that antiwoman, and especially antiprostitute, attitudes engender. The abstract for the study, which was presented at the Fifth International AIDS Conference, reads:

Efficacy of Nonoxynol–9 in Preventing HIV Transmission

Kreiss, Joan*; Ruminjo, I**; Ngugi, E**; Roberts, P*; Ndinya-Achola, J**; Plummer F***. *U. of Washington, Seattle, USA, **U. of Nairobi, Kenya, ***U. of Manitoba, Winnipeg, Canada.

Objective. To assess the efficacy of N–9 in preventing HIV transmission. [*N–9 is the active ingredient in many commercially available spermicides.*]

Method. A prospective randomized placebo-controlled study was conducted among HIV seronegative prostitutes in Nairobi, Kenya.

Results. Ninety-eight women were enrolled, assigned to the use of N–9 contraceptive sponges [*something like the Today Sponge commercially available in the U.S.*] (51) or placebo vaginal suppositories (47), and followed for a mean of 10 months (range 1–22). N–9 use was associated with a higher incidence of genital ulcers (17 vs 7% of exams, $p > .001$) and fungal vulvitis (19 vs 10%, $p > .001$) and a lower incidence of gonorrhea (21 vs 36%, $p > .001$). HIV infection occurred in 20 women in the N–9 group and 15 in the placebo group. Excluding women who were lost to follow-up or who seroconverted within 2 months of enrollment [*and therefore were already infected before the study*], 16 (46%) of 35 N–9 users and 10 (28%) of 35 placebo users developed HIV Abs by ELISA and WB (p = NS). . . .

    Conclusion. In this study of Nairobi prostitutes, we have failed to demonstrate efficacy of N–9 use in preventing heterosexual transmission of HIV. N–9 use was associated with an increased frequency of genital ulcers and of genital ulcer-associated seroconversion. Spermicide studies in other high risk populations are needed before recommendations regarding spermicide use can be knowledgeably made. [*Abstract M.A.O.36—this study was orally presented to hundreds of researchers.*]

"High risk" from where, we might ask? Unethical researchers? No one recommends use of N–9 sponges alone, and the only basis on which to study N–9 versus nothing (as opposed to a control group of condom users, a known "improvement" over "nothing") is the assertion that "Africans won't use condoms." In fact, there is a highly successful, prostitute-run condom promotion project in Nairobi, which began in 1986. The executors of the above study knew this, since they are also the researchers evaluating that project, which they reported on the day after presenting the study above. That study showed marked increase in condom use by the women's clients (the most frequent reason for non-use of condoms was customer refusal), and STD rates tracked among males in the surrounding region were reduced during the first year in which the project was run to less than half their 1981 level. Indeed, a report from the U.S. Agency for International Development (the major condom supplier in developing nations) presented in Montreal suggested that supply, not resistance to usage, was the major problem in HIV prevention. The report shows that if all 120 million condoms supplied to developing nations had gone only to Nigeria, less than six percent of the men aged fifteen to forty-nine could have been supplied with condoms for a year. The reality of condom access problems was brought home to me when I was in Youande, Cameroon at an AIDS education conference. A young woman approached me and asked if I was attending the AIDS conference, and when I replied yes, she asked if I could give her condoms. The condoms placed on display at the conference hall were almost immediately taken by the army guards and civilian cafeteria workers, and soldiers asked conference attendees if we could bring more.

    In 1988, scientists quietly dropped the anal sex differential argument in favor of the theory that sexually active Africans are afflicted by genital ulcers which increase the potential for transmission of the virus from women to men. Conference visual aids during the genital ulcers era were never complete without pictures of diseased genitals—projected to six or eight feet high to get over the point that the equipment of men and women in African is "different." What remained unspoken here was that those differences occur, not at the level of sexual, but of medical practice—at the level, that is, of differences in the availability of STD health care services (which incidentally vary as much in the U.S. as they do in other countries). The implication of this STD-ulcer research was, however, once again that STD-infected individuals were somehow able to produce HIV *sui generis*. This continuing attempt to locate gender differentials between the U.S. and Africa in the bodies of self-reported heterosexual Africans rather than in the social processes which create the economy of sexualities once again distorts both the demographics and sociology of HIV in Africa, and thus inhibits properly directed risk reduction campaigns.

The persistent conflation of HIV with secondary factors in Africa, particularly its linking with poverty and sexuality, has finally led researchers to hunt for differences in heterosexual practices instead of recognizing the existence of male homosexuality in countries and cultures where male-male sex is practiced under another name. In fact, a number of African cultures have long-standing, culturally specific structures of male-male sexual practice; yet there is inconsistent data on the existence of "homosexuality" in Africa, largely because of the categories and stereotypes of Western researchers who understand homosexuality as a preference or identity in Western terms, rather than as a form of social or economic bond. Zulu gay activist Alfred Machela has described the male-male sex structure widespread in his own and in geographically adjacent cultures. Male-male sex is part of a social/paramilitary bond of serious dimensions but is not considered "homosexuality," a category which is taboo and recognized as a Western or Arabic perversion. He suggests that when Western researchers ask about the incidence of homosexuality in African nations, the governments' prudish "not here" reply is a self-protective denial of European concepts of homosexuality, rather than a denial of male-male sex practices, which remain unspoken or ritualized in social or economic bonds. As Gill Shepard has noted, there were a wide variety of homosexual roles and relations articulated in precolonial cultures. Many of these were subsequently banned by Christian, colonial governments, who condemned them as "perversions" or "primitive" seductions. For colonized peoples, denying homosexuality could be seen therefore as a means of evading the legal and moral sanctions of the administrative state. In some cases, the strength and values of homosexual relations were totally destroyed during the colonial period. In other cases, as in Zulu culture, homosexual practices remain, but are doubly coded, in some contexts as perversions, in others as ritualized forms of male bonding.

Gay theorists have argued that gay identity and the notion of homosexuality are historically specific concepts in the West whose emergence coincided with the appearance of psychological explanations of sexuality. And indeed, current studies of sexual practice, launched worldwide in attempts to provide an epidemiological basis for HIV education, suggest boringly little difference in heterosexual and homosexual activities, in rates of partner change, or in acceptance of the new sexual practices of "safer sex." It is sexual identity and the relation between identity and "risk" that vary so dramatically around the world. The social arrangement and meaning of sexual acts differ from city to city, country to country, era to era; yet the acts themselves, even when Western definitions are used for what "counts" as sex, remain more or less the same. Unfortunately of course, the virus follows the routes of particular acts, regardless of whether they are considered homosexual acts, acts of male dominance, of sodomy (irrespective of gender), acts of economic exchange, acts of romantic male bonding or of species perpetuation. The virus enters any given locale through an accident of history, and slowing down the transmission of HIV depends on understanding the exact interrelationship between sexual actors of whatever gender or sexuality, whatever national or political formations. The key question, then, is how to understand the interrelation of sexualities internationally, and we should address this question, not as voyeurs or guardians of sexually overdetermined "Others," but as equal participants in an economy of pleasures. We should also understand what is at stake politically in current representations of "Other" sexualities.

Beneath the dramatic media accounts of Africa as a continent devastated by a virus lies the vision of a continent experiencing medical and scientific exploitation. Beyond the postcolonial and postrevolutionary administrations fighting for credibility and political survival on a global, Western-defined stage are people interrelating and seeking pleasures in their bodies. Cultural organizing to fight HIV must work in micronetworks to enable people both to recognize the acts which allow transmission of HIV, and to sustain and resymbolize those cultural/sexual practices which prevent transmission. We must also understand the political and social difference between the Western closet which circumscribes in order to *occlude deviance* and the traditional cultures which articulate homosexualities into economic and social and religious bonds in order to *sustain difference*.

Internationally, AIDS is constructed through a deadly set of assumptions about cultural and political difference. AIDS is mapped directly onto preexisting national and cultural formations. But HIV knows no geographical boundaries. HIV traces a geography unrecognized by governments intent on reducing sexualities which subvert economic production, thwart social control or merely stand as politically embarrassing reminders of richly symbolic and less rigidly conformist ways of life, once characteristic of traditional cultures, but now labeled as perverted and as a political liability by Western discourse. HIV follows the lines of transportation created by capital investment and traces a geography of bodily pleasures that defies the medical cops who police every country's border, no matter how many tests they devise. The HIV epidemic poses a unique moral challenge and will reform both the meaning of sexuality and the meaning of local and international cooperation.

The scientists, policymakers and media tycoons have the power to produce masks of otherness which create discrimination against people with HIV and AIDS. They have the power to thwart prevention by allowing people to ignore the necessity of speaking about sexual practices out of a false sense that HIV is somewhere else, in the bodies of others. Local activists—who slowly find each other through the improbable routes of international scientific conferences, ex-lovers, and FAX machines—will transform the meaning of geographical boundaries. Though many of us will die in this epidemic, the network of survivors will form a new, supranational community of resistance.

Bowers v. Hardwick

Justice WHITE delivered the opinion of the Court.

In August 1982, respondent Hardwick (hereafter respondent) was charged with violating the Georgia statute criminalizing sodomy[1] by committing that act with another adult male in the bedroom of respondent's home. After a preliminary hearing, the District Attorney decided not to present the matter to the grand jury unless further evidence developed.

Respondent then brought suit in the Federal District Court, challenging the constitutionality of the statute insofar as it criminalized consensual sodomy.[2] He asserted that he was a practicing homosexual, that the Georgia sodomy statute, as administered by the defendants, placed him in imminent danger of arrest, and that the statute for several reasons violates the Federal Constitution. The District Court granted the defendants' motion to dismiss for failure to state a claim, relying on *Doe v. Commonwealth's Attorney for the City of Richmond*, 403 F.Supp. 1199 (ED Va. 1975), which this Court summarily affirmed, 425 U.S. 901, 96 S.Ct. 1489, 47 L.Ed.2d 751 (1976).

A divided panel of the Court of Appeals for the Eleventh Circuit reversed. 760 F.2d 1202 (1985). The court first held that, because *Doe* was distinguishable and in any event had been undermined by later decisions, our summary affirmance in that case did not require affirmance of the District Court. Relying on our decisions in *Griswold v. Connecticut*, 381 U.S. 479, 85 S.Ct., 1678, 14 L.Ed.2d 510 (1965); *Eisenstadt v. Baird*, 405 U.S. 438, 92 S.Ct. 1029, 31 L.Ed.2d 349 (1972); *Stanley v. Georgia*, 394 U.S. 557, 89 S.Ct. 1243, 22 L.Ed.2d 542 (1969); and *Roe v. Wade*, 410 U.S. 113, 93 S.Ct. 705, 35 L.Ed.2d 147 (1973), the court went on to hold that the Georgia statute violated respondent's fundamental rights because his homosexual activity is a private and intimate association that is beyond the reach of state regulation by reason of the Ninth Amendment and the Due Process Clause of the Fourteenth Amendment. The case was remanded for trial, at which, to prevail, the State would have to prove that

117

the statute is supported by a compelling interest and is the most narrowly drawn means of achieving that end.

[1] Because other Courts of Appeals have arrived at judgments contrary to that of the Eleventh Circuit in this case,[3] we granted the Attorney General's petition for certiorari questioning the holding that the sodomy statute violates the fundamental rights of homosexuals. We agree with petitioner that the Court of Appeals erred, and hence reverse its judgment.[4]

[2] This case does not require a judgment on whether laws against sodomy between consenting adults in general, or between homosexuals in particular, are wise or desirable. It raises no question about the right or propriety of state legislative decisions to repeal their laws that criminalize homosexual sodomy, or of state-court decisions invalidating those laws on state constitutional grounds. The issue presented is whether the Federal Constitution confers a fundamental right upon homosexuals to engage in sodomy and hence invalidates the laws of the many States that still make such conduct illegal and have done so for a very long time. The case also calls for some judgment about the limits of the Court's role in carrying out its constitutional mandate.

We first register our disagreement with the Court of Appeals and with respondent that the Court's prior cases have construed the Constitution to confer a right of privacy that extends to homosexual sodomy and for all intents and purposes have decided this case. The reach of this line of cases was sketched in *Cary v. Population Services International*, 431 U.S. 678, 685, 97 S.Ct. 2010, 2016, 52 L.Ed.2d 675 (1977). *Pierce v. Society of Sisters*, 268 U.S. 510, 45 S.Ct. 571, 69 L.Ed.1070 (1925), and *Meyer v. Nebraska*, 262 U.S. 390, 43 S.Ct. 625, 67 L.Ed.1042 (1923), were described as dealing with child rearing and education; *Prince v. Massachusetts*, 321 U.S. 158, 64 S.Ct. 438, 88 L.Ed. 645 (1944), with family relationships; *Skinner v. Oklahoma ex rel. Williamson*, 316 U.S. 535, 62 S.Ct. 1110, 86 L.Ed. 1655 (1942), with procreation; *Loving v. Virginia*, 388 U.S. 1, 87 S.Ct. 1817, 18 L.Ed.2d 1010 (1967), with marriage; *Griswold v. Connecticut, supra*, and *Eisenstadt v. Baird, supra*, with contraception; and *Roe v. Wade*, 410 U.S. 113, 93 S.Ct. 705, 35 L.Ed.2d 147 (1973), with abortion. The latter three cases were interpreted as construing the Due Process Clause of the Fourteenth Amendment to confer a fundamental individual right to decide whether or not to beget or bear a child. *Carey v. Population Services International, supra*, 431 U.S., at 688–689, 97 S.Ct., at 2017–2018.

Accepting the decisions in these cases and the above description of them, we think it evident that none of the rights announced in those cases bears any resemblance to the claimed constitutional right of homosexuals to engage in acts of sodomy that is asserted in this case. No connection between family, marriage, or procreation on the one hand and homosexual activity on the other has been demonstrated, either by the Court of Appeals or by respondent. Moreover, any claim that these cases nevertheless stand for the proposition that any kind of private sexual conduct between consenting adults is constitutionally insulated from state proscription is unsupportable. Indeed, the Court's opinion in *Carey* twice asserted that the privacy right, which the *Griswold* line of cases found to be one of the protections provided by the Due Process Clause, did not reach so far. 431 U.S., at 688, n. 5, 694, n. 17, 97 S.Ct., at 2018, n. 5, 2021, n. 17.

Precedent aside, however, respondent would have us announce, as the Court of Appeals did, a fundamental right to engage in homosexual sodomy. This we are quite unwilling to do. It is true that despite the language of the Due Process Clauses of the Fifth and Fourteenth Amendments, which appears to focus only on the processes by which life, liberty, or property is taken, the cases are legion in which those Clauses have been interpreted to have substantive content, subsuming rights that to a great extent are immune from federal or state regulation or proscription. Among such cases are those recognizing rights that have little or no textual support in the constitutional language. *Meyer, Prince,* and *Pierce* fall in this category, as do the privacy cases from *Griswold* to *Carey.*

Striving to assure itself and the public that announcing rights not readily identifiable in the Constitution's text involves much more than the imposition of the Justices' own choice of values on the States and the Federal Government, the Court has sought to identify the nature of the rights qualifying for heightened judicial protection. In *Palko v. Connecticut,* 302 U.S. 319, 325, 326, 58 S.Ct. 149, 151, 152, 82 L.Ed. 288 (1937), it was said that this category includes those fundamental liberties that are "implicit in the concept of ordered liberty," such that "neither liberty nor justice would exist if [they] were sacrificed." A different description of fundamental liberties appeared in *Moore v. East Cleveland,* 431 U.S. 494, 503, 97 S.Ct. 1932, 1937, 52 L.Ed.2d 531 (1977) (opinion of POWELL, J.), where they are characterized as those liberties that are "deeply rooted in this Nation's history and tradition." *Id.,* at 503, 97 S.Ct. at 1938 (POWELL, J.). See also *Griswold v. Connecticut,* 381 U.S., at 506, 85 S.Ct., at 1693.

It is obvious to us that neither of these formulations would extend a fundamental right to homosexuals to engage in acts of consensual sodomy. Proscriptions against that conduct have ancient roots. See generally, Survey on the Constitutional Right to Privacy in the Context of Homosexual Activity, 40 U.Miami L.Rev. 521, 525 (1986). Sodomy was a criminal offense at common law and was forbidden by the laws of the original thirteen

States when they ratified the Bill of Rights.[5] In 1868, when the Fourteenth Amendment was ratified, all but 5 of the 37 States in the Union had criminal sodomy laws.[6] In fact, until 1961,[7] all 50 States outlawed sodomy, and today 24 States and the District of Columbia continue to provide criminal penalties for sodomy performed in private and between consenting adults. See Survey, U.Miami L.Rev., *supra*, at 524, n. 9. Against this background, to claim that a right to engage in such conduct is "deeply rooted in this Nation's history and tradition" or "implicit in the concept of ordered liberty" is, at best, facetious.

[3] Nor are we inclined to take a more expansive view of our authority to discover new fundamental rights imbedded in the Due Process Clause. The Court is most vulnerable and comes nearest to illegitimacy when it deals with judge-made constitutional law having little or no cognizable roots in the language or design of the Constitution. That this is so was painfully demonstrated by the face-off between the Executive and the Court in the 1930s, which resulted in the repudiation of much of the substantive gloss that the Court had placed on the Due Process Clauses of the Fifth and Fourteenth Amendments. There should be, therefore, great resistance to expand the substantive reach of those Clauses, particularly if it requires redefining the category of rights deemed to be fundamental. Otherwise, the Judiciary necessarily takes to itself further authority to govern the country without express constitutional authority. The claimed right pressed on us today falls far short of overcoming this resistance.

Respondent, however, asserts that the result should be different where the homosexual conduct occurs in the privacy of the home. He relies on *Stanley v. Georgia*, 394 U.S. 557, 89 S.Ct. 1243, 22 L.Ed.2d 542 (1969), where the Court held that the First Amendment prevents conviction for possessing and reading obscene material in the privacy of one's home: "If the First Amendment means anything, it means that a State has no business telling a man, sitting alone in his house, what books he may read or what films he may watch." *Id.*, at 565, 89 S.Ct., at 1248.

Stanley did protect conduct that would not have been protected outside the home, and it partially prevented the enforcement of state obscenity laws; but the decision was firmly grounded in the First Amendment. The right pressed upon us here has no similar support in the text of the Constitution, and it does not qualify for recognition under the prevailing principles for construing the Fourteenth Amendment. Its limits are also difficult to discern. Plainly enough, otherwise illegal conduct is not always immunized whenever it occurs in the home. Victimless crimes, such as the possession and use of illegal drugs, do not escape the law where they are committed at home. *Stanley* itself recognized that its holding offered no protection for the possession in the home of drugs, firearms, or stolen goods. *Id.*, at 568, n. 11, 89 S.Ct., at 1249, n. 11. And if respondent's submission is limited to the voluntary sexual conduct between consenting adults, it would be difficult, except by fiat, to limit the claimed right to homosexual conduct while leaving exposed to prosecution adultery, incest, and other sexual crimes even though they are committed in the home. We are unwilling to start down that road.

[4] Even if the conduct at issue here is not a fundamental right, respondent asserts that there must be a rational basis for the law and that there is none in this case other than the presumed belief of a majority of the electorate in Georgia that homosexual sodomy is immoral and unacceptable. This is said to be an inadequate rationale to support the law. The law, however, is constantly based on notions of morality, and if all laws representing essentially moral choices are to be invalidated under the Due Process Clause, the courts will be very busy indeed. Even respondent makes no such claim, but insists that majority sentiments about the morality of homosexuality should be declared inadequate. We do not agree, and are unpersuaded that the sodomy laws of some 25 States should be invalidated on this basis.[8]

Accordingly, the judgment of the Court of Appeals is
Reversed.

Chief Justice BURGER, concurring.

I join the Court's opinion, but I write separately to underscore my view that in constitutional terms there is no such thing as a fundamental right to commit homosexual sodomy.

As the Court notes, *ante*, at 2844, the proscriptions against sodomy have very "ancient roots." Decisions of individuals relating to homosexual conduct have been subject to state intervention throughout the history of Western civilization. Condemnation of those practices is firmly rooted in Judeo-Christian moral and ethical standards. Homosexual sodomy was a capital crime under Roman law. See Code Theod. 9.7.6; Code Just. 9.9.31. See also D. Bailey, Homosexuality and the Western Christian Tradition 70–81 (1975). During the English Reformation when powers of the ecclesiastical courts were transferred to the King's Courts, the first English statute criminalizing sodomy was passed. 25 Hen. VIII, ch. 6. Blackstone described "the infamous *crime against nature*" as an offense of "deeper malignity" than rape, a heinous act "the very mention of which is a disgrace to human nature," and "a crime not fit to be named." 4 W. Blackstone, Commentaries *215. The common law of England, including its prohibition of sodomy, became the received law of Georgia and the other Colonies. In 1816 the Georgia Legislature passed the statute at issue here, and that statute has been continuously in force in one form or another since that time. To hold that the act of homosexual sodomy is somehow protected as a fundamental right would be to cast aside millennia of moral teaching.

This is essentially not a question of personal "preferences" but rather of the legislative authority of the State. I find nothing in the Constitution depriving a State of the power to enact the statute challenged here.

Justice POWELL, concurring.

I join the opinion of the Court. I agree with the Court that there is no fundamental right—i.e., no substantive right under the Due Process Clause—such as that claimed by respondent Hardwick, and found to exist by the Court of Appeals. This is not to suggest, however, that respondent may not be protected by the Eighth Amendment of the Constitution. The Georgia statute at issue in this case, Ga.Code Ann. §16–6–2 (1984), authorizes a court to imprison a person for up to 20 years for a single private, consensual act of sodomy. In my view, a prison sentence for such conduct—certainly a sentence of long duration—would create a serious Eighth Amendment issue. Under the Georgia statute a single act of sodomy, even in the private setting of a home, is a felony comparable in terms of the possible sentence imposed to serious felonies such as aggravated battery, §16–5–24, first-degree arson, §16–7–60, and robbery §16–8–40.[1]

In this case, however, respondent has not been tried, much less convicted and sentenced.[2] Moreover, respondent has not raised the Eighth Amendment issue below. For these reasons this constitutional argument is not before us.

Justice BLACKMUN, with whom Justice BRENNAN, Justice MARSHALL, and Justice STEVENS join, dissenting.

This case is no more about "a fundamental right to engage in homosexual sodomy," as the Court purports to declare, *ante*, at 2844, than *Stanley v. Georgia*, 394 U.S. 557, 89 S.Ct. 1243, 22 L.Ed.2d 542 (1969), was about a fundamental right to watch obscene movies, or *Katz v. United States*, 389 U.S. 347, 88 S.Ct. 507, 19 L.Ed.2d 576 (1967), was about a fundamental right to place interstate bets from a telephone booth. Rather, this case is about "the most comprehensive of rights and the right most valued by civilized men," namely, "the right to be let alone." *Olmstead v. United*

States, 277 U.S. 438, 478 48 S.Ct. 564, 572, 72 L.Ed. 944 (1928) (Brandeis, J., dissenting).

The statute at issue, Ga.Code Ann. §16–6–2 (1984), denies individuals the right to decide for themselves whether to engage in particular forms of private, consensual sexual activity. The Court concludes that §16–6–2 is valid essentially because "the laws of . . . many States . . . still make such conduct illegal and have done so for a very long time." *Ante*, at 2843. But the fact that the moral judgments expressed by statutes like §16–6–2 may be " 'natural and familiar . . . ought not to conclude our judgment upon the question whether statutes embodying them conflict with the Constitution of the United States.' " *Roe v. Wade*, 410 U.S. 113, 117, 93 S.Ct. 705, 709, 35 L.Ed.2d 147 (1973), quoting *Lochner v. New York*, 198 U.S. 45, 76, 25 S.Ct. 539, 547, 49 L.Ed. 937 (1905) (Holmes, J., dissenting). Like Justice Holmes, I believe that "[i]t is revolting to have no better reason for a rule of law than that so it was laid down in the time of Henry IV. It is still more revolting if the grounds upon which it was laid down have vanished long since, and the rule simply persists from blind imitation of the past." Holmes, The Path of the Law, 10 Harv.L. Rev. 457, 469 (1897). I believe we must analyze Hardwick's claim in the light of the values that underlie the constitutional right to privacy. If that right means anything, it means that, before Georgia can prosecute its citizens for making choices about the most intimate aspects of their lives, it must do more than assert that the choice they have made is an " 'abominable crime not fit to be named among Christians.' " *Herring v. State*, 119 Ga. 709, 721, 46 S.E. 876, 882 (1904).

I

In its haste to reverse the Court of Appeals and hold that the Constitution does not "confe[r] a fundamental right upon homosexuals to engage in sodomy," *ante*, at 2843, the Court relegates the actual statute being challenged to a footnote and ignores the procedural posture of the case before it. A fair reading of the statute and of the complaint clearly reveals that the majority has distorted the question this case presents.

First, the Court's almost obsessive focus on homosexual activity is particularly hard to justify in light of the broad language Georgia has used. Unlike the Court, the Georgia Legislature has not proceeded on the assumption that homosexuals are so different from other citizens that their lives may be controlled in a way that would not be tolerated if it limited the choices of those other citizens. Cf. *ante*, at 2842, n. 2. Rather, Georgia has provided that "[a] person commits the offense of sodomy when he performs or submits to any sexual act involving the sex organs of one person and the mouth or anus of another." Ga. Code Ann. §16–6–2(a) (1985). The sex or status of the persons who engage in the act is irrelevant as a matter of state law. In fact, to the extent I can discern a legislative purpose for Georgia's 1968 enactment of §16–6–2, that purpose seems to have been to broaden the coverage of the law to reach heterosexual as well as homosexual activity.[1] I therefore see no basis for the Court's decision to treat this case as an "as applied" challenge to §16–6–2, see *ante*, at 2842, n. 2, or for Georgia's attempt, both in its brief and at oral argument, to defend §16–6–2 solely on the grounds that it prohibits homosexual activity. Michael Hardwick's standing may rest in significant part on Georgia's apparent willingness to enforce against homosexuals a law it seems not to have any desire to enforce against heterosexuals. See Tr. of Oral Arg. 4–5; cf. 760 F.2d 1202, 1205–1206 (CA11 1985). But his claim that §16–6–2 involves an unconstitutional intrusion into his privacy and his right of intimate association does not depend in any way on his sexual orientation.

Second, I disagree with the Court's refusal to consider whether §16–6–2 runs afoul of the Eighth or Ninth Amendments or the Equal Protection Clause of the Fourteenth Amendment. *Ante*, at 2847, n. 8. Respondent's complaint expressly invoked the Ninth Amendment, see App. 6, and he relied heavily before this Court on *Griswold v. Connecticut*, 381 U.S. 479, 484, 85 S.Ct. 1678, 1681, 14 L.Ed.2d 510 (1965), which identifies that Amendment as one of the specific constitutional provisions giving "life and substance" to our understanding of privacy. See Brief for Respondent Hardwick 10–12; Tr. of Oral Arg. 33. More importantly, the procedural posture of the case requires that we affirm the Court of Appeals' judgment if there is *any* ground on which respondent may be entitled to relief. This case is before us on petitioner's motion to dismiss for failure to state a claim, Fed.Rule Civ.Proc. 12(b)(6). See App. 17. It is a well-settled principle of law that "a complaint should not be dismissed merely because a plaintiff's allegations do not support the particular legal theory he advances, for the court is under a duty to examine the complaint to determine if the allegations provide for relief on any possible theory." *Bramlet v. Wilson*, 495 F.2d 714, 716 (CA8 1974); see *Parr v. Great Lakes Express Co.*, 484 F.2d 767, 773 (CA7 1973); *Due v. Tallahassee Theatres, Inc.*, 333 F.2d 630, 631 (CA5 1964); *United States v. Howell*, 318 F.2d 162, 166 (CA9 1963); 5 C. Wright & A. Miller, Federal Practice and Procedure §1357, pp. 601–602 (1969); see also *Conley v. Gibson*, 355 U.S. 41, 45–46, 78 S.Ct. 99, 101–102, 2 L.Ed.2d 80 (1957). Thus, even if respondent did not advance claims based on the Eighth or Ninth Amendments, or on the Equal Protection Clause, his complaint should not be dismissed if any of those provisions could entitle him to relief. I need not reach either the Eighth Amendment or the Equal Protection Clause issues because I believe that Hardwick has stated a cognizable claim that §16–6–2 interferes with constitutionally protected interests in privacy and freedom of intimate association. But neither the Eighth Amendment nor the Equal Protection Clause is so clearly irrelevant that a claim resting on either provision should be peremptorily dismissed.[2] The Court's cramped reading of the issue before it makes for a short opinion, but it does little to make for a persuasive one.

II

"Our cases long have recognized that the Constitution embodies a promise that a certain private sphere of individual liberty will be kept largely beyond the reach of government." *Thornburgh v. American College of Obstetricians & Gynecologists*, 476 U.S. 747, 772, 106 S.Ct. 2169, 2184, 90, L.Ed.2d 779 (1986). In construing the right to privacy, the Court has proceeded along two somewhat distinct, albeit complementary, lines. First, it has recognized a privacy interest with reference to certain *decisions* that are properly for the individual to make. *E.g., Roe v. Wade*, 410 U.S. 113, 93, S.Ct. 705, 35 L.Ed.2d 147 (1973); *Pierce v. Society of Sisters*, 268 U.S. 510, 45 S.Ct. 571, 69 L.Ed. 1070 (1925). Second, it has recognized a privacy interest with reference to certain *places* without regard for the particular activities in which the individuals who occupy them are engaged. *E.g., United States v. Karo*, 468 U.S. 705, 104 S.Ct. 3296, 82 L.Ed.2d 530 (1984); *Payton v. New York*, 445 U.S. 573, 100 S.Ct. 1371, 63 L.Ed.2d 639 (1980); *Rios v. United States*, 364 U.S. 253, 80 S.Ct. 1431, 4 L.Ed.2d 1688 (1960). The case before us implicates both the decisional and the spatial aspects of the right to privacy.

A

The Court concludes today that none of our prior cases dealing with various decisions that individuals are entitled to make free of governmental interference "bears any resemblance to the claimed constitutional right of homosexuals to engage in acts of sodomy that is asserted in this case." *Ante*, at 2844. While it is true that these cases may be characterized by their connection to protection of the family, see *Roberts v. United States Jaycees*, 468 U.S. 609, 619, 104 S.Ct. 3244, 3250, 82 L.Ed.2d 462 (1984), the Court's conclusion that they extend no further than this boundary ignores the warning in *Moore v. East Cleveland*, 431 U.S. 494, 501, 97 S.Ct. 1932, 1936, 52 L.Ed.2d 531 (1977) (plurality opinion), against "clos[ing] our eyes to the basic reasons why certain rights associated with the family have been accorded shelter under the Fourteenth Amendment's Due Process Clause." We protect those rights not because they contribute, in some direct and material way, to the general public welfare, but because they form so central a part of an individual's life. "[T]he concept of privacy embodies the moral fact that a person belongs to himself and not others nor to society as a whole." *Thornburgh v. American College of Obstetricians & Gynecologists*, 476 U.S., at 777, n. 5, 106 S.Ct. at 2187, n. 5 (STEVENS, J., concurring), quoting Fried, Correspondence, 6 Phil & Pub. Affairs 288–289 (1977). And so we protect the decision whether to marry precisely because marriage "is an association that promotes a way of life, not causes; a harmony in living, not political faiths; a bilateral loyalty, not commercial or social projects." *Griswold v. Connecticut*, 381 U.S., at 486, 85 S.Ct., at 1682. We protect the decision whether to have a child because parenthood alters so dramatically an individual's self-definition, not because of demographic considerations or the Bible's command to be fruitful and multiply. Cf. *Thornburgh v. American College of Obstetricians & Gynecologists*, supra, 476 U.S., at 777, n. 6, 106 S.Ct., at 2188, n. 6 (STEVENS, J., concurring). And we protect the family because it contributes so powerfully to the happiness of individuals, not because of a preference for stereotypical households. Cf. *Moore v. East Cleveland*, 431 U.S., at 500–506, 97 S.Ct., at 1936–1939 (plurality opinion). The Court recognized in *Roberts*, 468 U.S., at 619, 104 S.Ct., at 3250, that the "ability independently to define one's identity that is central to any concept of liberty" cannot truly be exercised in a vacuum; we all depend on the "emotional enrichment from close ties with others." *Ibid.*

Only the most willful blindness could obscure the fact that sexual intimacy is "a sensitive, key relationship of human existence, central to family life, community welfare, and the development of human personality," *Paris Adult Theatre I v. Slaton*, 413 U.S. 49, 63, 93 S.Ct. 2628, 2638, 37 L.Ed.2d 446 (1973); see also *Carey v. Population Services International*, 431 U.S. 678, 685, 97 S.Ct. 2010, 2016, 52 L.Ed.2d 675 (1977). The fact that individuals define themselves in a significant way through their intimate sexual relationships with others suggests, in a Nation as diverse as ours, that there may be many "right" ways of conducting those relationships, and that much of the richness of a relationship will come from the freedom an individual has to *choose* the form and nature of these intensely personal bonds. See Karst, The Freedom of Intimate Association, 89 Yale L.J. 624, 637 (1980); *cf. Eisenstadt v. Baird*, 405 U.S. 438, 453 92 S.Ct. 1029, 1038, 31 L.Ed.2d 349 (1972); *Roe v. Wade*, 410 U.S., at 153, 93 S.Ct., at 726.

In a variety of circumstances we have recognized that a necessary corollary of giving individuals freedom to choose how to conduct their lives is acceptance of the fact that different individuals will make different choices. For example, in holding that the clearly important state interest in public education should give way to a competing claim by the Amish to the effect that extended formal schooling threatened their way of life, the Court declared: "There can be no assumption that today's majority is 'right' and the Amish and others like them are 'wrong.' A way of life that is odd or even erratic but interferes with no rights or interests of others is not to be condemned because it is different." *Wisconsin v. Yoder*, 406 U.S. 205, 223–224, 92 S.Ct. 1526, 1537, 32 L.Ed.2d 15 (1972). The Court claims that its decision today merely refuses to recognize a fundamental right to engage in homosexual sodomy; what the Court really has refused to recognize is the fundamental interest all individuals have in controlling the nature of their intimate associations with others.

B

The behavior for which Hardwick faces prosecution occurred in his own home, a place to which the Fourth Amendment attaches special significance. The Court's treatment of this aspect of the case is symptomatic of its overall refusal to consider the broad principles that have informed our treatment of privacy in specific cases. Just as the right to privacy is more than the mere aggregation of a number of entitlements to engage in specific behavior, so too, protecting the physical integrity of the home is more than merely a means of protecting specific activities that often take place there. Even when our understanding of the contours of the right to privacy depends on "reference to a 'place,' " *Katz v. United States*, 389 U.S., at 361, 88 S.Ct., at 516 (Harlan, J., concurring), "the essence of a Fourth Amendment violation is 'not the breaking of [a person's] doors, and the rummaging of his drawers,' but rather is 'the invasion of his indefeasible right of personal security, personal liberty and private property.' " *California v. Ciraolo*, 476 U.S. 207, 226, 106 S.Ct. 1809, 1819, 90 L.Ed.2d 210 (1986) (POWELL, J., dissenting) quoting *Boyd v. United States*, 116 U.S. 616, 630, 6 S.Ct. 524, 532, 29 L.Ed. 746 (1886).

The Court's interpretation of the pivotal case of *Stanley v. Georgia*, 394 U.S. 557, 89 S.Ct. 1243, 22 L.Ed.2d 542 (1969), is entirely unconvincing. *Stanley* held that Georgia's undoubted power to punish the public distribution of constitutionally unprotected, obscene material did not permit the State to punish the private possession of such material. According to the majority here, *Stanley* relied entirely on the First Amendment, and thus, it is claimed, sheds no light on cases not involving printed materials. *Ante*, at 2846. But that is not what *Stanley* said. Rather, the *Stanley* Court anchored its holding in the Fourth Amendment's special protection for the individual in his home:

> " 'The makers of our Constitution undertook to secure conditions favorable to the pursuit of happiness. They recognized the significance of man's spiritual nature, of his feelings and of his intellect. They knew that only a part of the pain, pleasure and satisfactions of life are to be found in material things. They sought to protect Americans in their beliefs, their thoughts, their emotions and their sensations.' . . .
>
> These are the rights that appellant is asserting in the case before us. He is asserting the right to read or observe what he pleases—the right to satisfy his intellectual and emotional needs in the privacy of his own home." 394 U.S., at 564–565, 89 S.Ct., at 1248, quoting *Olmstead v. United States*, 277 U.S., at 478, 48 S.Ct., at 572 (Brandeis, J., dissenting).

The central place that *Stanley* gives Justice Brandeis' dissent in *Olmstead*, a case raising *no* First Amendment claim, shows that *Stanley* rested as much on the Court's understanding of the Fourth Amendment as it did on the First. Indeed, in *Paris Adult Theatre I v. Slaton*, 413 U.S. 49, 93 S.Ct. 2628, 37 L.Ed.2d 446 (1973), the court suggested that reliance on the Fourth Amendment not only supported the Court's outcome in *Stanley* but actually was *necessary* to it: "If obscene material unprotected by the First Amendment in itself carried with it a 'penumbra' of constitutionally protected privacy, this Court would not have found it necessary to decide *Stanley* on the narrow basis of the 'privacy of the home,' which was hardly more than a reaffirmation that 'a man's home is his castle.' " 413 U.S., at 66, 93 S.Ct., at 2640. "The right of the people to be secure in their . . . houses," expressly guaranteed by the Fourth Amendment, is perhaps the most "textual" of the various constitutional provisions that inform our understanding of the right to privacy, and thus I cannot agree with the Court's statement that "[t]he right pressed upon us here has no . . . support in the text of the Constitution," *ante*, at 2846. Indeed, the right of an individual to conduct intimate relationships in the intimacy of his or her own home seems to me to be the heart of the Constitution's protection of privacy.

III

The Court's failure to comprehend the magnitude of the liberty interests at stake in this case leads it to slight the question whether petitioner, on behalf of the State, has justified Georgia's infringement on these interests. I believe that neither of the two general justifications for §16–6–2 that petitioner has advanced warrants dismissing respondent's challenge for failure to state a claim.

First, petitioner asserts that the acts made criminal by the statute may have serious adverse consequences for "the general public health and welfare," such as spreading communicable diseases or fostering other criminal activity. Brief for Petitioner 37. Inasmuch as this case was dismissed by the District Court on the pleadings, it is not surprising that the record before us is barren of any evidence to support petitioner's claim.[3] In light of the state of the record, I see no justification for the Court's attempt to equate the private, consensual sexual activity at issue here with the "possession in the home of drugs, firearms, or stolen goods," *ante*, at 2846, to which *Stanley* refused to extend its protection. 394 U.S., at 568, n. 11, 89 S.Ct., at 1249, n. 11 None of the behavior so mentioned in *Stanley* can properly be viewed as "[v]ictimless," *ante*, at 2846: drugs and weapons are inherently dangerous, see, *e.g., McLaughlin v. United States*, 476 U.S. 16, 106 S.Ct. 1677, 90 L.Ed.2d 15 (1986), and for property to be "stolen," someone must have been wrongfully deprived of it. Nothing in the record before the Court provides any justification for finding the activity forbidden by §16–6–2 to be physically dangerous, either to the persons engaged in it or to others.[4]

The core of petitioner's defense of §16–6–2, however, is that respondent and others who engage in the conduct prohibited by §16–6–2 interfere with Georgia's exercise of the " 'right of the Nation and of the States to maintain a decent society,' " *Paris Adult Theater I v. Slaton*, 413 U.S., at 59–60, 93 S.Ct., at 2636, quoting *Jacobellis v. Ohio*, 378 U.S. 184, 199, 84 S.Ct. 1676, 1684, 12 L.Ed.2d 793 (1964) (Warren, C.J., dissenting). Essentially, petitioner argues, and the Court agrees, that the fact that the acts described in §16–6–2 "for hundreds of years, if not thousands, have been uniformly condemned as immoral" is a sufficient reason to permit a State to ban them today. Brief for Petitioner 19; see *ante*, at 2843, 2844–2846, 2847.

I cannot agree that either the length of time a majority has held its convictions or the passions with which it defends them can withdraw legislation from this Court's scrutiny. See, *e.g., Roe v. Wade*, 410 U.S. 113, 93 S.Ct. 705, 35 L.Ed.2d 147 (1973); *Loving v. Virginia*, 388 U.S. 1, 87 S.Ct. 1817, 18 L.Ed.2d 1010 (1967); *Brown v. Board of Education*, 347 U.S. 483, 74 S.Ct. 686, 98 L.Ed. 873 (1953).[5] As Justice Jackson wrote so eloquently for the Court in *West Virginia Board of Education v. Barnette*, 319 U.S. 624, 641–642, 63 S.Ct. 1178, 1187, 87 L.Ed. 1628 (1943), "we apply the limitations of the Constitution with no fear that freedom to be intellectually and spiritually diverse or even contrary will disintegrate the social organization. . . . [F]reedom to differ is not limited to things that do not matter much. That would be a mere shadow of freedom. The test of its substance is the right to differ as to things that touch the heart of the existing order." See also Karst, 89 Yale L.J., at 627. It is precisely because the issue raised by this case touches the heart of what makes individuals what they are that we should be especially sensitive to the rights of those whose choices upset the majority.

The assertion that "traditional Judeo-Christian values proscribe" the conduct involved, Brief for Petitioner 20, cannot provide an adequate justification for §16–6–2. That certain, but by no means all, religious groups condemn the behavior at issue gives the State no license to impose their judgments on the entire citizenry. The legitimacy of secular legislation depends instead on whether the State can advance some justification for its law beyond its conformity to religious doctrine. See, *e.g., McGowan v. Maryland*, 366 U.S. 420, 429–453, 81 S.Ct. 1101, 1106–1119, 6 L.Ed.2d 393 (1961); *Stone v. Graham*, 449 U.S. 39, 101 S.Ct. 192, 66 L.Ed.2d 199 (1980). Thus, far from buttressing his case, petitioner's invocation of Leviticus, Romans, St. Thomas Aquinas, and sodomy's heretical status during the Middle Ages undermines his suggestion that §16–6–2 represents a legitimate use of secular coercive power.[6] A State can no more punish private behavior because of religious intolerance than it can punish such behavior because of racial animus. "The Constitution cannot control such prejudices, but neither can it tolerate them. Private biases may be outside the reach of the law, but the law cannot, directly or indirectly, give them effect." *Palmore v. Sidoti*, 466 U.S. 429, 433, 104 S.Ct. 1879, 1882, 80 L.Ed.2d 421 (1984). No matter how uncomfortable a certain group may make the majority of this Court, we have held that "[m]ere public intolerance or animosity cannot constitutionally justify the deprivation of a person's physical liberty." *O'Connor v. Donaldson*, 422 U.S. 563, 575, 95 S.Ct. 2486, 2494, 45 L.Ed.2d 396 (1975). See also *Cleburne v. Cleburne Living Center, Inc.* 473 U.S. 432, 105 S.Ct. 3249,

87 L.Ed.2d 313 (1985); *United States Dept. of Agriculture v. Moreno*, 413 U.S. 528, 534, 93 S.Ct. 2821, 2825, 37 L.Ed.2d 782 (1973).

Nor can §16–6–2 be justified as a "morally neutral" exercise of Georgia's power to "protect the public environment," *Paris Adult Theatre I*, 413 U.S., at 68–69, 93 S.Ct., at 2641. Certainly some private behavior can affect the fabric of society as a whole. Reasonable people may differ about whether particular sexual acts are moral or immoral, but "we have ample evidence for believing that people will not abandon morality, will not think any better of murder, cruelty and dishonesty, merely because some private sexual practice which they abominate is not punished by the law." H.L.A. Hart, Immorality and Treason, reprinted in The Law as Literature 220, 225 (L. Blom-Cooper ed. 1961). Petitioner and the Court fail to see the difference between laws that protect public sensibilities and those that enforce private morality. Statutes banning public sexual activity are entirely consistent with protecting the individual's liberty interest in decisions concerning sexual relations: the same recognition that those decisions are intensely private which justifies protecting them from governmental interference can justify protecting individuals from unwilling exposure to the sexual activities of others. But the mere fact that intimate behavior may be punished when it takes place in public cannot dictate how States can regulate intimate behavior that occurs in intimate places. See *Paris Adult Theatre I*, 413 U.S., at 66, n. 13, 93 S.Ct., at 2640, n. 13 ("marital intercourse on a street corner or a theater stage" can be forbidden despite the constitutional protection identified in *Griswold v. Connecticut*, 381 U.S. 479, 85 S.Ct. 1678, 14 L.Ed.2d 510 (1965)).[7]

This case involves no real interference with the rights of others, for the mere knowledge that other individuals do not adhere to one's value system cannot be a legally cognizable interest, *cf. Diamond v. Charles*, 476 U.S. 54, 65–66, 106 S.Ct. 1697, 1705, 90 L.Ed.2d 48 (1986), let alone an interest that can justify invading the houses, hearts, and minds of citizens who choose to live their lives differently.

IV

It took but three years for the Court to see the error in its analysis in *Minersville School District v. Gobitis*, 310 U.S. 586, 60 S.Ct. 1010, 84 L.Ed. 1375 (1940), and to recognize that the threat to national cohesion posed by a refusal to salute the flag was vastly outweighed by the threat to those same values posed by compelling such a salute. See *West Virginia Board of Education v. Burnette*, 319 U.S. 624, 63 S.Ct. 1178, 87 L.Ed.

1628 (1943). I can only hope that here too, the Court soon will reconsider its analysis and conclude that depriving individuals of the right to choose for themselves how to conduct their intimate relationships poses a far greater threat to the values most deeply rooted in our Nation's history than tolerance of nonconformity could ever do. Because I think the Court today betrays those values, I dissent.

Justice STEVENS, with whom Justice BRENNAN and Justice MARSHALL join, dissenting.

Like the statute that is challenged in this case,[1] the rationale of the Court's opinion applies equally to the prohibited conduct regardless of whether the parties who engaged in it are married or unmarried, or are of the same or different sexes.[2] Sodomy was condemned as an odius and sinful type of behavior during the formative period of the common law.[3] That condemnation was equally damning for heterosexual and homosexual sodomy.[4] Moreover, it provided no special exemption for married couples.[5] The license to cohabit and to produce legitimate offspring simply did not include any permission to engage in sexual conduct that was considered a "crime against nature."

The history of the Georgia statute before us clearly reveals this traditional prohibition of heterosexual, as well as homosexual sodomy.[6] Indeed, at one point in the 20th century, Georgia's law was construed to permit certain sexual conduct between homosexual women even though such conduct was prohibited between heterosexuals.[7] The history of the statutes cited by the majority as proof for the proposition that sodomy is not constitutionally protected, *ante*, at 2844–2846, and nn. 5 and 6, similarly reveals a prohibition on heterosexual, as well as homosexual, sodomy.[8]

Because the Georgia statute expresses the traditional view that sodomy is an immoral kind of conduct regardless of the identity of the persons who engage in it, I believe that a proper analysis of its constitutionality requires consideration of two questions: First, may a State totally prohibit the described conduct by means of a neutral law applying without exception to all persons subject to its jurisdiction? If not, may the State save the statute by announcing that it will only enforce the law against homosexuals? The two questions merit separate discussion.

I

Our prior cases make two propositions abundantly clear. First, the fact that the governing majority in a State has traditionally viewed a particular practice as immoral is not a sufficient reason for upholding a law prohibiting the practice; neither history nor tradition could save a law prohibiting miscegenation from constitutional attack.[9] Second, individual decisions by married persons, concerning the intimacies of their physical relationship, even when not intended to produce offspring, are a form of "liberty" protected by the Due Process Clause of the Fourteenth Amendment. *Griswold v. Connecticut*, 381 U.S. 479, 85 S.Ct. 1678, 14 L.Ed.2d 510 (1965). Moreover, this protection extends to intimate choices by unmarried as well as married persons. *Carey v. Population Services International*, 431 U.S. 678, 97 S.Ct. 2010, 52 L.Ed.2d 675 (1977); *Eisenstadt v. Baird*, 405 U.S. 438, 92 S.Ct. 1029, 31 L.Ed.2d 329 (1972).

In consideration of claims of this kind, the Court has emphasized the individual interest in privacy, but its decisions have actually been animated by an even more fundamental concern. As I wrote some years ago:

> "These cases do not deal with the individual's interest in protection from unwarranted public attention, comment, or exploitation. They deal, rather, with the individual's right to make certain unusually important decisions that will affect his own, or his family's destiny. The Court has referred to such decisions as implicating 'basic values,' as being 'fundamental' and as being dignified by history and tradition. The character of the Court's language in these cases brings to mind the origins of the American heritage of freedom—the abiding interest in individual liberty that makes certain state intrusions on the citizen's right to decide how he will live his own life intolerable. Guided by history, our tradition of respect for the dignity of individual choice in matters of conscience and the restraints implicit in the federal system, federal judges have accepted the responsibility for recognition and protection of these rights in appropriate cases." *Fitzgerald v. Porter Memorial Hospital*, 523 F.2d 716, 719–720 (CA7 1975) (footnotes omitted); cert. denied, 425 U.S. 916, 96 S.Ct. 1518, 47 L.Ed.2d 768 (1976).

Society has every right to encourage its individual members to follow particular traditions in expressing affection for one another and in gratifying their personal desires. It, of course, may prohibit an individual from imposing his will on another to satisfy his own selfish interests. It also may prevent an individual from interfering with, or violating, a legally sanctioned and protected relationship, such as marriage. And it may explain the relative advantages and disadvantages of different forms of intimate expression. But when individual married couples are isolated from observation by others, the way in which they voluntarily choose to conduct their intimate relations is a matter for them—not the State—to decide.[10] The essential "liberty" that animated the development of the law in cases like *Griswold, Eisenstadt,* and *Carey* surely embraces the right to engage in nonreproductive, sexual conduct that others may consider offensive or immoral.

Paradoxical as it may seem, our prior cases thus establish that a State may not prohibit sodomy within "the sacred precincts of marital bedrooms," *Griswold,* 381 U.S., at 485, 85 S.Ct., at 1682, or, indeed, between unmarried heterosexual adults. *Eisenstadt,* 405 U.S., at 453, 92 S.Ct., at 1038. In all events, it is perfectly clear that the State of Georgia may not totally prohibit the conduct proscribed by §16–6–2 of the Georgia Criminal Code.

II

If the Georgia statute cannot be enforced as it is written—if the conduct it seeks to prohibit is a protected form of liberty for the vast majority of Georgia's citizens—the State must assume the burden of justifying a selective application of its law. Either the persons to whom Georgia seeks to apply its statute do not have the same interest in "liberty" that others have, or there must be a reason why the State may be permitted to apply a generally applicable law to certain persons that it does not apply to others.

The first possibility is plainly unacceptable. Although the meaning of the principle that "all men are created equal" is not always clear, it surely must mean that every free citizen has the same interest in "liberty" that the members of the majority share. From the standpoint of the individual, the homosexual and the heterosexual have the same interest in deciding how he will live his own life, and, more narrowly, how he will conduct himself in his personal and voluntary associations with his companions. State intrusion into the private conduct of either is equally burdensome.

The second possibility is similarly unacceptable. A policy of selective application must be supported by a neutral and legitimate interest—something more substantial than a habitual dislike for, or ignorance about, the disfavored group. Neither the State nor the Court has identified any such interest in this case. The Court has posited as a justification for the Georgia statute "the presumed belief of a majority of the electorate in Georgia that homosexual sodomy is immoral and unacceptable." *Ante,* at 2846. But the Georgia electorate has expressed no such belief—instead, its representatives enacted a law that presumably reflects the belief that *all sodomy* is immoral and unacceptable. Unless the Court is prepared to conclude that such a law is constitutional, it may not rely on the work product of the Georgia Legislature to support its holding. For the Georgia statute does not single out homosexuals as a separate class meriting special disfavored treatment.

Nor, indeed, does the Georgia prosecutor even believe that all homosexuals who violate this statute should be punished. This conclusion is evident from the fact that the respondent in this very case has formally acknowledged in his complaint and in court that he has engaged, and intends to continue to engage, in the prohibited conduct, yet the State has elected not to process criminal charges against him. As Justice POWELL points out, moreover, Georgia's prohibition on private, consensual sodomy has not been enforced for decades.[11] The record of nonenforcement, in this case and in the last several decades, belies the Attorney General's representations about the importance of the State's selective application of its generally applicable law.[12]

Both the Georgia statute and the Georgia prosecutor thus completely fail to provide the Court with any support for the conclusion that homosexual sodomy, *simpliciter*, is considered unacceptable conduct in that State, and that the burden of justifying a selective application of the generally applicable law has been met.

III

The Court orders the dismissal of respondent's complaint even though the State's statute prohibits all sodomy; even though that prohibition is concededly unconstitutional with respect to heterosexuals; and even though the State's *post hoc* explanations for selective application are belied by the State's own actions. At the very least, I think it clear at this early stage of the litigation that respondent has alleged a constitutional claim sufficient to withstand a motion to dismiss.[13]

I respectfully dissent.

1. Georgia Code Ann. §16–6–2 (1984) provides, in pertinent part, as follows:

    "(a) A person commits the offense of sodomy when he performs or submits to any sexual act involving the sex organs of one person and the mouth or anus of another.

    . . .

    "(b) A person convicted of the offense of sodomy shall be punished by imprisonment for not less than one nor more than 20 years. . . ."

2. John and Mary Doe were also plaintiffs in the action. They alleged that they wished to engage in sexual activity proscribed by §16–6–2 in the privacy of their home, App. 3, and that they had been "chilled and deterred" from engaging in such activity by both the existence of the statute and Hardwick's arrest. *Id.*, at 5. The District Court held, however, that because they had neither sustained, nor were in immediate danger of sustaining, any direct injury from the enforcement of the statute, they did not have proper standing to maintain the action. *Id.*, at 18. The Court of Appeals affirmed the District

Court's judgment dismissing the Does' claim for lack of standing, 760 F.2d 1202, 1206–1207 (CA11 1985), and the Does do not challenge that holding in this Court.

The only claim properly before the Court, therefore, is Hardwick's challenge to the Georgia statute as applied to consensual homosexual sodomy. We express no opinion on the constitutionality of the Georgia statute as applied to other acts of sodomy.

3. See *Baker v. Wade*, 769 F.2d 289, reh'g denied, 774 F.2d 1285 (CA5 1985) (en banc); *Dronenburg v. Zech*, 239 U.S.App.D.C. 229, 741, F.2d 1388, reh'g denied, 241 U.S.App.D.C. 262, 746 F.2d 1579 (1984).

4. Petitioner also submits that the Court of Appeals erred in holding that the District Court was not obligated to follow our summary affirmance in *Doe*. We need not resolve this dispute, for we prefer to give plenary consideration to the merits of this case rather than rely on our earlier action in *Doe*. See *Usery v. Turner Elkhorn Mining Co.*, 428 U.S. 1, 14, 96 S.Ct. 2882, 2891, 49 L.Ed.2d 752 (1976); *Massachusetts Board of Retirement v. Murgia*, 427 U.S. 307, 309, n. 1, 96 S.Ct. 2562, 2565, n. 1, 49 L.Ed.2d 520 (1976); *Edelman v. Jordan*, 415 U.S. 651, 671, 94 S.Ct. 1347, 1359, 39 L.Ed.2d 662 (1974). *Cf. Hicks v. Miranda*, 422 U.S. 332, 344, 95 S.Ct. 2281, 2289, 45 L.Ed.2d 223 (1975).

5. Criminal sodomy laws in effect in 1791:

Connecticut: 1 Public Statute Laws of the State of Connecticut, 1808, Title LXVI, ch. 1 § 2 (rev. 1672).

Delaware: 1 Laws of the State of Delaware, 1797, ch 22, § 5 (passed 1719).

Georgia had no criminal sodomy statute until 1816, but sodomy was a crime at common law, and the General Assembly adopted the common law of England as the law of Georgia in 1784. The First Laws of the State of Georgia, pt 1, p. 290 (1981).

Maryland had no criminal sodomy statute in 1791. Maryland's Declaration of Rights, passed in 1776, however, stated that "the inhabitants of Maryland are entitled to the common law of England," and sodomy was a crime at common law. 4 W. Swindler, Sources and Documents of United States Constitutions 372 (1975).

Massachusetts: Acts and Laws passed by the General Court of Massachusetts, ch 14, Act of Mar. 3, 1785.

New Hampshire passed it first sodomy statute in 1718. Acts and Laws of New Hampshire 1680–1726, p. 141 (1978).

Sodomy was a crime at common law in New Jersey at the time of the ratification of the Bill of Rights. The State enacted its first criminal sodomy law five years later. Acts of the Twentieth General Assembly, Mar. 18, 1796, ch. DC, § 7.

New York: Laws of New York, ch. 21 (passed 1787).

At the time of ratification of the Bill of Rights, North Carolina had adopted the English statute of Henry VIII outlawing sodomy. See Collection of the Statutes of the Parliament of England in Force in the State of North Carolina, ch. 17, p. 314 (Martin ed. 1792).

Pennsylvania: Laws of the Fourteenth General Assembly of the Commonwealth of Pennsylvania, ch. CLIV, § 2 (passed 1790).

· Rhode Island passed its first sodomy law in 1662. The Earliest Acts and Laws of the Colony of Rhode Island and Providence Plantations 1647–1719, p. 142 (1977).

South Carolina: Public Laws of the State of South Carolina, p. 49 (1790).

At the time of the ratification of the Bill of Rights, Virginia had no specific statute outlawing sodomy, but had adopted the English common law. 9 Hening's Laws of Virginia, ch. 5, § 6, p. 127 (1821) (passed 1776).

6. Criminal sodomy statutes in effect in 1868:

Alabama: Ala. Rev. Code § 3604 (1867).

Arizona (Terr.): Howell Code, ch. 10, § 48 (1865).

Arkansas: Ark.Stat., ch. 51, Art. IV, § 5 (1858).

California: 1 Cal.Gen.Laws, ¶ 1450, § 48 (1865).

Colorado (Terr.): Colo.Rev.Stat., ch. 22, §§ 45, 46 (1868).

Connecticut: Conn.Gen.Stat., Tit. 122, ch. 7, § 124 (1866).

Delaware: Del.Rev.Stat., ch. 131, § 7 (1893).

Florida: Fla.Rev.Stat., div. 5, § 2614 (passed 1868) (1892).

Georgia: Ga.Code §§ 4286, 4287, 4290 (1867).

Kingdom of Hawaii: Haw.Penal Code, ch. 13, § 11 (1869).

Illinois: Ill.Rev.Stat. div. 5, §§ 49, 50 (1845).

Kansas Terr.: Kan.Stat., ch. 53, § 7 (1855).

Kentucky: 1 Ky.Rev.Stat., ch. 28, Art. IV, § 11 (1860).

Louisiana: La.Rev.Stat., Crimes and Offences, § 5 (1856).

Maine: Me.Rev.Stat., Tit. XII, ch. 160, § 4 (1840).

Maryland: 1 Md.Code, Art. 30, § 201 (1860).

Massachusetts: Mass.Gen.Stat., ch. 165, § 18 (1860).

Michigan: Mich.Rev.Stat., Tit. 30, ch. 158, § 16 (1846).

Minnesota: Minn.Stat., ch. 96, § 13 (1859).

Mississippi: Miss.Rev.Code., ch. 64, § LII, Art. 238 (1857).

Missouri: 1 Mo.Rev.Stat., ch. 50, Art. VIII, § 7 (1856).

Montana (Terr.): Mont.Acts, Resolutions, Memorials, Criminal Practice Acts, ch. IV, § 44 (1866).

Nebraska (Terr.): Neb.Rev.Stat., Crim.Code, ch. 4, § 47 (1866).

Nevada (Terr.): Nev.Comp.Laws, 1861–1900, Crimes and Punishments, § 45.

New Hampshire: N.H.Laws, Act of June 19, 1812, § 5 (1815).

New Jersey: N.J.Rev.Stat., Tit. 8, ch. 1, § 9 (1847).

New York: 3 N.Y.Rev.Stat., pt. 4, ch. 1, Tit. 5, § 20 (5th ed. 1859).

North Carolina: N.C.Rev.Code, ch. 34, § 6 (1854).

Oregon: Laws of Ore., Crimes—Against Morality, etc., ch. 7, § 655 (1874).

Pennsylvania: Act of Mar. 31, 1860, § 32, Pub.L. 392, in 1 Digest of Statute Law of Pa. 1700–1903, p. 1011 (Purdon 1905).

Rhode Island: R.I.Gen.Stat., ch. 232, § 12 (1872).

South Carolina: Act of 1712, in 2 Stat. at Large of S.C. 1682–1716, p. 493 (1837).

Tennessee: Tenn.Code, ch. 8, Art. 1, § 4843 (1858).

Texas: Tex.Rev.Stat., Tit. 10, ch. 5, Art. 342, (1887) (passed 1860).

Vermont: Acts and Laws of the State of Vt. (1779).

Virginia: Va.Code, ch. 149, § 12 (1868).

West Virginia: W.Va.Code, ch. 149, § 12 (1860).

Wisconsin (Terr.): Wis.Stat. § 14, p. 367 (1839).

7. In 1961, Illinois adopted the American Law Institute's Model Penal Code, which decriminalized adult, consensual, private, sexual conduct. Criminal Code of 1961, §§ 11–2, 11–3, 1961 Ill. Laws, pp. 1985, 2006 (codified as amended at Ill.Rev.Stat., ch. 38, ¶¶ 11–2, 11–3 (1983) (repealed 1984)). See American Law Institute, Model Penal Code § 213.2 (Proposed Official Draft 1962).

8. Respondent does not defend the judgment below based on the Ninth Amendment, the Equal Protection Clause, or the Eighth Amendment.

JUSTICE POWELL

1. Among those States that continue to make sodomy a crime, Georgia authorizes one of the longest possible sentences. See Ala.Code § 13A–6–65(a)(3) (1982) (1-year maximum);

Ariz.Rev.Stat.Ann. §§ 13–1411, 13–1412 (West Supp. 1985) (30 days); Ark.Stat.Ann. § 41–1813 (1977) (1-year maximum); D.C.Code § 22–3502 (1981) (10-year maximum); Fla.Stat. § 800.02 (1985) (60-day maximum); Ga.Code Ann. § 16–6–2 (1984) (1 to 20 years); Idaho Code § 18–6605 (1979) (5-year maximum); Kan.Stat.Ann. § 21–3505 (Supp. 1985) (6-mouth maximum); Ky.Rev.Stat. § 510.100 (1985) (90 days to 12 months); La.Rev.Stat.Ann. § 14:89 (West 1986) (5-year maximum); Md.Ann.Code, Art. 27, §§ 553–554 (1982) (10-year maximum); Mich.Comp.Laws § 750.158 (1968) (15-year maximum), 750.338a–750.338b (1968) (5-year maximum); Minn.Stat. § 609.293 (1984) (1-year maximum); Miss.Code Ann. § 97–29–59 (1973) (10-year maximum); Mo.Rev.Stat. § 566.090 (Supp. 1984) (1-year maximum); Mont.Code Ann. § 45–5–505 (1985) (10-year maximum); Nev.Rev.Stat. § 201.190 (1985) (6-year maximum); N.C.Gen.Stat. § 14–177 (1981) (10-year maximum); Okla.Stat., Tit. 21, § 886 (1981) (10-year maximum); R.I.Gen.Laws §11–10–1 (1981) (7 to 20 years); S.C.Code § 16–15–120 (1985) (5-year maximum); Tenn.Code Ann. § 39–2–612 (1982) (5 to 15 years); Tex.Penal Code Ann. § 21.06 (1974) ($200 maximum fine); Utah Code Ann. § 76–5–403 (1978) (6-month maximum); Va.Code § 18.2–361 (1982) (5-year maximum).

2. It was conceded at oral argument that, prior to the complaint against respondent Hardwick, there had been no reported decision involving prosecution for private homosexual sodomy under this statute for several decades. See *Thompson v. Aldredge*, 187 Ga 467, 200 S.E. 799 (1939). Moreover, the State has declined to present the criminal charge against Hardwick to a grand jury, and this is a suit for declaratory judgment brought by respondents challenging the validity of the statute. The history of nonenforcement suggests the moribund character today of laws criminalizing this type of private, consensual conduct. Some 26 States have repealed similar statutes. But the constitutional validity of the Georgia statute was put in issue by respondents, and for the reasons stated by the Court, I cannot say that conduct condemned for hundreds of years has now become a fundamental right.

JUSTICE BLACKMUN

1. Until 1968, Georgia defined sodomy as "the carnal knowledge and connection against the order of nature, by man with man, or in the same unnatural manner with woman." Ga.Crim.Code § 26–5901 (1933). In *Thompson v. Aldredge*, 187 Ga. 467, 200 S.E. 799 (1939), the Georgia Supreme Court held that § 26–5901 did not prohibit lesbian activity. And in *Riley v. Garrett*, 219 Ga. 345, 133 S.E.2d 367 (1963), the Georgia Supreme Court held that § 26–5901 did not prohibit heterosexual cunnilingus. Georgia passed the act-specific statute currently in force "perhaps in response to the restrictive court decisions such as *Riley*," Note, The Crimes Against Nature, 16 J.Pub.L. 159, 167, n. 47 (1967).

2. In *Robinson v. California*, 370 U.S. 660, 82 S.Ct. 1417, 8 L.Ed.2d 758 (1962), the Court held that the Eighth Amendment barred convicting a defendant due to his "status" as a narcotics addict, since that condition was "apparently an illness which may be contracted innocently or involuntarily." *Id.*, at 667, 82 S.Ct., at 1420. In *Powell v. Texas*, 392 U.S. 514, 88 S.Ct. 2145, 20 L.Ed.2d 1254 (1968), where the Court refused to extend *Robinson* to punishment of public drunkenness by a chronic alcoholic, one of the factors relied on by Justice MARSHALL, in writing the plurality opinion, was that Texas had not "attempted to regulate appellant's behavior in the privacy of his own home." *Id.*, at 532, 88 S.Ct., at 2154. Justice WHITE, wrote separately:

"Analysis of this difficult case is not advanced by preoccupation with the label 'condition.' In *Robinson* the Court dealt with 'a statute which makes the "status" of narcotic addiction a criminal offense. . . .' 370 U.S., at 666 [82 S.Ct., at 1420]. By precluding criminal conviction for such a 'status' the Court was dealing with a condition brought about by acts remote in time from the application of the criminal sanctions contemplated, a condition which was relatively permanent in duration, and a condition of great magnitude and significance in terms of human behavior and values. . . . If it were necessary to distinguish between 'acts' and 'conditions' for purposes of the Eighth Amendment, I would adhere to the concept of 'condition' implicit in the opinion in *Robinson*. . . . The proper subject of inquiry is whether volitional acts brought about the 'condition' and whether those acts are sufficiently proximate to the 'condition' for it to be permissible to impose penal sanctions on the 'condition.' " *Id.*, 392 U.S., at 550–551, n. 2, 88 S.Ct., at 2163, n. 2.

Despite historical views of homosexuality, it is no longer viewed by mental health professionals as a "disease" or disorder. See Brief for American Psychological Association and American Public Health Association as *Amici Curiae* 8–11. But, obviously, neither is it simply a matter of deliberate personal election. Homosexual orientation may well form part of the very fiber of an individual's personality. Consequently, under Justice WHITE's analysis in *Powell*, the Eighth Amendment may pose a constitutional barrier to sending an individual to prison for acting on that attraction regardless of the circumstances. An individual's ability to make constitutionally protected "decisions concerning sexual relations," *Cary v. Population Services International*, 431 U.S. 678, 711, 97 S.Ct. 2010, 2029, 52 L.Ed.2d 675 (1977) (POWELL, J., concurring in part and concurring in judgment), is rendered empty indeed if he or she is given no real choice but a life without any physical intimacy.

With respect to the Equal Protection Clause's applicability to § 16–6–2, I note that Georgia's exclusive stress before this Court on its interest in prosecuting homosexual activity despite the gender-neutral terms of the statute may raise serious questions of discriminatory enforcement, questions that cannot be disposed of before this Court on a motion to dismiss. See *Yick Wo v. Hopkins*, 118 U.S. 356, 373–374, 6 S.Ct. 1064, 1072–1073, 30 L.Ed.2d 220 (1886). The legislature having decided that the sex of the participants is irrelevant to the legality of the acts, I do not see why the State can defend § 16–6–2 on the ground that individuals singled out for prosecution are of the same sex as their partners. Thus, under the circumstances of this case, a claim under the Equal Protection Clause may well be available without having to reach the more controversial question whether homosexuals are a suspect class. See, *e.g.*, *Rowland v. Mad River Local School District*, 470 U.S. 1009, 105 S.Ct. 1373, 84 L.Ed.2d 392 (1985) (BRENNAN, J., dissenting from denial of certiorari); Note, the Constitutional Status of Sexual Orientation: Homosexuality as a Suspect Classification, 98 Harv.L.Rev. 1285 (1985).

3.   Even if a court faced with a challenge to § 16–6–2 were to apply simple rational-basis scrutiny to the statute, Georgia would be required to show an actual connection between the forbidden acts and the ill effects it seeks to prevent. The connection between the acts prohibited by § 16–6–2 and the harms identified by petitioner in his brief before this Court is a subject of hot dispute, hardly amenable to dismissal under Federal Rule of Civil Procedure 12(b)(6). Compare, *e.g.*, Brief for Petitioner 36–37 and Brief for David Robinson, Jr., as *Amicus Curiae* 23–28, on the one hand, with *People v. Onofre*, 51 N.Y.2d 476, 489, 434 N.Y.S.2d 947, 951–952, 415 N.E.2d 936, 941 (1980); Brief for the Attorney General of the State of New York, joined by the Attorney General of the State of California, as *Amici Curiae* 11–14; and Brief for the American Psychological

Association and American Public Health Association as *Amici Curiae* 19–27, on the other.

4. Although I do not think it necessary to decide today issues that are not even remotely before us, it does seem to me that a court could find simple, analytically sound distinctions between certain private, consensual sexual conduct, on the one hand, and adultery and incest (the only two vaguely specific "sexual crimes" to which the majority points, *ante*, at 2846), on the other. For example, marriage, in addition to its spiritual aspects, is a civil contract that entitles the contracting parties to a variety of governmentally provided benefits. A State might define the contractual commitment necessary to become eligible for these benefits to include a commitment of fidelity and then punish individuals for breaching that contract. Moreover, a State might conclude that adultery is likely to injure third persons, in particular, spouses and children of persons who engage in extramarital affairs. With respect to incest, a court might well agree with respondent that the nature of familial relationships renders true consent to incestuous activity sufficiently problematical that a blanket prohibition of such activity is warranted. See Tr. of Oral Arg. 21–22. Notably, the Court makes no effort to explain why it has chosen to group private, consensual homosexual activity with adultery and incest rather than with private, consensual heterosexual activity by unmarried persons or, indeed, with oral or anal sex within marriage.

5. The parallel between *Loving* and this case is almost uncanny. There, too, the State relied on a religious justification for its law. Compare 388 U.S., at 3, 87 S.Ct., at 1819 (quoting trial court's statement that "Almighty God created the races while, black, yellow, malay and red, and he placed them on separate continents. . . . The fact that he separated the races shows that he did not intend for the races to mix"), with Brief for Petitioner 20–21 (relying on the Old and New Testaments and the writings of St. Thomas Aquinas to show that "traditional Judeo-Christian values proscribe such conduct"). There, too, defenders of the challenged statute relied heavily on the fact that when the Fourteenth Amendment was ratified, most of the States had similar prohibitions. Compare Brief for Appellee in *Loving v. Virginia*, O.T. 1966, No. 395, pp. 28–29, with *ante*, at 2844–2845, and n. 6. There, too, at the time the case came before the Court, many of the States still had criminal statutes concerning the conduct at issue. Compare 388 U.S., at 6, n. 5, 87 S.Ct., at 1820, n. 5 (noting that 16 States still outlawed interracial marriage), with *ante*, at 2845–2846 (noting that 24 States and the District of Columbia have sodomy statutes). Yet the Court held, not only that the invidious racism of Virginia's law violated the Equal Protection Clause, see 388 U.S., at 7–12, 87 S.Ct., at 1821–1823, but also that the law deprived the Lovings of due process by denying them the "freedom of choice to marry" that had "long been recognized as one of the vital personal rights essential to the orderly pursuit of happiness by free man." *Id.*, at 12, 87 S.Ct., at 1824.

6. The theological nature of the origin of Anglo-American antisodomy statutes is patent. It was not until 1533 that sodomy was made a secular offense in England. 25 Hen. VIII, ch. 6. Until that time, the offense was, in Sir James Stephen's words, "merely ecclesiastical." 2 J. Stephen, A History of the Criminal Law of England 429–430 (1883). Pollock and Maitland similarly observed that "[t]he crime against nature . . . was so closely connected with heresy that the vulgar had but one name for both." 2 F. Pollock & F. Maitland, The History of English Law 554 (1895). The transfer of jurisdiction over prosecutions for sodomy to the secular courts seems primarily due to the alterations of ecclesiastical jurisdiction attendant on England's break with the Roman Catholic Church, rather than to any new understanding of the sovereign's interest in preventing or punishing the behavior involved. Cf. 6 E. Coke, Institutes, ch. 10 (4th ed. 1797).

7. At oral argument a suggestion appeared that, while the Fourth Amendment's special protection of the home might prevent the State from enforcing § 16–6–2 against individuals who engage in consensual sexual activity there, that protection would not make the statute invalid. See Tr. of Oral Arg. 10–11. The suggestion misses the point entirely. If the law is not invalid, then the police *can* invade the home to enforce it, provided, of course, that they obtain a determination of probable cause from a neutral magistrate. One of the reasons for the Court's holding in *Griswold v. Connecticut*, 381 U.S. 479, 85 S.Ct. 1678, 14 L.Ed.2d 510 (1965), was precisely the possibility, and repugnancy, of permitting searches to obtain evidence regarding the use of contraceptives. *Id.*, at 485–486, 85 S.Ct., at 1682. Permitting the kinds of searches that might be necessary to obtain evidence of the sexual activity banned by § 16–6–2 seems no less intrusive, or repugnant. *Cf. Winston v. Lee*, 470 U.S. 753, 105 S.Ct. 1611, 84 L.Ed.2d 662 (1985); *Mary Beth G. v. City of Chicago*, 723 F.2d 1263, 1274 (CA7 1983).

JUSTICE STEVENS

1. See Ga.Code Ann. § 16–6–2(a) (1984) ("A person commits the offense of sodomy when he performs or submits to any sexual act involving the sex organs of one person and the mouth or anus of another").

2. The Court states that the "issue presented is whether the Federal Constitution confers a fundamental right upon homosexuals to engage in sodomy and hence invalidates the laws of the many States that still make such conduct illegal and have done so for a very long time." *Ante*, at 2843. In reality, however, it is the indiscriminate prohibitions of sodomy, heterosexual as well as homosexual, that has been present "for a very long time." See nn. 3, 4, and 5, *infra*. However, the reasoning the Court employs would provide the same support for the statute as it is written as it does for the statute as it is narrowly construed by the Court.

3. See, *e.g.*, 1 W. Hawkins, Pleas of the Crown 9 (6th ed. 1787) ("All unnatural carnal copulations, whether with man or beast, seem to come under the notion of sodomy, which was felony by the antient common law, and punished, according to some authors, with burning; according to others, . . . with burying alive"); 4 W. Blackstone, Commentaries * 215 (discussing "the infamous *crime against nature*, committed either with man or beast; a crime which ought to be strictly and impartially proved, and then as strictly and impartially punished").

4. See 1 E. East, Pleas of the Crown 480 (1803) ("This offence, concerning which the least notice is the best, consists in a carnal knowledge committed against the order of nature by man with man, or in the same unnatural manner with woman, or by man or woman in any manner with beast"); J. Hawley & M. McGregor, The Criminal Law 287 (3d ed. 1899) ("Sodomy is the carnal knowledge against the order of nature by two persons with each other, or of a human being with a beast. . . . The offense may be committed between a man and a woman, or between two male persons, or between a man or a woman and a beast").

5. See J. May, The Law of Crimes § 203 (2d ed. 1893) ("Sodomy, otherwise called buggery, bestiality, and the crime against nature, is the unnatural copulation of two persons with each other, or of a human being with a beast. . . . It may be committed by a man with a man, by a man with a beast, or by a woman with a beast, or by a man with a woman—his wife, in which case, if she consent, she is an accomplice").

6. The predecessor of the current Georgia statute provided: "Sodomy is the carnal knowledge and connection against the order of nature, by man with man, or in the same unnatural manner with woman." Ga.Code, Tit. 1, Pt. 4, § 4251 (1861). This prohibition of heterosexual sodomy was not purely hortatory. See, *e.g., Comer v. State*, 21 Ga.App. 306, 94 S.E. 314 (1917) (affirming prosecution for consensual heterosexual sodomy).

7. See *Thompson v. Aldredge*, 187 Ga. 467, 200 S.E. 799 (1939).

8. A review of the statutes cited by the majority discloses that, in 1791, in 1868, and today, the vast majority of sodomy statues do not differentiate between homosexual and heterosexual sodomy.

9. See *Loving v. Virginia*, 388 U.S. 1, 87 S.Ct. 1817, 18 L.Ed.2d 1010 (1967). Interestingly, miscegenation was once treated as a crime similar to sodomy. See Hawley & McGregor, The Criminal Law, at 287 (discussing crime of sodomy); *id.*, at 288 (discussing crime of miscegenation).

10. Indeed, the Georgia Attorney General concedes that Georgia's statute would be unconstitutional if applied to a married couple. See Tr. of Oral Arg. 8 (stating that application of the statute to a married couple "would be unconstitutional" because of the "right of marital privacy as identified by the Court in *Griswold*"). Significantly, Georgia passed the current statute three years after the Court's decision in *Griswold*.

11. *Ante*, at 2848, n. 2 (POWELL, J., concurring). See also Tr. of Oral Arg. 4–5 (argument of Georgia Attorney General) (noting, in response to question about prosecution "where the activity took place in a private residence," the "last case I can recall was back in the 1930s or 40s").

12. It is, of course, possible to argue that a statute has a purely symbolic role. Cf. *Carey v. Population Services International*, 431 U.S. 678, 715, n. 3, 97 S.Ct. 2010, 2031, n. 3, 52 L.Ed.2d 675 (1977) (STEVENS, J., concurring in part and concurring in judgment) ("The fact that the State admittedly has never brought a prosecution under the statute . . . is consistent with appellants' position that the purpose of the statute is merely symbolic"). Since the Georgia Attorney General does not even defend the statute as written, however, see n. 10, *supra*, the State cannot possibly rest on the notion that the statute may be defended for its symbolic message.

13. Indeed, at this stage, it appears that the statute indiscriminately authorizes a policy of selective prosecution that is neither limited to the class of homosexual persons nor embraces all persons in that class, but rather applies to those who may be arbitrarily selected by the prosecutor for reasons that are not revealed either in the record of this case or in the text of the statute. If that is true, although the text of the statute is clear enough, its true meaning may be "so intolerably vague that evenhanded enforcement of the law is a virtual impossibility." *Marks v. United States*, 430 U.S. 188, 198, 97 S.Ct. 990, 996, 51 L.Ed.2d 260 (1977) (STEVENS, J., concurring in part and dissenting in part).

Out in the City

David Shannon

I climbed into my seat at the end of the bar, aware that the conversation was well under way. My friend A. looked deep into his glass. He had been going through a bit of a topsy-turvy time lately, but managed to maintain a brave composure. Free association had taken him in a conversational direction far from what was really on his mind. A. was anxious to bring attention back to his dilemma.

A.'s flare for performance always made him a pleasure to watch. He took a grand sip of beer, shifted his weight in such a way as to indicate boredom with his friend's lack of concern. "Back to *my* situation," he blurted out. "I just don't know what to do."

He and his companion D. exchanged weighty glances. I think it was for my sake—since I arrived in the middle of their conversation, I was not yet aware that this was a serious discussion.

D. took charge. "Well, you see A. has a new friend . . . *aaand,*" here he looked me straight in the eye, leaning slightly forward, "he's only seventeen." All eyes were now on me, waiting to record my shock or delight. Frankly, I was still waiting for the point.

"Do you like him?" I asked.

"Yes!" said A.

"Does he like you? Are you having good sex?"

"Yes, yes."

Help me out here, I thought, what's all this drama for? "So what's the problem?" D. jumped in frustration that I had not played my part.

Aaaah, it was becoming clear now, they were operating under false assumptions, victims of too many American television shows. Now I could take my place on stage and play to the balcony. Following A.'s cue, I too took a sip of my beer, put the glass down and looked at A. with a smile. "A. dear, the age of consent in Canada is fourteen."

They gasped in shock. A. was at once thrilled and annoyed. Thrilled that he was not going to be hauled off and branded a pederast, annoyed that his crisis was for naught. There was now a garbled chorus of "fourteen? I didn't know—you see you had nothing to worry about—when did it change—fourteen?"

I was saving the best for last. "The law was quietly changed several years ago. Not only was the age of consent made equal for men and women, but also for queers and straights. But there was one restriction. I guess the committee which drew up the legislation felt they had to be antisex in some fashion, so they decided to restrict consent for anal sex to people eighteen and over."

A. was getting nervous all over again, exactly as I had hoped. "This caveat was mostly directed at gays. They probably thought that to pop the Hershey cherry, you should also be able to take copious amounts of legal drink. More likely it was just another way to keep us in place. But, a couple of weeks ago, the Ontario Court of Appeals overturned the outdated part of the legislation, stating it was an undue restriction on a consenting couple's behavior. The couple was straight by the way."

Everyone was delighted by now, and A. ordered another round.

The Politics of the Closet: Towards Equal Protection for Gay, Lesbian and Bisexual Identity

Janet E. Halley

In the summer of 1986, the U.S. Supreme Court made it resoundingly clear that no fundamental privacy right attaches to consensual homosexual sodomy.[1] *Bowers v. Hardwick* forged an equally indubitable link between the question of homosexual rights under the Constitution and the proper scope of judicial review of legislative decisions. Invoking the specter of *Lochner v. New York*[2] and "the face-off between the Executive and the Court in the 1930s," Justice White's majority opinion argued that "[t]he Court is most vulnerable and comes nearest to illegitimacy when it deals with judge-made constitutional law having little or no cognizable roots [sic] in the language or design of the Constitution."[3] Chief Justice Burger concluded in his concurring opinion, "[t]his is essentially not a question of personal 'preferences' but rather of [sic] the legislative authority of the State."[4] By refusing to extend its substantive due process jurisprudence, the Court remanded gay men and lesbians[5] to the political arena to combat sodomy laws and their discriminatory enforcement through the majoritarian political process.

The history of the United States testifies eloquently to the fact that, when a despised minority must fend for itself in the tumult of electoral and legislative politics, the majority may deny it a fair chance. Ever since *United States v. Carolene Products*,[6] the Supreme Court has acknowledged the constitutional dimension of this fact by committing itself to ensuring that the political process is not unfairly rigged. *Carolene Products* announced a rejection of the doctrine that legislative impositions on trade would be presumed unconstitutional, holding instead that they would be presumed to meet the requirements of the due process clause. In the "most celebrated footnote in constitutional law,"[7] Justice Stone warned that the Court, though

145

forswearing the power to make substantive law under the rubric of due process, did not intend to abrogate its duty to enforce constitutional guarantees that the majoritarian process would not be poisoned.

> There may be narrower scope for operation of the presumption of constitutionality when legislation appears on its face to be within a specific prohibition of the Constitution, such as those of the first ten amendments, which are deemed equally specific when held to be embraced within the Fourteenth.
>
> It is unnecessary to consider now whether legislation which restricts those political processes which can ordinarily be expected to bring about repeal of undesirable legislation, is to be subjected to more exacting judicial scrutiny under the general prohibitions of the Fourteenth Amendment than are most other types of legislation. . . . Nor need we enquire whether similar considerations enter into the review of statutes directed at particular religious, or national, or racial minorities: whether prejudice against discrete and insular minorities may be a special consideration, which tends seriously to curtail the operation of those political processes ordinarily to be relied upon to protect minorities, and which may call for a correspondingly more searching judicial inquiry.[8]

Though Footnote Four is discreetly phrased as dictum[9] and purports to canvass questions irrelevant to the present controversy, it remains the touchstone of process-based judicial review. The footnote foresees that judicial interference with legislative decisions may be justified in three situations: (1) violations of terms of the Constitution; (2) direct interferences with the political process; and (3) indirect interferences with the political process, in the form of laws disadvantaging minorities.[10] Placed back into its context, as a footnote to one of the line of cases jettisoning the jurisprudence of substantive due process, Footnote Four implicitly sets forth a vision of a renovated judiciary. No longer the intestine enemy of republican government, the judiciary is to be its champion; federal courts, while strictly restrained from frustrating the will of the people as expressed through the legislative process, are charged with a responsibility to interfere whenever that process has broken down. Judges must not usurp a power, under the due process clause, to void substantive legislative decisions made by political majorities; but neither may they abdicate a duty to guarantee that majorities will be formed and will exercise their powers in consonance with the Constitution.

The Court in *Bowers v. Hardwick*, far from rejecting the Footnote Four tradition, drew on its characterization of the judicial role. It made a constitutional promise to the very gay men and lesbians it spurned—a promise to guarantee us a full and unimpeded opportunity to advocate repeal of the sodomy statutes.

This article attempts to clear the ground for such protection by demonstrating that sexual identity is produced by social interaction, and that that activity of production is so fundamental to the development of a genuine and fair public debate about the wisdom of the sodomy statutes that, under the mandate of the equal protection clause, courts are obliged to protect it.[11] To adopt the trichotomy proposed in Footnote Four, advocates of gay and lesbian rights can look to the Bill of Rights for protection of rights expressly granted there; they can look to a rich constitutional tradition prohibiting direct interferences with the political process for protection of political speech *about* homosexuality; but when they voluntarily adopt or involuntarily bear the public identity "homosexual," and for that reason lose their employment and other public benefits, housing, custody of children, resident alien status, medical insurance and even physical safety, they are hindered and deterred from entering the public debate surrounding the sodomy laws. The harms they suffer interfere sharply, albeit indirectly, with the political process. The *Carolene* formulation has determined that, when confronted with this third form of process failure, would-be advocates of legislative change can call on the equal protection clause.

To recognize the direct implication of both the majority and concurring opinions in *Bowers v. Hardwick* is to acknowledge that *Hardwick* is not an equal protection case. This point requires emphasis because several courts have held that *Hardwick* is binding precedent in the equal protection context.[12] As a panel of the Ninth Circuit observed in rejecting the argument that *Hardwick* is binding in the equal protection context, these cases vastly oversimplify the structure of the Fourteenth Amendment, which not only provides a guarantee of due process but also poses "an independent obligation on government not to draw invidious distinctions among its citizens."[13]

Even if the two clauses are accorded the distinct analysis which clearly established precedent demands, however, one can interpret *Hardwick* to dictate the denial of heightened scrutiny under the equal protection clause by making a certain definition of the class of homosexuals. The argument turns on the relationship between homosexual identity and homosexual acts—specifically, the acts prohibited by statute in seven states.[14] If criminal or criminalizable sodomy is the inevitable consequence or the essential characteristic of homosexual identity, then the class of homosexuals is coterminous with a class of criminals or at least of persons whose shared behavior is criminalizable. In *Padula v. Webster*, for example, the holding that *Hardwick* requires a rejection of any heightened scrutiny for homosexuals under the equal protection clause, turns on a finding that sodomy is "the behavior that defines the class."[15] It is a short step from this act of definition to the reasoning advanced in *Phyler v. Doe*, where the Supreme Court rejected out of hand any argument that "illegal aliens" constitute a suspect class because "entry into the class is itself a crime."[16]

The reading of *Hardwick* as binding precedent in equal protection cases has brought new urgency to a project that has, until now, seemed rather academic: the project of ascertaining how the class of homosexuals is constituted. This article argues that homosexual identity is the product not of sodomitic acts *simpliciter*, but of a complex political discourse that is threatened, in ways that the *Carolene Products* formulation prohibits, by antihomosexual discrimination. Such an argument has already been adopted by two carefully argued decisions: *Watkins v. United States Army*[17] and *benShalom v. Marsh*.[18]

The full implications of this post-*Hardwick* equal protection jurisprudence cannot be understood without a recognition that recent, expansive readings of *Hardwick*, with their crudely essentialist notion of how the class of homosexuals is established, sound a weird echo of an argument repeatedly adopted by advocates of gay and lesbian rights. For until recently, gay rights advocates have fairly consistently argued that homosexual orientation is so unitary, fundamental, irresistible and inalterable that homosexuals meet a supposed requirement of suspect classifications, that of immutability. After *Hardwick*, the argument for heightened scrutiny under the equal protection clause is now undermined, not bolstered, by claims that homosexuality is a fixed and immutable attributable of a rigidly demarcated class.

In the pre-*Hardwick* setting, the immutability argument was not only legally but also rhetorically *a propos*. To many, it seemed a necessary riposte to the majority's fears that some of its numbers might become gay unless the cost of doing so was quite high. As it directly allays such anxieties on their own terms, the exonerating power of the immutability argument has struck a popular nerve. A father fought homophobia on behalf of his lesbian daughter, for instance, by revealing that Parents and Friends of Lesbians and Gays have learned "that we did not 'cause,' and our children did not 'choose,' their homosexuality—that sexual orientation, like warts or perfect pitch, is a matter of biological roulette."[19] And Jeffrey W. Levi of the National Gay and Lesbian Task Force, testifying before the Senate Judiciary Committee, engaged in the following illuminating exchange with Senator Strom Thurmond:

> MR. THURMOND: Does your organization advocate any kind of treatment for gays and lesbians to see if they can change them and make them normal like other people?

MR. LEVI: Well, Senator, we consider ourselves to be quite normal, thank you. We just happen to be different from other people. . . . To . . . answer the question more seriously, the predominant scientific viewpoint is that homosexuality is probably innate, if not innate then formed very early in life[.][20]

Confronted with the supposed requirement for heightened scrutiny that the proposed classification be based on an *immutable* trait, advocates of gay, lesbian, and bisexual rights have almost uniformly—though often with visible qualms—embraced the argument that homosexuality is immutable.[21] Judges supporting gay rights have often justified doing so by pointing to the immutability of homosexuality.[22] But other courts have based their decisions to deny protection to homosexuals on the supposed mutability of sexual preference.[23] The desirability of deterring children from imitating the homosexuality of those around them has loomed large in child custody, child care and education settings.[24] As I show below, both sides are empirically right: homosexuality is sometimes mutable and sometimes not. Given the prevailing failure of legal analysts to grapple with this less than simple empirical phenomenon, perhaps the best judicial responses to date have been cases upholding gay rights without reliance on the immutability argument.[25]

Expansive readings of *Hardwick* should draw new, skeptical attention to the immutability argument. Clearly, it is time for gay advocates to rethink that argument—but even if it were not, the sheer facts demand that the argument be abandoned.[26] In fact, the problem of the mutability of homosexual inclination is far more complex than the legal discourse has yet acknowledged. The patterns that emerge from recent empirical and theoretical work on the subject compel the conclusion that homosexual identity, far from being the equivalent of sodomy, is constituted in precisely the political process which, under the equal protection clause, the courts are pledged to protect. Far from closing constitutional debate on this issue, *Hardwick* opened it.

To make the case for heightened scrutiny of official acts punishing and deterring the public acknowledgment of gay, lesbian and bisexual identity, this article pursues a tripartite argument. Part I demonstrates that, in fact, immutability is not required by the Court's equal protection precedents, which focus instead on process implications often associated with apparently immutable traits. A proper reading of these precedents demonstrates that the equal protection clause vigilantly protects not monolithic groups but rather the dialogue that generates group identity and suggests that gay rights advocates and courts attend not to product but to process, not to the class but to the *classification* of homosexuals. Part II surveys the empirical literature on sexual orientation and the constitutive behavior of individuals in the legal process, to demonstrate that gay, lesbian and bisexual identity are produced by a discourse so intrinsically political that it merits the most careful judicial scrutiny. Part III invokes the sociology of the political process developed under the first amendment in order to demonstrate that equal protection review committed to preserving that process will not only protect the public disclosure or assignment of gay or homosexual identity but also delimit the courts' role in protecting minorities from the will of the majority.

Immutability Doctrine and the Political Process

Legal lore has it that a group must be defined by an immutable characteristic before the Supreme Court will even consider whether it should be regarded as a suspect class. The contradiction implicit in this claim is perhaps most concisely expressed in the oxymoron "suspect class"—for it is surely not the class, but the classification, that is suspect. And classifications are highly contingent products of social relations, subject to change not only in their definitions but also in the roster of persons they can marshal at any given moment. I argue in this section that the Supreme Court has, quite properly, repudiated the supposed requirement of immutability and focused its attention instead on the social process in which classifications are produced and policed.

Race and Immutability

If immutability were a requirement for strict scrutiny under the equal protection clause, race could not be a suspect classification. As the Supreme Court has shown in two recent cases recognizing that Arabs and Jews have a cause of action under 42 U.S.C. Sections 1981 and 1982, the very conception of race, and the taxonomy of "races," are products of culture rather than of nature.[27] In *Shaare Tefila Congregation v. Cobb* and *Saint Francis College v. Al-Khazraji*, the Court sought evidence that Jews and Arabs were racial groups within the meaning of the civil rights statutes. It conceded that it could not look to any "distinctive physiognomy"[28] or to any sound modern scientific conception of race:[29] instead, it had to turn to late-nineteenth-century dictionaries and floor debates before the passage of sections 1981 and 1982.[30] The mere evidence relied on by the Court reveals that race is historically contingent, that its contours have changed radically since the passage of the Civil Rights Amendments. If the boundaries between races can shift, the racial categorization of individuals can shift—a profound source of mutability.[31]

Shaare Tefila and *Saint Francis* expose a dynamic in the *creation* of race which, even as the Civil Rights Acts were being enacted, was perhaps most acutely revealed in the law of miscegenation. As Eva Saks has shown,[32] these laws were an effort to maintain, at the crucial boundary of access to property rights through marriage, a rigid and apparently natural line of division between races: they were racist not only in their purpose but in their method. They pitted the conception of race as an immutable and unambiguous biological given—"blood"—against an instrumental and highly contingent negotiation of race classifications in statutory definitions of race and in criminal prosecutions. The latter often won, revealing the former to be a social and legal (and racist) construction. In *Ferrall v. Ferrall*,[33] for example, a man wished to divorce his wife, with whom he had had several children, for miscegenation. The court refused to find that she was "of negro descent to the third generation inclusive," and in a concurring opinion Judge Clark described the constructive activity that the plaintiff had urged the court to perform:

> The law may not permit him thus to bastardize his own innocent children, but he would *brand them for all time by the judgment of a court as negroes.* . . . [The court contemned] this husband and father, who for the sake of a divorce would *make negroes of his wife and children, hitherto white.*[34]

Racial identity is recognized here to be the product of a social process, and to be subject to sudden and precipitous change by the exercise of instrumental power. Indeed, Judge Clark declared that the plaintiff's real obligations to his wife and children, if he did discover in them "any minute strain of colored origin," was to "keep to himself that of which the public was unaware"[35]—to maintain the admitted illusion that skin color reliably indicates one's race. Clearly, it is not just exceptional cases like John Howard Griffin, the renowned author of *Black Like Me*,[36] that prove race to be mutable: the very law creating race lines recognizes its own artificiality, extending an open invitation to those who can contrive to "pass"[37] to exploit the mutability of race within the frame of their own lives.

The Displacement of Immutability by Process Analysis

The paradigm of race is so fundamental to equal protection doctrine that we should be disposed rather to discard a requirement of immutability for suspect classification, than to insist on it at the cost of the entire doctrinal tradition. But no such choice is even posed by the precedents set out by the Supreme Court: immutability is neither a necessary nor a sufficient precondition for the recognition of a suspect classification, and where it has appeared as a factor in the Court's analysis, it has always been shorthand for inquiry into the fairness of the political process burdening the group.

In *San Antonio Independent School District v. Rodriguez*, the Court defined the "traditional indicia of suspectness" as those marking a class "saddled with such disabilities, or subjected to such a history of purposeful unequal treatment, or relegated to such a position of political powerlessness as to command extraordinary protection from the majoritarian political process."[38] Under this standard, heightened protection has been extended even without a showing of immutability, and denied even with it. Aliens, a group formally excluded from the electoral process, have been held to merit special protection despite the fact that alienage is a legal relationship subject to change.[39] Even where the Court has explicitly found that a group (for instance, the mentally disabled) is differentiated from the majority by an immutable characteristic, the doctrinal focus has remained on the question whether the political history of that characteristic is marked by oppressive abuses of the political power of the majority—and the Court has answered "no."[40] In determining how stringent its review must be, the Court looks for acute vulnerability in the political process, not the immutability of any trait uniting or defining the group. This vulnerability—not immutability— is what makes other suspect classifications "like race."[41]

Where immutability does feature in the Court's analyses, it is merely a factor in the Court's review of two different sorts of process failure: mere irrationality and a pervasive prejudice that distorts the relationship of majority to minority. The Court has acknowledged, further, that the former inquiry is more properly invoked under the rational basis test, while the process failure implicated in the latter is just as likely to be signaled by mutability as by immutability of a target group's distinctive characteristic.

IMMUTABILITY AND RATIONALITY

First, immutability can call into question the rationality of laws apparently aimed at deterring class membership. In *Frontiero v. Richardson*, a plurality of the Court reasoned that, because one's sex is "an immutable characteristic, determined solely by the accident of birth," it cannot fairly trigger discriminatory burdens in a system embracing "the basic concept . . . that legal burdens should bear some relationship to individual responsibility."[42] The commitments underlying this rather cryptic argument are made clearer in a line of cases determining whether and when strict scrutiny is triggered by legislation burdening children on the basis of statuses imposed on them by their parents and the state.

In *Parham v. Hughes*, the Court was confronted with a state statute denying to the father of an illegitimate child the right to sue for a child's wrongful death. A plurality of the Court distinguished this statute from those attaching disadvantages to illegitimacy where the Court had exercised heightened scrutiny[43] by noting that fathers, unlike their children, had it in their power to legitimate:

> The basic rationale of these decisions is that it is *unjust and ineffective* for society to express its condemnation of procreation outside the marital relationship by punishing the illegitimate child who is in no way responsible for his situation and is unable to change it. . . . [T]he appellant here was responsible for . . . failing to change [his illegitimate child's] status.
> . . . The justifications for judicial sensitivity to the constitutionality of differing legislative treatment of legitimate and illegitimate children are simply absent when a classification affects only the fathers of deceased illegitimate children.[44]

The logic expressed here is not a judgment on the merits, that the burden imposed is in some sense fundamentally unfair,[45] but rather, a determination that statutes attempting to deter people from bearing immutable characteristics are often *irrational*.

As the Court held in *Plyler v. Doe*, a statute excluding the children of aliens illegally present in the U.S. from public education "is directed against children, and imposes its discriminatory burden on the basis of a legal characteristic over which children can have little control. It is thus difficult to conceive of a *rational justification* for penalizing these children for their presence within the United States."[46] The Court discerns no logical reason to deprive the children of undocumented aliens of a public education. Instead it discovers a scheme that promises to make of those children a "permanent caste," a politically disenfranchised, economically defenseless "underclass."[47] Such a profound threat to the political process, it holds, warrants the strictest judicial scrutiny.

If immutability is merely a trope for undeterrability, and undeterrability a clue to process failure, one might ask: why not strike immutability from the constitutional lexicon and get to the point? Twice the Court has suggested that it favors such a simplification. As a panel of the Ninth Circuit has noted, the court in *Cleburne* "cast[] doubt on immutability theory."[48] Noting that the mentally retarded are "different, immutably so," from the majority that voted to impose special burdens on them, the Court nevertheless rejected an invitation to exercise strict scrutiny. In doing so, it adopted with approval Professor Ely's argument that immutability was an unreliable indicator of impermissible legislative hostility and an unsuitable substitute for careful examination of a statute's rationality.[49] The Court laid the foundation for this rather offhand repudiation of the immutability/ deterrence line of reasoning in *Mathews v. Lucas*, where it ruled that heightened scrutiny for laws burdening illegitimate children is not mandated by immutability alone, because immutability in these cases suggests nothing more than the arbitrariness and irrationality which rational basis scrutiny is specifically designed to discover.[50] Note that this case quotes the *Rodriguez* test in full[51] and determines that illegitimate children have never suffered the history of discrimination that has been saddled on Blacks and women:[52] as the talisman of immutability is debunked, the focus properly returns to social history and its effect on the political process.

IMMUTABILITY AND PREJUDICE

A second function of immutability is to serve as a rough index of the sort of "prejudice" that, Footnote Four suggests, unconstitutionally disables minorities in the political process. Perhaps the clearest example of this use of immutability appears in *Massachusetts Board of Retirement v. Murgia*,[53] where the Court held that a rule mandating retirement of police officers at the age of fifty does not call for strict scrutiny. After involving the *Rodriguez* test, the Court concludes:

> [E]ven old age does not define a "discrete and insular" group, *United States v. Carolene Products Co.*, in need of "extraordinary protection from the majoritarian political process." Instead, it marks a stage that each of us will reach if we live out our normal span.[54]

The Court's reasoning here is quite compressed. Because all of us expect to be old (or *are* old), we are likely to take our future (or present) welfare into account when we vote on proposals that old people shall make sacrifices for our benefit. Furthermore, old people are not set apart from the rest of us, are not "discrete and insular," so they have not been boxed out of political discourse about their duties and entitlements. The mutability of age classifications calls to the Court's attention both the peculiarity of age groups as political actors and the attitude of the "younger majority" towards them.

These implications of mutability parallel the exfoliations of *Carolene* doctrine accomplished by Professors Bruce Ackerman and John Hart Ely in their pivotal commentaries on Footnote Four. According to Ackerman, the key phrase in the *Carolene* formulation is "discrete and insular minorities," for these words imply that the sociology of the pluralistic process must be examined to identify groups that are unfairly disadvantaged.[55] According to Professor Ely, on the other hand, the key term is "prejudice," for it implies a determination that that impermissible legislative motive is very likely at work when groups subject to it are disproportionately harmed by legislation.[56] Ackerman focuses on the internal politics of the minority; Ely examines the "psychology of decision"[57] among the majority. Both views of process-based analysis demote immutability to a mere factor in the analysis of political interactions. Neither analysis recognizes the extent to which it is incomplete without the other, and the extent to which it mistakes the political significance of a group's apparent mutability or immutability because it ignores half of the whole composed of minority and majority. This more complete vision of the political process is what the Court has articulated in the *Rodriguez* test, with its dual inquiry into the majority's "purposeful unequal treatment" and the minority's "position of political powerlessness."[58] To get this right is to see how immutability *and* mutability can serve as indicators of constitutionally prohibited failures of the political process.

Ackerman argues that the real crux of the process-based review outlined by Footnote Four is the organizational capacity of the burdened minority. Justice Stone mistakenly guessed that discrete and insular minorities would always be the groups faced with the steepest political odds: anonymous and diffuse groups are at least as incapacitated to fend for themselves. The Footnote assumes that political isolation from a hostile majority and ready visibility of group members operate to exclude discrete and insular minorities from the bargaining table; what it does not contemplate, Ackerman asserts, is that discreteness and insularity can help a group to consolidate its bargaining position, while the obverse characteristics of anonymity and diffuseness can be politically debilitating. An insular group can corral free riders by drawing on a sense of group solidarity and by taking advantage of social occasions for applying sanctions to free riding; it enjoys lower costs of organizing and of identifying and evaluating its own leaders than a diffuse group; and it is more likely than a diffuse group to constitute a local majority in a few congressional districts and to be able to send its own people to the bargaining table.[59] Members of a discrete group cannot disguise their group membership, and are thus unable to escape the burdens imposed on their fellows. In contrast to group members who can evade classification with the group by pretending not to belong and keeping quiet, they have less to lose when asked to speak out for their group's interests.[60] Homosexuals, in fact, constitute one of Ackerman's paradigm anonymous-and-diffuse groups: they must deal with free riders, organization costs and the challenge of local representation without the advantages of insularity, and they must persuade other homosexuals voluntarily to incur discrimination as the price of speaking out.

Footnote Four's insistence on discreteness and insularity amounts to an insistence on immutability—on the power of observers unambiguously to associate individuals with the minority, on the inability of individuals to drift out of the minority to which they are assigned. On Ackerman's analysis it is the precise converse of such immutability—it is *mutability*—that disables minorities to play pluralist hardball. We know that, historically, both analyses have been true. Indeed, as Saks has demonstrated in her analysis of miscegenation, the oppression of Blacks has exploited both the apparently natural fact of their immutable identity as Black, and a strange mixture of fear at and connivance with the unspoken fact of their (unevenly distributed) power to "pass." Finally, miscegenation law demonstrates that mutability and immutability can be the product and the mechanism, rather than the cause of constitutionally intolerable domination.

Ackerman's minority-based approach thus implicates an analysis of the motives and strategies of the corresponding majority. For this, however, we must turn to Ely's psychology of prejudice. Ely discovers that legislators are both more likely to sympathize with groups aligned by a mutable characteristic, like those based on age,[61] *and* more likely to sympathize with groups identified by immutable characteristics, "feel[ing] sorry" for those "disabled by something [they] can't do anything about."[62] I do not intend to cavil at this contradiction, for both elements are surely at work. Its converse is presumably true, too: a legislator is likely to feel unconstitutional animus towards unremittingly strange and different "Others" but may also discover that her preexisting animus is neatly justified by legislation *making* a group "Other." The two motives can feed one another in a vicious circle, generating the social "fact" of an oppressive category's simultaneous mutability and immutability and setting in motion both the organizational disabilities foreseen by Justice Stone and those pinpointed by Professor Ackerman. Thus the very instability of race, once slavery ceased to give it a rigid social form, generated the White anxiety underlying miscegenation statutes, while its apparent fixity justified horror at interracial unions. Marked by a simultaneously immutable and mutable characteristic, Blacks could be excluded from the political process by being culturally and geographically isolated "as Blacks" or, wherever that proved impossible, by being appropriated and coopted "as Whites." The whole complex insured that no one was situated to challenge the very referentiality of racial descriptors or to propose that racial culture in the United States was no simple question of Black and White.

Mutability in the Social Context of Sexual Identity

To display, or not to display; to tell or not to tell; to let on or not to let on; to lie or not to lie; and in each case, to whom, how, when and where.[63]

Bowers v. Hardwick having indelibly drawn the link between judicial restraint and the question of homosexual rights, homosexual advocates must reconsider their litigation strategy. Heretofore homosexual rights advocates have argued almost uniformly for suspect classification status on the grounds that homosexuality is immutable.[64] Certainly they have been right when they have argued that homosexual orientation is not amenable to any recognized therapeutic "cure" and that the halting attempts at conversion sometimes undertaken are not only profoundly traumatic and expensive but are totally futile for all but a small population of "highly motivated" individuals of quavering sexual identity.[65] This argument, however germane to a "fundamental fairness" version of the immutability doctrine, in fact misses the point of the Supreme Court's actual jurisprudence of immutability and process failure. Moreover, it is factually inaccurate for the vast range of sexual identity—from personal self-description to the public disclosure of or subjection to homosexual or heterosexual identity—that is the proper object of constitutional process analysis.

Strict scrutiny must be triggered by the dynamics of mutability and immutability implicit in that empirical and analytical peculiarity of antihomosexual discrimination, the closet. Antihomosexual discrimination encourages people to manipulate the identity they attach to themselves, both in the secrecy of their own minds and on the public stage, in what I shall call their subjective and their public identities. It ensures that personal desires, sexual behavior, subjective identity and public identity will frequently get out of sync with each other. However carefully an individual disposes these elements, they are all subject to sudden, either joyous or catastrophic, rearrangement. That is to say, they are mutable. In this section I review the ways in which homosexual—and heterosexual—identities are changeable, first by reviewing the empirical literature—historical, psychological and sociological—on the formation of subjective homosexual identity, and second, by examining the ways in which the legal enforcement of antihomosexual laws and policies both generates the social fact of immutability and rings changes throughout the arena of public sexual identity.

Subjective Identity: The Empirical Literature

If you want to keep a secret you have to keep it from yourself.[66]

Renewed attention to the mutability of homosexuality reveals that empirical claims that homosexuality is immutable vastly oversimplify the findings of researchers. The psychological literature, often relied upon in arguments claiming that homosexuality is immutable, in fact presents a complex picture of what mutability is and how it is distributed. The conclusion most readily drawn from this literature is that immutability characterizes the sexual orientation of *some*, perhaps most, homosexuals, but that many individuals, homosexual and heterosexual alike, are capable of making decisions as to their sexual orientation.

Purely psychological analysis often creates a deeply misleading picture of the social meaning of this phenomenon, moreover, by ignoring the role of social activities of interpretation in destabilizing the categories "homosexual" and "heterosexual." For example, homosexuals who experience their sexual desire as immutably oriented towards persons of their own sex nevertheless may be coerced to pretend that they conform to the norm of heterosexuality.[67] Such a result is no mere fib: it is a change. To be sure, what has changed is not the supposed *essence* of sexual orientation, but the *representation* of it available for social interpretation. But essences, conceding for a moment their existence, are not visible to legislatures, judges, employers or police. Social agents work with social meaning; the fairness and indeed the constitutionality of their acts must be measured in the context of the practical, not the ideal, epistemology of their decision-making. A full evaluation of the usefulness of the mutability doctrine in assessing antihomosexual discrimination must rest, then, not only on psychological but also on sociological and hermeneutic studies, and must examine not only homosexual orientation but homosexual *identity*.

THE HISTORICAL AND HISTORIOGRAPHICAL PROBLEM

The idea that homosexuality is a fixed propensity that fundamentally characterizes individuals who desire or participate in homosexual acts is not shared by all cultures. It appeared in Western culture only in the late nineteenth century. Acts of sodomy had been described, decried, tolerated, practiced and praised since the earliest periods of Western civilization, but "the homosexual" as psychological or medical pathology appeared late. Towards the end of the nineteenth century, a group of "sexologists"—particularly Richard von Krafft-Ebing and Havelock Ellis—fundamentally altered the conception of homosexuality in Western culture by shifting the focus from transient acts to character or personality.

This work, while widely read as providing a pathological model of homosexuality (or "inversion") that renders it an immutable "condition," was deeply ambivalent as to whether the source of causation was social or biological.[68] Krafft-Ebing advanced a theory of congenital "inversion" and found himself forced to save appearances by creating, for cases of social causation, the additional category of "perversion."[69] Havelock Ellis hypothesized hormones as a biological cause of inversion, but proceeded to analyze social practices that could "excite the latent predisposition," finally calling them "exciting cause[s] of inversion."[70] Freud, on the other hand, preferred a social explanation in early childhood development, but held the door open for a biological cause.[71] Advocates of equal treatment for homosexuals quickly recognized that the concept of homosexuality as a medical or psychological condition offered a strong argument for tolerance. But the recognition of social causes, by silently acknowledging the importance of social interaction in which the homosexual plays an active role in forming her own sexuality, made any claim as to predetermination and immutability problematic. This originating body of literature inaugurated a tension that has become fundamental to the modern problem of defining and identifying the "homosexual."

Historians have sharply debated whether the sexologists' contribution was in fact something new under the sun. At stake in these debates is whether a pure and natural "essential homosexuality" can be posited for study. The strongest argument for historical relativism has been made by Michel Foucault, who declared:

> As defined by the ancient civil or canonical codes, sodomy was a category of forbidden acts; their perpetrator was nothing more than the juridical subject of them. The nineteenth-century homosexual became a personage, a past, a case history, and a childhood, in addition to being a type of life, a life form, and a morphology, with an indiscreet anatomy and possibly a mysterious physiology. . . . The sodomite had been a temporary aberration; the homosexual was now a species.[72]

This formulation completely denies that the term "homosexual" refers to anything in natural reality. When the sexologists coined the term, Foucault asserts, they constituted the form of existence it purports to refer to: it is simply "more text," and individuals are understood to inscribe themselves or, worse luck, to be inscribed into that already existing discourse. Few historians, to borrow John Boswell's handy terms, are willing so completely to abandon realism and embrace nominalism.[73] Even Jeffrey Weeks and Kenneth Plummer, perhaps the historians of homosexuality most firmly committed to the view that forms of sexuality are historically specific cultural products, refuse to jettison the assumption that socially constructed categories are most often experienced as real.[74]

On the other hand, Boswell, an exemplary realist historian of homosexuality, acknowledges that changing cultural conceptions of sexual identity invalidate blithe generalizations about its persistence as a transhistorical category. Even as he resists the tradition Foucault represents, Boswell is unable to reject it entirely. Arguing for the possibility of a unified history of homosexuality, Boswell acknowledges that historians wishing to make descriptions of "the bedrock of [actual] sexuality" must first carefully sift different historical "conceptualizations" of sexuality. The realist historian finds that he must incorporate rather than reject the nominalist project.[75]

The sexologists, though they sought a model of human sexual orientation that rested on purely natural, predetermined and immutable categories, found themselves forced to acknowledge the formative importance of cultural norms and symbolic interactions. The original contradiction is extrapolated in the tensions that both divide and strengthen the growing body of work on the history of homosexuality. Opposed to essentialism, realism and a conviction that social categories and lived experience must cohere, we find constructionism, nominalism and a conviction that social categories and lived experience can clash or even develop independently of one another. These opposing positions, moreover, never appear in a pure form: responsible scholars today seek to accommodate both the natural and the cultural models in a more complex conception that is more adequate than either to the historical record and current reality.[76] Legal analysis, when it describes homosexuality as purely mutable or purely immutable, ignores the fact that analysis itself is located within this historical debate. It ignores its own intellectual context at the price not only of appearing jejune but also of occluding from view its own production of homosexual identity.

EMPIRICAL STUDIES

Empirical research that answers the question, "Is homosexuality mutable?" arises from three distinct schools: the aetiological school, which attempts to discover the causes of sexual orientation; the behavioral school, which quantifies people's actual behavior; and the social-constructionist school, which focuses on the ways in which individuals' behavior and social identities are interrelated. Taken as a whole, this research demonstrates that for some individuals, sexual desires and sexual behavior are indeed immutable—and that for others they are not. It demonstrates, moreover, that both mutability and immutability, wherever they appear, are the products not only (if at all) of congenital or early childhood givens, but also (or predominantly) of the social interactions that generate social identity.

AETIOLOGICAL RESEARCH

Searches for the cause or causes of homosexuality have absorbed psychologists since Krafft-Ebing and Ellis. Whether they look for early childhood or congenital causes, these efforts have consistently hypothesized immutability. Although these studies have provided equivocal and questionable evidence of the *causes* of sexual preference,[77] they clearly demonstrate that, for many individuals, sexual orientation is indeed fixed immutability before puberty.[78] But one need examine only the most recent major study in this school to discover that the statistics do not support a conclusion that sexual orientation is *always* immutable.[79]

The latest report of the Alfred C. Kinsey Institute for Sex Research summarizes statistics gathered from 979 homosexual and 477 heterosexual men and women. The authors, Alan P. Bell, Martin S. Weinberg and Sue Kiefer Hammersmith, conclude that "[b]y the time boys and girls reach adolescence, their sexual preference is likely to be already determined"[80] and suggest that "our findings are not inconsistent with what one would expect to find if, indeed, there were a biological basis for sexual preference."[81] The authors argue, as we might expect, that such a conclusion "would reaffirm that discrimination against homosexuals is clearly no more justified than discrimination against redheads or blue-eyed persons."[82]

These latter-day Kinsey Institute researchers undermine their confident prediction by building it on three methodological fallacies. First, they make their prediction of immutability in the face of their own admission that their evidence provides no indication as to whether the preadolescent determination of sexual preference arises from a social learning process or a congenital propensity.[83] As long as social processes are possibly implicated, there exists a lively potential that cultural, historical and experiential particularities will exert their transforming effects on the putatively stable process of determination—precisely the same potential that, as we noted above, qualified the early sexologists' conclusion that homosexuality was immutable. Second, the authors are able to conclude only that sexual orientation is *"likely"* to be fixed by adolescence: for fully twenty-four percent of the study's subjects, no predetermining feature was discoverable.[84] The full spectrum of possibilities suggested by these uncertainties remains unexplored precisely because the study presupposes an irresistable cause. Finally, the study crudely classifies each study subject into one of two categories—homosexual or heterosexual—without regard to changes in personal desire or sexual behavior after age nineteen, and, more importantly, without regard to contradictions between desire and conduct. Remarkably, it does this by a destructive adaptation of Alfred C. Kinsey's scale.[85] But if Kinsey's figures have any validity at all, they fundamentally undermine any attempt to determine the cause of sexual preference on the basis of an assumption that people can be accurately described by the ideal types, "homosexual" and "heterosexual."

BEHAVIORAL RESEARCH

Alfred C. Kinsey attempted to jettison the concept central to the study of homosexuality since Freud and the late-nineteenth-century sexologists, the concept of "the homosexual." Instead, he sought information about homosexual *behavior*, about acts alone. Though the strategy purported to be pretheoretical and purely empirical—a means of evading or at least dulling the horns of the dilemma posed by the Freudian tradition—it inevitably imported a theoretical commitment. Kinsey's unspoken assumption was that homosexuality existed neither as pathology nor as historical identity. As Jeffrey Escoffier states it, Kinsey "believed that there were no homosexual persons, only homosexual acts."[86]

The astonishment with which Kinsey's figures were greeted is a measure of his success in removing the lens of character through which his contemporaries viewed homosexuality. For on a seven-point scale (not a bipolar opposition), Kinsey found relatively few exclusive lifelong homosexuals (four percent of White men and one to three percent of women) *and* surprisingly few exclusive lifelong heterosexuals (sixty-three percent of men and as few as sixty-one percent of single women and eighty-nine percent of married women). Almost all the remaining study subjects reported some mixture in their histories of heterosexual and homosexual experiences leading to orgasm.[87] Kinsey's scale permitted him to acknowledge that, regardless of the public or personal identity his subjects assumed, significant numbers of them belonged in practice to one of his five "bisexual" categories. Some of the more salient figures, noting actual behavior among men over a period of at least three years between the ages of 16 and 55:

Category No. 1 (largely heterosexual but with incidental homosexual history): 22.9%;

Category No. 2 (largely heterosexual but with a distinct homosexual history): 19.6%;

Category No. 3 (equally heterosexual and homosexual): 13.7%;

Category No. 4 (largely homosexual but with a distinct heterosexual history): 10.4%;

Category No. 5 (largely homosexual but with incidental heterosexual history): 8%;

Category No. 6 (exclusively homosexual): 6.2%.[88]

A bipolar opposition has dominated scientific, popular and legal conceptions of human sexual orientation since the late nineteenth century. Until Kinsey (and, as we have seen, even after him), students of sexual orientation have assumed that the world of phenomena can be captured by the two mutually exclusive categories, heterosexual and homosexual. Kinsey's studies put us on notice that those categories are simply incapable of describing what *people actually do*. Moreover, his figures notify us that what they do—what we do—is to mix homosexual behavior much more liberally into our apparently exclusively heterosexual lives than we let on. Kinsey's findings implicitly point to a complex form of mutability—the possibility for change in the ways people conceptualize and label their sexual behavior.

This groundbreaking work, of course, displays the defects of its virtues. The conception that the human world is bifurcated into homosexual and heterosexual may be distorting, but it is, in modern American life, virtually ubiquitous. Surely none of Kinsey's subjects were unaware that, however equivocal their own sexual histories, everyone but Kinsey expected them to manifest one of the two medical/psychological categories; surely many of them shaped their behavior or their understanding of it in response to that categorical imperative. Indeed, Kinsey seems to have recognized this inadequacy by diluting the purity of his research focus on behavior, expanding his inquiry into sexual orientation to examine not only "overt experience" but also "psychologic reactions."[89] But one wants to know more: how, for instance, would Kinsey's subjects explain the striking fact that so many of them reduced or abandoned homosexual behavior as they advanced into middle age?[90] Did desires change, or did middle age evoke a changed response to cultural norms?

SOCIAL-CONSTRUCTIONIST RESEARCH

Researchers into the social construction of sexual identity have carried on with Kinsey's refutation of the aetiological research program, but simultaneously strive to fill the gap he created when he excluded social interaction from his purview. This work reverses Kinsey's approach by taking the categories "homosexual" and (less insistently) "heterosexual" as the central objects of inquiry; it simultaneously seeks to reverse the medical/psychological model by asking not how these categories are determined by nature but rather how individuals respond and adapt to them.[91] Though the tendency has been to see this approach as polemically opposed to the psychological model first advanced by the sexologists,[92] it is the first school to grasp one horn of the dilemma posed by that earlier model, by undertaking to examine the social development of sexual identity. Drawing on the work of symbolic interactionists[93] and labeling theorists,[94] work in this tradition examines the social interactions that endow the names "homosexual," "gay," "lesbian" and so on, with personal and historical meaning.[95]

The focus is on the processes by which individuals either assume a stigmatized identity or find it imposed upon them. Mary McIntosh, in a pivotal early article, argued that homosexuality in modern society functions not as a condition but as a "role," a set of generally held expectations. The crucial point is that these expectations may, without any public recognition, go unfulfilled—that the content of the "role" may differ sharply from actual behavior. McIntosh notes, for example, that the homosexual role rests primarily on the incorrect assumption that homosexuality is a fixed condition marked by exclusively homosexual desires and behavior—an assumption which Kinsey's findings stoutly contradict.[96] The converse, of course, is also true: the "heterosexual role" purports to identify individuals of purely heterosexual desires and behavior, and is attributed, with more indifference than we typically acknowledge, to individuals' actual sexual practices. Hence everyone's surprise when Kinsey revealed so many practicing bisexuals in the putatively "heterosexual" population.

McIntosh's work has enabled students of sexual orientation to describe the slippages between desire and behavior on the one hand, and socially modulated sexual roles on the other. For example, Kinsey's data reveals that individuals frequently revise the ways in which they combine or abandon homosexual and heterosexual activity, but it does not tell us whether those with a potential for both interests enter adulthood with a recognition of their bisexuality or homosexuality, whether or how they evaluate the stigma attached to such a recognition, and, finally, whether individual management of the homosexual role is as mutable as Kinsey has shown desire and behavior to be. Only after an examination of how individuals negotiate a life story, weaving together the elements of their own erotic desires and experiences with the explanations and labels offered to them by their culture, can we begin to answer these questions.

In applying McIntosh's insight, researchers have found that individuals' *responses* to socially imposed "roles," even in the secrecy of their subjective self-assessments, are subject to change. Empirical studies of gay men and lesbians demonstrate clearly that some—not all—homosexuals have virtually always recognized themselves to be homosexual; and that some—again, not all—adopt a subjective identity by an exercise of self-definition that is in some senses elective. In one study, Barry M. Dank found that 386 self-professed gay men had labeled themselves gay at widely different ages: only twelve percent between the ages of eight and fourteen; thirty-five percent between the ages of fifteen and nineteen; thirty-one percent between the ages of twenty and twenty-four; and twenty-two percent sometime after age twenty-five.[97]

The diversity suggested by Dank's figures for gay men is confirmed by Carla Golden's findings after several years' discussions with college-aged, self-professed lesbians. Two major categories emerged: "primary lesbians," who felt that they simply always had been attracted to females and had never had any choice in the matter, and "elective lesbians," who recognized themselves to have chosen, for political and erotic reasons, their lesbian identity.[98] Elective lesbians differed among themselves, moreover, on how to accommodate the fixity of their lesbian identity with the fact that they adopted it by choice. Some experienced the self-ascription of a lesbian identity as the discovery of their true sexual nature, an unchangeable and previously suppressed aspect of themselves; for others, their change was enduring and stable but did not implicate any "essential or unchanging aspect of who they were."[99] Finally, Golden's surveys of older lesbians revealed that an elective lesbian's understanding of the fixity of her lesbian identity was itself subject to revision: some elective lesbians who, in their early twenties, had experienced their lesbian identity as essential and unchanging later described it as fluid, while others ascribed their earlier sense of a shifting and changeable sexual identity to the exploratory quality of youthful sexuality and felt that they had "grown into" a more mature, immutable sexual identification as lesbians.[100]

The formation of a gay or lesbian subjective identity bears no simple, univocal relation to sexual behavior. Golden found, for example, that both primary and elective lesbians adopted their lesbian identity whether or not they had ever had sex with a woman or with a man.[101] Gary McDonald, surveying 199 self-identified gay men, found that "18% of the sample labelled themselves 'homosexual' in the absence of any overt same-sex sexual experience; 22% arrived at homosexual self-definitions while participating in a long-term relationship with another man; 23% adopted homosexual self-definitions only *after* involvement in such a relationship."[102] That is, some homosexuals adopt a gay subjective identity without having had *any* homosexual sex; others fail to do so despite well-settled homosexual experience. Thomas S. Weinberg has formalized this recognition in his study of a much smaller sample of gay men, in which he notes the different sequences in which his respondents labelled themselves as gay (L), engaged in homosexual behavior (E), and suspected that they were gay (S). Weinberg found a wide variety of personal narratives. Some respondents first engaged in homosexual activity, then suspected they were gay, and finally labelled themselves gay (E—S—L). Others engaged in homosexual sex first, then labelled themselves gay, never having passed through a period of suspicion (E—L). Some entertained suspicions that they might be gay, engaged in homosexual sex, and only then labelled themselves gay (S—E—L), and still others passed through a period of suspicion, then labelled themselves gay, and finally participated in homosexual sex (S—L—E).[103]

These findings support Weinberg's distinction between homosexual behavior and homosexual identity, between "doing" and "being" gay, and allow us to infer that many individuals engaged in the project of managing their sexual identities behave as though they have some choice in the matter. McDonald concludes that "coming out is an arduous developmental process that may extend well into adulthood[,] . . . an active process involving individual choices that have profound consequences for one's emerging self-concept."[104] Both Golden and McDonald, moreover, challenge the assumption that these choices inevitably tend to the adoption of a subjective identity that coheres with exclusively homosexual or heterosexual desires and behavior.[105] Golden observed: "It appears to be the case . . . that sexual feelings and activities change; they can be fluid and dynamic. And furthermore, the reality is that feelings, activities, and self-conscious identities may not at all times be congruent."[106]

The act of assuming a gay or lesbian subjective identity is, for many individuals, a socially contingent one, often postponed until quite late stages in a person's sexual career, and sometimes never undertaken at all. Golden found that the resulting incongruence of sexual desires and behavior with subjective identity was neither uncommon nor distressful to the lesbian and bisexual women she interviewed.[107] It appears, then, that a high degree of mutability can characterize the subjective identity of perfectly content and well-adjusted individuals. But often, as McDonald emphasizes, the adoption of a gay subjective identity is made traumatic and arduous, and for some individuals impossible, by the stigma attached to the homosexual role.[108] The legal and social burdens imposed on homosexual identity deter the individuals whose desires and behavior are entirely or partially homosexual from acknowledging that fact.

I will discuss below the implications of this phenomenon for legal doctrine. Here it is enough to note that it makes virtually impossible empirical research into a crucial phenomenon: the denial of subjective homosexual or bisexual identity by individuals whose erotic desires or erotic experience is, to some degree, homosexual. The statistical studies demonstrate that many self-identified homosexuals toil long and hard to revise the "spoiled identity"[109] their culture has prepared for them, before they can apply it to themselves. These are the subjects who turn up in studies of self-identified homosexuals. Others, less likely to find their way into a survey of professed gays or lesbians, find the poisonous social image so irrelevant to their highly valued experience of same-sex love that they simply ignore it. Prominent among these are many women and apparently fewer men who are involved in a single, intense and protracted love relationship with a person of their own sex: as one study notes, "[a] woman may see herself as 'a person who loves this particular woman' without thinking that this makes her a lesbian."[110]

But perhaps the most important class is comprised of self-identified heterosexuals who totally deny the importance of their own homosexual desires and behavior. These uncounted individuals manage to maintain themselves within the pale of heterosexual normalcy, either by prohibiting to themselves same-sex fantasies or contacts or by refusing to acknowledge the homoeroticism of their sexual lives.[111] It is a truism in the gay and lesbian communities that such self-identified heterosexuals, in order to maintain their counterfactual denial of their own homoerotic experience, zealously foment the very stigma they are so concerned to avoid. They, more than any other group, are concerned that the line between gay and straight be rigid, immovable, bright.

Public Identity: The Legal Recognition of Sexual Identities

Interrogatory No. 30. . . . In other words, how many members of the Navy, identified as "homosexuals" have been retained in the Navy?

Answer No. 30: The use of the term "identified" makes this question impossible to answer. The term is imprecise. More information is needed.

—Interrogatory of Plaintiff James Miller and Answer of Defendant
U.S. Navy, in *Beller v. Middendorf*[112]

To borrow the language of semiology, the public status "heterosexual" is an unmarked signifier, the category to which everyone is assumed to belong. Something has to *happen* to mark an individual with the identity "homosexual."[113] Though this marking is accomplished only in complex social interactions, we can roughly distinguish two basic narratives: (1) an individual, acting in some sense voluntarily, publicly assumes a gay or lesbian identity; and (2) some other agent—a friend, parent, employer, prosecutor, judge—ascribes or imposes a gay or lesbian identity on an individual, with or without her consent. In the discussion that follows, I treat these categories as distinct, though it will repeatedly become apparent that, in the interpretive interactions that make up the world, they are inextricably intertwined.[114]

HOMOSEXUAL IDENTITY IMPOSED

The legal burdens imposed on homosexuality in our society deter people from *appearing* gay. Of the total number of self-identified gays and lesbians, only a fraction will voluntarily "come out," and of the remaining "closeted" gays, only a fraction will become subject to the public ascription of gay identity. Furthermore, because the assumption of heterosexuality applies in virtually every social interaction—from the encounter of teacher with student, salesperson with shopper, mother with daughter, Supreme Court Justice with clerk—even the most forthright and fearless gay man or lesbian cannot "come out" once and for all in a single public disclosure; as she moves from one social setting to another, she will have to come out afresh or acquiesce in the assignment to her of a nonreferential public identity. The public identity "homosexual" at any one moment, then, is vastly underinclusive of self-identified gay men and lesbians. It is, therefore, an even less accurate indicator of individuals who entertain homoerotic desires or have had homosexual experiences without labelling themselves gay or lesbian.

Simultaneous counterforces are at work to ensure that the public identity "homosexual" is overinclusive, encompassing individuals who do not (or do not very often) feel or act on homoerotic desires and who do not denominate themselves gay or lesbian. Consider, for instance, the process and criteria for assigning homosexual public identity which the Sixth Circuit approval in *Gay Inmates of Shelby County Jail v. Barksdale*.[115] Enforcing a county jail's policy of segregating all homosexual inmates, the intake officer is authorized to "make a purely subjective judgement," and to segregate (among others) inmates who "appear[] weak, small or effeminate."[116] The problem here is not only that the lack of physical strength or monumental build has no reliable correlation to gay male identity.[117] Nor do we exhaust the error by pointing out the fallacy, inscribed into the homosexual role, that men who desire men must be like women. The scene at the Shelby County Jail emphasizes a more profound element of public homosexual identity that is too often forgotten: in order for the sign to "mean" the signified, there must be an *interpreter*, and the interpreter cannot escape the web of signifiers that purport to indicate public sexual identity. If he is small himself, or delicate of build; if he is a behemoth; if he is just an average guy; no matter how many pounds of flesh lie on his bones, he will exercise his power of interpretation to channel interpretations of his own body. As Martha Minow has observed, "[i]n assigning the label of difference, the group confirms not only its identity, but also its superiority, and displaces doubts and anxieties onto the person now called 'different'."[118]

Two forms of immutability are being created in such interactions: the segregated inmate is marked—irrevocably for many social purposes[119]— as homosexual, and the officer so marking him confirms his own heterosexuality. Neither form of the immutability of public identity, however, is at all stable.

Nowhere is this phenomenon so clear as in the case law attempting to define homosexuality and to justify the current regime of judicial restraint. Courts, legislators and regulators have encountered intractable difficulties in their efforts to write coherent definitions of the homosexuals upon whom legal burdens may be placed. Consider the morass into which the D.C. Circuit strides when it announces that sodomy provides a definition of the class, homosexuals. In *Padula v. Webster*,[120] the court reasons that *Bowers v. Hardwick*,[121] by refusing to hold that the constitutional right to privacy extends to homosexual sodomy, foreclosed arguments that "practicing homosexuals" constitute a suspect classification. Crucial to this wide leap from due process to equal protection is the assertion that sodomy statutes "criminalize the behavior that defines the class."[122] But do they?

The statute upheld in *Hardwick* defined sodomy as "any sexual act involving the sex organs of one person and the mouth or anus of another."[123] Let us take the act of definition in *Padula* seriously. Lesbians who forego cunnilingus, the many gay men who have abandoned fellatio and anal intercourse to protect themselves and their lovers from AIDS, self-identified gay men and lesbians who remain celibate—the *Padula* court has determined that none of these groups belongs to the class "homosexual."[124] The court fails to observe that it may well have defined the lesbian plaintiff before it out of the class "homosexual" that it both creates and contemns. Note, furthermore, that not all states define sodomy as Georgia does.[125] The definition imposed in *Padula* produces the amusing result that the contours of the class "homosexuals" vary from state to state. And some states do not criminalize homosexual sodomy at all:[126] how, in those states, is the class to be defined?

The *Padula* definition offers an interpretation of homosexual identity:

indeed, the decision as an act of judicial violence[127] makes its interpretation, in an important sense, real. Its almost completely nonreferential definition of the class "homosexuals" provides an outstanding example of the imposition of a putatively clear, fixed, and rigid identity on gay men and lesbians. It also exemplifies the tendency of such rigid classifications to crumble under even light pressure from empirical fact.

Other courts, legislatures and regulators have attempted to contain these deconstructive forces by tempering legal definitions of the homosexual person more carefully, but have wound up with the same contradictions that lie under the surface of *Padula*'s clear equation of status with act. When the New Hampshire legislature, in an effort to exclude homosexuals from adoption, foster care and daycare center employment, proposed a definition of homosexuals virtually identical to that advanced in *Padula*,[128] the New Hampshire Supreme Court determined in an advisory opinion that exceptions had to be made to save the bill's constitutionality. It construed the bill to exclude victims of homosexual rape and made an exception for acts not "committed or submitted to on a current basis reasonably close in time to the filling of the application. . . . This interpretation thus excludes from the definition of homosexual those persons who, for example, had one homosexual experience during adolescence, but who now engage in exclusively heterosexual behavior."[129] The court maintains a conviction, which we have seen contradicted by the empirical findings, that homosexual status is occupied exclusively by persons who have engaged in homosexual acts. It reproduces without noting the underinclusiveness problems so apparent in the *Padula* definition.

Interestingly, the court is worried instead about the overinclusiveness of a definition that fails to distinguish as heterosexual individuals who, though they engaged in the physical acts described in the bill, did not *intend* them in such a way as to merit the label "homosexual." Those who gave no consent to an act of homosexual sex (rape victims), and those who consented *but only once*, stand out in the court's mind as true heterosexuals. As we have already seen, the patterns of intention in the latter category are deeply problematic. The category includes individuals whose desires may be predominantly homosexual, who have acted on them, but who have determined to mask these facts from themselves by embracing a purely heterosexual subjective identity, and from others by passing as straight. The court's example forgives these lies and builds them into the scheme of state enforcement. Furthermore, the "only once"[130] heterosexual is merely the example forwarded by the court of a much broader category, much more sweepingly permissive of heterosexual self-deception and self-protection: all those whose homosexual acts are not "committed on a current basis reasonably close in time to the filing of the application" shall be deemed to be heterosexual. Even as the New Hampshire Supreme Court, like the D.C. Circuit in *Padula*, attempts to erect a conceptual structure that will render the status "homosexual" rigid and immutable, it recognizes and privileges certain kinds of changes. The mutability of sexual identity is recognized, and its civil advantages are accorded exclusively to currently self-identified heterosexuals.

An attempt to avoid the difficulties that entangle the New Hampshire justices appears in regulations adopted by the Navy in 1978. These regulations further limit the exception for one-time-only sodomites—but in doing so they display a whole new range of contradictions inherent in the project of imposing a public homosexual identity on the complexity of living human beings. Before 1978, the Navy expressly mandated that any member found to have engaged even in a single homosexual act be processed for discharge.[131] Like the New Hampshire Supreme Court, it found this absolute-act-based definition of homosexuals too broad, and in 1978 adopted a new regulation providing for discretionary retention of "[a] member who has solicited, attempted or engaged in a homosexual act on a single occasion *and who does not profess or demonstrate proclivity to repeat such an act.*"[132] Two new limiting elements are introduced: demonstrated proclivity to homosexual acts and professed proclivity to homosexual acts. The Navy has embroiled itself in another series of epistemological difficulties here, but in order to discern them, it is helpful to understand the problems it was attempting to solve.

Before reformulating its regulations, the Navy defended a series of actions brought to challenge discharges made under the old rules, those equating act with status. In *Beller v. Middendorf*,[133] an appeal consolidating three such cases, one plaintiff posed a particularly sharp challenge to the definitional process. Both the hearing board convened to consider James Miller's discharge and the Senior Medical Officer who examined him balked at applying the strict act/status equation to Miller. The board found that he had committed homosexual acts while in service but recommended that he be retained.

It is not clear from the published opinion whether this vote expressed a view that Miller was an erring heterosexual, a harmless homosexual, or a human being who could not be fit into rigid ideal categories. The appellate opinion's report of the Senior Medical Officer's evaluation suggests the more critical third alternative. According to Judge (now Justice) Kennedy's opinion, the medical expert found that Miller "did not *appear* to be '*a homosexual*'."[134] The typography here recognizes the social artifice of the category "homosexual." And the careful reference to the problem of appearance points to the problem of interpreting social signals that is occluded—but evidently not eliminated—by the rigid equation of act with status. Judge Kennedy was able to render these highly equivocal reports legally nugatory and to stabilize the legal assignment of homosexual identity to plaintiff Miller only by interpreting the old rules as creating absolutely no discretion in those charged with carrying them out.[135] In contrast to the other plaintiffs, Kennedy concludes, "[t]he case of Miller is closer but no less clear."[136] Clarity here is surely the product of legerdemain, but Judge Kennedy showed rare judicial honesty in including within his opinion the procedural history that belies it.

We may surmise that the 1978 regulations, by recognizing the possibility of exceptions to the strict act/status equation, were intended to mitigate its procrustean crudity. But there need be no doubt that they merely reformulate the same old epistemological crises. The official Navy evaluations of plaintiff Miller's status show how uncharted are the waters opened up for decision-makers by the 1978 regulations, with their exception for "once-only" heterosexuals who "[do] not demonstrate proclivity to repeat such an act." All the uncertainties of interpretation that pestered the hearing board and Senior Medical Officer in Miller's case are here invited back into the new regulatory scheme.

Moreover, by cognizing the self-descriptions of accused servicepersons in the exception for "once-only" heterosexuals who "[do] not profess . . . proclivity to repeat such an act," the new regulations give new life to a second, perhaps deeper, and certainly more disturbing ambiguity of the Miller case. Plaintiff Miller admitted to committing homosexual acts while on leave in Taiwan and at some unspecified earlier time, yet he also "has at various times denied being homosexual and expressed regret or repugnance at his acts."[137]

It is tempting to see Miller's confession as a clear indication of some frame of mind or strategy proper to him. As we have seen, the stigma and deprivations attached to the status of homosexual—a good example being involuntary discharge from the Navy—deter individuals who engage in same-sex behavior from acknowledging to themselves that they have any component of homosexuality in their makeup. But Miller's statements are not fragments of an internal process of self-assessment, however inchoate: he made them to Navy officials under the threat of compulsory punishment. We oversimplify again if we conclude that Miller cynically declared himself a true heterosexual revolted by his inconsistent actions in order to dupe his inquisitors and obtain an undeserved clemency. For by the inquisitorial interaction recorded here, Miller and the Navy create for him a *new public identity*. The possibility of sincerity is simply foregone by such an utterance.

Instead, the process of social construction, the interaction in which an individual interprets himself to a world interpreting him, has reached a crisis at which, Robert Cover has suggested, both interpretation and language itself break down:

> Taken by itself, the word "interpretation" may be misleading. "Interpretation" suggests a social construction of an interpersonal reality through language. But pain and death have quite other implications. Indeed, pain and death destroy the world that "interpretation" calls up. . . .
> The deliberate infliction of pain in order to destroy the victim's normative world and capacity to create shared realities we call torture. . . . [T]orturers almost always require betrayal—a demonstration that the victim's intangible normative world has been crushed by the material reality of pain and its extension, fear. The torturer and victim do end up creating their own terrible "world," but this world derives its meaning from being imposed upon the ashes of another. The logic of that world is complete domination, though the objective may never be realized.[138]

As I have argued elsewhere,[139] the relationship Cover calls "complete domination" is not static but continues to unfold over time. As it does so, it manifests patterns of interaction and mutual interpretation, but everyone now understands—or should understand—that the utterances of the confessor and the categories imposed by the inquisitor have lost all referential power. In the case of plaintiff James Miller, the possibility of discovering any "true" sexual orientation, if it ever existed, has now been destroyed.

In this epistemological crisis, the knower of others' sexual identities can be expected to act a little defensively. In particular, he or she will attempt to render invisible the processes by which official knowledge is produced, while refusing to cognize any answering subterfuge in the object of official description. A striking example of these protective strategies is Judge Bork's opinion in *Dronenburg v. Zech*"[140]—fittingly, a Navy discharge case that arose under the revised, 1978 regulations and that replays the crisis of *Beller v. Middendorf*. Rejecting the argument that the privacy rights established by Supreme Court precedents encompass homosexual acts, Judge Bork declares: "*It need hardly be said* that none of these [privacy rights established by Supreme Court precedents] *covers* a right to homosexual conduct."[141] Bork here asserts his own right to say nothing, to remain inscrutable and silent, even as he determines that existing privacy doctrine does not hide from official view—does not "cover"—homosexual conduct. Homosexual conduct must be visible to a knower who is not to be known.

The doctrinal result of such a dynamic has been judicial endorsement of definitions of homosexuality that are not definitions at all. It only seems old-fashioned to declare, as a Texas court did in 1909, that a statute prohibiting "the *abominable and detestable crime against nature*" is perfectly sufficient because "the charge was too horrible to contemplate and too revolting to discuss."[142] Much more recently Maryland's prohibition of oral/genital contact and of "any other unnatural or perverted practice"[143] was held not to be unconstitutionally vague because the language employed conveyed "a clear legislative intention to cover the whole field of unnatural and perverted practices"; the state court of appeals "thought it unnecessary to describe in detail practices which are matters of common knowledge."[144] And in 1986, Chief Justice Burger placed his *imprimatur* on such definitions, intoning with approval: "Blackstone described 'the infamous crime against nature' as an offense of 'deeper malignity' than rape, an heinous act 'the very mention of which is a disgrace to human nature' and 'a crime not fit to be named'."[145] Well within this tradition of reticence, silence and modest submergence in "common knowledge," Judge Bork's opinion in *Dronenburg v. Zech* repeatedly deploys locutions which both assert that his position is patently obvious and mark his reluctance to expose it. His articulations are either unnecessary ("It need hardly be said that. . . ."; "To ask the question is to answer it."), redundant (evidence may be drawn from "common sense and common experience"), or reluctantly ceded to the exigencies of the moment (" . . . and, it must be said. . . . ").[146]

These gestures create the character of the official knower, a man whose "common sense and common experience" render him unexceptionably a member of a stable, common majority that knows without having to find out. The *Dronenburg* opinion nevertheless admits the epistemological difficulties that its magisterial epistemology pretends to negate. Providing the list of dangers which the Navy policy might rationally be supposed to redress—precisely the list that has been declared needless—Judge Bork supposes the need to obviate encounters that might "make personal dealings uncomfortable where the relationship is sexually ambiguous."[147] Discomfort with such ambiguity could hardly arise if heterosexual identity were as absolute and secure as the unnameability trope suggests. Indeed, Judge Bork deepens his suggestion that antihomosexual discrimination functions not to punish and separate a clear and preexisting class of homosexuals but to secure the confident subjective and public identities of heterosexuals when he concludes his list of dangers thus: "Episodes of this sort are certain, . . . it must be said, given the powers of military superiors over their inferiors, to enhance the possibility of homosexual seduction."[148] Judge Bork is not worried about homosexual rape, in which the victim is *ex hypothesi* an unwilling partner. Instead, his anxious concern focuses on the heterosexual sailor who *can be seduced* into a homoerotic encounter. A key rationale for antihomosexual discrimination, then, is anxiety about the ambiguity of heterosexual interactions, about a potential for mutability that undermines heterosexual identity. Lest the change actually take place, "known" homosexuals must be segregated.

HOMOSEXUAL IDENTITY ASSUMED

Some individuals are "exposed" as gay or lesbian; others expose themselves. Official discovery of individuals *in flagrante delicto* and the reports of former sex partners will rarely be available to provide evidence of homosexual conduct and give color to the official conclusion that an individual is "homosexual." It is much easier to rely on the professions of homosexuals themselves. Acts of discrimination in this setting seem to avoid the epistemological difficulties that undermine rules founded on homosexual conduct. After all, the open lesbian or gay man has inserted her- or himself into the legally defined class.

Miriam benShalom, for example, while a member of the U.S. Army Reserves, "publicly acknowledged her homosexuality during conversations with fellow reservists, in an interview with a reporter for her division newspaper, and in class, while teaching drill sergeant candidates."[149] In response to this candor the Army moved to discharge her, invoking a regulation providing for the discharge of any soldier who "evidences homosexual tendencies, desire, or interest, but is without overt homosexual acts."[150] This interaction is apparently unequivocal, benShalom and the Army agreeing as to her status and merely disagreeing as to its substantive value and consequences.

In fact, a series of cases involving self-professed homosexuals and bisexuals suggests that, to the contrary, legal strictures on sexual orientation carefully manage passage in and out of the closet, giving new and often unwanted meaning to sojourns on either side of the threshold. *Doe v. Casey*[151] offers a complex example of the legal meaning of secrecy in the context of homosexual stigma. The plaintiff, "out of the closet but under cover," was dismissed from his employment as a CIA agent after he voluntarily presented himself as homosexual to a CIA security officer. As the appellate opinion carefully notes, "John Doe is proceeding under a pseudonym only because his status as a CIA employee cannot be publicly acknowledged, not because of any embarrassment about his homosexuality."[152] The context reminds us that legally enforced secrecy can often be a vigorously persued government goal.

The court held that if Doe's dismissal arose from a CIA policy of firing all homosexuals, the key to his due process claim was whether that action burdened him with a stigma.[153] In a congested and difficult passage, it denied that Doe, as a self-professed homosexual, could be stigmatized by his dismissal. Because the "real stigma imposed by [the government employer's] action . . . is the charge of homosexuality,"[154] and "[b]ecause Doe himself does not view homosexuality as stigmatizing—and indeed, admits that he is a homosexual," the court ruled that Doe would not be stigmatized by the CIA's disclosure to other government agencies that he was dismissed on the grounds of his homosexuality.[155] The court purports to view the problem of stigma from Doe's point of view: if he disclosed his homosexuality, he clearly sees nothing scandalous in it; and if he sees nothing scandalous in his homosexuality, he has no liberty interest in evading its legal consequences. The apparent respect paid here to Doe's self-conception and self-description is revealed as a sham if we note the implication of the court's reasoning: a self-identified homosexual in government employment in order to retain a liberty interest in his or her job, must (1) subjectively regard his or her homosexuality as degrading and (2) hide it.

This reasoning creates a new form of the public identity "homosexual" for individuals who, like Doe, reject this invitation to self-denigrating secrecy. The court construes men and women who choose not to remain closeted to have made a simultaneous choice to wear whatever badge the majority determines is appropriate for them. Even as the court monopolizes the power to define and control the subjective experience of stigma, it simultaneously establishes the legal fiction that those harmed by government discrimination have chosen their injury.[156] As an alternative to this violent appropriation of the public identity of a self-professed homosexual, the case opens a pocket of legal protection for individuals who obey a prohibition on homosexuality not by eschewing homosexual acts or rejecting a homosexual subjective identity, but by appearing straight. One cost to them of accepting that protection is that they must also accept the public meaning of their equivocal position—the court's equation of their closetedness with the assumption that they have internalized the substantive determination that homosexuality is degrading to them.

Legal deterrence of homosexuality thus anticipates that many self-identified homosexuals, if allowed to pass as heterosexual, would rather switch than fight. It does all it can to motivate people to change their public self-presentations, fostering a pervasive and unquantifiable regime of mutability. Moreover, because control over the meaning of public identity is kept firmly in the hands of the antihomosexual majority, that majority retains the power to dictate still more changes.

Department of Defense regulations for granting security clearances recognize how profoundly volatile the closet can be by providing for deeply skeptical review of any applicant who, because she has concealed *anything* about her homosexual conduct or identity, is deemed to be susceptible to blackmail. The regulations regard as a disqualifying factor "the fact that an applicant has concealed or attempted to conceal his homosexuality from his employer or from his immediate family members, close associates, supervisors or coworkers."[157] As a federal court observes in upholding a challenge to these regulations, they obligate individuals to reveal not only sodomy, not only the very loosely defined group of acts deemed by the regulations to be "homosexual," but even desires: "because the policy relates to sexual preference itself, a person who is merely attracted to people of his own sex, but engages in no activity with them, must reveal his preference to all immediate family members, close associates, coworkers, or supervisors."[158] It is not even clear that, in the Department of Defense's eyes, full public disclosure of homosexuality protects one from the transformative power of blackmail: in *High Tech Gays* the Department of Defense offered as evidence of the homosexual's susceptibility to blackmail, the fact that plaintiff Timothy Dooling, an openly gay man, was approached for purposes of blackmail—even though Dooling had "unequivocally rejected" the offer.[159]

On the threshold between the closet and public homosexual identity, anything can happen. The beliefs of others can suddenly be transformed into one's public identity. Killian Swift, a White House stenographer, lost his job after his employer asked his immediate supervisor whether he was homosexual. She "confirmed that, *to her knowledge*, he is,"[160] and he was dismissed. The threshold is broad indeed, appearing under the feet even of the noncommittal and the inquisitive. Mere advocacy of homosexual rights and even mere investigation into the issue of sexual orientation can trigger suppositions that one is gay, and suppositions can become public reality. When the Army imposed the regulation contested in *benShalom v. Secretary of the Army*, requiring discharge of any soldier who "evidences homosexual tendencies, desire, or interest," it formalized this interaction. As the District Court recognized in that case, under such a regime of sexual identity

> [n]o soldier would dare be caught reading anything that might be construed as a homosexually-oriented book or magazine. No soldier would want to be observed in the company of any person suspected of being a homosexual. Most importantly, no soldier would even want to make any statements that might be interpreted as supporting homosexuality.[161]

The rapidity with which an individual can lose control of the secret of her sexual orientation and find it transformed into the opprobrium and civil disabilities of imposed public identity is illustrated by the story of Marjorie Rowland. Employed as a nontenured guidance counselor in a public high school, Rowland confidentially disclosed to a coworker that she was bisexual; the coworker reported her disclosure to the school's principal. Some time later, Rowland upset a parent by advising her not to panic at her child's confusion over sexual identity, and, fearing that her job might be threatened, confided the story, and her bisexuality, to the school's vice principal. Soon her sexual identity became a matter of public knowledge, the object of a local effort to get her fired. Throughout the growing turmoil, and with increasing publicity, Rowland continued to make confessions of her sexual identity. Finally she lost her job.[162]

The majority opinion of the Sixth Circuit classified Rowland's first two disclosures as mere private utterances on matters of personal interest,[163] and denied them the protection granted to public speech. In concluded: "[P]laintiff has attempted to make homosexual rights the issue in this case. However, her personal sexual orientation is not a matter of public concern."[164] Having once attempted to keep her bisexuality secret, Rowland could never join a public discourse about her own dismissal. This amputation of part of the body politic results from a view of sexual identity as a *thing*, immutably present prior to discussion of it. But the chain of events that led to Rowland's dismissal, more clearly than any other narrative I have found in gay rights case law, demonstrates that the disclosure of homosexual identity, no matter how secretive, *is always* a political act.

Justice Brennan, dissenting from the Supreme Court's denial of certiorari in *Rowland v. Mad River Local School District*, carefully delineates the false distinctions on which the Sixth Circuit's holding rests. First, no one can disclose personal homosexual or bisexual identity, even in the most secretive circumstances, without engaging in the current public debate over sexual orientation: "[t]he fact of petitioner's bisexuality, *once spoken*, necessarily and ineluctably involved her in that debate."[165] And second, that act of speech cannot then be distinguished from the sexual identity it reveals: "petitioner's First Amendment and equal protection claims may be seen to converge, because it is realistically impossible to separate her spoken statements from her status."[166]

Sexual Identity and the Processes of Mutability

It is important to recognize how thoroughly both the immutability and the mutability of sexual identity can poison the political process. This complex phenomenon can be crudely represented by a "mutability spectrum," along which individuals with the public identities "homosexual" *and* "heterosexual" may move. At various points along this spectrum are located at least the following hypothetical stations:

> *Station 1:* homosexuals who can neither change their sexual orientation nor cease to manifest their homosexuality;
>
> *Station 2:* homosexuals who cannot change their sexual orientation but who can be bribed by heavy sanctions into disguising it;
>
> *Station 3:* bisexuals who can be bribed by heavy sanctions to live as heterosexuals but are now living as homosexuals;
>
> *Station 4:* bisexuals who for political or affectional reasons live as homosexuals;
>
> *Station 5:* bisexuals who have been bribed by heavy sanctions to live as heterosexuals;
>
> *Station 6:* bisexuals who for political or affectional reasons live as heterosexuals;
>
> *Station 7:* heterosexuals who can neither change their sexual orientation nor cease to manifest their heterosexuality.

At each of these stations, special effects of mutability and immutability are noticeable:

1. At every stage of the spectrum, individuals remain vulnerable to the assignment of a rigid, immutable homosexual identity. We have seen just how arbitrary that assignment can be, threatening to catch up even heterosexuals holding on for dear life to stations 6 and 7 and transforming, for all public purposes, the self-disclosing lesbian, gay or bisexual identity of individuals willing to take their chances in stations 1 through 5. This arbitrary form of mutability underlies the whole spectrum, making it impossible to discern exactly what it is that antihomosexual discrimination is intended to deter.[167]

2. Only stations 1 and 7 represent perfect immutability of harmonized and coherent personal and public sexual identity. But we have seen the dynamics that make it impossible to be sure that anyone inhabits either of these categories. Because heterosexuality is assumed to be a universal norm, gay men and lesbians, no matter how "out," must constantly resist assimilation into the class of heterosexuals, and so constantly must make decisions about the price they are willing to pay to do so. They may decide they must resist at important sites in their lives—family, job, classroom—but allow a false ascription of heterosexuality to go uncorrected when they are buying stamps at the post office. It would be virtually impossible to

resist so consistently that one *never was heterosexual* in the sense of bearing that social identity.

The epistemological instability of station 7 arises from a converse dynamic. Because homosexuality is so stigmatized, individuals are encouraged to maintain a self-deceptively unambiguous heterosexual subjective identity and to protect it eagerly from ambiguities that arise from within as well as from without. As long as coercive antihomosexual discrimination remains at work, and as long as it justifies both social and internal surveillance, an individual's unvarying heterosexual self-presentation can signify genuinely coherent heterosexual identity, compliance with a powerful social force, or some complex mixture of the two. Under these circumstances a pure and coherent heterosexual person is possible, but identifying such an individual is made difficult indeed.

The vexation to which these categories is subject results in distinct distortions in the political process. The fluidity of gay identity at one extreme of the spectrum means that it is always threatened with invisibility and political ineffectiveness; the stability of straight identity at the other extreme is so fragile that is encourages defensive, phobic abuses of majority power.

3. Throughout the middle range of the spectrum. where most if not all of us actually live, sexual orientation is mutable not only in its practice but also in its manifestation. Moreover, throughout that wide middle range the fundamental effect of legal deterrents is to foster mutability, to encourage individuals to act or appear heterosexual despite the actual complexity of their sexual lives. Only for those homosexuals who freely choose homosexuality (station 4) and who are never intimidated into disguising their choice—if any such exist—can it be said that legal burdens on homosexuality played no role in creating mutability. Every change of this sort makes heterosexuality appear more universal, makes homosexuality appear more—well—queer, compounding the difficulty of establishing a normative public vote for sexual difference. Mutability of this sort is a product of antihomosexual discrimination and should not be allowed to become a justification for the denial of equal protection.

Equal Protection, Equal Process and the Specter of Substantive Review: Placing Limits on the Process-Based Equal Protection of Homosexual Identity

> For each was so surprised at the quickness of the other's sympathy, and
> it was to each such a revelation that a woman could be as tolerant and

free-spoken as a man, and a man as strange and subtle as a woman,
that they had to put the matter to the proof at once.
And so they would go on *talking*. . . . [168]

The critics of process-based equal-protection review have argued that
all judicial efforts to preserve the fairness of the legislative process are
founded on substantive commitments, and charge that the *Carolene Products* tradition disingenuously denies those substantive implications.[169] The
arguments they advance acknowledge, moreover, that the conflict between
the rights of homosexuals and the power of legislatures to deter homosexuality continually exemplifies these underlying substantive problems.[170] These
critiques challenge the Court and its advisory board of academics to abandon
their pretense that process theories avoid substantive review, and to take
up the job of crafting a theory of substantive judicial review that leaves some
substantive legislative decisions—let's say a statute prohibiting burglary—
beyond its scope. *Bowers v. Hardwick* makes it virtually impossible to
imagine the Court taking up this challenge in the context of gay rights,
sending those who would obtain some measure of constitutional justice
back to the process theory assumed by the Court in that case. But the
critiques of process theories require that any argument based on them
carefully limit its invitation to the Court to reject substantive decisions of
the political branches.

The critiques typically arrange themselves as responses to Ely's *Democracy and Distrust*, where antihomosexual legislation short of prohibitions
of sodomy itself is seen as a proper object of process-based review because
it combines "the factors of prejudice and hideability."[171] Ely finds himself
forced to conclude, however, that sodomy laws may reflect not "prejudice"—which he defines as "a simple desire to injure the parties involved"—
but "a sincerely held moral objection to the act"—a quintessentially substantive motive."[172] The problem is not simply that Ely's exception swallows
his rule. His argument virtually invites Dean Brest's observation that the
most pernicious forms of discrimination have arisen from, and been justified
by, sincerely held moral beliefs: if judges must not interfere in such cases,
the political process will be left unprotected precisely from its most virulent
attacks. "The alternative," Brest observes, "is to be *selective* in determining
which beliefs to accept and which to deny. But this, of course, requires
judicial judgments of social values."[173] Distinguishing between prejudice
and legitimate disapprobation requires reference to some substantive system
of values, some "substantive vision of proper conduct,"[174] "principles," or
"normative judgments" which the Constitution has placed "beyond the pale
of legitimacy."[175] Brest observes that insults to dignity may be deemed

morally wrong, permissible or even desirable, and concludes: "The reason that homophobic legislation is so constitutionally troublesome is that our society is currently riven about which of these categories insults to homosexuals should be placed in."[176]

Both proponents and critics have involved themselves in the fallacy of *nil tertium quid*: judicial review is conceived as *either* entirely procedural (and therefore unproblematic) *or* pervasively substantive (and therefore a source of incurable vertigo).[177] A third term remains, however, and it offers a possibility of principled judicial restraint: judicial review of substantive legislative choices that impinge on the process of majoritarian decision-making. The presence of substantive values in the motivating context of discriminatory legislation does not oust procedural concerns: indeed, granting *arguendo* the moral legitimacy of a state's decision to deter the public formation of gay or lesbian identity, such laws exemplify how substantive aims can be intertwined with devastating effects on the political process. They also require us to recall that the bogey of *Lochner* properly overlooks the due process clause, whose terms arguably authorize judicial review of process *only*: here, by contrast, we are examining the scope not of equal process but of equal *protection*.

In the concluding section of this article, I propose that an intelligible line can be drawn between antihomosexual discrimination that blocks the political process and is properly subject to heightened judicial scrutiny and legislative decisions to deter homosexuality that remain unreviewable because they do not interfere with the public debate. That line has already been drawn, in the first amendment precedents distinguishing conduct from speech.[178]

Conduct and Speech

I turn to the distinction between conduct and speech, looking for a more progressive, more accurately descriptive and legally more eloquent analysis than that offered by the distinction between act and status. In doing so I acknowledge that gay rights advocates have argued that homosexuality is a status, legally similar to drug addiction and, under *Robinson v. California*,[179] immune from criminal sanction.[180] The act/status argument offers some strategic advantages. It directly parries the logic that would make *Hardwick* binding in an equal protection context: sodomy, like buying and selling drugs, may be criminalized without constitutional violation, but the status of homosexual, like the status of drug addict, is so inextricably intertwined with "the very fiber of an individual's personality,"[181] so "central" or "essential to personhood,"[182] that is cannot be the object of the legal sanction. In another sense, however, this view is extremely vulnerable after *Hardwick*: if a majority can criminalize what this essentializing viewpoint describes as "intimacies inherent in a homosexual orientation" and "the behavior that forms part of the very definition of homosexuality,"[183] what constitutional duty can that majority owe to restrain its moral indignation when confronted not with the act but with the personhood that inevitably produces it?

Personhood arguments, moreover, unwittingly assimilate from the doctrine of *Robinson* the counterfactual assertion that homosexuality, as a status, is immutable, and forego the substantial protection to gay identity under process theories. The strategic drawback of the process arguments, of course, is that sodomy itself quite possibly cannot be brought within the magic circle of political discourse. If tactical disabilities are to be compared, however, personhood arguments improvidently invite the Court to engage in a substantive evaluation—and *Hardwick* demonstrates its determination to resist such invitations—in an intensely controversial area—and in this area *Hardwick* demonstrates which way the Court's knee jerks.

In turning from the criminal distinction between act and status, with its essentialist and, I think, epistemologically overconfident declarations about the nature of the person, to the First Amendment doctrine distinguishing conduct from speech, we find a legally authoritative analysis capable of describing not isolated individuals but social interactions—precisely the activities, as we have seen, that constitute public sexual identity. This should be no surprise. The guarantee of free speech, after all, has provided the Court with its most ample opportunity to reflect on our political life, the cumulative result being a constitutional sociology of the majoritarian process. Indeed, the Court repeatedly states its protection of free speech as arising not from rights vested in individuals, but from a collective right we all share to participate in the wars of political truth. In *Terminiello v. Chicago*[184] the Court recognized that "[t]he vitality of civil and political institutions in our society depends on free discussion. . . . [I]t is only through free debate and free exchange of ideas that government remains responsive to the will of the people and peaceful change is effected."[185] In *New York Times v. Sullivan*,[186] the Court reaffirmed "a profound national commitment to the principle that debate on public issues should be uninhibited, robust, and wide open, and that it may well include vehement, caustic, and sometimes unpleasantly sharp attacks on government and political officials."[187]

The first amendment thesis that we are safe from tyranny only so long as we engage (as speakers or listeners) in open social dialogue implicates a recognition that the protection of minority voices will be a most crucial function of the courts. In *Tinker v. Des Moines School District*,[188] the Court acknowledged that even speech so unpopular with the majority that it might feed fears of a physically violent reaction made a fundamental contribution to our collective effort at democratic self-government:

> [I]n our system, undifferentiated fear or apprehension of disturbance is not enough to overcome the right to freedom of expression. . . . Any word spoken, in class, in the lunchroom, or on the campus, that deviates from the views of another person may start an argument or cause a disturbance. But our Constitution says we must take this risk; and our history says that it is this sort of hazardous freedom . . . that is the basis of our national strength. . . .[189]

Thus, when the first amendment precedents providing positive law drawing the distinction between conduct and speech articulate a process rationale for protection of the latter, we are justified in expecting that light will be shed on the process protected by the equal protection clause as well. At this point, to borrow Justice Brennan's expression in his dissent from the denial of certiorari in *Rowland v. Mad River Local School District*, first amendment and equal protection concerns converge,[190] as the process commitments of the two constitutional provisions meet.

First amendment cases involving the political speech of gay activists, and indeed of anyone resisting homophobia, have acknowledged the fundamental process dangers imposed by the legal coercion of expression about sexual identity. As Judge Williams of the Northern District of California has recognized, the first amendment association rights of an acutely controversial gay-rights organization implicate precisely the process concerns that Justice Stone had in mind when he penned Footnote Four. Refusing to grant discovery of the membership list of Solidarity (a gay rights group sued by Adolph Coors Company), Judge Williams recognized the danger that "civil lawsuits could be misused as coercive devices to cripple, or subdue, vocal opponents," and took particular note that forcing the gay men and lesbians of Solidarity out of the closet would violate the first amendment because it constituted a "threat[] aimed at suppressing an attempted exercise of political rights" precisely of the kind foreseen by Justice Stone in *Carolene Products*.[191]

Even in the face of the repeated equation of speech about homosexuality with homosexual conduct, courts have recognized that the First Amendment protects groups organized to promote understanding of sexual orientation and to advocate gay rights, and have carefully distinguished political speech from unprotected conduct. An Oklahoma statute, for instance, provided that no public school teacher could gain or retain employment if she were found to have engaged in "public homosexual conduct," defined as follows: "advocating, soliciting, imposing, encouraging or promoting public or private homosexual activity in a manner that creates a substantial risk that such conduct will come to the attention of school children or school employees."[192]

In *National Gay Task Force v. Board of Education*,[193] the Tenth Circuit rejected this pathetic reduction of every species of speech to "conduct," ruling that first amendment "speech" extended to all advocacy short of public acts of criminal homosexual sodomy.[194] This determination realizes the promise of a long line of First Amendment precedents carefully parsing the distinction between speech and conduct, and vigorously protecting speech wherever the line is difficult to draw. Only where criminal conduct itself "manifests absolutely no element of protected expression" is the state free to act notwithstanding incidental effects on speech.[195] Where criminal conduct and protected speech are mixed, however, as they were when David Paul O'Brien burned his draft card, the law requires a searching inquiry into the power of the state to control the conduct and the substantiality of its interest in doing so; even if these standards are met, the state must not intend to suppress speech, and must adopt the means least likely to produce that effect.[196] The conception of political discourse embedded in these holdings may result in holdings that sodomy itself bears no elements of speech, but they clearly prohibit any determination that antihomophobic advocacy is not speech.

The *National Gay Task Force* court further articulated the relationship between protected speech and criminal conduct by invoking the rule established in *Brandenburg v. Ohio*:[197] "[T]he constitutional guarantees of free speech and free press do not permit a State to forbid or proscribe advocacy of . . . law violation except where such advocacy is directed to inciting or producing imminent lawless action and is likely to incite or produce such action."[198] The Court recognizes that speech advocating any element of homosexual identity short of criminal sodomy is intrinsic to political discourse. And, under well-settled First Amendment law, such speech retains its purely discursive character even if it advocates the commission of criminal sodomy, unless it is intended to *and* is likely to incite someone to commit that crime *right away*.[199] Otherwise it comes within the broad First Amendment commitment to vigorous, even if disturbing and unsettling, advocacy. This rule responds directly to the underlying rationale of antihomosexual discrimination: that the state is justified in silencing gay advocacy because of its interest in preventing heterosexuals from falling away. In the vision of political discourse attributed to the Constitution under the first amendment, the potential mutability of heterosexual behavior and identity—if it is an evil at all—is one that must be cured not by silence, but by more speech.

Sexual Identity as Political Discourse

When Skadden, Arps, Slate, Meagher & Flom and a number of other prominent law firms, corporations, and unions sponsored a benefit for the Lambda Legal Defense and Education Fund in May of 1987, the *New York Times* reported that their support signaled the entry of the gay rights organization into the political mainstream. But it also noted that "newspaper photographers were restricted in the pictures they could take because, according to . . . the organizer of the benefit, some participants feared that if their presence at [it] became known, others would assume that they were homosexual."[200] After *Rowland v. Mad River Local School District*, both heterosexual friends of gay rights and homosexual advocates of their own safety and security must divert energy, and advocacy, from political debate to the painstaking management of the mutability and immutability of homosexual identity. Public homosexual identity is so volatile, so problematically referential to a history of genital homosexual conduct, and so relentlessly controversial that it has become an element of political discourse distinguishable from the conduct that, *Hardwick* informs us, states may constitutionally criminalize.

When courts have denied to gay rights advocates protection for gay *identity*, they have made painfully clear the costs that discrimination exacts from the political process. These courts, like the audience feared by Skadden, Arps, conflate the opinions and the sexual identities of gay rights advocates and require that homosexual advocates keep both secret. James Michael McConnell, for instance, a gay man employed in the library of a public university, applied for a marriage license with his male companion, an "antic," the Eighth Circuit notes with gratuitous contempt, that "generated at least four news articles in the local press."[201] Although the court noted that McConnell did not arrange for the media attention his action attracted, it nevertheless upheld the withdrawal of his offer of public employment on the grounds that he had failed to keep his sexual orientation secret: "this is not a case involving mere homosexual propensities on the part of a prospective employee. Neither is it a case in which an applicant is excluded from employment because of a desire clandestinely to pursue homosexual conduct."[202] Like Rowland's, McConnell's sexual orientation irresistably became the object of public interest and debate the moment he took a step to disclose it. Under these circumstances, identity is inevitably public advocacy; and if the *Rowland* court held that advocacy can be barred because the identity is intolerable, the court here holds that the identity can be barred because advocacy is unprotected. Indeed, the court suggests that, in a contest between public employer and gay employee, one must always be the silent bearer of the other's message: "[McConnell] demands . . . the right to pursue an activist role in *implementing* his unconventional ideas concerning the societal status to be accorded homosexuals and, thereby, to foist tacit approval of this socially repugnant concept upon his employer."[203] Rather than force a helpless university to blazon its employee's political views, the court insists that the employee must remain silent about them and, by semiotic default, proclaim the ubiquity and normalcy of heterosexuality.[204] But as the Supreme Court declared in *West Virginia Board of Education v. Barnette*: "If there is any fixed star in our constitutional constellation, it is that no official, high or petty, can prescribe what shall be orthodox in politics, nationalism, religion, or other matters of opinion or force citizens to confess by word or act their faith therein."[205]

The "excruciating system of double binds"[206] into which lesbians and gay men are cinched by rulings that ignore the lesson of *Barnette* is suggested by the decisional biography of Joseph Acanfora, a teacher transferred from his post when his employer learned, through the news media, that he had successfully challenged a previous, job-related episode of discrimination based on his gay identity. The lower court held that, though the First Amendment protected him at the time of his transfer, he forwent its protection when he publicly protested the job action. The Fourth Circuit, on appeal, ruled that Acanfora had not only a constitutional right to publicize his transfer, but a legal duty (which he had breached at the time of his application for employment) to disclose a gay political affiliation to his employer. Of course, it was that affiliation that had precipitated the first employment snafu, the first suit, and the media coverage that sparked his transfer.[207] The only way Acanfora could have avoided participating in this grotesque plot would have been to ensure the absolute secrecy of his gay identity—a task to be accomplished, we learn from *Rowland* and *McConnell*, by disclosing it to no one and doing nothing about it.

These holdings prohibit not only gay advocacy but also gay identity.[208] *McConnell* and *Acanfora* are simply bad First Amendment law: the court in *High Tech Gays v. Defense Industrial Security Clearance Office* properly held that individuals may not be penalized in their government employment for belonging to "gay organizations" unless that membership directly threatens a "paramount" and "vital" government interest.[209] Beyond that, however, these cases—along with the Skadden, Arps festivities—point to the problem addressed by process-based review of discrimination based on gay identity. The mere disclosure of one's gay, lesbian or bisexual identity ineluctably accumulates political significance, while one's mere participation in political action to alter laws affecting gays and lesbians can precipitously earn one a public homosexual identity. These legal and social prohibitions hobble everyone's discourse about gay rights, producing a process failure of constitutional magnitude. It is not the class of gays, lesbians and bisexuals, but the classification of homosexuals—a group that could include anyone participating in the antihomophobic argument—that requires heightened scrutiny under the equal protection clause.

Equal Protection of Gay Identity

This article has shown that the political circumstances that produce both the closet and gay, lesbian and bisexual identity pervasively infect the process by which antihomosexual legislation—including the sodomy laws—has been adopted. It argues that this infection is so severe that process-based equal protection scrutiny is at once necessary and justified.[210] But will the exercise of that scrutiny revive the bogey of *Lochner*?

The problem here is to define the limits of the courts' power to protect the political process. This article has concentrated on one question: if homosexual sodomy can be criminalized, are not courts foreclosed from any interference with popular decisions to condemn homosexuality? But now we confront its converse: if we grant to courts the power to review substantive law condemning homosexuality, haven't we granted them the power to reject all our substantive choices—for instance, our determination that burglary shall be a crime?

The distinction between speech and conduct provides an answer to this question. It not only grounds in the Constitution an understanding of the political process that requires heightened scrutiny of antihomosexual discrimination: it also limits judicial review. It stipulates that conduct is not speech, and is not part of the political process—at least, not a part that courts may protect under the theory of Footnote Four.

The question, then, becomes: What is conduct? Imagine five relations a person might assume to burglary, each implicating a distinctive mixture of substantive and procedural concerns: a person might (1) exhort a crowd to burgle; (2) announce that she was in favor of burglary as a general proposition; (3) declare that she was a burglar; (4) disclose that she had burgled; or (5) get caught red-handed. This list suggests a circle, which would be closed by speech threatening so imminently to produce crime that it can itself be criminalized. But if we assume that the exhortation of stage (1) falls short of this constitutional limit, the list as a whole displays a direct relationship between the proportion of speech to deed and the proportion of procedural to substantive value. Impassioned political rhetoric urging a crowd to break the law need not but can present that most urgent moment of political speech protected under the First Amendment: to interfere with it is to halt the political process precisely when it is working at top speed. Speech and process are both calmer, but equally pure, at stage (2). Once our agent declares she is a burglar, however, something has changed: though she claims a personal identity, it is a identity almost always understood to rest exclusively on the past commission of a crime. She might mean something different from that—perhaps she thinks it is burglary to pick someone's pocket or perhaps she thinks of herself as a burglar because she intends to commit burglary—but it is very unlikely that she is proposing that burglars are involved in a *licit* activity. At the fourth stage one cause of doubt drops out, and at the fifth all is clear: the circumstances might vary, but the essential elements of burglary are *ex hypothesi* settled. As our agent descends through these stages, we lose our suspicion that her speech does not refer to the commission of a crime; and as that happens her contribution to political debate about the merits and debits of burglary degenerates until it almost disappears.[211]

Quite different shifts are implicated if we attempt to imagine a self-identified lesbian working her way down the scale. At stage (1), what shall we imagine she is urging on her eager crowd? That they begin to entertain homosexual desires? That they admit to themselves that they already feel homosexual desires? That they admit this to others? That they act on those desires? In fantasy? By holding someone's hand? By committing sodomy? Clearly "exhorting a crowd to adopt homosexuality" points in a number of directions, only one of them criminal. If "exhorting a crowd to commit burglary" manifests a high proportion of speech and of process, our lesbian's incitement manifests even more—and the same thing can be said for stage (2). For these same reasons, however, the declaration "I am a lesbian" differs strikingly from the announcement "I am a burglar." The former statement manifests a much wider scope for problematically referential speech, and is thus more intrinsically involved in a political process, than the latter: the possibilities we entertained on hearing "I am a burglar" recur (the speaker might not know what the word means legally; she might refer to some intended future action), but we also know that a person can adopt the label "lesbian" on the basis of desires, of sexual acts not including sodomy, and of political affiliation notwithstanding personal sexual orientation.[212] The problem of stage (4) is more directly indicated by a glance at stage (5): the image of our lesbian at this point is uncertain in a way that the image of our red-handed burglar can never be. For even when burglary has almost completely exhausted its store of discourse, "homosexual acts" retain their power to escape the bounds of a sodomy statute. Finally, homosexual sodomy itself involves a discourse of genders, requiring for its commission the articulation of two bodies *as the same*.[213] and though burglary can be similarly expressive of possession and ownership, categorizations based on sex have been deemed to warrant heightened scrutiny while those founded on property have not.

Hardwick may well be reversible on an equal protection analysis alert to these discursive implications, without creating any necessary implication that criminal prohibitions in constitutionally less sensitive areas are barred. But even if we assume that *Hardwick* was decided correctly, the "homosexual acts" encompassed by that case's holding are almost never at issue when government imposes burdens on homosexual *identity*. Here, the proportion of political speech to conduct—and of procedural to substantive review—is so high that heightened judicial scrutiny is not only proper but necessary.

Notes

I wish to thank Akhil Reed Amar, Paul Gewirtz, Andrew Koppelman, Sandra E. Lundy, Martha McCluskey and Eve Kosofsky Sedgwick for their useful comments on earlier drafts of this Article, and Beth A. Solerno for expert bibliographical assistance. At this time I also wish to remember an episode of gay-bashing at Yale Law School, in which the contours of the closet as I have tried to describe them here were revealed to me as under a spotlight; and to thank the students, faculty and administration of Yale Law School for rising to the occasion.

1. *Bowers v. Hardwick*, 478 U.S. 186, reh'g denied, 487 U.S. 1039 (1986).

2. 198 U.S. 45 (1905).

3. *Hardwick*, 478 U.S. at 194.

4. *Id.* at 197.

5. Recent academic writing on homosexuality almost always begins with an acknowledgment that the words we use to describe same-sex love inevitably reflect and shape our political commitments on this volatile subject. This article can be no exception. As adjectives, "gay," "lesbian," "bisexual," "homosexual" and "heterosexual" are relatively uncontroversial. I draw attention only to the resistance I offer to the tendency to conflate "bisexual" and "lesbian" into the adjective "gay."

   It is when these terms are used as *nouns*, and thus imply essences or states of being, that they implicate really intractable problems. Most antihomophobic writers abjure these nouns, but I cannot do so because my purpose is to argue that the widely held conception that homosexuality is a state of being has constitutionally significant effects on the political debate about gay rights. I therefore continue to use these scandalous nouns in this article, but with an inflection that registers their intra- and intersubjective constitution. Thus, "gays" and "gay men and lesbians" refer to people who have acknowledged, at least to themselves, that their sexual desires or practices are often, predominantly or entirely homoerotic. The noun "homosexual" usefully refers to the hypostasized social conception that some people are uniformly, exclusively and immutably inclined to same-sex eroticism, and the noun "heterosexual" handily indicates the converse. People are just as likely to apply these nouns to themselves as to others: whenever these labels are adopted or applied, they become part of our political reality.

6. 304 U.S. 144 (1938).

7. Powell, "*Carolene Products* Revisited," 82 *Colum. L. Rev.* 1087, 1087 (1982).

8. *Carolene Products*, 304 U.S. at 152 n.4 (citations omitted).

9. *Kovacs v. Cooper*, 336 U.S. 77, 90–91 (1949) (Frankfurter, J., concurring); Powell, *supra* note 7, at 1092; Lusky "Footnote Redux: A *Carolene Products* Reminiscence," 82 *Column. L. Rev.* 1093, 1098 (1982).

10. Whether the third step of the *Carolene* analysis offers special protection *only* to racial, religious and national minorities, or protects as well other "discrete and insular minorities," has been the object of some textual debate. Justice Powell, speaking informally, advocated the former reading of Footnote Four. *See* Powell, *supra* note 7, at 1088, 1091. Professor Lusky, who served as Justice Stone's clerk at the time Footnote Four was being drafted, rejects Justice Powell's reading. He assumes that the term "discrete and insular minorities" is not defined by the first clause of the sentence but rather requires additional interpretation. Lusky, *supra* note 9, at 1105 n.72. Justice Stone's initial draft of Footnote Four, which Lusky prints in his article, classified laws burdening religions and national and racial minorities with interferences with the right to vote and peaceably to assemble as "comparable" to other interferences with the repeal process. Prejudice against discrete and insular minorities appeared in this draft in a separate sentence, *see id.* at 1096–97, a classification that the final version of the footnote does not unambiguously refute.

These nice questions are rendered moot by equal protection law, which has recognized that a number of quite dissimilar groupings are constitutionally suspect. See *Graham v. Richardson*, 403 U.S. 365, 372 (1971) (alienage); *Loving v. Virginia*, 388 U.S. 1, 11 (1967) (race); *Korematsu v. United States*, 323 U.S. 214, 216 (1944) (national origin). But see *Ambach v. Norwich*, 441 U.S. 68, 72–75 (1979). Several other groupings, though not meriting the most stringent scrutiny, may reflect unconstitutional discrimination. See *Plyler v. Doe*, 457 U.S. 202 (1982) (children of illegal aliens); *Lalli v. Lalli,* 439 U.S. 259, 265 (1978) (illegitimacy); *Craig v. Boren*, 429 U.S. 190 (1976) (sex); *Frontiero v. Richardson*, 411 U.S. 677 (1973) (sex); *Reed v. Reed*, 404 U.S. 71 (1971) (sex). Chief Justice Rehnquist's plea that heightened equal protection scrutiny should be limited to the groups named in Footnote Four has not carried the day. See *Trimble v. Gordon*, 430 U.S. 762 (1977) (Rehnquist, J., dissenting).

11. For an argument that sodomy laws themselves violate the equal protection guarantee. See Note, "The Miscegenation Analogy: Sodomy Law as Sex Discrimination," 98 *Yale L.J.* 145 (1988).

12. The argument from *Hardwick* is specifically advanced in *Padula v. Webster*, 822 F.2d 97 (D.C. Cir. 1987); *Gay Inmates of Shelby County Jail v. Barksdale*, No. 84–5666

(6th Cir. June 1, 1987) (Westlaw, Allfeds database); *Dronenburg v. Zech*, 741 F.2d 1388, 1391 (D.C. Cir. 1984); State v. Walsh, 713 S.W.2d 508, 511 (Mo. 1986); *In re Opinion of the Justices*, 129 N.H. 290, 295, 530 A.2d 21, 24 (1987). Other courts conclude that *Hardwick* "lends support" to the foreclosure of meaningful equal protection. See *Gay and Lesbian Students Ass'n v. Gohn*, 656 F. Supp. 1045, 1057 (W.D. Ark. 1987). For anticipations of this line of reasoning, see *Commonwealth v. Bonadio*, 490 Pa. 91, 97–98, 415 A.2d 47, 51 (1980). But see *Bowers v. Hardwick*, 487 U.S. at 202 (Blackmun, J., dissenting); *Watkins v. United States Army*, 837 F.2d 1428, reh'g granted, 847 F.2d 1362 (9th Cir. 1988) (*en banc*); *Doe v. Casey*, 796 F.2d 1508, 1522 (D.C. Cir. 1986), aff'd in part and rev'd in part on other grounds, *sub nom. Webster v. Doe*, 108 S.Ct. 2047 (1988); *benShalom v. Marsh*, No. 88–G468 (E.D. Wis. 1989) (LEXIS Genfed library, Dist file); *High Tech Gays v. Defense Indus. Sec. Clearance Office*, 668 F. Supp. 1361, 1369 (N.D. Cal 1987); *Swift v. United States*, 649 F. Supp. 596, 601 (D.D.C. 1986); *benShalom v. Secretary of the Army*, 489 F. Supp. 964 (E.D. Wis. 1980).

13. *Watkins v. United States Army*, 837 F.2d at 1431–40 n.20. Cass R. Sunstein has constructed a sustained critique of arguments conflating due process with equal protection analysis in this context. See Sunstein, "Sexual Orientation and the Constitution: A Note on the Relationship between Due Process and Equal Protection," 55 *U. Chi. L. Rev.* 1161 (1988).

14. Seven states maintain statutes that criminalize homosexual sodomy, all providing different definitions of the crime. Ark. Code Ann. 5–14–122 (Michie 1987) ("penetration . . . of the anus or mouth of . . . a person by the penis of a person of the same sex" or "penetration . . . of the vagina or anus of . . . a person by any body member of a person of the same sex"); Kan Stat. Ann. §§21–3501(2), 21–3505 (Supp. 1987) ("sodomy between persons who are members of the same sex"; sodomy defined as "oral or anal copulation; . . . or any penetration of the anal opening by any body part or object"); Ky. Rev. Stat. Ann. §§510.010(1), 510.100 (1985) ("deviate sexual intercourse with another person of the same sex" where deviate sexual intercourse is "any act of sexual gratification . . . involving the sex organs of one (1) person and the mouth or anus of another"); Mo. Ann. Stat. §566.090.1(3) (Vernon 1979) ("deviate sexual intercourse with another person of the same sex"); Mont. Code Ann. §§45–2–101(20), 45–5–505(1) (1987) ("deviate sexual conduct" defined as "sexual contact or sexual intercourse between two persons of the same sex"); Nev Rev. Stat. Ann. §201.190 (Michie 1986) ("the infamous crime against nature" defined as "anal intercourse, cunnilingus or fellatio between consenting adults of the same sex"); Tex. Penal Code Ann. §§21.06, 21.01(1) (Vernon 1974 & Supp. 1988) ("deviate sexual intercourse with another individual of the same sex" where deviate sexual intercourse is "any contact between any part of the genitals of one person and the mouth or anus of another person" or "the penetration of the genitals or anus of another person with an object").

15. *Padula v. Webster*, 822 F.2d at 103.

16. *Plyler v. Doe*, 457 U.S. 202, 219 n.19 (1982).

17. *Watkins v. United States Army*, 837 F.2d 1928, reh'g granted, 847 F.2d 1362 (9th Cir. 1988) (*en banc*).

18. *benShalom v. Marsh*, No. 88–C–468 (E.D. Wis. Jan. 10, 1989) (LEXIS, Genfed library, Dist. file).

19. Bernstein, "My Daughter is a Lesbian," *New York Times* (February 24, 1988), p. A27, col. 1

20. Thurmond on Homosexuality, *New York Times* (August 2, 1986), p. 6, col. 1.

21. All of the following important academic contributions to the gay rights polemic have claimed that homosexuality is immutable and therefore eligible for heightened scrutiny: Delgado, "Fact, Norm, and Standard of Review—The Case of Homosexuality," 10 *U. Dayton L. Rev.* 575, 583–85 (1985); Lasson, "Civil Liberties for Homosexuals: The Law in Limbo," 10 *U. Dayton L. Rev.* 645, 656–57 (1985); Miller, "An Argument for the Application of Equal Protection Heightened Scrutiny to Classifications Based on Homosexuality," 57 *S. Cal. L. Rev.* 797, 817–21 (1984); Note, "Marital Status Classifications: Protecting Homosexual and Heterosexual Cohabitors," 14 *Hastings Const. L.Q.* 111, 120, 127–28 (1986); Note, "The Legality of Homosexual Marriage," 82 *Yale L.J.* 573, 576 (1973). The argument is reluctantly adopted by Arriola, "Sexual Identity and the Constitution: Homosexual Persons as a Discrete and Insular Minority," 10 *Women's Rts. L. Rep.* 143, 154–55 (1988). Three publications assert that the immutability argument is empirically or doctrinally problematic in arguments urging the protection of homosexual rights. Chaitin and Lefcourt ,"Is Gay Suspect," 8 *Lincoln L. Rev.* 24 (1973); Note, "The Constitutional Status of Sexual Orientation: Homosexuality as a Suspect Classification," 98 *Harv. L. Rev.* 1285, 1302 (1985); and Comment, "*Bowers v. Hardwick*: Balancing the Interests of the Moral Order and Individual Liberty," 16 *Cumb. L. Rev.* 555, 588 (1986). The last of these argues that, because homosexuality is not known to be immutable, it cannot form a suspect classification.

22. See *Baker v. Wade*, 774 F.2d 1285 (5th Cir. 1985) (sexual orientation of many homosexuals immutable and therefore not deterrable); *Gay Rights Coalition of Georgetown Univ. Law Center v. Georgetown Univ.*, 536 A.2d 1, 36 (D.C. App. 1987); *Commonwealth v. Bonadio*, 490 Pa. 91, 95, 415 A.2d 47, 50 (Pa. 1980) (rejecting marriage-promotion justification); *Doe v. Commonwealth's Attorney*, 403 F. Supp. 1199, 1205 (E.D. Va. 1975) (Merhige, J., dissenting) (rejecting argument that antihomosexual legislation promotes marriage), aff'd mem., 425 U.S. 901 (1976).

23. See *In re Opinion of the Justices*, 129 N.H. 290, 295, 530 A.2d 21, 24 (1987) (rejecting strict or intermediate scrutiny because "sexual preference is not a matter necessarily tied to gender, but rather to inclination, whatever the source thereof").

24. See *National Gay Task Force v. Bd. of Educ.*, 729 F.2d 1270 (10th Cir. 1984), aff'd by an equally divided court, 470 U.S. 903 (1985); *In re Opinion of the Justices*, 129 N.H. at 290, 530 A.2d at 21; Note, "Custody Denials to Parents in Same-Sex Relationships: An Equal Protection Analysis," 102 *Harv. L. Rev.* 617 (1989); Comment, "Assessing Children's Best Interests When a Parent is Gay or Lesbian: Toward a Rational Custody Standard," 32 *UCLA L. Rev*, 852, 881–84 (1985); Comment, "Burdens on Gay Litigants and Bias in the Court System: Homosexual Panic, Child Custody, and Anonymous Parties," 19 *Harv. C.R.-C.L. L. Rev.* 497, 515–46 (1984).

25. See *High Tech Gays v. Defense Indus. Sec. Clearance Office*, 668 F. Supp. 1361 (N.D. Cal. 1987); see also *Watkins v. United States Army*, 837 F.2d 1428, 1446–47 (sex, alienage and race—all held to establish suspect classifications—are not entirely mutable but rather very difficult or painful to change; that requirement is met by homosexuality) reh'g granted, 847 F.2d 1362 (9th Cir. 1988) (*en banc*).

26. For a fascinating example of self-censorship by a scholar who recognized that the social dynamics of sexual orientation are more complex than the "immutability argument"

acknowledges, but who feared that disclosure of her results would weaken the case for repeal of England's sodomy statutes, see "Postscript: The 'Homosexual Role' Revisited: Jeffrey Weeks and Kenneth Plummer Interview Mary McIntosh," in *The Making of the Modern Homosexual* 44–45 (K. Plummer, ed. 1981) [hereinafter *Modern Homosexual*].

27. *Shaare Tefila Congregation v. Cobb*, 481 U.S. 615 (1987); *Saint Francis College v. Al-Khazraji*, 481 U.S. 604 (1987).

28. *Saint Francis*, 481 U.S. at 613.

29. *Id.*

30. *Id.*, pp. 610–13.

31. In a disturbing contradiction, the Court held that its intentionalist reading of the civil rights statutes required that it adopt and enforce the late-nineteenth-century conception that race is determined by ancestry, by derivation from a common "stock." *Saint Francis*, 481 U.S. at 611. Martha Minow has subjected these opinions to stern criticism, for elevating to binding precedent an outdated and racist conception of race. See Minow, "The Supreme Court 1986 Term, Forward: Justice Engendered," 101 *Harv. L. Rev.* 10, 19–22, 37–38 (1987).

    Regulators have the jump on the Supreme Court in developing an adequate inquiry into race identity. The National Science Foundation requests grant applicants to indicate their "ethnic/racial status" as American Indian, Asian, Black, Hispanic or White, and identifies a person belonging to any of these groups as "having origins"—not his or her *origin*—in the geographical areas historically associated with the group. The cultural complexity of racial identity is emphasized by the definition of American Indian or Alaskan Native: "A person having origins in any of the original peoples of North America, *and who maintains cultural identification through tribal affiliation or community recognition*." National Science Foundation, *Grants for Research and Education in Science and Engineering* 17 (1987) (emphasis added). An applicant whose origins can be found in more than one of the proposed racial categories is asked to mark the one "that most closely reflects [his or her] recognition in the community." *Id.*

32. Saks, "Representing Miscegenation Law," 8 *Raritan* 39 (Fall 1988). The following reading of miscegenation law draws heavily on Saks's work.

33. 153 N.C. 174, 69 S.E. 60 (1910).

34. *Id.* at 180–81, 69 S.E. at 62–63 (Clark, C.J., concurring) (emphasis added; citations omitted).

35. *Id.* at 180, 69 S.E. at 62.

36. John Howard Griffin, *Black Like Me* (1977), cited as an example of the mutability of race in *Watkins v. United States Army*, 837 F.2d 1428, 1446 reh'g granted, 847 F.2d 1362 (9th Cir. 1988) (*en banc*).

37. Patricia J. Williams tells the story of a Black woman who, giving up her dark-skinned daughter to be raised by equally dark-skinned relatives, "passed for White" during her decades of marriage to a White man and returned to her Black family only upon his death. Williams, "On Being the Object of Property," 14 *Signs: J. of Women and Soc.* 5, 12–13 (1988).

38. *San Antonio Indep. School Dist. v. Rodriguez*, 411 U.S. 1, 28 (1973).

39. *Graham v. Richardson*, 403 U.S. 365 (1971). Professor Lusky expressed amazement at the Supreme Court's holding in *Graham*: "Indeed, considering that we are a nation of aliens and the descendents of aliens, that our 'melting pot' is a source of national pride, . . . and that naturalization is broadly available, the abrupt announcement in the *Graham* case is incomprehensible." Lusky, *supra* note 9, at 1105 n.72

40. See *City of Cleburne v. Cleburne Living Center*, 473 U.S. 432 (1985).

41. But see *Parham v. Hughes*, 441 U.S. 347, 351 (1979) (dictum) (attributing immutability to race, national origin, alienage, illegitimacy and gender).

42. *Frontiero v. Richardson*, 411 U.S. 677, 686 (1973) (quoting *Weber v. Aetna Casualty & Surety Co.*, 406 U.S. 164, 175 (1972)); *see also* J. Ely, *Democracy and Distrust: A Theory of Judicial Review* 154–55 (1980).

43. The cases distinguished are *Trimble v. Gordon*, 430 U.S. 762 (1977); *Weber v. Aetna Casualty & Surety Co.*, 406 U.S. 164 (1972).

44. *Parham v. Hughes*, 441 U.S. at 352–53. Justice Powell's concurrence, which completes the majority rejecting the challenge to the statute, focuses solely on its gender classification.

45. But see *Watkins v. United States Army*, 837 F.2d 1428, 1446 (Supreme Court precedents regard immutability as a rough indicator of "gross unfairness"), reh'g granted, 847 F.2d 1362 (9th Cir. 1988) (*en banc*).

46. *Plyler v. Doe*, 457 U.S. 202, 221 (1982) (emphasis added).

47. *Id.* at 219–20.

48. *Watkins*, 837 F.2d at 1446.

49. The Supreme Court took special note of this passage:

> Surely one has to feel sorry for a person disabled by something he or she can't do anything about, but I'm not aware of any reason to suppose that elected officials are unusually unlikely to share that feeling. Moreover, classifications based on physical disability and intelligence are typically accepted as legitimate, even by judges and commentators who assert that immutability is relevant. The explanation, when one is given, is that *those* characteristics (unlike the one the commentator is trying to render suspect) are often relevant to legitimate purposes. At that point there's not much left of the immutability theory, is there?

J. Ely, *supra* note 42, at 150 (footnote omitted), *cited in City of Cleburne v. Cleburne Living Center*, 473 U.S. 432, 442–43 n.10 (1985).

50. 427 U.S. 495, 505 (1976).

51. *Id.* at 506 n.13.

52. *Id.* at 507.

53. 427 U.S. 307 (1976).

54. *Id.* at 307, 313–14 (1976) (citations omitted). The Court associates immutability with Footnote Four prejudice in *Plyler v. Doe*, 457 U.S. 202, 217 n.14 (1982).

55. Ackerman, "Beyond *Carolene Products*," 98 *Harv. L. Rev.* 713 (1985).

56. Ely, *supra* note 42, at 152–53.

57. *Id.* at 153.

58. *San Antonio Indep. School Dist. v. Rodriguez*, 411 U.S. 1, 28 (1973).

59. Ackerman, *supra* note 55, at 724–28.

60. *Id.* at 729–31.

61. Ely, *supra* note 42, at 160.

62. *Id.* at 150.

63. E. Goffman, *Stigma: Notes on the Management of Spoiled Identity* 42 (1963).

64. See *supra* note 21.

65. An extensive bibliography is provided in Note, "An Argument for the Application of Equal Protection Heightened Scrutiny to Classifications Based on Homosexuality," 57 *S. Cal. L. Rev.* 797, 820–21 nn.147–48 (1984). See also *Watkins v. United States Army*, 837 F.2d 1428, 1446, reh'g granted, 847 F.2d 1362 (9th Cir. 1988) (*en banc*); Hart, "Theoretical Explanations in Practice," in *The Theory and Practice of Homosexuality* 48–58 (J. Hart & D. Richardson eds. 1981).

66. G. Orwell, *1984* (1949).

67. See S. Terkel, *The Good War: An Oral History of World War Two* 180 (1984) (Terkel interview with Ted Allenby, a Marine dishonorably discharged for his homosexuality: TERKEL: "Did you take part in the banter?" ALLENBY: "Of course. You have to, otherwise somebody'd suspect you. You develop quite a repertory of tricks to prevent detection. Be even more vociferous than everybody else.").

68. In the brief review that follows, I necessarily simplify a complex historical tension. For a more thorough exposition of debates over congenital and social causes, see generally J. Weeks, *Coming Out: Homosexual Politics in Britain from the Nineteenth Century to the Present* (1977).

69. R. von Krafft-Ebing, *Psychopathia Sexualis, with Special Reference to the Antipathic Sexual Instinct: A Medico-Forensic Study* 286–461 (F. Rebman trans. 1925); see also McIntosh, "The Homosexual Role," in *Modern Homosexual, supra* note 26, at 31–44 (McIntosh's article first appeared in 16 *Soc. Problems* 182 (1968)).

70. H. Ellis, *Studies in the Psychology of Sex: Sexual Inversion* 315–17, 322 (3d ed. 1929).

71. S. Freud, "Three Essays on the Theory of Sexuality," in *On Sexuality* 45–60 (1977).

72. M. Foucault, *The History of Sexuality: An Introduction* 43 (R. Hurley trans. 1980).

73. Boswell, "Towards the Long View: Revolutions, Universals and Sexual Categories" 58–59 *Salmagundi* 89, 91–96 (1982–1983).

74. See, e.g., J. Weeks, *Coming Out: Homosexual Politics in Britain from the Nineteenth Century to the Present* 31 (1977); Plummer, "Homosexual Categories: Some Research Problems in the Labelling Perspective of Homosexuality," in *Modern Homosexual, supra* note 26, at 53; Weeks, "Discourse, Desire and Social Deviance: Some Problems in a History of Sexuality," in *Modern Homosexual, supra* note 26, at 53.

75. Boswell, *supra* note 73, at 105.

76. See D. Greenberg, *The Construction of Homosexuality* 482–99 (1988); Epstein, "Gay Politics, Ethnic Identity: The Limits of Social Constructionism," 17 *Socialist Rev.* 9

(1987); Escoffier, "Sexual Revolution and the Politics of Gay Identity," 15 *Socialist Rev.* 119 (July–Oct. 1985).

77. See McIntosh, *supra* note 69, at 31; Boswell, *supra* note 73, at 96.

78. See J. Spada, *The Spada Report* 23–27 (1979); Whitam, "The Homosexual Role: A Reconsideration," 13 *J. Sex Res.* 1 (1977).

79. See Plummer, *supra* note 74, at 69–70.

80. A. Bell, M. Weinberg and S. Kiefer Hammersmith, *Sexual Preference: Its Development in Men and Women* 186 (1981) (emphasis omitted).

81. *Id.* at 216 (emphasis omitted).

82. *Id.* at 219.

83. *Id.* at 187.

84. *Id.* at 186.

85. *Id.* at 32. The study asked subjects to rate their feelings and their behavior on Kinsey's seven-point scale, from exclusively heterosexual (0) to exclusively homosexual (6). See *infra* notes 87–90 and accompanying text. Those whose average score was 2 or more were classified as homosexual; all others were grouped as heterosexual. The greater the divergence between a person's feelings and behavior, the more procrustean the categorization.

86. Escoffier, *supra* note 76, at 126.

87. A. Kinsey, W. Pomeroy and C. Martin, *Sexual Behavior in the Human Male* 650–51 (1948) [hereinafter *Human Male*]; A. Kinsey, W. Pomeroy, C. Martin and P. Gebhard, *Sexual Behavior in the Human Female* 488 (1953) [hereinafter *Human Female*]. Differences in analytic emphasis between these two studies make intelligible comparisons of women and men almost impossible.

88. *Human Male, supra* note 87, at 654 (Table 150.

89. *Id.* at 639; *Human Female, supra* note 87, at 471–72.

90. *Human Male, supra* note 87, at 652, Table 148. For a social-interactionist interpretation of these figures, see McIntosh, *supra* note 69, at 41.

91. A useful articulation of this shift in focus appears in J. Gagnon and W. Simon, *Sexual Conduct: The Social Sources of Human Sexuality* 137, 215–16 (1973).

92. See, e.g., J. Weeks, *Sexuality and Its Discontents* 194, 301 n.26 (1985).

93. E.g., P. Berger and T. Luckmann, *The Social Construction of Reality* (1967).

94. E.g., H. Becker, *Outsiders: Studies in the Sociology of Deviance* (1963); E. Goffman, *supra* note 63.

95. For theoretical assessments of this social-psychological research, see K. Plummer, *Sexual Stigma: An Interactionist Account* (1975); J. Weeks, *supra* note 92; *Modern Homosexual, supra* note 26; D'Emilio, "Capitalism and Gay Identity," in *Powers of Desire: The Politics of Sexuality* (A. Snitow, C. Stansell and S. Thompson eds. 1983); Epstein, *supra* note 76; Escoffier, *supra* note 76.

96. McIntosh, *supra* note 69, at 33, 38–43.

97. See Dank, "The Homosexual," in *Sexual Deviance and Sexual Deviants* 182 (E. Goode & R. Troiden eds. 1974); see also de Monteflores & Schultz, "Coming Out: Similarities

and Differences for Lesbians and Gay Men," 34 *J. Soc. Issues* 59, 62 (Summer 1978) (concluding from such figures that, whether or not one can "choose to be gay," "one can choose whether or not to express same-sex feelings in behavior, to label oneself gay or homosexual, or to disclose one's identity to others").

98. Golden, "Diversity and Variability in Women's Sexual Identities," in *Lesbian Psychologies: Explorations and Challenges* 19, 25 (Boston Lesbian Psychologies Collective ed. 1987). Golden draws her terminology here from B. Ponse, *Identities in the Lesbian World* (1978).

99. Golden, *supra* note 98, at 26–27.

100. *Id*. at 27–28.

101. *Id*. at 25–27.

102. McDonald, "Individual Differences in the Coming Out Process for Gay Men: Implications for Theoretical Models," 8 *J. Homosexuality* 47, 47 (Fall 1982) (emphasis added).

103. See Weinberg, "On 'Doing' and 'Being' Gay: Sexual Behavior and Homosexual Male Self Identity," 4 *J. Homosexuality* 143, 148–49 (1978); T. Weinberg, *Gay Men, Gay Selves: The Social Construction of Homosexual Identities* (1983).

104. McDonald, *supra* note 102, at 54.

105. *Id*. at 48. Proponents of the "stage sequential" model include: Cass, "Homosexual Identity Formation: A Theoretical Model," 4 *J. Homosexuality* 219 (1979); Lee, "Going Public: A Study in the Sociology of Homosexual Liberation," 3 *J. Homosexuality* 49 (1977); Schäfer, "Sexual and Social Problems of Lesbians," 12 *J. Sex Res.* 50 (1976).

106. Golden, *supra* note 98, at 29.

107. *Id*. at 31.

108. McDonald, *supra* note 102, at 58; see also Kimmel, "Adult Development and Aging: A Gay Perspective," 34 *J. Soc. Issues* 113, 116–17 (1978); de Monteflores & Schultz, *supra* note 97, at 69.

109. The term is Goffman's. E. Goffman, *supra* note 63.

110. de Monteflores & Schultz, *supra* note 97, at 68.

111. Cass, *supra* note 105, at 223.

112. *Beller v. Middendorf*, 632 F.2d 788, 804 n.13 (9th Cir. 1980) cert. denied, sub nom *Beller v. Lehman*, 452 U.S. 905, cert. denied, 454 U.S. 855 (1981).

113. Broadly accepted stereotypes of homosexual behavior or appearance do not destroy but rather refute, for those who are deemed to bear them, the assumption that everyone is heterosexual. Gay men and lesbians who adopt these signifiers, though they threaten the assumption, have not yet managed to dismantle it. Their effort to control their categorization by others will fail whenever they encounter a naif who does not know the meaning assigned to the sign they have adopted, or a sophisticate who understands how multivalent such signs have become.

114. For an exposition of the peculiarly unstable dynamics that attend the disclosure or discovery of gay identity, see Sedgwick, "Epistemology of the Closet," 7 *Raritan* 39 (1988).

115. *Gay Inmates of Shelby County Jail v. Barksdale*, No. 84-5666 (6th Cir. June 1, 1987) (Westlaw, Allfeds database).

116. *Id.* at 3–4.

117. Indeed, urban gay men set out to debunk this stereotype in the early 1980s, with their often parodic celebration of bodybuilding and "macho." Gay male culture's response to AIDS has further complicated this metaphoric nexus.

118. Minow, *supra* note 31, at 51 n.201.

119. Inmates at the Shelby County Jail may be classified as homosexual if they have been so classified in the past. *Gay Inmates*, No. 84–5666 at 4. Even without this policy, peers of an inmate classified as a homosexual are not likely to forget it.

120. 822 F.2d 97 (D.C. Cir. 1987).

121. 478 U.S. 186 (1986).

122. *Padula*, 822 F.2d at 103.

123. Ga. Code Ann. §26–2002(a) (Harrison 1983).

124. See *Baker v. Wade*, 553 F. Supp. 1121, 1134 (N.D. Tex 1982) (Texas sodomy statute prohibiting contacts of the sex organs of one person with the mouth or anus of another does "not prohibit homosexuals from kissing or sexually stimulating their partner with hands and fingers"), rev'd, 769 F.2d 289 (5th Cir. 1985), cert. denied, 478 U.S. 1022 (1986).

125. See *supra* note 14.

126. These statutes criminalize sodomy without reference to the gender of the participants: Ala. Code §13A–6–65(a)(3) (1982); Ariz. Rev. Stat. Ann. §§13–1411, 13–1412 (Supp. 1987); D.C. Code Ann. §22–3502 (1981); Idaho Code §18–6605 (1987); La. Rev. Stat. Ann. §14:89 (West 1986); Md. Crim. Law Code Ann. §§553–554 (1987); Mich. Comp. Laws §750.158 (1981); Minn. Stat. §609.293 (1987); Miss. Code Ann. §97–29–59 (1973); N.C. Gen. Stat. §14–177 (1981); Okla. Stat. tit. 21 §886 (1983); R.I. Gen Laws §11–10–1 (1981); S.C. Code Ann. §16–15–120 (Law Co-op 1985); Tenn. Code Ann. §39–2–612 (1982); Utah Code Ann. §76–5–403 (Supp. 1987); Va. Code Ann. §18.2–361 (1982). The following jurisdictions have repealed their homosexual sodomy statutes: Arkansas, California, Colorado, Connecticut, Delaware, Hawaii, Illinois, Maine, New Mexico, North Dakota, Ohio, Oregon and Washington.

127. See Cover, "Violence and the Word," 95 *Yale L.J.* 1601 (1986).

128. New Hampshire House Bill 70 defined "a homosexual" as "any person who performs or submits to any sexual act involving the sex organs of one person and the mouth or anus of another person of the same gender." *In re Opinion of the Justices*, 129 N.H. 290, 293, 530 A.2d 21, 22 (1987).

129. *In re Opinion of the Justices*, 129 N.H. at 295, 530 A.2d at 24.

130. Many readers of this article in manuscript have queried my use of this term—a phenomenon which nicely emphasizes that sexual identity is indeed exceedingly problematic. Here, we are confronted with a hypothetical person who *ex hypothesi* presents him- or herself as heterosexual, contradicting some element of his or her sexual biography. To call such a person "heterosexual" is not only to insist on the reality of this social self-presentation but also to destabilize the referentiality of the term "heterosexual." These consequences of the terminological choices made in *supra* note 5, I think, repay the difficulties involved in my admittedly unconventional use of the term.

131. The Navy's Personnel Manual, Bupersman §340220, quoted in *Beller v. Middendorf*, 632 F.2d 788, 803 n.11 (9th Cir. 1980), cert. denied, sub nom. *Beller v. Lehman*, 452 U.S. 905, cert denied, 454 U.S. 855 (1981).

132. SEC/NAV Instruction 1900.9C ¶6b (Jan. 20, 1978) (emphasis added), quoted in *Dronenburg v. Zech*, 741 F.2d 1388, 1389 n.1 (D.C. Cir. 1984).

133. 632 F.2d 788 (9th Cir. 1980), cert. denied, sub nom. *Beller v. Lehman*, 452 U.S. 905, cert. denied, 454 U.S. 855 (1981).

134. *Id.* at 794 (emphasis added).

135. *Id.* at 801–05.

136. *Id.* at 802 n.9.

137. *Id.*

138. Cover, *supra* note 127, at 1602–03 (footnotes omitted).

139. Halley, "Heresy, Orthodoxy, and the Politics of Religious Discourse: The Case of the English Family of Love," 15 *Representations* 98 (1986), reprinted in *Representing the English Renaissance* 303 (S. Greenblatt ed. 1988).

140. 741 F.2d 1388 (D.C. Cir. 1984).

141. *Id.* at 1395–96 (emphasis added).

142. *Baker v. Wade*, 553 F. Supp. 1121, 1148 (1982) (quoting Tex. Penal Code, art. 342 (1860) (current version at Tex. Penal Code Ann. §§21.06, 1.05, 21.01 (Vernon 1974); *Harvey v. State*, 55 Tex. Crim. 199, 113 S.W. 1193 (1909).

143. Md. Crim. Law Code Ann. §554 (1987).

144. *Hughes v. State*, 14 Md. App. 497, 500 n.3, 287 A.2d 299, 302 n.3 (citing *Blake v. State*, 210 Md. 459, 124 A.2d 273 (1956)), cert. denied, 409 U.S. 1025 (1972).

145. *Bowers v. Hardwick*, 478 U.S. 186, 197 (1986) (Burger, C. J., concurring) (quoting 4 W. Blackstone, *Commentaries on the Laws of England* 215 (1769)).

146. 741 F.2d 1388, 1395–96, 1398 (D.C. Cir. 1984).

147. *Id.* at 1398.

148. *Id.*

149. *benShalom v. Secretary of the Army*, 489 F. Supp. 964, 969 (E.D. Wis. 1980).

150. Army Regulations Ch. 7-5b(6), 135–178, quoted in *benShalom*, 489 F. Supp. at 969.

151. 796 F.2d 1508 (D.C. Cir. 1986), aff'd in part, rev'd in part on other grounds, sub nom. *Webster v. Doe*, 108 S. Ct. 2047 (1987).

152. *Id.* at 1512 n.2.

153. Under the rule of *Bd. of Regents v. Roth*, 408 U.S. 564 (1972), a government employee adversely affected in her employment can seek due process protection of her liberty interests only if she can show an actual change of status and an accompanying "injury to the employee's good name, reputation, honor or integrity, or the imposition of a similar stigma." *Doe v. Casey*, 796 F.2d at 1522–23 (citing *Board of Regents v. Roth*, 408 U.S. 564 (1972), and *Doe v. United States Dept. of Justice*, 753 F.2d 1092, 1105 (D.C. Cir. 1985)).

154. *Doe v. Casey*, 796 F.2d at 1523 n.66 (quoting *Beller v. Middendorf*, 632 F.2d 788, 806 (9th Cir. 1980), cert. denied, sub nom. *Beller v. Lehman*, 452 U.S. 905, cert. denied, 454 U.S. 855 (1981)).

155. *Doe v. Casey*, 796 F.2d at 1523.

156. *Cf. Plessy v. Ferguson*, 163 U.S. 537, 551 (1896) (If "the enforced separation of the two races stamps the colored race with a badge of inferiority[,] . . . it is not by reason of anything found in the act, but solely because the colored race chooses to put that construction upon it.")

157. Department of Defense Personnel Security Program Regulation, 32 C.F.R. §154. app. H (1987), quoted in *High Tech Gays v. Defense Indus. Sec. Clearance Office*, 668 F. Supp. 1361, 1365 (N.D. Cal. 1987).

158. *High Tech Gays*, 668 F. Supp. at 1376.

159. *Id.* at 1375.

160. *Swift v. United States*, 649 F. Supp. 596, 597 (D.D.C. 1986) (emphasis added).

161. *benShalom v. Secretary of the Army*, 489 F. Supp. 964, 974 (E.D. Wis. 1980).

162. *Rowland v. Mad River Local School Dist.*, 730 F.2d 444 (6th Cir. 1984), cert. denied, 470 U.S. 1009 (1985). The full story has to be gleaned from the Sixth Circuit's majority and dissenting opinions and from Justice Brennan's dissent from the Supreme Court's denial of certiorari.

163. *Id.* at 449. The court here applies the rule set forth in *Connick v. Myers*, 461 U.S. 138, 147 (1983) ("[w]hen a public employee speaks not as a citizen upon matters of public concern, but instead as an employee upon matters only of personal interest, absent the most unusual circumstances, a federal court is not the appropriate forum in which to review the wisdom of a personnel decision taken by a public agency allegedly in reaction to the employee's behavior.").

164. *Rowland*, 730 F.2d at 451.

165. *Rowland*, 470 U.S. at 1012 (Brennan, J., dissenting) (emphasis added).

166. *Id.* at 1016 n.11.

167. Consider the thought-befuddling implications of the following letter, mailed by a campus group entitled the Great White Brotherhood of the Iron Fist to the parents of students who participated in Gay and Lesbian Alliance activities at the University of Chicago (not all of whom, it is fair to assume, are self-identified homosexuals):

> Dear parents of ———: We have some unpleasant news for you. We have recently discovered that your son/daughter is homosexual, and possibly a carrier of AIDS. We are very concerned that he/she may be endangering his/her life through his/her frequent sexual contact with people of the same gender, many of whom must be infected by AIDS.
>
> Please help pull him/her out of this reckless existence! We are convinced that he/she can be cured of his/her homosexuality, given psychiatric and religious help at an early enough time. . . .
>
> Unless your son/daughter renounces his/her deviant sexuality, we will be forced to take further actions concerning him/her to protect the community from the AIDS threat.
>
> Please help your child before it is too late!

Harper's Magazine (Sept. 1987), p. 16.

168. V. Woolf, *Orlando: A Biography* 258 (1956) (emphasis added). I adopt, with thanks, the italicization of this passage from S. Knopp, *"If I Saw You Would You Kiss Me?"*: *Sapphism and the Subversiveness of Virginia Woolf's* Orlando, 103 *PMLA* 24, 31 (1988).

169. Justice Powell anxiously summarizes the critique as follows:

> The problem is this: in a democratic society there inevitably are both winners and losers. The fact that one group is disadvantaged by a particular piece of legislation, or action of government, therefore does not prove that the process has failed to function properly. To infer otherwise—that the process has been corrupted by invidious discrimination—a judge must have some *substantive* vision of what results the process should have yielded. Otherwise he has no way to know that the process was unfair.
>
> Here I must pause to wonder. If I am correct about the implicit link between a substantive judgment and a malfunction of process, then one may inquire whether we have not returned in some cases to a kind of substantive due process.

Powell, *supra* note 7, at 1091 (emphasis in original).

170. For responses to this impasse and the more general question it raises, see Ackerman, *supra* note 55; Brest, "The Fundamental Rights Controversy: The Essential Contradictions of Normative Constitutional Scholarship," 90 *Yale L.J.* 1063 (1981); Brest, "The Substance of Process," 42 *Ohio St. L.J.* 131 (1981) [hereinafter Brest, "Substance"]; Brilmayer, *"Carolene,* Conflicts, and the Fate of the 'Inside-Outsider'," 134 *U. Pa. L. Rev.* 1291 (1986); Tribe, "The Puzzling Persistence of Process-Based Constitutional Theories," 89 *Yale L.J.* 1063 (1980). With the single exception of Brilmayer, all of these focus on the problem of antihomosexual legislation.

171. J. Ely, *supra* note 42, at 163.

172. *Id*. at 256, n.92.

173. Brest, "Substance," *supra* note 170, at 136 (emphasis in original).

174. Tribe, *supra* note 170, at 1076 (emphasis deleted).

175. Ackerman, *supra* note 55, at 740.

176. Brest, "Substance," *supra* note 170, at 141; see also Tribe, *supra* note 170, at 1075–76:

> Legislators may see homosexuals as "different" not out of ignorance, but on principle—on the basis of a morality that treats certain sexual practices as repugnant to a particular view of humanity, and thus regards people who engage in those practices as "other." Such legislation can be rejected only on the basis of a principle that is equally substantive: a view of what it means to be a person, and to have a sexual identity.

177. See Note, "The Constitutional Status of Sexual Orientation: Homosexuality as a Suspect Classification," 98 *Harv. L. Rev.* 1285, 1303–04 (1985), for such a rejection of process-based arguments urging equal protection for gays, lesbians and bisexuals.

178. For an exposition of the first amendment as a shield for gay personhood and gay speech—an argument not attempted here—see Gomez, "The Public Expression of Lesbian/Gay Personhood as Protected Speech," 1 *J. Law and Inequality* 121 (1983).

179. 370 U.S. 660 (1962).

180. See L. Tribe, *American Constitutional Law* 1424 n.32 (2d ed. 1988).

181. *Bowers v. Hardwick*, 478 U.S. 186, 203 n.2 (Blackmun, J., dissenting).

182. Note, *supra* note 177, at 1300.

183. L. Tribe, *supra* note 180, at 1424 n.32, 1428.

184. 337 U.S. 1 (1949).

185. *Id.* at 4.

186. 376 U.S. 254 (1964).

187. *Id.* at 270.

188. 393 U.S. 503 (1969).

189. *Id.* at 508–09 (citation omitted).

190. *Rowland v. Mad River Local School Dist.*, 470 U.S. 1009, 1016 (1985) (Brennan, J., dissenting); see also text accompanying note 165, *supra*.

191. *Adolph Coors Co. v. Wallace*, 570 F. Supp. 202, 209 & n.24 (N.D. Cal. 1983).

192. Okla. Stat. Ann. tit. 70 §6–103.15(A)(2) (West 1972).

193. 729 F.2d 1270 (10th Cir. 1984), aff'd mem. by an equally divided Court, 470 U.S. 903 (1985).

194. *Id.* at 1274.

195. *Arcara v. Cloud Books, Inc.*, 478 U.S. 697, 705 (1986).

196. *United States v. O'Brien*, 391 U.S. 367 (1968).

197. 395 U.S. 444 (1969).

198. *Id.* at 447.

199. Where sodomy is not a crime, even this limit on speech disappears. For an astonishing case *contra*, see *State ex rel. Grant v. Brown*, 39 Ohio St. 2d 112, 313 N.F.2d 847 (1974), cert. denied, 420 U.S. 916 (1975) (gay rights advocacy group refused articles of incorporation on grounds that its advocacy was unlawful, though legislature had repealed sodomy law).

200. "Concern Over AIDS Helps Rights Unit," *New York Times* (May 3, 1987), §1 at 43, col. 1.

201. *McConnell v. Anderson*, 451 F.2d 193, 195 n.4 (8th Cir. 1971), cert. denied, 405 U.S. 1046 (1972).

202. *Id.* at 196.

203. *Id.* (emphasis in original).

204. See also *Singer v. United States Civil Serv. Comm'n*, 530 F.2d 247 (9th Cir. 1976), vacated and remanded, 429 U.S. 1035 (1977) (public employee who fails to remain closeted, but actively participates in political advocacy of gay rights, may be dismissed because his activity "reflects discredit on the Federal Government" and harms its efficiency); *Gish v. Bd. of Educ.*, 145 N.J. Super. 96, 366 A.2d 1337 (1976), cert.

denied, 434 U.S. 879 (1977) (high school teacher deemed to "deviat[e] from normal . . . mental health" because he presided over gay political group and participated in its media efforts).

205. *West Virginia State Bd. of Educ. v. Barnette*, 319 U.S. 624, 642 (1943).

206. Sedgwick, *supra* note 114, at 43.

207. *Acanfora v. Bd. of Educ.*, 359 F. Supp. 843 (D.C. Md. 1973), aff'd on other grounds, 491 F.2d 498 (4th Cir.), cert. denied, 419 U.S. 836 (1974).

208. See *Gay Law Students Ass'n v. Pacific Tel. & Tel.*, 24 Cal. 3d 458, 595 P.2d 592, 156 Cal Rptr. 14 (1979) (statute barring utility from interfering with "the fundamental right of employees . . . to engage in political activity" prohibits job discrimination against "manifest homosexuals"); Warner, "Homophobia, "Manifest Homosexuals" and Political Activity: A New Approach to Gay Rights and the "Issue" of Homosexuality," 11 *Golden Gate U.L. Rev.* 635 (1981).

209. 668 F. Supp. 1361, 1377–78 (N.D. Cal. 1987) (citing *Elrod v. Burns*, 427 U.S. 347, 362 (1976)). The court relies here on a plurality opinion, the reasoning of which was adopted and extended in *Branti v. Finkel*, 445 U.S. 507 (1980) (test is whether "an employee's private political beliefs would interfere with the discharge of his public duties"). Courts have carefully scrutinized the government employer's claim that an employee's constitutionally protected activity or affiliation interfered with the efficient execution of public business. *Rankin v. McPherson*, 483 U.S. 378 (1987); *Elrod*, 427 U.S. at 364–65 (1976); *Hollon v. Pierce*, 257 Cal. App. 2d 468, 64 Cal. Rptr. 808 (1967).

210. For the more limited argument that the invisibility of gays spoils the political process and would justify special protection under civil rights legislation, see R. Mohr, *Gays/Justice: A Study of Ethics, Society and Law* 162–87 (1988).

211. On the possibility that simple burglary might also be political speech, see D. Hay, P. Linebaugh, J. Rule, E. Thompson and C. Winslow, *Albion's Fatal Tree: Crime and Society in Eighteenth-Century England* 14 (1975) ("social crime" and "crime without reservation" distinguishable).

212. Rich, "Compulsory Heterosexuality and Lesbian Existence," 5 *Signs* 631 (1980) (a "lesbian continuum" unites women who resist male dominance and forced heterosexuality, regardless of their sexual desires or practices).

213. See Saks, *supra* note 32, at 88–89 n.51; Note, *supra* note 11.

II

Pleasures and Dangers

Philosophy in the Bedroom

The Marquis de Sade
Translated by Richard Seaver and Austryn Wainhouse

DOLMANCÉ . . . in all the world there is no mode of pleasure-taking preferable to this; I worship it in either sex; but I'll confess a young lad's ass gives me yet more pleasure than a girl's. *Buggers* is the appellation designating those who are this fancy's adepts; now, Eugénie, when one goes so far as to be a bugger, one must not stop halfway. To fuck women in the rear is but the first part of buggery; 'tis with men Nature wishes men to practice this oddity, and it is especially for men she has given us an inclination. Absurd to say the mania offends Nature; can it be so, when 'tis she who puts it into our head? can she dictate what degrades her? No, Eugénie, not at all; this is as good a place to serve her as any other, and perhaps it is there she is most devoutly worshiped. Propagation owes its existence to her forbearance. How could she have prescribed as law an act which challenges her omnipotence, since propagation is but a consequence of her primary intentions, and since new constructions, wrought by her hand, were our species to be destroyed absolutely, would become again primordial intentions whose accomplishment would be far more flattering to her pride and to her power?

MADAME DE SAINT-ANGE: Do you know, Dolmancé, that by means of this system you are going to be led to prove that totally to extinguish the human race would be nothing but to render Nature a service?

DOLMANCÉ: Who doubts of it, Madame?

MADAME DE SAINT-ANGE: My God! wars, plagues, famines, murders would no longer be but accidents, necessary to Nature's laws, and man, whether instrumental to or the object of these effects, would hence no longer be more a criminal in the one case that he would be a victim in the other?

DOLMANCÉ: Victim he is, without doubt, when he bends before the blows of ill fortune; but criminal, never. We shall have more to say about all these things; for the moment, in the lovely Eugénie's behalf, let's analyze sodomistic pleasures, which presently are the subject of our discussion. In this mode of pleasure-seeking, the posture most commonly adopted by the woman is for her to lie belly down upon the edge of the bed, the buttocks well spread, the head as low as possible; after having mused for an instant upon the splendid prospect of a ready and beckoning ass, after having patted it, slapped it a bit, handled it, sometimes after having beaten or whipped it, pinched and bitten it, the rake moistens with his mouth the pretty little hole he is about to perforate, and prepares his entry with the tip of his tongue; in similar wise, he wets his engine with saliva, or with pomade, and gently presents it to the aperture he intends to pierce; he guides it with one hand, with the other he lays wide open the cheeks of his delight; immediately he feels his member penetrate, he must thrust energetically, taking all due care not to give ground; then it is, occasionally, the woman suffers, if she is new, or young; but, totally heedless of the pangs which are soon to change into pleasures, the fucker must be lively and drive his engine ahead, inch by inch, gradually, but with determination, till at last he is arrived at his objective, till, that is to say, his device's hairs precisely rub the anal rim of the embuggered party. Then may he give free rein to himself; all the thorns are plucked from out his path, there remain roses only there. To complete the metamorphosis into pleasures of what distresses his object still experiences, if it be a boy, let him seize his prick and frig it; let him twiddle her clitoris, if 'tis a girl; the titillations of the pleasure he will cause to be born will in turn work a prodigious contraction in the patient's anus, and will double the delight of the agent who, overwhelmed with comfort, will soon dart, to the very depths of the ass of his delight, a sperm quite as abundant as thick, thus determined by so many lubricious details. There are some who do not care to have the patient take pleasure in the operation; an attitude we will account for in good time.

MADAME DE SAINT-ANGE: Allow me to be the scholar for a moment, and let me ask you, Dolmancé, in what state the patient's ass must be in order to ensure the agent a maximum of pleasure?

DOLMANCÉ: Full, by all means; 'tis essential the object in use have the most imperious desire to shit, so that the end of the fucker's prick, reaching the turd, may drive deep into it, and may more warmly and more softly deposit there the fuck which irritates and sets it afire.

MADAME DE SAINT-ANGE: I fear the patient's pleasure is less.

DOLMANCÉ: Error! This method of pleasure-taking is such that there exists no possibility of the fucker's receiving hurt nor of the employed object's failing to be transported into seventh heaven. No other matches this in value, no other can so completely satisfy each of the protagonists, and they who have tasted of it know a great difficulty in abandoning it for another. Such, Eugénie, are the best ways of taking pleasure with a man if the perils of pregnancy are to be avoided; for one enjoys—and be very certain of it—not only offering a man one's ass, also sucking and frigging him, etc., and I have known libertine ladies who often had an higher esteem for this byplay than for real pleasures. The imagination is the spur of delights; in those of this order, all depends upon it, it is the mainspring of everything; now, is it not by means of the imagination one knows joy? is it not of the imagination that there come the most piquant delights? . . .

Were you, Eugénie, to desire some analysis of men's preferences when they resort to libertinage, we might, in order most lucidly to examine the question, generally reduce those tastes to three: *sodomy, sacrilegious fancies* and *penchants to cruelty*. The first of these passions is universal today; to what we have already said upon it, we shall join a few choice reflections. It divides into two classes, active and passive: the man who embuggers, be it a boy, be it a woman, acquits himself of an active sodomization; he is a passive sodomite when he has himself buggered. The question has often been raised, which of the two fashions of sodomistic behavior is the more voluptuous? assuredly, 'tis the passive, since one enjoys at a single stroke the sensations of before and behind; it is so sweet to change sex, so delicious to counterfeit the whore, to give oneself to a man who treats us as if we were a woman, to call that man one's paramour, to avow oneself his mistress! Ah! my friends, what voluptuousness! . . .

DOLMANCÉ: But how charming! Come here, little one, I'd whip thee a bit (*He strikes her ass.*) Kiss me, your turn is soon to come.

MADAME DE SAINT-ANGE: From now on we must occupy ourselves exclusively with her; consider her, brother, she's the prey; examine that charming maidenhead; 'twill soon belong to thee.

EUGÉNIE: Oh, no! not by the fore-end! 'twould hurt me overmuch; from behind as much as you please, as Dolmancé dealt with me a short while ago.

MADAME DE SAINT-ANGE: Naïve and delicious girl! She demands of you precisely what one has so much difficulty obtaining from others.

EUGÉNIE: Oh, 'tis not without a little remorse; for you have not entirely reassured me upon the criminal enormity I have always heard ascribed to this, especially when it is done between man and man, as has just occurred with Dolmancé and Augustin; tell me, Monsieur, tell me how your philosophy explains this species of misdemeanor. 'Tis frightful, is it not?

DOLMANCÉ: Start from one fundamental point, Eugénie: in libertinage, nothing is frightful, because everything libertinage suggests is also a natural inspiration; the most extraordinary, the most bizarre acts, those which most arrantly seem to conflict with every law, every human institution (as for Heaven, I have nothing to say), well Eugénie, even those are not frightful, and there is not one amongst them all that cannot be demonstrated within the boundaries of Nature; it is certain that the one you allude to, lovely Eugénie, is the very same relative to which one finds such a strange fable in the tasteless fictions of the Holy Writ, that tedious compilation of an untutored Jew during a Babylonian captivity; but the anecdote is false, wants all likelihood, all verisimilitude, when it is affirmed that in retribution for these depravities, those cities, those towns rather, perished by fire; having their site upon the craters of ancient volcanoes, Sodom, Gomorrah too, perished like the Italian cities Vesuvius' lavas submerged; and that's all there is to the miracle, yet, all the same, 'twas from this most simple event they departed in order barbarously to invent the torture of fire to be used against those unfortunate humans who, in one area of Europe, delivered themselves over to this natural fancy.

EUGÉNIE: Oh, 'tis natural?

DOLMANCÉ: Yes, natural, so I affirm it to be; Nature has not got two voices, you know, one of them condemning all day what the other commands, and it is very certain that it is nowhere but from her organ that those men who are infatuated with this mania receive the impressions that drive them to it. They who wish to denigrate the taste or proscribe its practice declare it is harmful to population; how dull-witted they are, these imbeciles who think of nothing but the multiplication of their kind, and who detect nothing but the crime in anything that conduces to a different end. Is it really so firmly established that Nature has so great a need for this overcrowding as they would like to have us believe? Is it very certain that one is guilty of an outrage whenever one abstains from this stupid propagation? To convince ourselves, let us for an instant scrutinize both her operations and her laws. Were it that Nature did naught but create, and never destroy, I might be able to believe, with those tedious sophists, that the sublimest of all actions would be incessantly to labor at production, and following that, I should grant with them, that the refusal to reproduce would be, would perforce have to be, a crime; however, does not the most fleeting glance at natural operations reveal that destructions are just as necessary to her plan as are creations? That the one and the other of these functions are interconnected and enmeshed so intimately that for either to operate the other would be impossible? That nothing would be born, nothing would be regenerated without destructions? Destruction, hence, like creation, is one of Nature's mandates.

This principle acknowledged, how may I offend Nature by refusing to create? the which, supposing there to be some evil in it, would appear infinitely less evil, no question about it, than the act of destruction, which latter is numbered among her laws, as I have but a moment ago proven. If on the one hand I admit the penchant Nature has given me to fabricate these losses and ruins, I must examine, on the other hand, to see whether they are not necessary to her and whether I do not conform with her will when I destroy; thus considered, where then, I ask you, is the crime? But, the fools and the populators continue to object—and they are naught but one—this procreative sperm cannot have been placed in your loins for any purpose other than reproduction: to misuse it is an offense. I have just proven the contrary, since this misuse would not even be equivalent to destruction, and since destruction, far more serious than misuse, would not itself be criminal. Secondly, it is false that Nature intends this spermatic liquid to be employed only and entirely for reproduction; were this true, she would not permit its spillage under any circumstance save those appropriate to that end. But experience shows that the contrary may happen, since we lose it both when and where we wish. Secondly, she would forbid the occurrence of those losses save in coitus, losses which, however, do take place, both when we dream and when we summon remembrances; were Nature miserly about this so precious sap, 'twould never but be into the vessel of reproduction she would tolerate its flow; assuredly, she would not wish this voluptuousness, wherewith at such moments she crowns us, to be felt by us when we divert our tribute; for it would not be reasonable to suppose she could consent to give us pleasures at the very moment we heaped insults upon her. Let us go further; were women not born save to produce—which most surely would be the case were this production so dear to Nature—would it happen that, throughout the whole length of a woman's life, there are no more than seven years, all the arithmetic performed, during which she is in a state capable of conceiving and giving birth? What! Nature avidly seeks propagation, does she; and everything which does not tend to this end offends her, does it! and out of a hundred years of life the sex destined to produce cannot do so during more than seven years! Nature wishes for propagation only, and the semen she accords man to serve in these reproducings is lost, wasted, misused wherever and as often as it pleases man! He takes the same pleasures in this loss as in useful employment of his seed, and never the least inconvenience! . . .

Let us cease, good friends, let us cease to believe in such absurdities: they cause good sense to shudder. Ah! far from outraging Nature, on the contrary—and let us be well persuaded of it—the sodomite and lesbian serve her by stubbornly abstaining from a conjunction whose resultant progeniture can be nothing but irksome to her. Let us make no mistake about it, this propagation was never one of her laws, nothing she ever demanded of us, but at the very most something she tolerated; I have told you so. Why! what difference would it make to her were the race of men entirely to be extinguished upon earth, annihilated! she laughs at our pride when we persuade ourselves all would be over and done with were this misfortune to occur! Why, she would simply fail to notice it. Do you fancy races have not already become extinct? Buffon counts several of them perished, and Nature, struck dumb by a so precious loss, doesn't so much as murmur! The entire species might be wiped out and the air would not be the less pure for it, nor the star less brilliant, nor the universe's march less exact. What idiocy it is to think that our kind is so useful to the world that he who might not labor to propagate it or he who might disturb this propagation would necessarily become a criminal! Let's bring this blindness to a stop and may the example of more reasonable peoples serve to persuade us of our errors. There is not one corner of the earth where the alleged crime of sodomy has not had shrines and votaries. The Greeks, who made of it, so to speak, a virtue, raised a statue unto Venus Callipygea; Rome sent to Athens for law, and returned with this divine taste.

And under the emperors, behold the progress it made! Sheltered by the Roman eagle, it spread from one end of the earth to the other; with the Empire's collapse, it took refuge near the diadem, it followed the arts in Italy, it is handed down to those of us who govern ourselves aright. We discover a hemisphere, we find sodomy in it. Cook casts anchor in a new world: sodomy reigns there. Had our balloons reached the moon, it would have been discovered there as well. Delicious preference, child of Nature and of pleasure, thou must be everywhere men are to be found, and wherever thou shalt be known, there shall they erect altars to thee! O my friends, can there be an extravagance to equal that of imagining that a man must be a monster deserving to lose his life because he has preferred enjoyment of the asshole to that of the cunt, because a young man with whom he finds two pleasures, those of being at once lover and mistress, has appeared to him preferable to a young girl, who promises him but half as much! He shall be a villain, a monster, for having wished to play the role of a sex not his own! Indeed! Why then has Nature created him susceptible of this pleasure?

Let us inspect his conformation; you will observe radical differences between it and that of other men who have not been blessed with this predilection for the behind; his buttocks will be fairer, plumper; never a hair will shade the altar of pleasure, whose interior, lined with a more delicate, more sensual, more sensitive membrane, will be found positively of the same variety as the interior of a woman's vagina; this man's character, once again unlike that of others, will be softer, more pliant, subtler; in him you will find almost all the vices and all the virtues native to women; you will recognize even their weaknesses there; all will have feminine manias and sometimes feminine habits and traits. Would it then be possible that Nature, having thuswise assimilated them into women, could be irritated by what they have of women's tastes? Is it not evident that this is a category of men different from the other, a class Nature has created in order to diminish or minimize propagation, whose overgreat extent would infallibly be prejudicial to her? . . . Ah, dear Eugénie, did you but know how delicate is one's enjoyment when a heavy prick fills the behind, when, driven to the balls, it flutters there, palpitating; and then, withdrawn to the foreskin, it hesitates, and returns, plunges in again, up to the hair! No, no, in the wide world there is no pleasure to rival this one: 'tis the delight of philosophers, that of heroes, it would be that of the gods were not the parts used in his heavenly conjugation the only gods we on earth should reverence!

EUGÉNIE: *very much moved.* Oh, my friends, let me be buggered! . . . Here, my buttocks stand ready. . . . I present them to you! . . . Fuck me, for I discharge! . . . (*upon pronouncing these words, she falls into the arms of Madame de Saint-Ange, who clasps her, embraces her, and offers the young lady's elevated flanks to Dolmancé.*) . . .

DOLMANCÉ: The penchant for sodomy is the result of physical formation, to which we contribute nothing and which we cannot alter. At the most tender age, some children reveal that penchant, and it is never corrected in them. Sometimes it is the fruit of satiety; but even in this case, is it less Nature's doing? Regardless of how it is viewed, it is her work, and, in every instance, what she inspires must be respected by men. If, were one to take an exact inventory, it should come out that this taste is infinitely more affecting than the other, that the pleasures resulting from it are far more lively, and that for this reason its exponents are a thousand times more numerous than its enemies, would it not then be possible to conclude that, far from affronting Nature, this vice serves her intentions, and that she is less delighted by our procreation than we so foolishly believe? Why, as we travel about the world, how many peoples do we not see holding women in contempt! Many are the men who strictly avoid employing them for anything but the having of the child necessary to replace them. The communal aspect of life in republics always renders this vice more frequent in that form of society; but it is not dangerous. Would the Greek legislators have introduced it into their republics had they thought it so? Quite the contrary; they deemed it necessary to a warlike race. Plutarch speaks with enthusiasm of the battalion of lovers; for many a year they alone defended Greece's freedom. The vice reigned amongst comrades-in-arms, and cemented their unity. The greatest of men lean toward sodomy. At the time it was discovered, the whole of America was found inhabitated by people of this taste. In Louisiana, amongst the Illinois, Indians in feminine garb prostituted themselves as courtesans. The Blacks of Benguéla publicly keep men; nearly all the seraglios of Algiers are today exclusively filled with young boys. Not content to tolerate love for young boys, the Thebans made it mandatory; the philosopher of Chaeronea prescribed sodomy as the surest way to a youth's affection.

We know to what extent it prevailed in Rome, where they had public places in which young boys, costumed as girls, and girls as boys, prostituted themselves. In their letters, Martial, Catullus, Tibullus, Horace, and Virgil wrote to men as though to their mistresses; and we read in Plutarch[1] that women must in no way figure in men's love. The Amasians of Crete used to abduct boys, and their initiation was distinguished by the most singular ceremonies. When they were taken with love for one, they notified the parents upon what day the ravisher wished to carry him off; the youth put up some resistance if his lover failed to please him; in the contrary case, they went off together, and the seducer restored him to his family as soon as he had made use of him; for in this passion as in that for women, one always has too much when one has had enough. Strabo informs us that on this very island, seraglios were peopled with boys only; they were prostituted openly.

Is one more authority required to prove how useful this vice is in a republic? Let us lend an ear to Jerome the Peripatetic: "The love of youths," says he, "spread throughout all of Greece, for it instilled in us strength and courage, and thus stood us in good stead when we drove the tyrants out; conspiracies were formed amongst lovers, and they were readier to endure torture than denounce their accomplices; such patriots sacrificed everything to the State's prosperity; it was beheld as a certain thing, that these attachments steadied the republic, women were declaimed against, and to entertain connections with such creatures was a frailty reserved to despots." Pederasty has always been the vice of warrior races. From Caesar we learn that the Gauls were to an extraordinary degree given to it. The wars fought to sustain the republic brought about the separation of the two sexes, and hence the propagation of the vice, and when its consequences, so useful to the State, were recognized, religion speedily blessed it. That the Romans sanctified the amours of Jupiter and Ganymede is well known. Sextus Empiricus assures us that this caprice was compulsory amongst the Persians. At last, the women, jealous and contemned, offered to render their husbands the same service they received from young boys; some few men made the experiment, and returned to their former habits, finding the illusion impossible. The Turks, greatly inclined toward this depravity Mohammed consecrated in the Koran, were nevertheless convinced that a very young virgin could well enough be substituted for a youth, and rarely did they grow to womanhood without having passed through the experience. Sextus Quintus and Sanchez allowed this debauch; the latter even undertook to show it was of use to procreation, and that a child created after this preliminary exercise was infinitely better constituted thanks to it. Finally, women found restitution by turning to each other. This latter fantasy doubtless has no more disadvantages than the other, since nothing comes of the refusal to reproduce, and since the means of those who have a bent for reproduction are powerful enough for reproduction's adversaries never to be able to harm population. Amongst the Greeks, this female perversion was also supported by policy: the result of it was that, finding each other sufficient, women sought less communication with men and their detrimental influence in the republic's affairs was thus held to a minimum. Lucian informs us of what progress this license promoted, and it is not without interest we see it exemplified in Sappho.

In fine, these are perfectly inoffensive manias; were women to carry them ever further, were they to go to the point of caressing monsters and animals, as the example of every race teaches us, no ill could possibly result therefrom, because corruption of manners, often of prime utility to a government, cannot in any sense harm it, and we must demand enough wisdom and enough prudence of our legislators to be entirely sure that no law will emanate from them that would repress perversions which, being determined by constitution and being inseparable from physical structure, cannot render the person in whom they are present any more guilty than the person Nature created deformed.

Note

1. The *Moralities*: "On Love."

Her Body, Mine, and His

Dorothy Allison

Frog fucking. Her hands on my hips; my heels against my ass, legs spread wide; her face leaning into my neck; my hands gripping her forearms. Her teeth are gentle. Nothing else about her is. I push up on the balls of my feet, rock my ass onto my ankles, reaching up for every forward movement of her thighs between mine. Her nipples are hard, her face flushed, feet planted on the floor while I arch off the edge of the bed, a water mammal, frog creature with thighs snapping back to meet her every thrust.

My labia swell. I can feel each hair that curls around the harness she wears. I imagine manta rays unfolding, great undulating labia-wings in the ocean, wrapping around the object of their desire. Just so my labia, the wings of my cunt. I reach for her with my hands, my mouth, my thighs, my great swollen powerful cunt.

Her teeth are set, hips are thrusting, shoving, head back, pushing, drawing back and ramming in. I laugh and arch up into her, curse her and beg her. My feet are planted. I can do anything. I lift my belly, push up even more. Fucking, fucking, fucking. I call this fucking. Call her lover, bastard, honey, sweetheart, nasty motherfucker, evil-hearted bitch, YOU GODDAMNED CUNT! She calls me her baby, her girl, her toy, her lover, hers, hers, hers. Tells me she will never stop, never let me go. I beg her. "Fuck me. Hard," I beg her. "You, you, you . . . Hard! Goddamn you! Do it! Don't Stop! Don't stop!"

jesus fucking christ don't stop.

don't stop.

I have been told that lesbians don't do this. Perhaps we are not lesbians? She is a woman. I am a woman. But maybe we are aliens? Is what we do together a lesbian act?

Paul took me out for coffee in New York and gave me a little silver claw holding a stone. "A little something for that poem of yours," he told me, "the one about the joy of faggots. I've been reading it everywhere." He drank herbal tea and told me about his travels, reading poetry and flirting with the tender young boys at all the universities—going on and on about how they kneel in the front row and look up to him—their lips gently parted and their legs pressed together. Sipping tea he told me. "They're wearing those loose trousers again, the ones with the pleats that always remind me of F. Scott Fitzgerald and lawn parties."

I drank the bitter coffee, admired his narrow moustache and told him how much I hate those blouson pants women are wearing instead of jeans. It's hell being an ass woman these days, I joked.

He started to laugh, called me a lech, looked away, looked back, and I saw there were tears in his eyes. Said, "Yes, those jeans, tight, shaped to the ass, worn to a pale blue-white and torn, like as not showing an ass cheek paler still. Said, "Yes, all those boys, those years, all the men in tight tight pants." Said, "Yes, those jeans, the pants so tight their cocks were clearly visible on the bus, the subway, the street, a shadow of a dick leading me on. Sometimes I would just lightly brush them, and watch them swell under the denim, the dick lengthening down the thigh." He stopped, tears all over his face, his hand on his cup shaking, coming up in the air to gesture, a profound sad movement of loss. "All gone," he whispered, the romantic poet in his suede professor's jacket. "I never do it any more, never. Never touch them, those boys, can't even imagine falling in love again, certainly not like I used to for twenty minutes a time on any afternoon."

I started to speak and he put his hand up. "Don't say it. Don't tell me I'm being foolish or cowardly or stupid or anything. I loved the way it used to be and I hate the fact that it's gone. I've not gone celibate, or silly, or vicious, or gotten religion, or started lecturing people in bars. It's those memories I miss, those boys on the street in the afternoon laughing and loving each other, the sense of sex as an adventure, a holy act."

He put his cup down, glared at it and then at me. Indignant, excited, determined. "But you still do it! Don't you? You dykes. You're out there all the time, doing it. Flirting with each other, touching, teasing, jerking each other off in bathrooms, picking each other up, and going to parties. Fucking and showing off and doing it everywhere you can. You are. Say you are, I know you are.

I said, "Yes." I said, "Yes." I lied, and said, "Yes." Paul, we are. "Yes."

She has named her cock "Bubba." Teases me with it. Calls it him, says talk to him, pet him. He's gonna go deep inside you. I start to giggle, slap

Bubba back and forth. Cannot take him too seriously, even though I really do like it when she straps him on. Bubba is fat and bent, an ugly pink color not found in nature, and he jiggles obscenely when she walks around the room. Obscene and ridiculous, still he is no less effective when she puts herself between my legs. Holding Bubba in one hand, I am sure that this is the origin of irony—that men's penises should look so funny and still be so prized.

She is ten years younger than me . . . sometimes. Sometimes I am eight and she is not born yet, but the ghost of her puts a hand on my throat, pinches my clit, and bites my breast. The ghost of her teases me, tells me how much she loves all my perversities. She says she was made for me, promises me sincerely that she will always want me. Sometimes I believe her without effort. Sometimes, I become her child, trusting, taking in everything she says. Her flesh, her body, her lust and hunger—I believe. I believe, and it is not a lie.

When I am fucking her I am a thousand years old, a crone with teeth, bone teeth grinding, vibrating down into my own hips. Old and mean and hungry as a wolf, or a shark. She is a suckling infant, soft in my hands, trusting me with her tender open places. Her mouth opens like an oyster, the lower lip soft under the tongue, the teeth pearls in the dim light. Her eyes are deep and dark and secret. She is pink, rose, red, going purple dark . . . coming with a cry and a shudder, and suddenly limp beneath my arms. I push up off her, and bite my own wrist. It is all I can do not to feed at her throat.

I drank too much wine at a party last fall, found myself quoting Muriel Rukeyser to Geoff Mains, all about the backside, the body's ghetto, singing her words "never to go despising the asshole nor the useful shit that is our clean clue to what we need." "The clitoris in her least speech," he sang back and I loved him for that with all my soul. We fed each other fat baby carrots and beamed at our own enjoyment.

"Ah, the Ass," Geoff intoned, "the temple of the gods." I giggled, lifted a carrot in a toast, and matched his tone. "And the sphincter—gateway to the heart."

He nodded, licked his carrot, reached down, shifted a strap, and inserted that carrot deftly up his butt. He looked up at me, grinned, rolled a carrot in my direction, and raised one eyebrow. "Least speech," I heard myself tell him. Then I hiked up my skirt and disappeared that carrot, keeping my eyes on his all the while. There was something about his expression, a look of arrogant conviction that I could not resist.

"Lesbians constantly surprise me," was all Geoff said, lining up a row of little baby carrots from the onion dip to the chips, pulling the dish of butter over as well. He handed me another carrot. I blinked, watched as he took another for himself. "I propose the carrot olympics, a cross-gender, mutually queer event." I started to laugh and he rolled buttery carrots between his palms. His face was full of laughter, his eyes so blue and pleased with himself they sparkled. "All right," I agreed. How could I not? I pulled up the hem of my skirt, tucked it into my waistband, took up the butter, and looked Geoff right in the eye. "Dead heat or one on one?"

FAGGOT! That's what he called me. The boy on the street with the baseball bat that followed me from Delores Park the week after I moved here. He called me a faggot. My hair is long. My hips are wide. I wear a leather jacket and walk with a limp. But I carry a knife. What am I exactly? When he called me a faggot I knew. I knew for sure who I was and who I would not be. From the doorway of the grocery at 18th and Guerrero, I yelled it at him. "Dyke! Get it right, you son of a bitch, I'm a dyke."

I am angry all the time lately, and being angry makes me horny, makes me itchy, makes me want to shock strangers and surprise the girls who ask me, please, out for coffee and to talk. I don't want to talk. I want to wrestle in silence. When I am like this, it is not sex I want, it is the intimacy of their bodies, the inside of them, what they are afraid I might see if I look too close. I look too close. I write it all down. I intend that things shall be different in my lifetime, if not in theirs.

Paul, Geoff, I am doing it as much as I can, as fast as I can. This holy act. I am licking their necks on Market Street, fisting them in the second-floor bathroom at Amelia's, in a booth under a dim wall lamp at the Box— coming up from her cunt a moment before the spotlight shifts to her greedy features. I have tied her to a rail in a garage down in Howard Street, let her giggle and squirm while I teased her clit. Then filled her mouth with my sticky fingers and rocked her on my hipbone till she roared. We have roared together. Everywhere I go the slippery scent of sweat and heat is in the air, so strong it could be me or the women I follow, the ones who follow me. They know who I am just as I know them. I have ripped open their jeans at the Powerhouse, put my heel between their legs at the Broadway Cafe, opened their shirts all the way down at Just Desserts, and pushed seedless grapes into their panties at the Patio Cafe. The holy act of sex, my sex, done in your name, done for the only, the best reason. Because we want it. I am pushing up off the bed into Alix's neck like a great cat with a gazelle in its teeth. I am screaming and not stopping, not stopping. Frog fucking, pussy creaming, ass clenching, drumming out, pumping in, I am doing it, boys and girls, I am doing it, doing it all the time.

The Philosopher-Villain

Pierre Klossowski
Translated by Alphonso Lingis

Sade's Critique of the Pervert, the Preliminary for the Creation of a Sadean Character

To arrive at his notion of integral monstrosity, and to create an original character type to represent it, Sade first had to undertake a critique of the pervert properly so-called.

The pathological sense of the term *perversion* is not to be found in Sade. His terminology in this domain remains that of moral psychology, of the *examination of conscience* developed by the casuists.

In *The 120 Days of Sodom* the different cases of perversion are designated as passions, advancing from *simple passions* to *complex passions*. The whole set forms that genealogical tree of vices and crimes already evoked in *Aline and Valcour*. The subject affected with perversity is termed vicious, depraved, a "lecherous criminal," indulging in "murders in debauchery." The recurring term that is closest to notions of modern pathology is the term *maniac*.

Indeed the pervert Sade observes and describes in *The 120 Days*—that is, in the narration of anecdotes about and episodes in brothels, which will serve as themes that the four principal characters will be able to vary and improvise on—the pervert thus observed and documented does behave essentially as a maniac. He subordinates his pleasure to the performing of one sole gesture.

The pervert is distinguished in the midst of ordinary licentious company by a specific *fixed idea*. This is not yet the "idea" in the sense that Sade will work out. In the context of what one now calls "libertinage" nothing is less free than the pervert's gesture. For if one means by libertinage the pure and simple propensity for orgy, as free of scruples as can be, the pervert's desire is sated only in the scrupulous taste for, and search for, a detail, sated only in a gesture that advances scrupulously to this detail. This kind of concern escapes those who deliver themselves over to outbursts of raw appetites.

The pervert pursues the performance of one sole gesture; it is done in a moment. The pervert's existence becomes the constant waiting for the moment in which this gesture can be performed.

The pervert as such can signify himself only by this gesture; the executing of this gesture counts for the whole of his existing. As a result, the pervert has nothing to say about his gesture that would be intelligible on the level of reciprocity between individuals. The pervert is both below and beyond the level of "individuals," which level constitutes a set of functions subordinated to the norms of the species. He presents an arbitrary subordination of the habitual life functions to one sole insubordinate function, a craving for an improper object. In this respect he is not yet at the level of the most crude individuals. But inasmuch as this insubordination of one sole function could only be concretized and thus become individuated in his case, he suggests to Sade's reflections a multifold possibility of the redistribution of the functions. Beyond individuals "normally" constituted, he opens a broader perspective, that of sensuous polymorphy. In the conditions of life of the human species, the pervert is one who can affirm himself only by destroying these conditions in himself. His existence consecrates the death of the species in him as an individual; his being is verified as a suspension of life itself. Perversion would thus correspond to a property of being, a property founded on the expropriation of life functions. An expropriation of one's own body and of others would be the meaning of this property of being.

The pervert—whatever the sort of perversion that affects him—seems to formulate by his gesture a definition of existence and a sort of judgment put on existence. For his gesture to verify in this way the fact of existing, it must correspond to a representation. What the gesture designates is not comprehensible in itself. Though it is produced in a sphere of license, the pervert's gesture can be understood only as diverted from its incomprehensible content. In this sphere one discerns in this gesture only a detour to the sating of an appetite, which then apparently finds the same solution as "normal" appetites.

In Sade's eyes, the perverse gesture must have a signification that gets obscured in the closed circuit of a particular case of perversion. The perverse gesticulation is a deaf-mute language. Deaf-mutes possess a memory of their code, but the pervert's gesture does not yet belong to any code. His perversity is its own memory. It is not so much the pervert that recalls his gesture so as to unleash it again as it is the gesture itself that recalls the pervert.

If this gesture signifies something intelligible, if it answers to a representation, if finally it is a judgment, this means that this gesture *interprets* something. To make it explicit, Sade will interpret the supposed interpretation of the pervert. He will do so on the basis of what he deciphers in the pervert's gesture.

An absolutely central case of perversity, which Sade will take as the basis for interpreting all others, as the principle of affinity in what will form integral monstrosity, is the case of sodomy.

This biblical term, consecrated by moral theology, covers an action that is not limited to homosexual practice. Homosexuality, which is not an intrinsic perversion, must be distinguished from sodomy, which is. Like heterosexual forms of behavior, homosexual practices admit of giving rise to an institution, as has been seen many times in the history of human societies. But sodomy is formulated by a specific gesture of countergenerality, the most significant in Sade's eyes—that which strikes precisely at the law of the propagation of the species and thus *bears witness to the death of the species in the individual*. It evinces an attitude not only of refusal but of aggression; in being the simulacrum of the act of generation, it is a mockery of it. In this sense it is also a simulacrum of the destruction that a subject dreams of ravaging on another of the same sex by a sort of reciprocal transgression of their limits. When perpetrated on a subject of the other sex, it is a *simulacrum of metamorphosis*, always accompanied by a sort of magic fascination. The sodomist gesture, transgressing the organic specificity of individuals, introduces into existence the principle of the metamorphosis of beings into one another, which integral monstrosity tends to reproduce and which universal prostitution, the ultimate application of atheism, postulates.

To decipher the pervert's gesture Sade will set up a code of perversion. Its key sign is revealed by the constitution of the sodomist gesture. For Sade, all things, close up or far off, gravitate about this gesture—the more absolute because of the mortal threat it poses for the norms of the species, and also because of a kind of immorality its repetition gives it; the more ambiguous in that it is conceivable only because of the existence of these norms; the more qualified for transgression, which can be brought about only through the obstacle constituted by these norms.

One can see that Sade in no way seeks to know the origin of perversion with respect to norms, nor to explain how these norms could become depraved in the individual. He takes perversion as a given (constitutional or congenital) phenomenon that, like everything manifested by nature, is to be explained rationally. This is why Sade introduces logically structured language into perversion, which is with respect to this language a structure apparently devoid of logic.

The code, now translated into words, will feel the effects specifically of the perverse gesture on which it will be structured, as also logical language will restructure the perverse gesture and shape Sade's written expression of it. What logical language, as the language of reason, will adapt to the coded gesture of the pervert is atheism, as an "act of good sense," of "common sense." On the other hand, what the perverse gesture thus coded introduces into the language of "common sense" is the nonlanguage of monstrosity, which subsists under this code. Here, between the rational language of norms and the anomaly, there is a sort of osmosis that Sade alone could carry off—atheism will become integral only inasmuch as perversion will set out to be rational, and only inasmuch as it will have set out to be rational will it become integral monstrosity.

Here Sade will inaugurate his original creation by a decisive masterstroke: to create the imaginative character corresponding to the type of the pervert he conceives, Sade takes the pervert out of conventional licentious society, and in particular out of the brothel. Here Sade breaks with the libertine literary tradition and introduces the theme of perversion into the depiction of common manners of life. Sade plants his character in the everyday world; he finds him in the midst of institutions, in the fortuitous circumstances of social life. Thus the world itself appears as the locus in which the secret law of the universal prostitution of beings is verified. Sade conceives the countergenerality to be thus already implicit in the existent generality, not in order to criticize institutions, but in order to demonstrate that of themselves institutions ensure the triumph of perversions.

Sade invents a type of pervert who speaks with his singular gesture *in the name of generality*. If this gesture counts as a judgement, the judgment is pronounced only at the moment when the notion of generality intervenes. For if the gesture is singular, undecipherable, it is so only with respect to the generality of gestures. The generality of gestures is one with speech. It is true that if his gesture has a meaning for the pervert, he has no need of speech to express what it signifies by itself. But the singular gesture of the pervert is precisely not the gesture formed in the medium of generality that may accompany speech, is sometimes substituted for the word, and sometimes even contradicts it. The singular gesture of the pervert *empties all content out of speech at once, since it is by itself the whole of existence for him.*

But once set up as Sade's character type, the pervert explicates his singular gesture in accordance with the generality of gestures. By the very fact that he speaks, he requires the reciprocity involved in persuasion and invokes his belongingness to the human species.

It follows that the moment he speaks, the singularity of the gesture that was the motive of his discourse is disavowed in that such singularity is taken to be proper to each one. The content of his gesture is then not singular, for in silence it still had no meaning—and now it acquires meaning in speech. If, as the pervert says, the singularity of his gesture is proper to each, he still has to show that each one can act in the singular way that he acts. Yet each time the pervert speaks, it is only because he is convinced of the contrary—that he is alone in acting in this way. From the very fact that he speaks, he is mistaken about the object of his demonstration and raises up the obstacle established in himself. For the pervert who speaks, the obstacle is not to be singular but to belong to generality in his own singularity. How can he overcome this obstacle? If he speaks, can he show, in the name of generality, that there is no generality and that the norms of the species have no real existence? If that were true, one could no longer say that this singularity is proper to each. How could one show that the norms do not exist? The singularity of the gesture is reestablished without its opaqueness being in any way cleared up. The only one to have to show the validity of his gesture, the pervert makes haste to perform that gesture.

The discourse of the pervert, owing to the very fact that it invokes one's adherence to common sense, remains a sophism in that one does not get away from the concept of normative reason. Persuasion can be brought about only if the interlocutor is in turn led to reject norms in himself. It is not by arguments that Sade's character can obtain the assent of his interlocutor but by complicity.

Complicity is the contrary of persuasion in accordance with universal understanding. Those who know themselves to be accomplices in aberration need no argument to understand one another. Yet the characters Sade depicts, despite the affinities they discover in one another through the unique gesture (of sodomy), owe it to themselves to proclaim each time the absence of a God, guarantor of norms, and thus to profess the integral atheism that they claim to bear witness to by their acts. But among themselves, the coded gesture is disengaged from the logically structured language that, as an oratorical precaution, is put over it, and the key sign that this gesture represents reappears in its true locus: the secret society. Here the gesture becomes a simulacrum, a rite, which the members of the secret society do not explain to one another otherwise than by the inexistence of the absolute guarantor of norms, an inexistence they commemorate as an event that one can represent only by this gesture.

In order for complicity with the pervert to emerge in the normal interlocutor, he *qua* "rational" individual must first be disintegrated. This is possible only by a leap of impulsion or of repulsion provoked in him by the word of the pervert.

How could the pervert recognize complicity in this "normal" interlocutor? By a gesture a subject makes in the generality of gestures, in contradiction to what he says. The interlocutor who rejects the sophism of the pervert makes a gesture that is in this sense contradictory, for, notwithstanding the disavowal it expresses, it physically, hence corporeally, bears witness to his own singularity—latent in him as in everyone. For if the rejection of the sophism is made in the name of the generality of common sense, what is the interlocutor, who at this moment has become a passive subject, defending himself against if not this latent singularity in himself? He can make this gesture of disavowal and defense only by thereby avowing his own singularity. The pervert lays in wait for this contradictory gesture, this reflex gesture, this corporeal, thus mute, gesture, which he deciphers in these terms: "Consider all the fatalities that unite us and see if Nature does not offer you a victim in my individual nature."

How Integral Monstrosity Constitutes a Space for Minds: The Ascesis of Apathy

For Sade, the sodomist act is the supreme form of the transgression of norms (which supposes their paradoxical maintenance); at the same time it must be the way to transgress the different cases of perversion and thus to constitute the principle of affinity among the perversions. For, like a callipygian test, this act suppresses the specific borders between the sexes and, according to Sade, constitutes the key sign for all perversions.

Having interpreted this act morally as a testimony of atheism and a declaration of war on the norms inherited from monotheism, Sade then projects perversion into the domain of thought. There integral monstrosity forms a sort of space for minds that communicate with one another by the mutual understanding of this key sign.

Whence the doctrinal character of Sade's work and of the didactic situations he lays out; whence above all the preliminary discrimination in effect in this singular academy by which the doctors of monstrosity recognize one another, distinguish themselves from the pervert shut up in his isolated case, and choose their disciples.

No candidate for integral monstrosity is recognized as qualified who has not conceived this way of acting as a profession of atheism; no atheist is recognized who is not capable of passing immediately into action. Once such disciples are chosen, they are subjected to a progressive initiation that culminates in the practice of an asceticism—the ascesis of apathy.

The practice of apathy, as Sade suggests it, supposes that what is named "soul," "consciousness," "sensibility," "the heart," are only diverse structures that the concentration of the same impulsive forces take on. These forces can set up the structure of an instrument of intimidation under the pressure of the institutional world or that of an instrument of subversion under the internal pressure of these forces, and they set up these structures in an instantaneous movement. But it is always the same impulses that intimidate us at the same time that they raise us up in revolt.

How does this intimidating insurrection or this insurrectional intimidation act in us? By the images that precede the acts, inciting us to act or to undergo, as well as by the images of acts committed or omitted that recur in us and make our conscience remorseful whenever the idleness of the impulses reconstitutes it. Thus the consciousness of oneself and of others is a most fragile and most transparent structure.

Since our impulses intimidate us in the form of "fear," "compassion," "horror," "remorse," by images of acts that have been or can be realized, it is the acts, whatever they be, that we must substitute for their repellent images whenever these images tend to substitute themselves for the acts and thus to forestall them.

Sade does not use the term *image* here; it is we who put this term in place of the terms *fear* and *remorse*, since his terms presuppose a representation of the act that has been or has to be committed. Yet an image intervenes not only in the form of remorse but also in the form of a project.

Reiteration is at first the condition required for the monster to remain on the level of monstrosity; if the reiteration is purely passionate it remains uncertain. For the monster to progress beyond the level that has been reached, he has first to avoid falling back shy of it; he can do so only if he reiterates his act in absolute apathy. This alone can maintain him in a state of permanent transgression. In putting this new condition on the candidate for integral monstrosity, Sade introduces a critique of the sensuous, and especially a critique of the primary benefit of transgression—the pleasure inseparable from the act.

How can the same act committed in intoxication, in delirium, be reiterated sober-mindedly? For there to be any possibility of reeffecting this act, must not the image which re-presents itself to the mind, however repellent it be, function as a lure, a promise of pleasure?

What Sade takes as understood beneath his maxim of the apathetic reiteration of an act we can reconstitute as follows: Sade recognizes the alternation of the diverse structures that the impulsive forces take on in their insurrectional and at the same time intimidating movement. But in one of these structures that these forces, individuated in the subject, have developed under the pressure of the institutional environment, that is, of norms, he seems also to have recognized a *self-consciousness*. This structure suffers variations and instability, though these become clear only after the event. Sometimes these forces put the subject *outside himself* and make him act *against himself;* they transgress the structure of consciousness and decompose it. Sometimes, in particular when they have made him act against himself, they recompose the (remembering) consciousness of the subject during his inaction; in this case these same forces are inverted. The inversion of the same forces constitutes the consciousness that *censors* the subject. What exercises censorship is the feeling the subject has that *being put outside of oneself* is a menace to the subject, who is dependent on the norms of the species. This censorship is exercised already in the very act of transgression and is the necessary motive for it. For Sade, moral conscience simply corresponds to an exhaustion of the impulsive forces (the "calm of the senses"); this state of exhaustion opens an interval in which the repellent image of the act committed represents itself in the form of "remorse."

In fact, from the first time the act was committed, it presented itself as a promise of pleasure because its image was repellent. And if now the reiteration of the same act is to "annihilate" conscience, it is because each time it is the same forces that, through their inversion, reestablish conscience. Inverted into a censorship, they will then provoke the act again.

Sade's formulation of apathetic reiteration is the expression of a deeper apprehension: Sade feels quite clearly that transgression is bound up with censorship, but the purely logical analysis that his formulation presupposes does not grasp the contradictory simultaneity of the two. Sade describes and decomposes this simultaneity into successive states: insurrection-transgression-intimidation; but intimidation and transgression remain in close interdependency, each provoking the other. This is why he wishes to eliminate intimidation by the apathetic reiteration of the act. He then apparently empties transgression of the benefit it would yield: pleasure.

The elimination of the sensuous element should then block the return of moral conscience. But in preventing its return, this ascesis seems to uproot the motive for transgression. The sodomist act (which forms the key sign of all perversion) has not significative act value save as a conscious transgression of the norms represented by conscience. The being cast *outside oneself* thus sought for is in practice equivalent to a disintegration of the conscience of the subject by means of thought. Thought must reestablish the primitive version of the impulsive forces, which the conscience of the subject has inverted. For the disciple who will practice the doctrine (not the pervert shut up in his own singular case), monstrosity is the zone of this being *outside oneself, outside conscience*; the monster can maintain himself in this zone only by the reiteration of the same act. The "voluptuous harshness" that, according to Sade, is its fruit is no longer something sensuous: the "harshness" presupposes a distinction between thought and moral conscience; the "voluptuousness" alludes to the ecstasy of thought in the representation of the act reiterated "in cold blood"—an ecstasy here opposed to its functional analogue, orgasm.

For the orgasmic moment amounts to a fall of thought outside its own ecstasy. It is this fall outside ecstasy that ends in the orgasm of the body's functions that Sade's character wishes to prevent through apathy. He knows that orgasm is but a tribute paid to the norms of the species and is thus a counterfeit of the ecstasy of thought. It is not enough that orgasm in the sodomist act is but a loss of forces, a *useless* pleasure; when the act, this time separate from orgasm, is reiterated, this useless pleasure is identified with the ecstasy of thought.

The apathetic reiteration of the act brings to light a new factor—number—and in particular the relationship between quantity and quality in sadism. The act passionately reiterated on the same object depreciates (or varies) in favor of the quality of the object. As the object is multiplied and as the number of objects depreciates them, so the quality of the act itself, reiterated in apathy, is the better affirmed. . . .

Androgyny in Sade's Representation

In Sade the principal types of perversion are generally represented only by men; the number of unnatural women found there do not really represent anomaly as such. Man, because traditionally he alone exercises reflection, represents the rational sex; he is also therefore alone called upon to give an account of reason. However monstrous, perverse, delirious a woman may be, she is never considered "abnormal," for it is written in the norms that by nature she lacks reflection, possesses no equilibrium or measure, and never represents anything but uncontrolled sensuous nature, more or less attenuated by a reflection prescribed by man. Indeed, the more monstrous or mad she is the more fully a woman she is, according to the traditional representation, always colored by misogyny. Yet she has resources that man will never possess, resources she shares with the pervert.

The integral monstrosity conceived by Sade has as its immediate effect the working of an exchange of the specific qualities of the sexes. The result is not just a simple symmetrical reversal of the schema of differentiation within each of the two sexes, with active and passive pederasty on the one side, lesbianism and tribadism on the other. In integral monstrosity as a didactic project for sensuous polymorphousness, the two representatives of the species, male and female, will in their relationship with one another face a twofold model. Each of the two sexes interiorizes this twofold model not only because of the ambivalence proper to each but also because of the embellishment Sade put on this ambivalence.

Man as the Sadean pervert type, although he apparently retains rational primacy, henceforth presents himself as the assertion of sensuous nature, but in the sense that sensuous nature offers itself to him in the perspective of the mind: the perspective of the imaginary. Perversion, we said at the beginning, insofar as it confirms the fact of its being by a suspension of the life functions, would correspond to a property of being whose meaning would be the expropriation of one's own body and the body of the other.

Integral atheism, the suppression of an absolute guarantor of norms, would corroborate this expropriation ideologically. For in abolishing the limits of the responsible and self-identical ego, it logically abolishes the identity of one's own body. In itself the body is the concrete product of the individuation of the impulsive forces realized according to the norms of the species. Since we are in fact dealing with denomination in language, we can say now that these impulsive forces speak to the pervert in these terms: The language of institutions has taken over this body, more particularly taken over what is functional in "*my*" body for the best preservation of the species. This language has assimilated the body that "I am" through this body to the point that "we" have been expropriated by institutions from the beginning. This body has only been restored to "me" corrected in certain ways—certain forces have been pruned away, others subjugated by language. "I" then do not possess "my" body save in the name of institutions; the language in "me" is just their overseer put in "me." Institutional language has taught "me" that this body in which "I am" was "mine." The greatest crime "I" can commit is not so much to take "his" body from the "other"; it is to break "my" body away from this "myself" instituted by language. What "I" gain by "myself" having a body, "I" immediately lose in reciprocal relations with the "other," whose body does not belong to "me."

The representation of having a body whose state is not that of one's own body is clearly specific to perversion. Although the pervert feels the alterity of the alien body, he feels much more the body of the other as being his own, and the body that normatively and institutionally is his he experiences as being really foreign to himself, that is, foreign to the insubordinate function that defines him. For him to be able to conceive the effect of his violence on the other, he must first inhabit the other. In the reflexes of another's body he verifies this foreignness; he experiences the irruption of an alien force within "himself." He is both within and without.

How can this be brought about? Not first, indeed not at all by recourse to violence that could go as far as murder, but rather by the imagination that precedes every violent act. The imaginary will have primacy over the rational. We can see this primacy of the imaginary in the representation of pleasure, where the impulse doubles up in the projecting of an image of itself, extending pleasure to organs excluded from the function of propagation and reducing the functional organs, thereby producing pleasure without utility.

The imagination prerequisite for the perverse gesture is constituted on correspondences between intensities that the functional reason had to exclude in order to set itself up on the basis of the subordination of the life functions of the species. While reason (logical language) expresses and also guarantees the equilibrium that the species found in its empirical habit, imagination apprehends the schemas of an illusory function in which the existing organ only serves to take the place of the absent—hence ideal— "functional" structure. In these schemas, the absence of the structure that is imagined is evidently the factor that excites; the existing structures offer a terrain in which outrage is inflicted in the name of something absent: the ideal structure of the androgynous one.

When the presence of this imaginary structure in the pervert and his disconnection from his body are strong enough for him to behave as a woman with his masculine counterpart, he will feel feminine passivity in himself more profoundly. He can then conduct himself *actively* only if he deals with his masculine counterpart as with a woman, or deals with a woman as with a boy.

Out of this latter case, Sade elaborates the synthetic simulacrum of the androgynous being—not a woman-man but a man-woman. He conceived Juliette as such a being. Contrary to man, more particularly contrary to the Sadean pervert, who, in integral monstrosity, functions as the definition of sensuous nature, the Sadean heroine sets forth reason. She makes use of reason only the better to recover possession of sensuous nature, which she originally and traditionally (according to the norms) is; she recovers possession of that sensuous nature only inasmuch as she progresses into insensibility. She presents the perfect example of the morality of apathy. This morality is one of the secret expedients of women, here set up as a doctrine; the morality of apathy is feminine frigidity methodically put to use. Finally, and most important, it is the Sadean heroine who carries atheism all the way to its integral affirmation, dissociating it from normative and anthropomorphic reason, freeing thought itself in the experimental sphere of monstrosity.

The abolition of norms, which this thought implies, is more important to the woman than to the pervert, in whom the norms exist only in a state of decay. As woman she remains subject to the norms at least organically, principally by reason of her fecundable condition. All the more then will she seek in apathy her line of conduct, the first effect of which is the extirpation of all maternal instinct. Here again we see verified the fact that the norms themselves (here corporeal norms) as institutions structure the forces that are to destroy them. "Normally" prostitutable, "normally" vicious, "normally" lesbian and tribade, it is again reason, here "good sense," that dictates to her that she be all this coldly. In learning to undergo coolly the perverse acts committed on her own body, she develops the virile energy of a consummate callipygian.

Thus Juliette presents herself to the Sadean pervert as the simulacrum of what the sodomist act designates. In this figure formed by the reversal of sensuous passivity into active intellection, the preeminent act of transgression finds the image complementary to it.

Towards an Irrecuperable Pederasty

Guy Hocquenghem
Translated by Chris Fox

At the end of the spring of 1972, just a year after its creation, the very success of the FHAR (Front Homosexual d'Action Révolutionnaire) began to fossilize a bit. The "miracle" which united libidinal and militant ties within groups and general meetings had ended. Little by little the militants withdrew into circles of friends or into isolated research groups. The general meeting of the FHAR was turning into nothing but a chance to cruise, so much so that it became completely unacceptable to the administration of the Ecole des beaux-arts where the meeting was held. The "Thursday meeting" became a huge public toilet, and ended up being shut down by the police.

By recalling the words of Lautréamont, this text intends to direct the movement toward goals other than the self-affirmation of homosexuality, so that it can take up the role of an unclassifiable inquisitor of heterosexuality.

. . . But in the meantime we wanted to prevent the fatal error of creating a sodomite movement resembling the Zionist movement and of rebuilding Sodom. The minute they arrived, the sodomites would leave the city so they wouldn't seem to be a part of it. . . . They would only go to Sodom at moments of desperate need, when their city was empty, at those times when hunger makes the wolf come out of the woods. . . .
—Marcel Proust

The ones who are *ashamed* reject and dismiss with the greatest care anything which might make them known for what they are. What is more, since they dress like everyone else, there is no way to reveal them. . . .
—Canler (former Parisian Chief of Safety, 1797–1865) *Memoirs*,
"The Typology of Homosexuals"

Homosexuality is traditionally linked directly to feelings of shame. At the end of the nineteenth century and the beginning of the twentieth, homosexuality was accepted only with shame. That, indeed, is the deeper meaning of Proust's claim. For Proust, the very idea of a homosexual "movement" contradicts homosexual experience. For the general public, homosexuality exists only in the press's revelations of a scandalous, secret and debauched underground. To this day, there has been no other state of mind toward homosexuality than the one which we see in the great morality trials of fifty years ago. An old high-society fag like the gossip columnist Peyrefitte worthily preserves this tradition of half-truths and avowals whispered to the already initiated. It is impossible to know whether this snake in the grass of the gossip columns is just a man with some casual homosexual contact, for instance, in a boarding school or in a barracks. The only people who have a real awareness of their homosexuality are those who become ashamed of it, not so much because of real obstacles (their families, the workplace, the police) as because, in capitalist society, the homosexual is *naturally* ashamed.

The spurt of feelings and ideas and the expression of a genuine willingness to fight which accompanied the creation of the FHAR in April 1971 (just the way it happened in the United States when similar movements were created) are explained first of all by this situation.

We are a Social Scourge

This veritable explosion was summed up in the slogan "We're homosexual and we're proud of it" and in the protest we shouted out in the demonstrations on May Day against being labeled a "social scourge" (homosexuality was declared to be a "social scourge" in 1960 under the sponsorship of that unmentionable legislator Mirguet). Four fundamental moves make up this explosion. It was directed, first of all, to others (to "straight people"). The first text in issue 12 of *Tout* was an "Address to those who consider themselves straight," with a theme which was to become the leitmotiv of the FHAR: You think you're not a part of it, but nevertheless you are our oppressors; you will not be able to do anything for us so long as you stay the way you are. In other words, the opposite of shame's self-repression is first of all to direct the fight against others by appealing to their good conscience.

On the other hand, what needed to be said to other homosexuals was this: you won't be able to admit to yourselves fully that you're homosexual unless you attack "straight" society as a whole. The first tract we delivered

to the mailboxes of homosexuals founded our unity as a homosexual movement on the refusal of a situation in which "we accept the hetero thought-
police propaganda which provides the conventional image of male and
female; we play our social roles in our workplaces. Face to face with the
heteropolice, we don't fit in."

These two moves, in a way, constitute the first spring which made the
FHAR pop out of its box with a suddenness that astonished all of the
elementary school leftists. To those initial moves we quickly added two
others, moves whose planning depended, first, on the existence of a political
terrain already cleared by the MLF (Mouvement Libération des Femmes),
and second, on the large number of ex-militants from leftist groups who
participated in the creation of the FHAR.

The homosexual revolt takes as its target the patriarchal capitalist family.
It proclaims itself straightaway to be on the side of women. Homosexuals
know that they take their own pleasure outside the system. Quite simply,
their sperm won't serve to create the reserve labor force of a society eager
to increase its number of workers and consumers. They come to realize
very quickly that they are traitors in the eyes of straight society—they have
the physical characteristics which are supposed to show a man's superiority
(the penis) and they are scorned, like women, to whom they know they
will be assimilated by "manly" men. They are therefore not unaware of
how things stand with sexual roles, and the importance of those roles to
society. Their situation is as paradoxical as the thesis of Valerie Solanas,
that notorious "flaming madwoman" who claims to have cut off men's
balls, and who explains that men oppress women by imparting to them
their own character traits. Of the two, she says, men are the weaker,
the more effeminate, the more treacherous, the more unstable, the more
dishonest, the more unfaithful, and so on.

The conception that the FHAR has of its own actions relies as a result
on an absolute right to self-contradiction, on the primacy of lived experiences, on the disorderly house of the general meetings and on the psychodra-
mas within the smaller groups. The theoretical bases remain more or less
explicit, but in general, they amount to this, that homosexuality is the
commonest thing in the world; only "society" represses it. Compare what
Freud has to say on the matter:

> Psychoanalysis considers that a choice of an object independently of its
> sex—freedom to range equally over male and female objects—as it is
> found in childhood, in primitive states of society and early periods of
> history, is the original basis from which, as a result of restriction in one
> direction or the other, both the straight and the inverted types develop.

Thus from the point of view of psychoanalysis the exclusive sexual interest felt by men for women is also a problem that needs elucidating and is not a self-evident fact based upon an attraction that is ultimately of a chemical nature.[1]

Our Assholes are Revolutionary

Repressed homosexual desire plays an important role in the repressive institutions of bourgeois society (the church, the army, and so on). The development of the aggressivity hidden by the mask of free competition, the valorization of virility as a sign of superiority, both belong to a civilization based on force. Homosexual experience properly understood is based on weakness. American homosexuals were able to denounce the Vietnam War as one of the forms of this cult of masculine violence. Marcuse himself was able to see the relationships between a refusal of the cult of virility, a certain feminization of American youths and American radical movements (the antiwar movement, the student movement, the women's movement and so on). Freud puts forth as a hypothesis towards the explanation of what he calls the social impulses of homosexuals that "the behavior towards men in general of a man who sees in other men potential love objects must be different from that of a man who looks upon other men in the first instance as rivals in regard to women."[2]

Let us note, in passing, that in Germany, for example, the defense of homosexuals by Hirschfeld and his committee of humanists was aimed above all at their social rehabilitation. Let us also remark that the community of men (all of humanity) is by instinct assimilated to the community of males, which is, after all, quite normal since responsibilities, such as those of politics, are reserved for men and forbidden to women. It is, moreover, perfectly true that the social relations of homosexuals concern other men far more than women. We will return to this.

Men, at least those who are proclaimed as such physiologically, have no other relationships with other men than those of rivalry, in regard to what has been proclaimed as the sole object of their sexual activity, that is, women. This is as true for their relationships in the bosom of their families with their fathers and their brothers as it is in political associations with their comrades. In the given framework of this male society, the homosexual inverts these relationships and finds himself displaced.

Jealousy (as much as the generalized paranoia in our society, with everything it supposes, such as relationships of possession and ownership) should be considered in relation to the self-repression of homosexuality.

Freud (again) speaks of the link between paranoid jealousy and the subject's protection against his homosexual desire toward his best friend who is fucking his wife. This can be expressed in that man's point of view with the formula: "I don't love him, she does."[3]

The asshole remains the one shameful part of the bourgeois body. It does not benefit from the penis's ambivalence. Even a heterosexual like Bataille felt this way. The anus is the private part par excellence of the bourgeois body. It is to the anus that this famous "sublimation" applies, which is, after all, only a way to deny any direct sexual implications to the political arena. "You sublimate, and then it is no longer your ass which is in question, because your ass is private, and it's nobody's business but yours. It has no place in socially admissible desire." Now, "it is not the anal which is meant for sublimation, but rather it is sublimation itself which is anal."[4] The use of the asshole is the touchstone of the conflict between the private and the public (the political). The practical discovery of revolutionary homosexuals is that the private is only a closet and that the political is only one libidinal expression among many. In other words, our assholes are neither shameful nor private; they are public and revolutionary.

Homosexual penetration, namely ass fucking, appears to be a two-way practice allowing the overstepping of roles, even if that isn't always the case in reality. The fact that submissive homosexuality involves a temptation to imitate the heterosexual penetrative relationship (a relationship of domination) changes nothing in the simple fact that it is, all the same, one man whom another man is fucking. Shit will never be like menstrual blood, and a proof of the existence of a true anal orgasm will not change the male homosexual into a woman. The theoretical impossibility of making a male homosexual into a woman without the threat of a renunciation of the inherent discriminatory value of the penis forces the bourgeois citizen to adopt the old reactionary theory of a third sex, which allows him to distinguish himself completely from homosexuals. For most people, homosexuals belong to a different race from "masculine" men.[5] As for the rest, those who tend more toward the left, homosexuals are divided into men and women, into pitchers and catchers. In that way they return to the traditional and fundamental division, and from then on they can charge homosexuals with a criminal love of the phallus. Some leftists, in fact, have not failed to reproach the FHAR for this. Now, it is false that an apparently masculine man's desire is directed naturally toward a woman or, lacking that, toward a homosexual who is sufficiently feminine to act as a substitute. We have all had the opportunity to observe that some effeminate men are heterosexual and that sometimes a masculine appearance hides a disposition to "passivity" in sexual matters. "When you say 'masculine,'" says Freud, "you usually mean 'active,' and when you say 'feminine,' you usually mean 'passive.' It seems to me to serve no useful purpose and adds nothing to our knowledge."[6]

This attitude is based upon the assimilation of object-choice to the sexual character of the desiring subject, an assimilation denounced by Freud[7] but which still allows people lazily to suppose that natural certainties determine the two roles: Men love women, so effeminate men must love masculine men, and so on. By making object-choice depend on these given roles, the variety of choices is closed, desire is canalized, whereas it goes in many directions, and obligatory analogies are drawn (the one fucked is effeminate, the one fucking, masculine, and so on).

We are not saying that none of this exists in reality, any more than we are saying that jealousy has no place in the homosexual universe. We are simply saying that these obligatory analogies (between object choice and sexual nature, between sexual relationships and jealousy) are only obligatory for a society which bases its sexual activity on the primacy of heterosexual relationships and the repression of homosexual relationships.

The heterosexual vision of a homosexual world teaches us that, if they cannot completely eliminate that world, they can, at least, attempt to imagine it according to the best model available, their own. Indeed, the heterosexual world does admit the existence of a homosexual world. But leftists should stop waving that "truth" in our faces as a proof of our possible social integration, and should instead see it for what it is, a collective mutilation.

It is clear then that the position of the conscious homosexual cannot be reduced to that of a revolutionary who happens to be homosexual. Otherwise we all would have joined in with the struggles of leftist movements, and even of the socialist PSU. That is why learning that the Trotskyites have, in all probability, included the right to homosexuality in their charter is good news for those, like me, who have had some problems with the Trotskyites, even though the same news makes the majority of us burst out laughing. It is needless to point out yet again that we are fundamentally not struggling for the recognition of our right to a sexual practice just like any other. If any of the above is valid, we can deduce that we are impelled by a concrete philosophical stance: that of a refusal of any normality, even one dressed up in leftist clothing. If the FHAR did in fact place itself on the fringes of the Left since it contests large, organized groups, it was not simply to obtain a modification of the status of these groups.[8] All of this to inform the readers of *Partisans*, a journal which, as everyone knows, is situated in the political ambit of the revolutionary left. We have tried to define the attitude of the revolutionary homosexual as a vision or as a homosexual view of the world. Unfortunately, these terms are already marked ideologically; we are not disciples of the philosopher Dilthey. It might therefore be better to speak of an attitude of refusing all worldviews, although such a refusal is still not enough. We wish to characterize ourselves through a permanent displacement (which transcribes what we all experience) and through a continual demolition of the images which form the basis for social conditioning.[9]

Some Justifications

What I have just sketched out sums up what was being said about the FHAR at the time. If I write "what was being said," of course it's not that people are not saying it anymore, it's just that I feel more or less outside the meetings where such things would be said today.

By taking up point for point the principal themes of the FHAR such as I have presented them, we will attempt to see how a system of thought which finally led to a set of impoundings and prohibitions was progressively instituted; how, progressively, in relation to women, to ourselves and to straight people, we have defined ourselves as a sort of homosexual "counternorm." But let's make it quite clear that I'm not interested in watering things down and saying, for example, that we went too far. . . . I'm interested in seeing why the FHAR, once it promoted and organized its fantasy, if not its reality, elaborated its theories in such a justificatory direction. Its very foundation was conceived as a privileged grouping of homosexuals, posing problems of inclusion and exclusion bordering on paranoia.

Let's take two examples. The text "Fags and the Revolution," which became the most commonly accepted point of reference within the FHAR as well as outside of it, is thought of as a sort of manifesto for our movement. Now, we can hardly attribute to journalistic convention the fact that it is presented in the form of "responses to objections." I am not saying that this text is without interest; on the contrary, it has been quite useful for us. I am, however, attempting to see why and at what moment the thought of the FHAR stumbled on the obstacle it was becoming. Responding to objections, in fact, presumes that one possesses a certain amount of objectivity and that the arguments put forth have a general enough validity that the real problem would be to force one's opponents (in this case, the Left) to agree.

Let's consider another text, "Some Reflections on Lesbianism as a Revolutionary Position." I would take as the pivotal point of its argument the following sentence: "Our homosexual relationships are, *by definition*, the negation of certain social relationships which are constitutive of patriarchy and capitalism." The constitutive bisexuality of men and women was our point of reference, leading us, finally, to the nature, as it were, of the sexual individual, backed by the support of Freud as our authority. Indeed, it is *by definition* that we were right, and the only problem from then on was answering objections. Moreover, I don't think it is by pure chance that advanced leftists were so appreciative of "Fags and Revolution." In some ways they found in it, to some degree, the style of their own addresses, in which concepts have exchange value and become tokens of recognition.

The contradictions which led to the FHAR's obstacles were tied in with the relationships between homosexuals and the Left, and not, as people were saying, those between homosexuality and the Revolution. The FHAR, in the beginning, adopted the following remark made by the psychiatrist André Morali-Daninos: "If homosexuality were to acquire a semblance of approval, even in theory, if it was regarded, even a little bit, outside the framework of pathology, we would quickly come to the abolition of the heterosexual couple and the family which are the basis of Western society."[10] Within our homosexual optic, by inverting the terms of this proposition, we found, of course, our position among leftists. Our ideological universe was thereby restricted. The first victim was our relations with women in the FHAR.

Farewell to Dykes

It's no secret to anyone that women had a predominant role in the creation of the FHAR, nor that, on the other hand, they participated very little in the working out of the ideas and writings which I have just discussed (we realized through the theoretical positions taken by the FHAR how poorly defined the place accorded to women really was). Nor was it, finally, any secret that women have almost completely given up on the general meetings of the FHAR. Some of these women responded to the article "Fags and the Revolution" and one in particular wrote "must you, implicitly, speak only to men just because you are men? And why, moreover, would you speak only to heterosexuals, since you are, after all, homosexuals like we are? Why refute their arguments? Why justify them? Or maybe you have been drawn as revolutionaries to discussions with other, heterosexual revolutionaries?"

I cite this text because it is important to understand the disengagement of women and the isolation of men within the FHAR. The MLF inspired our movement as it was beginning, and we might not have gotten started at all if the women had not begun before us. We copied their style and their mode of operation. We called ourselves brothers and sisters; we wanted peace among ourselves and war on everyone else; we drew up our manifesto for "The 343 sluts who were fucked up the ass by Arabs"; we held our general meetings according to the same principles and in the same places. We identified ourselves with the MLF even in our relationships with the Left, at least at first.

But still, even from our first moves, our relations with the MLF showed a curious mixture of imitation and independence. At each general meeting the situation got worse. On May Day, Mother's Day and at last November's demonstration, the debate became more and more paralyzed.[11] "What has the MLF decided to do?" "Let's not wait for the women to begin before we act," it was argued. "Let's not unquestioningly follow their decisions," and so on. We ended up arguing over absurd questions: "Should lesbians join the FHAR or the MLF?" "Is it possible to be a member of both?" and so on. Faced with a debate which came up again and again without any conclusion, lesbians were forced to keep answering by repeating their double status as homosexuals and as women. The more the FHAR defined itself subconsciously as a closed group, the more lesbians became representatives of the MLF within the FHAR, ambassadors representing one power in the court of another. Along this path which led from identification to active opposition, some homosexuals of the FHAR worked out a frenzy of "antigynocratic" measures which finally got them expelled. Even though these measures were unacceptable, they are understandable, not only because of a return to a "phallocratic" nature, but especially because of the impossibility of accepting within one group formed in the image of a second elements from that second group which were both foreign and familiar. Oedipus driven out in one direction returned from the other.

The MLF split the world of the Left in two: on the one side were leftists whose sexual life did not escape the criticisms of the MLF; on the other were the homosexuals, the only leftists whom women did not ask to renounce their ways. I see in this one of the major reasons why we managed to avoid a complete break with them. We had the immense advantage of driving the men of the Left who were so proud of their women crazy; indeed, we were suddenly transformed in their eyes into a privileged group with access to secret meetings from which all males were supposed to be barred. And, besides, we were doing the women a considerable favor by allowing them to insist that they were not systematically hostile to all men.

I once announced that we had finally found the form of true love, an egalitarian form which barred the horrible penetrative relationship, a form which was libidinal and not sexual in the bourgeois sense of the word. I am quite afraid today that it was more a question of a kind of friendly complicity completely dependent on a system of relationships between the Left and women of which we had no grasp. The pleasure derived from this situation came much more from a desire for vengeance on other men than from a real fondness for women. In the mechanics of this new arrangement in which we were an important cog, our position was only of value in comparison to that of other men on the Left.

Today, it is more or less certain that, even if they came together around the obstacles they wished to bring down, the homosexual movement and the lesbian movement are built on totally different ideological bases. The women's movement remains valid, especially in the sense of community which women establish among themselves, a community which is best realized when, among lesbians, the male oppressor is at least provisionally excluded from his dominant position. The women's movement, apparently, needs to put itself in a position of relative strength with respect to male society. The importance that they placed on the idea "love among us and war upon men" just proves my point.

Let's turn to that sense of love. From the beginning (and this caused some heated discussions with women), the FHAR made itself known as a sexual movement: we were interested in sex, we were only interested in sex, some women said, as if love and human relations meant nothing to us. I tend to think that is right. There is little or no place in a homosexual movement for a psychology of relationships based on a "truly humane love." If there is an antihumanist movement, then it is this one, in which the sex machine, with its plugs and connections, is just about our only interest. As we have been reproached again and again, we are orgasm machines.

Along the Way: From Autonomy to Closing

Along with incontestable successes in the fossilized political world of the Leninists, we all noticed a certain flagging of energy in what were called the autonomous movements (the MLF, the FHAR, the youths' FLJ and so on). A new form of praxis was founded on the juncture of irreducibly particular situations in these movements, those of women, youths and homosexuals. The working principle was to reach a revolutionary universal principle starting from particular experiences. This new idea caused a complete upheaval in a political world founded for the most part on putting forward general and "true" political theories, no matter where they came from (from Maoism, from Trotskyism and so on). In this new juncture, the place of the FHAR was all the more distant because its starting point was so particular; it was a political world which resembled an inverted pyramid, since the point was to overturn an order of things in which we were considered as the extreme of marginality. Even if the effects of our movement upon the ideological world of Parisian revolutionaries exceeded our wildest expectations, and that *is* our main achievement, in one year of existence the internal situation and realities of our movement got worse and worse. Some of our comrades were obsessed with the fear that the ferociously autonomous movements within our new cultural revolution would explode into so many contradictory "isolationisms." Without going quite that far, one could say that the speed with which we uttered our rallying cries very quickly locked us into a perpetual repetition where almost everything was already said, and where all that was left was to apply it. We affirmed our existence so quickly that we spared many of those who joined us the trouble of discovering themselves. This undoubtedly explains the vast split between the Parisian group and those of the rest of France. Our thought, in fact, became normative. A homosexual credo was thus established.

Once again, it is the outcome rather than the content of our beliefs that poses the problem. We saw that while our chant of "Plum, plum, tra la la, the fags are here" was surprising in May, it was expected at our every appearance by November. We lost a part of our power to disturb others (straight people) because they knew beyond the shadow of a doubt that the gulf between them and us was making us repeat the same lines over and over. Now that is obviously only true for those we actually reached with the propaganda, even indirectly, and it comes more from a dangerous tendency than from a definitive situation. Sometimes, however, it happens that we no longer take into account what is around us, either through a complete and systematic contempt for nonhomosexuals, or because it becomes tiring to repeat once again what we have already said so many times. When someone intervenes during a meeting, during a lecture or during any sort of gathering, he shouldn't have to "bear witness to our revolutionary homosexuality." Instead, he should explain the relationships that people can have with their own homosexuality, rather than having the very word "homosexual" be the definitive and crucial point of his intervention.

If we admit that the present crisis of the Left has much to do with its institutionalization and its transformation into a movement outside of people's daily lives, we see that that crisis has not spared us either. For us, particularly, it should be less an issue of enrolling people under our banner and teaching them right away the results we have come to, than of leading them to a way of thinking which would, finally, make them put their daily lives in question.

The Weakening of our Desire

I reminded my reader as I began that, like the MLF, we declared peace among ourselves and war on straight people. That is what I am questioning in part today. In the first two or three months, a great joy was expressed in the meetings of the FHAR; that joy came from the discovery of the multiplicity of our desires: anyone could desire anyone else and, for the first time, our libido was expressed without hypocrisy and was joined to a hope for collective liberation. Many of us made love with each other. That, too, has abated: those who come to cruise the FHAR often are only those people who remain outside of the group's project. Now, we hardly desire anyone within the group at all.

We wanted to do what the women had done, looking for the satisfaction of our desires within the group, the phallocrats be damned. But our desire finds sustenance everywhere.[12] Making love to someone is also a wish to change him. We underestimate that wish when we reduce homosexual desire simply to the desire to sleep with other men.

We wished to toss into the trash the weighty contexts, which from Proust to Gide, as I mentioned above, burden homosexuality, without seeing how deeply they marked us. We thought that it was enough to reverse the terms, so that what was shameful could become a source of pride. In that way, in our will to quickly construct a "counterideology," we even neglected to examine how the situation which was already available offered us possibilities of breaking away. Homosexual relationships cannot be reduced to amoral relationships which society would prevent from being made public. Before the creation of the FHAR, I used to see this complicity between two homosexuals out together as they would secretly point out to one another a boy who was a mutual object of their desire, even though for me more often than not he was a *confirmed* heterosexual.[13] We believed all too quickly that, by analyzing this complicity, it would be transformed into love. I think that our desire must be produced as scandalous in the reading of it; that is what gives it its subversive value. Proust considers homosexuals an accursed race. He sees in them a monstrous deviation since, he says, their desire can be admitted neither to their closest friends nor to their relatives. The homosexual, according to him, remains at the heart of an irresolvable contradiction which makes him desire those whom he knows to be contemptuous of him. This unhappy conception of a submissive homosexuality is not merely the sign of a social oppression which it would suffice to expose in order to destroy it. At the extreme, we might say, because we are proud to be homosexuals, we desire, more often than not, those who are contemptuous of us, the phallocrats. Far from seeing in that desire an irremediable weakness which we would do best to overcome, I believe our desire is our best weapon. We desire what is different from us, what we can no longer be or no longer wish to be, and we do not want to convert anyone, because then our desire would burn out in a universe consisting only of "flaming queens."

We have been trapped in a role of shame which we transformed into a role of pride. Such a change is only gilding the bars of our cage. Our desire does not force us to dream of establishing some kind of homosexual normality corresponding to "hetero" normality. Many of our comrades in the FHAR have come to avoid our initial slogan of "we are proud to be fags." Deep down, we are a bit ashamed to be proud of it. That kind of pride damages us, too, since it lets us believe that we are liberated by reversing the values of the straight world term for term, something our desire tells us is false. Our desires continuously call for new sustenance (hence our notorious sexual "instability"). The whole world is not too wide for us: from Arabs to Blacks, from young street things to swingers, sometimes even with women. We need gay bars as well as schools, factories as well as public toilets, the streets as well as our meeting places. Our withdrawal into ourselves stands in the way of these free associations of desire that make us who we are. We even need the supposed "straights," not so much to "convert" them (how bored we would all be in a purely homosexual world) as to put our tongues in their mouths, and our assholes, our dicks, our hands and our feet. . . .

We are not liberated homosexuals proud to be homosexual. Our homosexuality is not a revolutionary value that we must spread throughout the world, but a permanent state of questioning norms. A world where freedom of desire can be realized remains to be built.

Notes

1. *Three Essays on Sexuality* (Standard Edition), VII, p. 145n.

2. Freud, "Some Neurotic Mechanisms in Jealousy, Paranoia and Homosexuality," (Standard Edition, XVIII).

3. Freud, "Some Neurotic Mechanisms in Jealousy, Paranoia and Homosexuality."

4. Deleuze and Guattari, *Anti-Oedipus* (trans. Chris Fox).

5. "Indeed, what is important is that no one force us to hear the voice of the guilty man himself, that carnal and troubling voice which seduces the young, that breathless voice which mumbles through pleasure, that crude voice which kisses and tells. The faggot must remain an object, a flower, an insect, an inhabitant of ancient Sodom or faraway Uranus, . . . anything really, anything but my neighbor or me. For we *must* choose: if every man is every man, this pervert must be no more than a pebble or else he'll be me." J.-P. Sartre, *Saint Genet, Actor and Martyr* (trans. Chris Fox).

6. Freud, "Femininity" (Standard Edition, XXII).

7. In "The Psychogenesis of a Case of Female Homosexuality" (Standard Edition, XVIII).

8. Large, organized groups are opposed "libidinally" to small groups; the former represent an official, political stage of desire, while the latter (and in some ways the FHAR) represent a molecular stage of desire.

9. For a further treatment of this question, see "For a Homosexual Worldview" in *Statements against normality* published by the FHAR through Editions du Champ libre. The text is certainly open to criticism, but its essential position is that the "libidinal" is everywhere in the political, and the political is everywhere in the "libidinal." This is not through sublimation, but by a direct connection. The struggle of the Palestinians, for example, would be linked "libidinally" to our homosexual struggle.

10. *Sociology of Sexual Relations*, P.U.F., Collection "Que sais-je" (trans. Chris Fox).

11. This refers to the period between May 1970 and November 1971.

12. This is particularly true in our relationships with minors, which we have not sufficiently discussed, and which, moreover, is nearly the only aspect of homosexuality expressly forbidden by law. It would be necessary to study the social role of this prohibition on minors and, even more importantly, on prepubescent boys; we would need to analyze the exclusion of homosexuality from education, less by actual prohibition than by the reduction of homosexual experiences to unfortunate accidents caused by ignorance which will disappear of their own accord once mature "genitality" is reached. Schoolteachers do not so much tell kids not to be fags as they tell them that fags do not exist, that it is immature and needs to be outgrown.

13. Some women pointed out quite correctly that our May slogan, "Straights, unclench your butts" was never anything but the expression of a desire to reverse the relations of force, quite the opposite of our sexual desire. It was a way to avenge ourselves by repaying our humiliation in kind.

Reclaiming Sodom

Rocky O'Donovan

In the past, I have been deeply envious of lesbians because of one simple but vital factor in their existence; they have Lesbos—actual space which they can dream of and re-create and hope toward. All us Queer Boys are not as fortunate. I did not think that we had any such space/time to claim as our own. And then one day, the Goddess sent me a very distinct message. She told me that I should start calling myself a Sodomite-American. At first I balked, but then it grew on me after I had spent some time thinking about what it means to be a sodomite (and what good company I'm in!). And now I have realized that Sodom is potent/important space for us Queer Boys to (re)claim for our own de-signs.

There are four main mythologies concerning the destruction of the twin cities, Sodom and Gomorrah: the original myth found in the Hebrew scriptures (Genesis 19), other biblical interpretations of it, then the Momo/ Christian* interpretation(s) of it, and my own Queer mythology concerning Sodom.

The myth in Genesis describes how two "holy" men came from god to check out Sodom. Once they entered the town, they were surrounded by a bunch of men who wanted to gang-rape these two divine dudes. This guy named Lot offered his two daughters to the sexually ravenous crowd so they would not rape the "holy" men, and while they dick-ered over the two daughters, the "holy" men struck the people blind and the holy men and Lot's family made their escape from Sodom. Once outside Sodom, the "holy" men brought god's wrath down on it and Lot's wife looked back on her town, being turned into a phallic pillar of salt, as a reminder of the power of the Almighty Penis.

Other biblical writers interpreted Sodom's destruction to have been the result of the Sodomites' inhospitably to visiting strangers; thou shalt not make that which is different from yourself unwelcome and of no value.

---

*Momo = Mormon

247

Too bad the Momo/Christians didn't get that message out of the story. Instead, in the Momo/Christian myth, Sodom was a huge city (forget the fact that Sodom was probably nothing more than a small hamlet) full of depraved, psychotic, sybaritic queer men. God, in his justified anger, sent the two angels to destroy it merely because of our existence in that city. Joe Smith added his own little twist to the Christian myth by saying that there were actually three "holy" men who destroyed Sodom—obviously mirroring the trinity of the hetero/male godhead. And if god destroyed us abominations back then, he will do so again (i.e., AIDS). Of course, I am totally confused as to what gang rape of two or three angels (of unspecific gender?) has to do with modern, con/Sensual homosexuality. Go figure.

But I want to (re)claim Sodom all for our very own, so I speak a new myth. I want the tiny hamlet to be Queer Space—and really, it is ours whether we want it or not. So let's take it, claim it, speak it; enough of our blood has been spilled in its name to warrant ownership of that landscape several million times over. And all because that nasty old god hates us Queer Boys—would rather kill us than look at us. So that's new? That god, rabid with his own omnipotence and made in the image of the power-hungry, jealous, White, bourgeois, straight, able-bodied male, is no friend (let alone god) of mine.

Let Sodom be the symbol of what heterosexism and homophobia do to us, like the holocaust has become for the Jewish people. It's an interesting coincidence that "Sodom" and "holocaust" are literally synonyms—they both mean "burnt" in Hebrew and Greek, respectively. Burned, burns, will burn, all us little faggots, faggots for the fire of that god—our burning flesh is sweet incense to his nostrils. That power-hungry, White, jealous heterosexual, bourgeois, able-bodied, male god lives to burn us up and that burns me up, incenses me! All just because we don't fit in with (god)awful plan—all because we maybe would rather "dress and keep the garden" (namely interior designers, faabulous drag queens, artists, dancers, pagan faeries with our faggot/wands, burning bright, lighting up the dark-ness of the heterosexual world, casting shadows, spells, reflections in a mirror for heteros to see their own horror) rather than merely "multiply and replenish the earth" like we're just a bunch of ambulatory heteroinsemi-nators.

I like Sodom now. I feel comfortable there. Of course god destroyed it. That's what straight men like him do. And now Sodom is ours. Nobody else dares step foot/body/soul into that space. So let's take back Sodom. Let's rebuild there. They always give us wastelands and we always turn them into music and gardens, full of our passions, desires, beauties. In that space I can stand my ground. In that space I can speak my body without fear.

Is the Rectum a Grave?

Leo Bersani

I want to propose, instead of a denial of what I take to be important (if politically unpleasant) truths about male homosexual desire, an arduous representational discipline. The sexist power that defines maleness in most human cultures can easily survive social revolutions; what it perhaps cannot survive is a certain way of assuming, or taking on, that power. If, as Jeffrey Weeks puts it, gay men "gnaw at the roots of a male heterosexual identity," it is not because of the parodistic distance that they take from that identity, but rather because, from within their nearly mad identification with it, *they never cease to feel the appeal of its being violated.*

To understand this, it is perhaps necessary to accept the pain of embracing, at least provisionally, a homophobic representation of homosexuality. Let's turn for a moment to the disturbed harmonies of Arcadia, Florida, and try to imagine what its citizens—especially those who set fire to the Rays' home—actually saw when they thought about or looked at the Rays' three boys. The persecuting of children or of heterosexuals with AIDS (or who have tested positive for HIV) is particularly striking in view of the popular description of such people as "innocent victims." It is as if gay men's "guilt" were the real agent of infection. And what is it, exactly, that they are guilty of? Everyone agrees that the crime is sexual, and Watney,[1] along with others, defines it as the imagined or real promiscuity for which gay men are so famous. He analyzes a story about AIDS by the science correspondent of the *Observer* in which the "major argument, supported by 'AIDS experts in America,' [is] against 'casual sexual encounters.'" A London doctor does, in the course of the article, urge the use of condoms in such encounters, but "the main problem . . . is evidently 'promiscuity', with issues about the kinds of sex one has pushed firmly into the background" (p. 35). But the kinds of sex involved, in quite a different sense, may in fact be crucial to the argument. Since the promiscuity here is homosexual promiscuity, we may, I think, legitimately wonder if what is being done is not as important as how many times it is being done. Or, more exactly, the act being represented may itself be associated with insatiable desire, with unstoppable sex.

Before being more explicit about this, I should acknowledge that the argument I wish to make is a highly speculative one, based primarily on the exclusion of the evidence that supports it. An important lesson to be learned from a study of the representation of AIDS is that the messages most likely to reach their destination are messages already there. Or, to put this in other terms, representations of AIDS have to be X-rayed for their fantasmatic logic; they document the comparative irrelevance of information in communication. Thus the expert medical opinions about how the virus cannot be transmitted (information that the college-educated mayor of Arcadia and his college-educated wife have heard and refer to) is at once rationally discussed and occulted. SueEllen Smith, the Arcadia mayor's wife, makes the unobjectionable comment that "there are too many unanswered questions about this disease," only to conclude that "if you are intelligent and listen and read about AIDS you get scared when it involves your own children, because you realize all the assurances are not based on solid evidence." In strictly rational terms, this can of course be easily answered: there are indeed "many unanswered questions" about AIDS, but the assurances given by medical authorities that there is no risk of the HIV virus being transmitted through casual contact among schoolchildren is in fact based on "solid evidence." But what interests me most about the *New York Times* interview with the Smiths from which I am quoting (they are a genial, even disarming couple: "I know I must sound like a country jerk saying this," remarks Mr. Smith, who really never does sound like a country bumpkin) is the evidence that they have in fact received and thoroughly assimilated quite different messages about AIDS. The mayor said that "a lot of local people, including himself, believed that powerful interests, principally the national gay leaders, had pressured the Government into refraining from taking legitimate steps to help contain the spread of AIDS."[2] Let's ignore the charming illusion that "national gay leaders" are powerful enough to pressure the federal government into doing anything at all, and focus on the really extraordinary assumption that those belonging to the group hit most heavily by AIDS want nothing more intensely than to see it spread unchecked. In other words, those being killed are killers. Watney cites other versions of this idea of gay men as killers (their behavior is seen as the cause and source of AIDS), and he speaks of "a displaced desire to kill them all—the teeming deviant millions" (p. 82). Perhaps; but the presumed original desire to kill gays may itself be understandable only in terms of the fantasy for which it is offered as an explanation: homosexuals are killers. But what is it, exactly, that makes them killers?

The public discourse about homosexuals since the AIDS crisis began has a startling resemblance (which Watney notes in passing) to the representation of female prostitutes in the nineteenth century "as contaminated vessels, conveyancing 'female' venereal diseases to 'innocent' men" (pp. 33–34).[3] Some more light is retroactively thrown on those representations by the association of gay men's murderousness with what might be called the specific sexual heroics of their promiscuity. The accounts of Professor Narayan and Judge Wallach of gay men having sex twenty to thirty times a night, or once a minute, are much less descriptive of even the most promiscuous male sexuality than they are reminiscent of male fantasies about women's multiple orgasms. The Victorian representation of prostitutes may explicitly criminalize what is merely a consequence of a more profound or original guilt. Promiscuity is the social correlative of a sexuality physiologically grounded in the menacing phenomenon of the nonclimactic climax. Prostitutes publicize (indeed, sell) the inherent aptitude of women for uninterrupted sex. Conversely, the similarities between representations of female prostitutes and male homosexuals should help us to specify the exact form of sexual behavior being targeted, in representations of AIDS, as the criminal, fatal and irresistibly repeated act. This is of course anal sex (with the potential for multiple organisms having spread from the insertee to the insertor, who, in any case, may always switch roles and be the insertee for ten or fifteen of those thirty nightly encounters), and we must of course take into account the widespread confusion in heterosexual *and* homosexual men between fantasies of anal and vaginal sex. The realities of syphilis in the nineteenth century and of AIDS today "legitimate" a fantasy of female sexuality as intrinsically diseased; and promiscuity in this fantasy, far from merely increasing the risk of infection, is the *sign of infection*. Women and gay men spread their legs with an unquenchable appetite for destruction.[4] This is an image with extraordinary power; and if the good citizens of Arcadia, Florida, could chase from their midst an average, law-abiding family, it is, I would suggest, because in looking at three hemophiliac children they may have seen—that is, unconsciously represented—the infinitely more seductive and intolerable image of a grown man, legs high in the air, unable to refuse the suicidal ecstasy of being a woman.

But why "suicidal"? Recent studies have emphasized that even in societies in which, as John Boswell writes, "standards of beauty are often predicated on male archetypes" (he cites ancient Greece and the Muslim world) and, even more strikingly, in cultures that do not regard sexual relations between men as unnatural or sinful, the line is drawn at "passive" anal sex. In medieval Islam, for all its emphasis on homosexual eroticism, "the position of the 'insertee' is regarded as bizarre or even pathological," and while for the ancient Romans, "the distinction between roles approved for male citizens and others appears to center on the giving of seed (as opposed to the receiving of it) rather than on the more familiar modern active-passive division," to be anally penetrated was no less judged to be an "indecorous role for citizen males."[5] And in Volume II of *The History of Sexuality,* Michel Foucault has amply documented the acceptance (even glorification) *and* profound suspicion of homosexuality in ancient Greece. A general ethical polarity in Greek thought of self-domination and a helpless indulgence of appetites has, as one of its results, a structuring of sexual behavior in terms of activity and passivity, with a correlative rejection of the so-called passive role in sex. What the Athenians find hard to accept, Foucault writes, is the authority of a leader who as an adolescent was an "object of pleasure" for other men; there is a legal and moral incompatibility between sexual passivity and civic authority. The only "honorable" sexual behavior "consists in being active, in dominating, in penetrating, and in thereby exercising one's authority."[6]

In other words, the moral taboo on "passive" anal sex in ancient Athens is primarily formulated as a kind of hygienics of social power. *To be penetrated is to abdicate power.* I find it interesting that an almost identical argument—from, to be sure, a wholly different moral perspective—is being made today by certain feminists. In an interview published in 1982 in *Salmagundi,* Foucault said, "Men think that women can only experience pleasure in recognizing men as masters"[7]—a sentence one could easily take as coming from the pens of Catherine MacKinnon and Andrea Dworkin. These are unlikely bedfellows. In the same interview from which I have just quoted, Foucault more or less openly praises sadomasochistic practices for helping homosexual men (many of whom share heterosexual men's fear of losing their authority by "being under another man in the act of love") to "alleviate" the "problem" of feeling "that the passive role is in some way demeaning."[8] MacKinnon and Dworkin, on the other hand, are of course not interested in making women feel comfortable about lying under men, but in changing the distribution of power both signified and constituted by men's insistence on being on top. They have had quite a bit of bad press, but I think that they make some very important points, points that—rather unexpectedly—can help us to understand the homophobic rage unleashed by AIDS. MacKinnon, for example, argues convincingly against the liberal distinction between violence and sex in rape and pornography, a distinction that, in addition to denying what should be the obvious fact that violence *is* sex for the rapist, has helped to make pornography sound merely sexy, and therefore to protect it. If she and Dworkin use the word *violence* to describe pornography that would normally be classified as nonviolent (for example, porno films with no explicit sadomasochism or scenes of rape), it is because they define as violent the power relation that they see inscribed in the sex acts pornography represents. Pornography, MacKinnon writes, "eroticizes hierarchy"; it "makes inequality into sex, which makes it enjoyable, and into gender, which makes it seem natural." Not too differently from Foucault (except, of course, for the rhetorical escalation), MacKinnon speaks of "the male supremacist definition of female sexuality as lust for self-annihilation." Pornography "institutionalizes the sexuality of male supremacy, fusing the eroticization of dominance and submission with the social construction of male and female."[9] It has been argued that even if such descriptions of pornography are accurate, they exaggerate its importance: MacKinnon and Dworkin see pornography as playing a major role in constructing a social reality of which it is really only a marginal reflection. In a sense—and especially if we consider the size of the steady audience for hard-core pornography—this is true. But the objection is also something of a cop-out, because if it is agreed that pornography eroticizes—and thereby celebrates—the violence of inequality itself (and the inequality doesn't have to be enforced with whips to be violent: the denial to Blacks of equal seating privileges on public busses was rightly seen as a form of racial violence), then legal pornography is legalized violence.

Not only that: MacKinnon and Dworkin are really making a claim for the realism of pornography. That is, whether or not we think of it as constitutive (rather than merely reflective) of an eroticizing of the violence of inequality, pornography would be the most accurate description and the most effective promotion of that inequality. Pornography can not be dismissed as less significant socially than other more pervasive expressions of gender inequality (such as the abominable and innumerable TV ads in which, as part of a sales pitch for cough medicine and bran cereals, women are portrayed as slaves to the normal functioning of their men's bronchial tubes and large intestines), because only pornography tells us why the bran ad is effective: the slavishness of women is erotically thrilling. The ultimate logic of MacKinnon's and Dworkin's critique of pornography—and, however parodistic this may sound, I really don't mean it as a parody of their views—would be *the criminalization of sex itself until it has been reinvented*. For their most radical claim is not that pornography has a pernicious effect on otherwise nonpernicious sexual relations, but rather that so-called normal sexuality is already pornographic. "When violence against women is eroticized as it is in this culture," MacKinnon writes, "it is very difficult to say that there is a major distinction in the level of sex involved between being assaulted by a penis and being assaulted by a fist, especially when the perpetrator is a man."[10] Dworkin has taken this position to its logical extreme: the rejection of intercourse itself. If, as she argues, "there is a relationship between intercourse per se and the low status of women," and if intercourse itself "is immune to reform," then there must be no more penetration. Dworkin announces: "In a world of male power—penile power—fucking is the essential sexual experience of power and potency and possession; fucking by mortal men, regular guys."[11] Almost everybody reading such sentences will find them crazy, although in a sense they merely develop the implicit *moral* logic of Foucault's more detached and therefore more respectable formulation: "Men think that women can only experience pleasure in recognizing men as masters." MacKinnon, Dworkin and Foucault are all saying that a man lying on top of a woman assumes that what excites her is the idea of her body being invaded by a phallic master.

The argument against pornography remains, we could say, a liberal argument as long as it is assumed that pornography violates the natural conjunction of sex with tenderness and love. It becomes a much more disturbingly radical argument when the indictment against pornography is identified with an indictment against sex itself. This step is usually avoided by the positing of pornography's violence as either a sign of certain fantasies only marginally connected with an otherwise essentially healthy (caring, loving) form of human behavior, or the symptomatic by-product of social inequalities (more specifically, of the violence intrinsic to a phallocentric culture). In the first case, pornography can be defended as a therapeutic or at least cathartic outlet for those perhaps inescapable but happily marginal fantasies, and in the second case pornography becomes more or less irrelevant to a political struggle against more pervasive social structures of inequality (for once the latter are dismantled, their pornographic derivatives will have lost their raison d'être). MacKinnon and Dworkin, on the other hand, rightly assume the immense power of sexual images to orient our imagination of how political power can and should be distributed and enjoyed, and, it seems to me, they just as rightly mistrust a certain intellectual sloppiness in the catharsis argument, a sloppiness that consists in avoiding the question of how a center of presumably wholesome sexuality ever produced those unsavory margins in the first place. Given the public discourse around the center of sexuality (a discourse obviously not unmotivated by a prescriptive ideology about sex), the margins may be the only place where the center becomes visible.

Furthermore, although their strategies and practical recommendations are unique, MacKinnon's and Dworkin's work could be inscribed within a more general enterprise, one which I will call the *redemptive reinvention of sex*. This enterprise cuts across the usual lines on the battlefield of sexual politics, and it includes not only the panicky denial of childhood sexuality, which is being "dignified" these days as a nearly psychotic anxiety about child abuse, but also the activities of such prominent lesbian proponents of S & M sex as Gayle Rubin and Pat Califia, neither of whom, to put it mildly, share the political agenda of MacKinnon and Dworkin. The immense body of contemporary discourse that argues for a radically revised imagination of the body's capacity for pleasure—a discursive project to which Foucault, Weeks and Watney belong—has as its very condition of possibility a certain refusal of sex as we know it, and a frequently hidden agreement about sexuality as being, in its essence, less disturbing, less socially abrasive, less violent, more respectful of "personhood" than it has been in a male-dominated, phallocentric culture. The mystifications in gay activist discourse on gay male machismo belong to this enterprise; I will return to other signs of the gay participation in the redemptive sex project. For the moment, I want to argue, first of all that MacKinnon and Dworkin have at least had the courage to be explicit about the profound *moral revulsion* with sex that inspires the entire project, whether its specific program be antipornography laws, a return to the arcadian mobilities of childhood polysexuality, the S & M battering of the body in order to multiply or redistribute its loci of pleasure, or, as we shall see, the comparatively anodine agenda (sponsored by Weeks and Watney) of sexual pluralism. Most of these programs have the slightly questionable virtue of being indubitably saner than Dworkin's lyrical tribute to the militant pastoralism of Joan of Arc's virginity, but the pastoral impulse lies behind them all. What bothers me about MacKinnon and Dworkin is not their analysis of sexuality, but rather the pastoralizing, redemptive intentions that support the analysis. That is—and this is the second, major point I wish to argue—they have given us the reasons why pornography must be multiplied and not abandoned, and, more profoundly, the reasons for defending, for cherishing the very sex they find so hateful. Their indictment of sex—their refusal to prettify it, to romanticize it, to maintain that fucking has anything to do with community or love—has had the immensely desirable effect of publicizing, of lucidly laying out for us, the inestimable value of sex as—at least in certain of its ineradicable aspects—anticommunal, antiegalitarian, antinurturing, antiloving.

Let's begin with some anatomical considerations. Human bodies are constructed in such a way that it is, or at least has been, almost impossible not to associate mastery and subordination with the experience of our most intense pleasures. This is first of all a question of positioning. If the penetration necessary (until recently . . .) for the reproduction of the species has most generally been accomplished by the man's getting on top of the woman, it is also true that being on top can never be just a question of a physical position—either for the person on top or for the one on the bottom. (And for the woman to get on top is just a way of letting her play the game of power for awhile, although—as the images of porn movies illustrate quite effectively—even on the bottom, the man can still concentrate his deceptively renounced aggressiveness in the thrusting movement of his penis.)[12] And, as this suggests, there is also, alas, the question of the penis. Unfortunately, the dismissal of penis envy as a male fantasy rather than a psychological truth about women does not really do anything to change the assumptions behind that fantasy. For the idea of penis envy describes how many feel about having one, and, as long as there are sexual relations between men and women, this can not help but be an important fact *for women.* In short, the social structures from which it is often said that the eroticizing of mastery and subordination derive are perhaps themselves derivations (and sublimations) of the indissociable nature of sexual pleasure and the exercise or loss of power. To say this is not to propose an "essentialist" view of sexuality. A reflection on the fantasmatic potential of the human body—the fantasies engendered by its sexual anatomy and the specific moves it makes in taking sexual pleasure—is not the same thing as an *a priori,* ideologically motivated and prescriptive description of the essence of sexuality. Rather, I am saying that those effects of power which, as Foucault has argued, are inherent in the relational itself (they are immediately produced by "the divisions, inequalities and disequilibriums" inescapably present "in every relation from one point to another")[13] can perhaps most easily be exacerbated, and polarized into relations of mastery and subordination, in sex, and that this potential may be grounded in the shifting experience that every human being has of his or her body's capacity, or failure, to control and to manipulate the world beyond the self.

Needless to say, the ideological exploitations of this fantasmatic potential have a long and inglorious history. It is mainly a history of male power, and by now it has been richly documented by others. I want to approach this subject from a quite different angle, and to argue that a gravely dysfunctional aspect of what is, after all, the healthy pleasure we take in the operation of a coordinated and strong physical organism is the temptation to deny the perhaps equally strong appeal of powerlessness, of the loss of control. Phallocentrism is exactly that: not primarily the denial of power to women (although it has obviously also led to that, everywhere and at all times), but above all the denial of the *value* of powerlessness in both men and women. I don't mean the value of gentleness, or nonaggressiveness, or even of passivity, but rather of a more radical disintegration and humiliation of the self. For there is finally, beyond the fantasies of bodily power and subordination that I have just discussed, a transgressing of that very polarity which, as Georges Bataille has proposed, may be the profound sense of both certain mystical experiences and of human sexuality. In making this suggestion I am also thinking of Freud's somewhat reluctant speculation, especially in the *Three Essays on the Theory of Sexuality,* that sexual pleasure occurs whenever a certain threshold of intensity is reached, when the organization of the self is momentarily disturbed by sensations or affective processes somehow "beyond" those connected with psychic organization. Reluctant because, as I have argued elsewhere, this definition removes the sexual from the intersubjective, thereby depriving the teleological argument of the *Three Essays* of much of its weight. For on the one hand Freud outlines a normative sexual development that finds its natural goal in the post-Oedipal, genitally centered desire for someone of the opposite sex, while on the other hand he suggests not only the irrelevance of the object in sexuality but also, and even more radically, a shattering of the psychic structures themselves that are the precondition for the very establishment of a relation to others. In that curiously insistent, if intermittent, attempt to get at the "essence" of sexual pleasure—an attempt that punctuates and interrupts the more secure narrative outline of the history of desire in the *Three Essays*—Freud keeps returning to a line of speculation in which the opposition between pleasure and pain becomes irrelevant, in which the sexual emerges as the *jouissance* of exploded limits, as the ecstatic suffering into which the human organism momentarily plunges when it is "pressed" beyond a certain threshold of endurance. Sexuality, at least in the mode in which it is constituted, may be a tautology for masochism. In *The Freudian Body,* I proposed that this sexually constitutive masochism could even be thought of as an evolutionary conquest, in the sense that it allows the infant to survive, indeed to find pleasure in, the painful and characteristically human period during which infants are shattered with stimuli for which they have not yet developed defensive or integrative ego structures. Masochism would be the psychical strategy that partially defeats a biologically dysfunctional process of maturation.[14] From this Freudian perspective, we might say that Bataille reformulates this self-shattering into the sexual as a kind of nonanecdotal self-debasement, as a masochism to which the melancholy of the post-Oedipal superego's moral masochism is wholly alien, and in which, so to speak, the self is exuberantly discarded.[15]

The relevance of these speculations to the present discussion should be clear: the self which the sexual shatters provides the basis on which sexuality is associated with power. It is possible to think of the sexual as, precisely, moving between a hyperbolic sense of self and a loss of all consciousness of self. But sex as self-hyperbole is perhaps a repression of sex as self-abolition. It inaccurately replicates self-shattering as self-swelling, as psychic tumescence. If, as these words suggest, men are especially apt to "choose" this version of sexual pleasure, because their sexual equipment appears to invite by analogy, or at least to facilitate, the phallicizing of the ego, neither sex has exclusive rights to the practice of sex as self-hyperbole. For it is perhaps primarily *the degeneration of the sexual into a relationship that condemns sexuality to becoming a struggle for power*. As soon as persons are posited, the war begins. It is the self that swells with excitement at the idea of being on top, the self that makes of the inevitable play of thrusts and relinquishments in sex an argument for the natural authority of one sex over the other.

Far from apologizing for their promiscuity as a failure to maintain a loving relationship, far from welcoming the return to monogamy as a beneficent consequence of the horror of AIDS,[16] gay men should ceaselessly lament the practical necessity, now, of such relationships, should resist being drawn into mimicking the unrelenting warfare between men and women, which nothing has ever changed. Even among the most critical historians of sexuality and the most angry activists, there has been a good deal of defensiveness about what it means to be gay. Thus for Jeffrey Weeks the most distinctive aspect of gay life is its "radical pluralism."[17] Gayle Rubin echoes and extends this idea by arguing for a "theoretical as well as a sexual pluralism."[18] Watney repeats this theme with, it is true, some important nuances. He sees that the "new gay identity was constructed through multiple encounters, shifts of sexual identification, actings out, cultural reinforcements, and a plurality of opportunity (at least in large urban areas) for desublimating the inherited sexual guilt of a grotesquely homophobic society," and therefore laments the "wholesale de-sexualisation of gay culture and experience" encouraged by the AIDS crisis (p. 18). He nonetheless dilutes what I take to be the specific menace of gay sex for that "grotesquely homophobic society" by insisting on the assertion of "the diversity of human sexuality in *all* its variant forms" as "perhaps the most radical aspect of gay culture" (p. 25). *Diversity* is the key word in his discussions of homosexuality, which he defines as "a fluctuating field of sexual desires and behavior" (p. 103); it maximizes "the mutual erotic possibilities of the body, and that is why it is taboo" (p. 127).[19]

Much of this derives of course from the rhetoric of sexual liberation in the sixties and seventies, a rhetoric that received its most prestigious intellectual justification from Foucault's call—especially in the first volume of his *History of Sexuality*—for a reinventing of the body as a surface of multiple sources of pleasure. Such calls, for all their redemptive appeal, are, however, unnecessarily and even dangerously tame. The argument for diversity has the strategic advantage of making gays seem like passionate defenders of one of the primary values of mainstream liberal culture, but to make that argument is, it seems to me, to be disingenuous about the relation between homosexual behavior and the revulsion it inspires. The revulsion, it turns out, is all a big mistake: what we are really up to is pluralism and diversity, and getting buggered is just one moment in the practice of those laudable humanistic virtues. Foucault could be especially perverse about all this: challenging, provoking and yet, in spite of his radical intentions, somewhat appeasing in his emphases. Thus in the *Salmagundi* interview to which I have already referred, after announcing that he will not "make use of a position of authority while [he is] being interviewed to traffic in opinions," he delivers himself of the highly idiosyncratic opinions, first of all, that "for a homosexual, the best moment of love is likely to be when the lover leaves in the taxi" ("the homosexual imagination is for the most part concerned with reminiscing about the act rather than anticipating [or, presumably, enjoying] it") and, secondly, that the rituals of gay S & M are "the counterpart of the medieval courts where strict rules of proprietary courtship were defined."[20] The first opinion is somewhat embarrassing; the second has a certain campy appeal. Both turn our attention away from the body—from the acts in which it engages, from the pain it inflicts and begs for—and directs our attention to the romances of memory and the idealizations of the presexual, the courting imagination. That turning away from sex is then projected onto heterosexuals as an explanation for their hostility. "I think that what most bothers those who are not gay about gayness is the gay life-style, not sex acts themselves," and, "It is the prospect that gays will create as yet unforseen kinds of relationships that many people cannot tolerate."[21] But what is "*the* gay life-style"? Is there one? Was Foucault's life-style the same as Rock Hudson's? More importantly, can a nonrepresentable form of relationship really be more threatening than the representation of a particular sexual act—especially when the sexual act is associated with women but performed by men and, as I have suggested, has the terrifying appeal of a loss of the ego, of a self-debasement?

We have been studying examples of what might be called a frenzied epic of displacements in the discourse on sexuality and on AIDS. The government talks more about testing than it does about research and treatment; it is more interested in those who may eventually be threatened by AIDS than in those already stricken with it. There are hospitals in which concern for the safety of those patients who have not been exposed to HIV takes precedence over caring for those suffering from an AIDS-related disease. Attention is turned away from the kinds of sex people practice to a moralistic discourse about promiscuity. The impulse to kill gays comes out as a rage against gay killers deliberately spreading a deadly virus among the "general public." The temptation of incest has become a national obsession with child abuse by day-care workers and teachers. Among intellectuals, the penis has been sanitized and sublimated into the phallus as the originary signifier; the body is to be read as a language. (Such distancing techniques, for which intellectuals have a natural aptitude, are of course not only sexual: the national disgrace of economic discrimination against Blacks is buried in the self-righteous call for sanctions against Pretoria.) The wild excitement of fascistic S & M becomes a parody of fascism; gay males' idolatry of the cock is "raised" to the political dignity of "semiotic guerrilla warfare." The phallocentrism of gay cruising becomes diversity and pluralism; representation is displaced from the concrete practice of fellatio and sodomy to the melancholy charms of erotic memories and the cerebral tensions of courtship. There has even been the displacement of displacement itself. While it is undeniably right to speak—as, among others, Foucault, Weeks and MacKinnon have spoken—of the ideologically organizing force of sexuality, it is quite another thing to suggest—as these writers also suggest—that sexual inequalities are predominantly, perhaps exclusively, displaced social inequalities. Weeks, for example, speaks of erotic tensions as a displacement of politically enforced positions of power and subordination,[22] as if the sexual—involving as it does the source and locus of every individual's original experience of power (and of powerlessness) in the world: the human body—could somehow be conceived of apart from all relations of power, were, so to speak, belatedly contaminated by power from elsewhere.

Displacement is endemic to sexuality. I have written, especially in *Baudelaire and Freud*,[23] about the mobility of desire, arguing that sexual desire initiates, indeed can be recognized by, an agitated fantasmatic activity in which original (but, from the start, unlocatable) objects of desire get lost in the images they generate. Desire, by its very nature, turns us away from its objects. If I refer critically to what I take to be a certain refusal to speak frankly about gay sex, it is not because I believe either that gay sex is reducible to one form of sexual activity or that the sexual itself is a stable, easily observable or easily definable function. Rather, I have been trying to account for the murderous representations of homosexuals unleashed and "legitimized" by AIDS, and in so doing I have been struck by what might be called the aversion displacements characteristic of both those representations and the gay responses to them. Watney is acutely aware of the displacements operative in "cases of extreme verbal or physical violence towards lesbians and gay men and, by extension, the whole topic of AIDS"; he speaks, for example, of "displaced misogyny," of "a hatred of what is projected as 'passive' and therefore female, sanctioned by the subject's heterosexual drives" (p. 50). But, as I argued earlier, implicit in both the violence toward gay men (and toward women, both gay and straight) *and* the rethinking among gays (and among women) of what being gay (and what being a woman) means is a certain agreement about what sex should be. The pastoralizing project could be thought of as informing even the most oppressive demonstrations of power. If, for example, we assume that the oppression of women disguises a fearful male response to the seductiveness of an image of sexual powerlessness, then the most brutal machismo is really part of a domesticating, even sanitizing project. The ambition of performing sex as *only* power is a salvational project, one designed to preserve us from a nightmare of ontological obscenity, from the prospect of a breakdown of the human itself in sexual intensities, from a kind of selfless communication with "lower" orders of being. The panic about child abuse is the most transparent case of this compulsion to rewrite sex. Adult sexuality is split in two: at once redeemed by its retroactive metamorphosis into the purity of an asexual childhood, and yet preserved in its most sinister forms by being projected onto the image of the criminal seducer of children. "Purity" is crucial here: behind the brutalities against gays, against women and, in the denial of their very nature and autonomy, against children lies the pastoralizing, the idealizing, the redemptive project I have been speaking of. More exactly, the brutality is identical to the idealization.

The participation of the powerless themselves in this project is particularly disheartening. Gays and women must of course fight the violence directed against them, and I am certainly not arguing for a complicity with misogynist and homophobic fantasies. I am, however, arguing against that form of complicity that consists in accepting, even finding new ways to defend, our culture's lies about sexuality. As if in secret agreement with the values that support misogynist images of female sexuality, women call for a permanent closing of the thighs in the name of chimerically nonviolent ideals of tenderness and nurturing; gays suddenly rediscover their lost bathhouses as laboratories of ethical liberalism, places where a culture's ill-practiced ideals of community and diversity are authentically put into practice. But what if we said, for example, not that it is wrong to think of so-called passive sex as "demeaning," but rather that *the value of sexuality itself is to demean the seriousness of efforts to redeem it?* "AIDS," Watney writes, "offers a new sign for the symbolic machinery of repression, making the rectum a grave" (p. 126).

But if the rectum is the grave in which the masculine ideal (an ideal shared—differently—by men *and* women) of proud subjectivity is buried, then it should be celebrated for its very potential for death. Tragically, AIDS has literalized that potential as the certainty of biological death, and has therefore reinforced the heterosexual association of anal sex with a self-annihilation originally and primarily identified with the fantasmatic mystery of an insatiable, unstoppable female sexuality. It may, finally, be in the gay man's rectum that he demolishes his own perhaps otherwise uncontrollable identification with a murderous judgment against him.

That judgment, as I have been suggesting, is grounded in the sacrosanct value of selfhood, a value that accounts for human beings' extraordinary willingness to kill in order to protect the seriousness of their statements. The self is a practical convenience; promoted to the status of an ethical ideal, it is a sanction for violence.[24] If sexuality is socially dysfunctional in that it brings people together only to plunge them into a self-shattering and solipsistic *jouissance* that drives them apart, it could also be thought of as our primary hygienic practice of nonviolence. Gay men's "obsession" with sex, far from being denied, should be celebrated—not because of its communal virtues, not because of its subversive potential for parodies of machismo, not because it offers a model of genuine pluralism to a society that at once celebrates and punishes pluralism, but rather because it never stops re-presenting the internalized phallic male as an infinitely loved object of sacrifice. Male homosexuality advertises the risk of the sexual itself as the risk of self-dismissal, of *losing sight* of the self, and in so doing it proposes and dangerously represents *jouissance* as a mode of ascesis.

Notes

1. Simon Watney, *Policing Desire* (Minneapolis: University of Minnesota Press, 1987).

2. Jon Nordheimer, "To Neighbors of Shunned Family AIDS Fear Outweighs Sympathy," *New York Times,* August 31, 1987, p. A1.

3. See Charles Bernheimer's excellent *Figures of Ill Repute: Representing Prostitution in 19th Century France* (Cambridge: Harvard University Press, 1989) for further discussion.

4. The fact that the rectum and the vagina, as far as the sexual transmission of the HIV virus is concerned, are privileged loci of infection is of course a major factor in this

legitimizing process, but it hardly explains the fantasmatic force of the representations I have been discussing.

5. John Boswell, "Revolutions, Universals and Sexual Categories," *Salmagundi*, Nos. 58–59 (Fall 1982–Winter 1983), pp. 107, 102, and 110. See also Boswell's *Christianity, Social Tolerance and Homosexuality* (Chicago: University of Chicago Press, 1980).

6. Michel Foucault, *The Use of Pleasure*, trans. Robert Hurley (New York: Pantheon, 1985). This argument is made in chapter 4.

7. "Sexual Choice, Sexual Act: An Interview with Michel Foucault," *Salmagundi*, Nos. 58–59 (Fall 1982–Winter 1983), p. 21.

8. *Ibid.*

9. Catherine A. MacKinnon, *Feminism Unmodified: Discourses on Life and Law* (Cambridge, MA, and London, England; Harvard University Press, 1987), pp. 3 and 172.

10. *Ibid.*, p. 92.

11. Andrea Dworkin, *Intercourse* (New York: The Free Press, 1987), pp. 124, 137, 79.

12. The idea of intercourse without thrusting was proposed by Shere Hite in *The Hite Report* (New York: Macmillan, 1976). Hite envisaged "a mutual lying together in pleasure, penis-in-vagina, vagina-covering-penis, with female orgasm providing much of the stimulation necessary for male orgasm" (p. 141).

13. Michel Foucault, *The History of Sexuality, vol. 1, An Introduction*, trans. Robert Hurley (New York: Vintage Books, 1980), pp. 93–94.

14. See Leo Bersani, *The Freudian Body: Psychoanalysis and Art* (New York: Columbia University Press, 1986), chapter 11, especially pp. 38–39.

15. Bataille called this experience "communication," in the sense that it breaks down the barriers that define individual organisms and keep them separate from one another. At the same time, however, like Freud he seems to be describing an experience in which the very terms of a communication are abolished. The term thus lends itself to a dangerous confusion if we allow it to keep any of its ordinary connotations.

16. It might be pointed out that, unless you met your lover many, many years ago and neither you nor he has had sex with anyone else since then, monogamy is not that safe anyway. Unsafe sex a few times a week with someone carrying the HIV virus is undoubtedly like having unsafe sex with several HIV positive strangers over the same period of time.

17. Weeks, *Coming Out: Homosexual Politics in Britain* (London: Quartet, 1977), p. 218.

18. Gayle Rubin, "Thinking Sex: Notes for a Radical Theory of the Politics of Sexuality," in Carole Vance, ed., *Pleasure and Danger: Exploring Female Sexuality* (Boston, London, Melbourne, and Henley: Routledge & Kegan Paul, 1984), p. 309.

19. A frequently referred-to study of gay men and women by the Institute for Sex Research founded by Alfred C. Kinsey concluded that "homosexual adults are a remarkably diverse group." See Alan P. Bell and Martin S. Weinberg, *Homosexualities: A Study of Diversity among Men and Women* (New York: Simon and Schuster, 1978), p. 217. One can hardly be unhappy with that conclusion in an "official" sociological study, but, needless to say, it tells us very little—and the tables about gay sexual preferences in the same study are not much help here either—concerning fantasies of and about homosexuals.

20. "Sexual Choice, Sexual Act," pp. 11, 20.

21. *Ibid.,* p. 22.

22. See Weeks, p. 44.

23. University of California, 1977.

24. This sentence could be rephrased, and elaborated, in Freudian terms, as the difference between the ego's function of "reality-testing" and the superego's moral violence (against the ego).

Seeing Things: Representation, the Scene of Surveillance and the Spectacle of Gay Male Sex

Lee Edelman

In 1810 an angry London mob attacked a group of men who were being taken to the pillory after having been convicted of assault with the intent to commit sodomy in the back room of a Vere Street pub. As Louis Crompton observes in *Byron and Greek Love,* the journalistic reports detailing the violence wreaked by the thousands who participated in this scene prompted Louis Simond, a French visitor to England, to make the following notation in the journal he kept:

> We have just read in all the newspapers a full and disgusting account of the public and cruel punishment on the pillory of certain wretches convicted of vile indecencies. I can conceive of nothing more dangerous, offensive, and unwise, than the brutality and unrestrained publicity of such infliction. The imagination itself is sullied by the exposition of enormities, that ought never to be supposed to exist.[1]

These comments repudiate the virulence of the mob, but only by suggesting that such scenes of brutality make evident the brutalizing effects on the populace of any public discourse on sexual relations between men—effects that cannot be avoided even when such discourse is generated to make possible the prosecution of "wretches" who commit "vile indecencies." The horrifying spectacle of the riotous mob pelting the manacled convicts with, as one contemporary account reported, "mud, dead cats, rotten eggs, potatoes, and buckets filled with blood, offal, and dung,"[2] does not argue, in the passage from Simond, against the criminalizing of sodomitical relations, but functions, instead, as a displaced image of the interdicted sexual act: it figures forth, in other words, the infectious indecency of sodomy itself by reading the atrocities committed by the crowd as yet another effect of the "indecencies" that brought those "wretches" to the pillory in the first place. Such a sentiment was by no means unusual, of course; homosexuality, or more precisely, the bias toward sodomitical relations, already had assumed, by the time Simond wrote, its extraordinarily potent, though phobically charged, position within the signifying conventions of the West. It had already come to be construed, that is, as a behavior marked by a transgressive force that could be reproduced, not merely designated, by naming or discussing it. For it constituted, more than an assault upon the flesh, an assault upon the logic of social discourse, an assault so extreme that not only one's morals but even one's "imagination" could be sullied by the "exposition of enormities, that ought never to be supposed to exist."

It is worth pausing to consider the significance attached to this scandal of supposition in which horror and violent denial seem indissociable from the discursive representation of homosexuality itself. What wound, after all, can the scene of sodomy inflict to make its staging, if only in the space of the imagination, so dangerous to effect, and what within that scene has such power to implicate—and, by implicating, to sully—that such a scene, or even the possibility of such a scene, ought properly to be disavowed? Framed in these terms this scandal of supposition may begin to take shape in relation to the process whereby psychoanalysis articulates the constitution of masculine subjectivity: a process that centers on the crisis of representation through which the subject acquires knowledge of sexual difference. The sexual supposition that Simond would disallow may suggest, then, not only the undecidable question of presence or absence that inheres in any fetishistic supposition or belief, but also the male subject's normative interpretations or narrative accounts of sexual difference: the suppositions with which he responds to the "law" of castration and his retroactive understanding of what Freud defines as "the primal scene." I want to examine that scene and its framing in *From the History of an Infantile Neurosis*—Freud's analysis of the Wolf Man, as his patient has subsequently come to be known—both because that case engages explicitly the question of sexual supposition and because it does so by invoking the representation of a sodomitical encounter.

Let me be clear about my purpose at the outset, however; I aim neither to privilege nor to repudiate the psychoanalytic paradigm; rather, I hope to read its relationship to the inscriptions of sodomy in the primal scene as a response to the sodomitical implications of the scene of psychoanalysis itself. For that reason, along with Freud's account of the primal scene as one in which the supposition of homosexuality is embedded, I want to examine, if only briefly, passages from a number of other texts that suppose the scene of sodomy between men: passages from John Cleland's *Memoirs of a Woman of Pleasure,* Tobias Smollett's *Adventures of Peregrine Pickle* and Jacques Derrida's *The Post Card.* In each case a presumptively heterosexual spectator's unobserved surveillance of a sexual encounter between men occasions certain narrative and tropological effects that operate in Freud's case history as well; but rather than construing the Freudian analysis as a matter-discourse with which to illuminate the more explicitly literary passages, or, alternatively, using the literary passages to deconstruct Freudian psychoanalysis, I want to observe how in each of these texts homosexuality comes to signify as a distinctively literary or rhetorical operation in its own right. Though read differently at different historical moments, the inscription of homosexuality within a sodomitical scene proves scandalous in all of these quite different texts, not because it occupies a position *outside* the rules of social discourse, but precisely because it operates from *within* those rules to suggest the instability of positioning that is sexually itself.

Perhaps it is appropriate to try to make clear the direction from which I want to come at these issues by noting that the problem I want to address is the problem, at least in part, of how one comes at a problem: from what direction, that is, one approaches it and in what position one chooses to engage it. Freud's metapsychological theories, after all, repeatedly articulate a structural return to a trauma occasioned by an earlier event that has no existence *as a scene of trauma* until it is (re)presented—or (re)produced—as a trauma in the movement of return itself. His theories, in this way, define a psychic experience in which the most crucial and constitutive dramas of human life are those that can never be viewed head on, those that can never be taken in frontally, but only, as it were, approached from behind. As Mary Ann Doane has recently observed, "The psychical layer Freud designated perception-consciousness is frequently deceived, caught from behind by unconscious forces which evade its gaze."[3]

Not for nothing, therefore, in his analytic (re)construction of the Wolf Man's primal scene, does Freud propose that the sexual encounter observed (or fantasized) by the Wolf Man in his infancy involved his parents in what Freud envisions as an act of coitus *a tergo;* for along with the other ways in which this interpretation serves Freud's purpose, such a posture conveniently allegorizes both the retroactive understanding whereby the primal scene will subsequently generate its various effects, and the practice of psychoanalysis itself to the extent that it approaches experience from behind through the analyst's efforts to replicate the distinctive logic of the unconscious.[4] Psychoanalysis, in other words, not only theorizes about but also operates by means of the (re)construction or reinterpretation of earlier experiences in ways that evoke the temporal logic distinctive of deferred action; and as a result of what Laplanche and Pontalis describe as the "unevenness of its temporal development," human sexuality constitutes the most significant arena in which the effects of deferred action, or *Nachträglichkeit,* comes into play.[5] With this theory psychoanalysis refuses any unidirectional understanding of the temporality of psychic development; instead, it questions the logic of the chronological and the determinate relationship of cause and effect. If temporal revisions and inversions, then, mark the production of psychoanalytic narrative, the very articulation of psychoanalytic logic can be construed in terms of metalepsis, the rhetorical substitution of cause for effect or effect for cause, a substitution that disturbs the relationship of early and late, or before and behind.[6] And nowhere is this metaleptic structure—a structure I propose to discuss as "(be)hindsight" so as to figure its complicitous involvement in the sodomitical encounter— more evident than in Freud's theorization of the Wolf Man's primal scene.

Perhaps it is not irrelevant, then, to remind ourselves that the Wolf Man, in his earliest psychoanalytic transferences, believed that Freud himself desired to "use [him] from behind."[7] At the time that he made this comment, of course, the Wolf Man did not have access to what Freud would "uncover" as his primal scene—a scene in which, according to Freud, the Wolf Man observed at first hand what being used from behind entailed. Indeed, in Freud's formulation of it, the primal scene itself can never be recollected or brought forward into consciousness but only, at best, pieced together during the analytic process: "scenes, like this one in my present patient's case, which date from such an early period and exhibit a similar content, and which further lay claim to such an extraordinary significance for the history of the case, are as a rule not reproduced as recollections, but have to be divined—constructed—gradually and laboriously from an aggregate of indications."[8] Thus the supposition or construction of the primal scene is the effect of the analyst's interpretation of symptoms that subsequently will be determined to have been, themselves, effects of that constructed scene; this disarticulation of temporal logic in what I have chosen to call "(be)hindsight" exemplifies the metaleptic structure of the psychoanalytic hypothesis, especially when the trope of metalepsis is considered, as Marguerite Waller has aptly phrased it, as a "rhetorical Möbius loop."[9]

Now what distinguishes the Möbius loop, of course, is the impossibility of distinguishing its front from its back, a condition that has, as I have already implied, an immediate sexual resonance; but that indistinguishability bespeaks as well a crisis of certainty, a destabilizing of the foundational logic on which knowledge as such depends. Thus, if *From the History of an Infantile Neurosis,* in its elaboration of the primal scene, enacts a psychoanalytic method as metaleptic as the Möbius loop, the self-questioning hesitancy with which Freud responds to his own positing of that scene betrays the effects of the Möbius loop's epistemological disruptions; for no other case history testifies so powerfully to the psychoanalyst's inability to decide where to position himself with regard to his theoretical insights. As Nicholas Abraham and Maria Torok observe in discussing Freud's analysis of the Wolf Man: "Polemical in its explicit purpose, it also reflects another debate, that of the author with himself. Throughout this stirring account and within the meanderings of the theoretical discussion, attentive readers will sense a doubt—it is Freud's doubt regarding his own statements."[10] Indeed, throughout the case history of the Wolf Man the insistence of such doubt reflects Freud's deep anxiety that the primal scene occupying the very center of his analysis may prove to be only an illicit supposition of something that ought never to be supposed to exist.

Certainly the audacity of the scene Freud calls forth might justify such an anxiety: that the parents of a one-and-a-half-year-old boy—a boy who was suffering at the time from malaria—would engage in sexual relations three times while the child rested in the same room—let alone that those relations would feature penetration from behind—and that all of this would take place around five o'clock on a summer afternoon, represents, within its discursive context, so sensational an erotic vision that Freud must initially defend his construction by flatly denying that there is anything sensational in this scenario at all: "On the contrary," he writes, "such an event would, I think, be something entirely commonplace and *banal*" (38). Later, however, in an addition to the manuscript, when he undertakes to reconsider the primal scene's "reality," Freud proposes that prior to his dream of the wolves, the child may have witnessed "not copulation between his parents but copulation between animals, which he then displaced on to his parents" (57). Freud goes on to acknowledge that with this supposition "the demands on our credulity are reduced. We need no longer suppose that the parents copulated in the presence of their child (a very young one, it is true)—which was a disagreeable idea for many of us" (58). That Freud designates here as straining credulity what he first described as banal, that he now presents as a "disagreeable idea" what he first called "entirely commonplace," bespeaks the ambivalence of his position and the extent of what Abraham and Torok describe as his "doubt regarding his own statements."

Now Freud himself offered a provocative insight into the nature of such doubt and the etiology of such ambivalence in a letter written in another context to Lou Andreas-Salomé. "Your derivation of the phenomenon of doubt," he tells her, "is too intellectual, too rational. The tendency to doubt arises not from any occasion for doubt, but is the continuation of the powerful ambivalence tendencies in the pregenital phase, which from then on become attached to every pair of opposites."[11] In this Freudian genealogy, the doubt that attaches to such binary oppositions as cause and effect, or before and behind, represents the carrying forward of an ambivalence associated with the oral and anal stages of libidinal organization, stages in which, as Freud puts it, "it is . . . a question of *external* and *internal*. What is unreal, merely a presentation and subjective, is only internal; what is real is also there *outside*."[12] This description appears in Freud's essay on negation, or *Verneinung,* the psychic defense he employs in denying that the erotic spectacle he initially proposed as essential to the primal scene exceeds in any way the merely commonplace and banal. Freud's subsequent ambivalence, his expression of doubt about the status of the scene as either internal or external, imagined or real, bears the traces, therefore, of a pregenital survival according to his own analysis; and since the mobilization of that doubt seeks to expel or cast out an anxiety about the ontological condition of the most, as it were, *fundamental* theoretical construct at work in his reading of the Wolf Man, it carries more specifically the psychic inscription of the anal-erotic organization.[13]

It is all the more significant, therefore, that anal-erotic fixation and the tendency toward doubt that it is said to produce figure centrally in the Wolf Man's neurosis as Freud construes it in this case history. After all, Freud attempts to account not only for the Wolf Man's predilection for heterosexual relations in which he penetrates his partner from behind, but also for the patient's inability to move his bowels without an enema administered by a male attendant. Freud attributes to this anal fixation, moreover, the skepticism with which the Wolf Man first resisted his spiritual indoctrination into Christian piety. Freud sees in this questioning of orthodox belief the Wolf Man's desire to perpetuate his infantile erotic attachment to his father in the face of the overwhelming uncertainties and doubts occasioned by the dream of the wolves that Freud interprets as signaling the analysand's deferred understanding of the primal scene. These doubts find expression, tellingly enough, in the Wolf Man's need to determine whether or not Christ "had a behind" (63) and consequently experienced the necessity of defecation. "We catch a glimpse," Freud goes on to declare, "of [the Wolf Man's] repressed homosexual attitude in his doubting whether Christ could have a behind, for these ruminations can have had no other meaning but the question whether he himself could be used by his father like a woman— like his mother in the primal scene" (64); his doubt, that is, expresses an anxiety about his own desire to be used from behind—a desire whose fulfillment seems now necessarily to subject him to the law of castration. But we only "catch a glimpse" of this structure by coming at the primal scene itself through "(be)hindsight," and Freud's interrogation within this case history of his belief in the theoretical insights he produces by approaching the scene from this direction takes shape at once as a resistance to, and an unwitting reinscription of, the disorienting confusion between outside and inside, real and imagined, analyst and analysand in the articulation of the primal scene. Freud, to put it another way, tries to distance his method from the anal-eroticism he identifies as characteristic of the Wolf Man by casting doubt upon the coitus *a tergo* that Freud himself had initially envisioned in his approach to the primal scene through analytic "(be)-hindsight"; but that very doubt, however tendentiously it seeks to differentiate Freud's eros from the Wolf Man's, only reenacts the doubt or skepticism that Freud has already specified as an index of the Wolf Man's anal-eroticism. Freud's ambivalence about the vision of penetration from behind generates, in consequence, a certain defensiveness about the status of his own analytic hypothesis—a defensiveness that may tell us a great deal about the danger posed by the vision of the sodomitical scene.

For Freud exposes himself at his most self-protective when he responds, in a section of *From the History of an Infantile Neurosis* that he sets aside for just this purpose, to suggestions that what he labels as primal scenes are not "real occurrences" with a historical basis in the experience of the infant, but only "products of the imagination, which find their instigation in mature life" and thus constitute nothing more than fantasies that "owe their origin to a regressive tendency" (49). While acknowledging that such a "regressive tendency . . . [is] regularly confirmed by analysis," (53) and even going so far as to take credit for having been the one to identify such tendencies in the first place,[14] Freud denies that the theory of psychoanalysis demands that the primal scene be read as a mere retroactive fantasy. Defending his belief in the reality of such scenes, he argues instead that the early outbreak of the Wolf Man's obsessional neurosis demonstrably "limits the regressive part of the causation" and "brings into full view the portion of it which operates in a forward direction" (55).

What Freud, I would argue, feels called upon to limit in relation to this critical scene is a particular reading of the metaleptic structure that marks psychoanalysis as a coming from behind; he cannot allow the primal scene that he still views here as real and central to the course of the Wolf Man's neurosis to be interpreted as merely a *fantasmatic* effect of the effects it is alleged to have produced. He needs, instead, to affirm the possibility of its operation in a "forward direction"—an operation that Freud wants to "bring into full view" in the context of a case that will, if successful, "give a clear picture of this position of things" (55). Freud's defense of this theory of the primal scene thus depends upon his ability to "bring into full view" a "clear picture" of the "forward direction" of the effects produced by the primal scene, a scene that itself can only be constructed metaleptically, put together *a posteriori,* through the "aggregate indications" of those effects themselves. To complicate further the "clear picture" Freud would offer, the "forward direction" of the scene's effects must be viewed in the context of an erotic scene whose thematic content explicitly focuses on the question of what can or cannot be viewed, and on the specific positions that the actors must occupy in order for the observer to be able to view specific "things" without obstruction; it is a scene, therefore, that permits a "clear" view only when the act of intercourse at its center does not take place in a "forward direction" but occurs, instead, from behind. Only thus, after all, is it possible for the spectator to gain visual access to what later will register as the signifying presence of the father's penis in relation to what at that point will be construed as the problematical absence of the mother's, an absence that will be attributed, metaleptically, to the mother's submission to the father's desire.

Freud performs in this passage an elaborate dance of forward and backward, before and behind—not a fox-trot, but a Freudian Wolf-trot perhaps; and the rigorous confusion that characterizes this attempt to present a "clear picture of [the] position of things" expresses his concern that the mere envisioning of this scene, with its spectacular representation of penetration from behind, may color or call into question the position of the analyst— or even of psychoanalysis itself—in relation to the man on the analyst's couch. For the primal scene, as Freud reconstructs the perspective of the infant at the moment he observes it,[15] activates the pregenital supposition "that sexual intercourse takes place at the anus" (78). Thus in the first instance the primal scene is always perceived as sodomitical, and it specifically takes shape as a sodomitical scene between sexually undifferentiated partners, both of whom, fantasmatically at least, are believed to possess the phallus. In a sense, then, the primal scene as Freud unpacks it presupposes the imaginative priority of a sort of protohomosexuality, and it designates male heterosexuality, by contrast, as a later narcissistic compromise that only painfully and with difficulty represses its identification with the so-called "passive" position in that scene so as to protect the narcissistically invested penis from the fate that is assumed to have befallen the penis of the mother.[16] Insofar as the participants in the primal scene are as yet undifferentiated sexually to the infant who observes them—both, that is, in the logic of Freudian theory, are seen as phallic—it is small wonder that he has little difficulty in experiencing an identification with each of their positions; but insofar as that scene must thereafter bear traces of sodomitical fantasy and homosexual desire, it is small wonder that Freud has great difficulty indeed in allowing himself or his psychoanalytic practice to be implicated in the scene at all. The "(be)hindsight" of psychoanalysis produces a correspondence too close for comfort.

One pragmatic reason for such discomfort becomes apparent when Freud responds to the charge that the primal scene is not only a retroactive phantasy, but a phantasy whose origin must be attributed to the analyst rather than to the analysand. He ventriloquizes this line of reasoning as follows: "what is argued now is evidently that there are fantasies not of the patient but of the analyst himself, who forces them upon the person under analysis on account of some complexes of his own" (52). The supposition or imagining of the sodomitical scene so destabilizes the division between real and imagined, external and internal, patient and analyst, that the psychoanalyst's imagining of the scene itself can be read as a figural enactment of that scene: for the analyst is now subject to representation as one who "forces" himself surreptitiously "upon the person under analysis," imposing himself, like the unconscious, in a way that evades the patient's gaze. He is accused, that is, at bottom, of wanting to "use [his patient] from behind" not only by the Wolf Man in his early imaginary or transferential relation to the analyst, but also by real, external critics of psychoanalysis as he practices it.

This charge, to which Freud's text responds as it is leveled by such contemporaries as Jung and Adler, has received more recent formulation in an essay by Stanley Fish. "Freud reserves to himself," Fish argues, ". . . the pleasure of total mastery. It is a pleasure that is intensely erotic, . . . affording the multiple satisfactions of domination, penetration, and engulfment."[17] Though Fish identifies, correctly in my view, Freud's implication in the primal scene's coitus *a tergo,* neither pleasure nor mastery seems adequate as a description of his response to that implication. Rather, the fancy rhetorical footwork he performs in an effort to keep the forward and backward directions of psychoanalytic operations and sexual encounters from corresponding too exactly suggests the precariousness of his relation to a scene that cannot be viewed without wounding the nonhomosexually identified spectator who is positioned to observe it. After all, as Freud himself understands, no possible response can dissuade his accusers from reading the primal scene as a fantasy that reveals the analyst's psychological "complexes," his own "perverse" desires. "On the one side," he notes with resignation, "there will be a charge of subtle self-deception, and on the other of obtuseness of judgment; it will be impossible to arrive at a decision" (53).

If the supposition of the primal scene calls forth this radical indeterminacy that threatens to put the analyst in the position of the patient, that same indeterminacy more famously informs Freud's final remark concerning the ontological status of the scene itself: "I intend on this occasion," he declares, in a passage added after he had finished the manuscript of his text, "to close the discussion of the reality of the primal scene with a *non liquet,*" (60) that is, with a legal determination that the evidence is insufficient. But the Latin phrase thus appropriated by the law means literally "it is not clear," and this denial of clarity thus marks a return of the optical metaphor always at issue in the thematics of the primal scene. By affirming a lack of clarity in the perspective from which he would undertake to view or "catch a glimpse" of that theoretically indispensable scene, Freud situates himself unresolvedly before the very *analytic* scene in which the Wolf Man's primal scene was metaleptically constructed. His acknowledgment, in other words, of a conceptual opacity within the scene of psychoanalysis, an opacity that betokens a node of resistance internal to the *theorization* of the primal scene, reenacts the resistance of the Wolf Man, after his "recognition" of castration, to his spectatorial involvement in the primal scene as originally construed. In each case, a sexual theory undergoes revisionary rearticulation in order to protect the theorist from implication in the spectacle as he initially envisioned it.

Thus the Wolf Man's sexual theory, as Freud argues, at the moment he witnessed the primal scene, centered on his identification with the pleasure derived from (what he took to be) the penetration of the anus, a "penetration" that should be read as describing both the act of penetrating and the act of being penetrated. This double identification allowed him imaginatively to inhabit the positions of both his mother and his father in the spectacle of coitus *a tergo;*[18] but that theoretical positioning was psychically rewritten with the dream that insisted on castration as the price of gratifying what Freud defines as the patient's "homosexual enthusiasm" (78). And the dream that marks (and/or effects) this theoretical revision crucially features a reassignment of spectatorial positions as well, so that the child who viewed the primal scene (and in the process experienced the pleasure of multiple erotic identifications) dreams that he himself has now become the *object* of observation (and consequently experiences the paranoid fear that he must suffer for his earlier experience of spectatorial satisfaction). Similarly, the psychoanalyst whose theory makes the primal scene visible within the theater of analysis in order to "give a clear picture" of how psychological trauma can sneak up from behind, belatedly redefines as a "disagreeable idea" the coitus *a tergo* that he first described as "entirely commonplace and *banal.*" The theorist who sought to produce a "clear picture" produces, in response to the criticism of analysts who would turn his own methods against him and make him the object of their professional gaze, a theory in which the anxious-making "picture" of the primal scene must not be made too clear; for as the analytic scene and the primal scene uncontrollably collapse into one another, Freud can only conclude with a *non liquet,* declaring his inability to specify with any clarity the meaning of either one.

This inability testifies to the destabilization of definitional barriers and to the undoing of the logic of positionality effected by the sodomitical spectacle; it thus makes possible the identification of Freud with the infant who observes and identifies with both participants in the primal scene. It puts the Freud, that is, who fails to resolve the theoretical status of the primal scene in the position he imagines the infant occupying *within* that scene itself, a position from which real and imagined, inside and outside, active and passive are so deeply and inextricably interwoven that he simultaneously identifies with positions that only later become mutually exclusive (op)positions. I would argue that this disorientation of positionality is bound up with the danger historically associated in Euro-American culture with the spectacle or representation of the sodomitical scene between men, and that this can be demonstrated by attending to the ways in which the logic of spatiotemporal positioning insistently marks our culture's framing of homosexual relations.

I mean by this something more than the fact that we are accustomed to using a metaphorics of "in" or "out" to measure an aspect of lesbian and gay political identity; I mean something that can be approximated more closely by noting that modern masculinist heterosexual culture conceptualizes lesbian and gay male sexuality in terms of a phallocentric positional logic, insistently (and dismissively) articulating lesbianism as a form of extended, nonproductive foreplay and gay male sexual relations as a form of extended, nonproductive behind-play. The scene of sodomy comes to figure, therefore, both a spatial disturbance in the logic of positions and a temporal disturbance in the logic essential to narrative development. In "Jenny Cromwell's Complaint Against Sodomy" (1692), the complainant, for example, looks back to a time "When Britains did encounter face to face/And thought a back stroke trecherous and base"; but that lost time of "homely joys," was, as Jenny Cromwell tells us, before the "Reformation/ Turned all things Arsy-versy in the nation."[19] As this poem makes explicit, the practice of sodomy is construed as exemplifying a logic of reversal with widespread and uncontrollable implications—implications that reenact a "sodomitical" disturbance of temporal (and therefore narrative) positionality that threatens to reduce the play of history to the finality of an endgame.

Such disarticulations of positional logic find concise expression in a passage from John Cleland's *Memoirs of a Woman of Pleasure,* a novel in which Fanny Hill, that memorable woman of pleasure herself, celebrates all manner of erotic experience with the single and noteworthy exception of male-male sexual relations. Forced unexpectedly to amuse herself in a roadwide "publick-house," Fanny discovers a "paper patch" concealing an opening in the moveable partition that divides her room from the one adjoining it. Piercing the patch with a needle, she manages to spy upon "two young sparks romping . . . in frolic, and innocent play."[20] Before long, however, their play turns amorous, and Fanny is able to discover, as she knowingly puts it, "what they were" (158); for theirs, in Fanny's significant phrase, is a "project of preposterous pleasure" (157). I focus on this phrase in particular because it signally condenses the disturbance of positionality that is located in and effected by the sodomitical scene; sodomy, that is, gets figured as the literalization of the "preposterous" precisely insofar as it is interpreted as the practice of giving precedence to the posterior and thus as confounding the stability or determinacy of linguistic or erotic positioning. Not surprisingly, this defiance of the order of meaning articulated through relations like before and behind—a defiance like that inherent in the very structure of the Möbius loop—dominates Fanny's interest in the sexual spectacle played out before her, especially when she focuses on the erection sported by the young man being penetrated from the rear. "His red-topt ivory toy, that stood perfectly stiff," she scientifically notes, "shewed, that if he was like his mother behind, he was like his father before" (158).

The figural logic at work in this sentence must not pass unremarked, for the categories designated by "like his mother" and "like his father" bear a heavy conceptual burden. If Fanny's magnetized attention to the young man's "red-topt ivory toy" seems to specify exactly what she means in describing him as "like his father before," there remains, nonetheless, an element of opacity when she likens him to "his mother behind." Consider, for instance, that the syntax here allows as a perfectly proper interpretation of this sentence that the young man who, when seen from before, is like his father *when seen from before,* is simultaneously, when seen from behind, like his mother *when seen from behind;* the sentence, that is, could be construed to assert that where his penis represents a phallic endowment comparable in kind to that of his father, his buttocks represent a posterior endowment comparable in kind to that of his mother. But the sentence, as most readers of Cleland intuit, seems to signify something else instead: that the man who, from the front, is like his father from the front, is also from the back, like his mother *from the front.* The sodomite, therefore, like the Möbius loop, represents and enacts a troubling resistance to the binary logic of before and behind, constituting himself as a single-sided surface whose front and back are never completely distinguishable as such.

In order to bring fully into focus, however, the meaning of this metaphoric equation of the young man's anus and the mother's vagina, it is useful to remember that before and behind not only identify spatial positions, but gesture toward temporal relations as well. Psychoanalysis, of course, posits castration as the event that effects the temporal logic whereby what was perceived as phallic "before" becomes feminine "behind." Indeed, as Freud writes with specific reference to the Wolf Man's pathogenic dream, the eroticism associated with the posterior or the "behind" has, for men, a deep-seated relation to their emergent understanding of female sexuality in the wake of the castration complex:

> We have been driven to assume that during the process of the dream he understood that women are castrated, that instead of a male organ they have a wound which serves for sexual intercourse, and that castration is the necessary condition of femininity; we have been driven to assume that the threat of this loss induced him to repress his feminine attitude toward men, and that he awoke from his homosexual enthusiasm in anxiety. Now how can this comprehension of sexual intercourse, this recognition of the vagina, be brought into harmony with the selection of the bowel for the purpose of identification with women? Are not the intestinal symptoms based on what is probably an older notion, and one which in any case completely contradicts the dread of castration—the notion, namely, that sexual intercourse takes place at the anus? (78)

Obedient to the law of castration—the law that plays out the *fort/da* logic of presence and absence so that "before" and "behind" can elaborate a sequencing of loss into a coherent narrative that offers itself as the basis for the binary organization of all logic and all thought[21]—the male here must repudiate the pleasures of the anus because their fulfillment allegedly presupposes, and inflicts, the loss or "wound" that serves as the very definition of femaleness. Thus the male who is terrorized into heterosexuality through his internalization of this determining narrative must embrace with all his narcissistic energy the phantom of a hierarchically inflected binarism always to be defended zealously. His anus, in turn, will be phobically charged as the site at which he traumatically confronts the possibility of becoming "like his mother," while the female genitalia will always be informed by their signifying relation to the anal eroticism he has had to disavow—a relation underscored by the Wolf Man's reference to the vagina as the female's "front bottom" (25).[22]

The scandal of the sodomitical scene, therefore, as Cleland has Fanny describe it, derives from its repudiation of the binary logic implicit in male heterosexualization and from its all too *visible* dismissal of the threat on which the terroristic empire of male heterosexuality has so effectively been erected. For the sodomite, after all, to be "like his mother behind" and *still* to be "like his father before," is apparently to validate the sexual theories and the libidinal cathexes of the infant as he observes the primal scene. Playing out the possibility of multiple, nonexclusive erotic identifications and positionings, the spectacle of sodomy would seem to confirm precisely those infantile sexual speculations that the male, coerced by the bogey of castration, is expected to have put behind him. It threatens to bring out of the closet, that is, the realization that the narcissistic compromise productive of male heterosexuality, the sacrifice of "homosexual enthusiasm" to defend against the prospect of castration, might not have been necessary after all. Indeed, the sodomitical spectacle, when viewed from this perspective, cannot fail to implicate the heterosexual male situated to observe it since it constitutes an affront to the primary narrative that orients his theory of sexuality. From such a vantage point it generates a response that can be interpreted as the negative counterpart or inversion, as it were, of fetishism and the fetishistic overesteeming of the object: for if the problem engaged in the fetish is that of affirming a belief in presence over and against the knowledge of loss, the problem produced by the scene of sodomy is that of affirming a belief in loss over and against the knowledge of presence. In order to uphold the law of castration, the male homosexual must be cut off from the social prerogatives associated with maleness, signified by the penis, precisely because the vision of male-male sodomy shows that the penis has *not* been cut off as castration should demand. Its presence in the order of anatomy must be transformed into an absence in the order of culture, thus complying with the logic of the signifying processes that derive from the articulation of sexual difference through the agency of castration. The sodomitical scene, in consequence, must be overwritten with a code, one essentially legislative, that effects a psychic translation of "to have" into "to have not."

The disappropriation of "proper" relationship in the episode narrated in Cleland's novel extends, therefore, beyond the two men whom Fanny subjects to her surveillance until it encompasses Fanny herself as an observer of that scene. In this regard it is important to bear in mind Nancy K. Miller's suggestion that Fanny must be viewed as "a male 'I' in female drag."[23] While this is true throughout the novel, the sodomitical encounter calls forth a particularly insistent thematic emphasis on the reversal of gender roles and expectations and the concomitant destabilization of binary logic for Fanny as an observer of the spectacle as well as for the two young men more actively involved. Fanny's very spectatorial position, for example, confers upon her the power to see without becoming an object of scrutiny herself—a power culturally coded as the prerogative of the heterosexual male—and it places her in the position associated in the Freudian scenario with the analyst or the unconscious, a position from which she can come upon the sodomitical spectacle from behind. And as she gains access to this spectacle by appropriating a male-coded position in the erotics of vision, she achieves that position by figuratively enacting the male role in a heterosexual script: by piercing, that is, the paper patch on the wall, a sort of textual hymen, with the bodkin or needle she carries, thereby revealing a hole or "flaw" (157) in the partition allowing intercourse between the two rooms. Moreover, as one last instance of sodomy's power to implicate those stationed to observe it, when Fanny indignantly determines to "raise the house" upon the "miscreants" whose "preposterous pleasure" has shown her that they don't know which end is up, she catches her foot unexpectedly on some "nail or ruggedness in the floor," which "fl[ings] [her] on [her] face with such violence, that [she] f[alls] senseless to the ground" (159). Lying unconscious—face down, bottom up—on this suddenly unreliable ground, Fanny embodies the instability of positioning that radiates out from the sodomitical scene and demonstrates that it was not without reason that Cleland named her Fanny after all.

A similar dissemination of reversals could be traced in the sodomitical episode recounted by Smollett in *The Adventures of Peregrine Pickle*. When Peregrine's companion, Pallet, observes an Italian count making amorous overtures to a sleeping German baron, he is "scandalized" by "such expressions of tenderness," and, becoming "conscious of his own attractions, [and] alarmed for his person" he flees the room and "put[s] himself under the protection" of the novel's eponymous hero, explaining to Peregrine the particulars of the "indecency" he has so distressingly observed.[24]

> Peregrine, who entertained a just detestation for all such abominable practices, was incensed at this information; and stepping to the door of the dining-room where the two strangers were left together, saw with his own eyes enough to convince him, that Pallet's complaint was not without foundation, and that the baron was not averse to the addresses of the count. Our younger gentleman's indignation had well nigh prompted him to rush in, and take immediate vengeance on the offenders

> but, considering that such a precipitate step might be attended with
> troublesome consequences for himself, he resisted the impulse of his
> wrath, and tasked his invention with some method of inflicting upon
> them a disgrace suited to the grossness of their ideas. (242)

Despite his indignation at the "grossness" of this sodomitical vision, Peregrine dares not intervene for fear of "troublesome consequences to himself"—for fear, in other words, that any intervention, even if only to enact
his revenge on the practitioners of vice, will lead to his being implicated
in the "grossness" of the scene. But the very fact of his being prevented
from intervening in this way identifies in itself his implication in the
disturbances of positionality this spectacle effects; it demonstrates, that is,
how his sexual authority has been challenged by a sight that imposes upon
the male a disturbing "conscious[ness] of his own attractions" and thus an
awareness of his susceptibility to being taken as a potential sexual object
instead of an active sexual subject. Peregrine's implication in the sodomitical scene's disruption of gender-coded oppositions, however, is only reinforced by the strategy he adopts in order to vent his "wrath." Wary of
taking action himself, he arranges for his landlady, described as "a dame
of remarkable vivacity," to step into the next room in the belief that she
is carrying a message to its occupants.

> The lady very graciously undertook the office, and entering the apart-
> ment, was so much offended and enraged at the mutual endearments of
> the two lovers, that instead of delivering the message with which she
> had been entrusted, she set the trumpet of reproach to her mouth, and
> seizing the baron's cane, which she found by the side-table, belaboured
> them both with such eagerness of animosity, that they found themselves
> obliged to make a very disorderly retreat, and were actually driven down
> stairs, in a most disgraceful condition, by this exasperated virago. . . .
> (243)

If Peregrine, after witnessing the spectacle of male-male love, is effectively
unmanned by his inability to take action, the landlady becomes all the
more martial and virile as she sounds the trumpet of battle, wields the
baron's cane, and forces the two male lovers to make a "disorderly retreat."
And as if to signal that the landlady's transformation into an animated
"virago"—literally, her transformation into a simulacrum of a man—has
not put an end to the logical disturbances produced by the sodomitical scene,
Peregrine and Pallet celebrate the punishment of the amorous "offenders" by
attending a masquerade that night, with Pallet in full female drag.

   In each of these passages the scene of sodomy between men exposes
the impossibility of establishing the distance necessary to secure an "uncon-

taminated" spectatorial relation to that scene. The spectatorial position is destabilized, however, not because the scene is so alien or remote, but precisely because the vision of male-male sodomy looks uncannily familiar: as familiar, that is, as the primal scene that in Freudian theory only belatedly undergoes heterosexualization. Since gay male sexual relations thus threaten to disseminate what might be described as a generalized sodomitical effect—threaten, that is, to effect a contagious disturbance of positional logic—it should come as no surprise that the sodomitical passages in both these eighteenth-century texts should have been expurgated after their initial publication. Like Freud or Fanny or Peregrine, after all, the heterosexually identified reader has too much at stake in such an encounter with or representation of the sodomitical scene.

Just what that stake is may be illuminated from a different historical direction by catching a glimpse of one last spectator catching a glimpse of sodomy between men. In the section of *The Post Card* titled "Envois," Jacques Derrida, producing what he suggests may be a "satire of epistolary literature"[25]—a satire, that is, of a genre that includes *The Memoirs of a Woman of Pleasure*—focuses much of his attention on a medieval drawing of Plato and Socrates that he claims to have noticed on a post card in the gift shop at Oxford's Bodleian Library. Tellingly, his espial of the post card takes place, as Derrida recounts it, while he himself is being spied on and made a participant in a scene; for at the moment when his eye first falls upon the image of the two philosophers in the drawing, he has the sense that his companions, Jonathan Culler and Cynthia Chase, whom he imagines as having anticipated and arranged for this discovery, were, as he writes, "observing me obliquely, watching me look. As if they were spying on me in order to finish the effects of a spectacle they had staged (they have just married more or less)" (16). Thus it is as a third party in the company of newlyweds staging a "spectacle" before him—a spectacle in which he finds himself both conscripted and implicated—that Derrida encounters an image that represents philosophy's primal scene; perhaps it is not coincidental, then, that he reads the image on the post card as a graphic depiction of penetration from behind. "I see *Plato* getting an erection in *Socrates'* back," he writes, "and see the insane hubris of his prick, an interminable, disproportionate erection . . . slowly sliding, still warm, under *Socrates'* right leg" (18). For Derrida, as for Cleland and Smollett and Freud, this scene plays out a vertiginous reversibility of positions, specifically of the spatiotemporal positions on which Western philosophy rests: "Socrates, the one who writes—seated, bent over, a scribe or docile copyist, Plato's secretary, no? He is in front of Plato, no, Plato is *behind* him" (9).

This reversal of priority between Socrates and Plato extends its metaleptic reach across the whole of Western history so that Derrida can insist not only that "S. is P., Socrates is Plato, his father and his son, therefore the father of his father, his own grandfather and his own grandson" (47), but also, as the references to grandfather and grandson suggest through their evocation of *Beyond the Pleasure Principle,* that Freud too has a part to play in this unorthodox genealogy, this narrative of a temporality articulated otherwise: "as-I-show-in-my-book it is then Plato who is the inheritor, for Freud. Who pulls the same trick, somewhat, on Plato that Plato pulls on Socrates. This is what I call a catastrophe" (28). Catastrophe, "an overturning and inversion of relations" (22), as Derrida describes it, the condition of being "Arsy-versy" as in "Jenny Cromwell's Complaint," names for Derrida the deconstructive logic not only of the primal scene, but also of writing and philosophy as they are construed in the Western tradition: "S. does not see P. who sees S., but only (and here is the truth of philosophy) only *from the back.* There is only the *back,* seen from the back, in what is written, such is the final word. Everything is played out in *retro* and *a tergo*" (48). Thus for Derrida, as for Western philosophy, the sodomitical spectacle constitutes the primal scene of writing;[26] philosophy—and psychoanalysis as an offshoot of philosophy—ceaselessly elaborates itself by turning its back on its origin, only to turn back, through that very gesture, to the origin it seeks to deny.

This means, as I see it, something more than what Stanley Cavell, for instance, apparently intends when he writes, in an essay titled (by coincidence?) "Postscript (1989)": "I am from time to time haunted—I rather take it for granted that this is quite generally true of male heterosexual philosophers—by the origin of philosophy (in ancient Greece) in an environment of homosexual intimacy."[27] What haunts Derrida is not just (whatever "just" in this case might mean) the homophobic, homosocial, homoerotic and homosexual relations that endlessly circulate within—and as—"the philosophical tradition"; at issue for him is the irreducibility of both sodomy and writing to a binary logic predicated on the determinacy of presence or absence—a binary logic that Derrida defines as intrinsic to "phallogocentrism [which] is articulated on the basis of a determined situation (let us give this word all its imports) in which the phallus *is* the mother's desire to the extent that she does not have it."[28]

Casting doubt on the analyticophilosophical "system of the symbolic, of castration, of the signifier, of the truth" ("*Le facteur,*" 444), Derrida engages a structure of rigorously *in*determinate situations (and I give that word all its imports) that Freud, in a sentence cited earlier in part and offered now in its entirety, might gloss in the following way: "The tendency to doubt arises not from any occasion for doubt, but is the continuation of the powerful ambivalent tendencies in the pregenital phase, which from then on become attached to every pair of opposites that dresent [sic] themselves." If the logic of paired opposites generated through castration's institution of sexual difference supplants a pregenital ambivalence—which is to say, an overdetermined multiplicity of identifications—that makes such distinctions as inside or outside, imagined or real, problematic, it is important to note that only by adopting the perspective of castration can castration be seen as the "opposite" of pregenital ambivalence. Castration, that is, represents itself as the *knowledge* of antithetical positioning and thus positions itself in opposition to the indeterminacy of the primal scene; it does so, moreover, by constituting itself as the very *principle* of paired opposites, as the truth of "truth" as the either/or determination of presence or absence.

Yet in the passage quoted in the previous paragraph from Freud's letter to Lou Andreas-Salomé, the word rendered indeterminate through a "typographical" error in the English translation as published—and published in association with the Institute of Psycho-Analysis—is, suggestively, the word "present" itself. The "present" has thus been absented from this translation of the Freudian text through a Derridean "catastrophe," a sodomitical inversion or overthrow: "erroneously" positioned with its bottom up, the "p" has effected a sudden multiplication of its identity, has come out of the closet of typography in the disturbing drag of a "d."[29] In the context of *The Post Card*'s argument it is difficult not to speculate on the significance of this transformation; if "S. is P." according to Derrida, surely it is fair to meditate on this dislocation of "p" by "d": *P*lato, *p*hilosophy, *p*hallogocentrism, and *p*sychoanalysis *d*isarticulated by *D*errida and *d*econstruction? The fortifications of the *p*resent shown not to be a "fort" after all but a "*da*"? In this translation of the letters circulated between Freud and Lou Andreas-Salomé, letters that in many ways echo those included in Derrida's "Envois,"[30] the word "present" cannot present itself; it is defeated or deferred by a letter. Thus writing, performing a sodomitical reversal, gestures toward the persistence of a "pregenital" indeterminancy that the law of castration would deny through institutionalized categories of present and not present. The *différance* of the *p*resent figured by the "p" with its bottom up allegorizes the insistence of the *b*ehind (another inversion: "p" as "b"?) in the very act of making present. Thus both philosophy and psychoanalysis insist on coming back to the back, returning to the behind that is always at the forefront of the "dresent": "Before all else it is a question of turning one's back," as Derrida observes, "[o]f turning the back of the post card (what is *Socrates'* back when he turns his back to *Plato*—a very amorous position, don't forget—? this is also the back of the post card: as we remarked one day, it is equally legitimate to name it recto or verso). . . . To turn one's back is the analytic position, no?" (178).

Such reversals, inversions or conflations of (putative op)positions recur throughout Derrida's writing and mark the organization of his text; hence the "Envois," which designates a concluding passage in poetry or prose, is located at the front of *The Post Card,* a text in which Derrida has written, "I owe it to you to have discovered homosexuality" (53). What this means, of course, has everything to do with the figuration of sodomy in terms evocative of the (il)logical structure of the möbius loop, the (il)logic that dislocates such spatiotemporal "situations" as "pre" and "post," or before and behind. For sodomy and writing insist on the (il)logical possibility that what is behind can also, and properly, come before: "In the beginning," as Derrida phrases it, "in principle, was the post" (29). If we can say of such an observation that it is, to be precise, "preposterous," we can add that what makes it "preposterous" also makes it precisely—and even "in principle"—sodomitical.

Perhaps, too, we can understand better, in relation to this principle of the preposterous, why Louis Simond might have feared the imagination's susceptibility to being "sullied by the exposition of enormities, that ought never to be supposed to exist." The (il)logic by which exposition exposes its implication in such enormities, the (il)logic by which narrative produces the "crime" that it apparently only reports, the (il)logic of metalepsis that locates the cause as the effect of its effects, is, after all, an (il)logic that refutes all possibility of defining clear identities or establishing the security of fixed positions. It discovers, instead, within the either/or logic that Freud, *as a heterosexual man,* enshrines as the law of castration, the scandalous presence of another logic, the sodomitical (il)logic of the primal scene that comes always both before and behind it. Thus for Cleland and Smollett, Simond and Derrida, as for countless others who intervene more oppressively in the politics of discursive practices, any representation of sodomy between men is a threat to the epistemological security of the observer—whether a heterosexual male himself or merely heterosexual-male-identified—for whom the vision of the sodomitical encounter refutes the determinacy of positional distinctions and compels him to confront his too-clear implication in a spectacle that, from the perspective of castration, can only be seen as a "catastrophe."

Notes

This essay was first presented, in a shorter form, at the 1989 conference on Lesbian and Gay

Studies held at Yale University. Joanne Feit Diehl, D. A. Miller and, as always, Joseph Litvak read versions of this essay and offered valuable support and advice.

1. Louis Crompton, *Byron and Greek Love: Homophobia in 19th-Century England* (Berkeley: University of California Press, 1985), p. 169.

2. *Trying and Pilloring of the Vere Street Club* (London: J. Brown, 1810), cited in Crompton, *Byron and Greek Love*, p. 166.

3. Mary Ann Doane, "Veiling over Desire: Close-ups of the Woman," *Feminism and Psychoanalysis*, eds. Richard Feldstein and Judith Roof (Ithaca: Cornell University Press, 1989), p. 105. Similarly, Kaja Silverman, in her excellent essay "Too Early/ Too Late: Subjectivity and the Primal Scene in Henry James," notes that the Freudian model of the psyche in *The Interpretation of Dreams* "rests precisely upon the possibility of forward and backward movement between the unconscious and the preconscious/ conscious system" (*Novel* 21 [Winter/Spring 1988], p. 149). Silverman touches on a number of issues related to those that I am examining here. Although she uses Freud as the source of a psychic model that she then applies to James, her account of James's inscriptions of anality can itself be "turned around" upon Freud. In any case, despite its differences from mine, her project constitutes an important source for anyone working toward the possibility of reenvisioning the primal scene.

4. See, for instance, Freud's remark in *From the History of an Infantile Neurosis:* "Of the physician's point of view I can only declare that in a case of this kind he must behave as 'timelessly' as the unconscious itself, if he wishes to learn anything or to achieve anything," in *The Standard Edition of the Complete Psychological Works of Sigmund Freud*, ed. James Strachey (London: The Hogarth Press, 1955), vol. 17, p. 10. All subsequent references to this case history will be given in the text.

5. J. Laplanche and J.-B. Pontalis, *The Language of Psychoanalysis*, trans. Donald Nicholson-Smith (London: The Hogarth Press, 1983), p. 112.

6. Though his focus is quite different from mine, Jonathan Culler provides an excellent discussion of metaleptic narrative structures, and frames them briefly in terms of Freud's analysis of the Wolf Man, in "Story and Discourse in the Analysis of Narrative," *The Pursuit of Signs: Semiotics, Literature, Deconstruction* (Ithaca: Cornell University Press, 1981), see especially pp. 172–82.

7. Quoted in Peter Gay, *Freud: A Life for Our Time* (New York: W. W. Norton & Co., 1988), p. 287.

8. Freud, *From the History of an Infantile Neurosis*, p. 51. See also his earlier assertion that "these scenes from infancy are not represented during the treatment as recollections, they are the products of construction" (p. 50–51).

9. Marguerite Waller, "Academic Tootsie: The Denial of Difference and the Difference It Makes," *Diacritics* 17, No. 1 (Spring 1987), p. 2.

10. Nicholas Abraham and Maria Torok, *The Wolf Man's Magic Word: A Cryptonymy,* trans. Nicholas Rand (Minneapolis: University of Minnesota Press, 1986), p. 2.

11. Sigmund Freud, *The Letters of Sigmund Freud and Lou Andreas-Salomé*, ed. Ernst Pfeiffer, trans. William and Elaine Robson-Scott (London: The Hogarth Press and the Institute of Psychoanalysis, 1972), p. 77.

12. Sigmund Freud, "Negation," *The Standard Edition of the Complete Psychological Works*, vol. 19 (1961), p. 237.

13. Stanley Fish has persuasively read this case history as an "allegory of persuasion" (938) in his essay, "Withholding the Missing Portion: Power, Meaning and Persuasion in Freud's 'The Wolf-Man,' " *Times Literary Supplement* (August 29, 1986), pp. 935–38. He too focuses on Freud's anal-erotisim, though he sees its inscription not in Freud's manifestations of uncertainty or doubt, but in his management of information, his withholding and then delivering of crucial interpretive details at strategic moments in his narrative. Fish's insights have been valuable to me in formulating my reading, though I am primarily interested in reading the discursive logic of Freud's positioning in relation to the primal scene, a logic of which Freud is not the master and which bears a determining relation to the discourse of homosexuality, while Fish undertakes to examine Freud's rhetoric as a sign precisely of his insistent mastery over the reader, however much that rhetoric may have its "sources in his deepest anxieties" (938).

14. "I was the first—a point to which none of my opponents have [sic] referred—to recognize both the part played by phantasies in symptom-formation and also the 'retrospective phantasying' of late impressions into childhood and their sexualization after the event," *From the History of an Infantile Neurosis*, p. 103, n. 1.

15. The use of the masculine pronoun here is intended to signify that my reading of the primal scene, like Freud's, focuses on an experience whose implications are emphatically affected by gender. In the case under discussion here, the gender of the subject in question is male.

16. The primal scene, to put this another way, always starts as the mobilization of libidinal energies that will be defined, after the fact, as homosexual; the scene only later becomes heterosexualized, and that heterosexualization induces the horror and anxiety that the Wolf Man experiences in his pathogenic dream.

17. Fish, "Withholding the Missing Portion," p. 938.

18. It should be recalled that Freud insists that the infant signals this dual libidinal identification by passing a stool and interrupting his parents' lovemaking with a scream. Reading this activity as a "sign of [the infant's] sexual excitement," Freud argues that it "is to be regarded as characteristic of his congenital sexual constitution. He at once assumed a passive attitude, and showed more inclination towards a subsequent identification with women than with men" (81).

19. "Jenny Cromwell's Complaint Against Sodomy," cited in Dennis Rubini, "Sexuality and Augustan England: Sodomy, Politics, Elite Circles and Society," *The Pursuit of Sodomy: Male Homosexuality in Renaissance and Enlightenment Europe,* eds. Kent Gerard and Gert Hekma (New York: Harrington Park Press, 1989), p. 381.

20. John Cleland, *Memoirs of a Woman of Pleasure,* ed. Peter Sabor (New York: Oxford University Press, 1985), p. 157. All subsequent references to this work will be given in the text.

21. In the psychic economy of the heterosexualized male, the *narrative* of castration, however frightening its content, achieves a fetishistic, recuperative status to the extent that its explanatory coherence domesticates the violence that it thematizes. It becomes, in effect, a primal screen to obscure the primal scene. Jacques Derrida offers a related observation in "Le facteur de la vérité": "In this sense castrationtruth is the opposite of fragmentation, the very antidote for fragmentation: that which is missing from its place has in castration a fixed, central place, freed from all substitution" (*The Post Card: From Socrates to Freud and Beyond,* trans. Alan Bass [Chicago: University of

Chicago Press, 1987], p. 441; all subsequent references to this work will be given in the text).

22. Eve Kosofsky Sedgwick provides a powerful reading of such figurations in "A Poem is Being Written," *Representations* 17 (Winter 1987), pp. 110–136. In particular, she analyzes the significance of the fact that in colloquial discourse "women's *genital* receptivity is described as 'ass,' as in 'a piece of' " (129).

23. Nancy K. Miller, " 'I's' in Drag: The Sex of Recollection," *The Eighteenth Century* 22, No. 1 (1981), p. 53.

24. Tobias Smollett, *The Adventures of Peregrime Pickle,* ed. James L. Clifford (New York: Oxford University Press, 1964), p. 242. All subsequent references to this work will be given in the text.

25. This phrase appears in the "letter" printed on the back cover of *The Post Card.*

26. Throughout *The Post Card* and particularly in the "Envois," Derrida elaborates a theory of textual rivalry within the philosophical tradition that echoes Harold Bloom's formulations of literary revisionism and the anxiety of influence. Derrida suggests, for example, that "In compromising Socrates Plato was seeking to kill him, to eliminate him, to neutralize the debt while looking as if he were taking on the entire burden. In *Beyond,* . . . precisely on the subject of Aristophanes' discourse, Freud starts it all over, he forgets Socrates, erases the scene and indebts up to Plato" (146). This implies the need to reconsider the Bloomian scenario of Oedipal rivalry in relation to a sodomitical scene that presents a more complicated network of anxieties, identifications and desires.

27. Stanley Cavell, "Postscript (1989): To Whom It May Concern," *Critical Inquiry* 16 (1990), p. 256.

28. Derrida, "Le facteur de la vérité," *The Post Card,* p. 480.

29. This can be seen by paying attention to the serifs of the letters "p" and "d" in the text. It is worth adding that both Freud and Derrida provide justifications in their writings for taking errors of transcription, typing or typesetting seriously. See, for instance, Derrida, "Du Tout," *The Post Card,* p. 513–15; an important discussion of typographical distortions and Freud's relation to the Wolf Man can be found in Maria Torok, "Afterword: What is Occult in Occultism? Between Sigmund Freud and Sergei Pankeiev Wolf Man," *The Wolf Man's Magic Word: A Cryptonomy.*

30. Compare for instance the recurrent anxieties about the reliability of the post in both collections. Freud writes, "Let us hope that the postal authorities will not continue to be unfavorably disposed toward us. My lost letter contained all the details that were meant for you better than I can repeat them today" (*Sigmund Freud and Lou Andreas-Salomé: Letters,* p. 148); Derrida writes, "Hound them at the post office. Does the search go through them? No, I will never rewrite it, that letter" ("Envois," p. 57). Or compare Freud's comment that "not every arrow reaches its mark" (172) with Derrida's famous assertion, "A letter can always not arrive at its destination" ("Le facteur," p. 444).

Evidence: 1870

Neil Bartlett

Among the many extraordinary cases which are from time to time brought before the public, none have created more sensation, or a greater degree of dismay in the respectable portion of the community, than the astounding, and, we fear, too-well-founded charges against Boulton and Park, and the outrages of which they have been guilty; the social crime, for so it is, which they have openly perpetrated, cannot be too strongly condemned.

We speak firmly, and without the slightest hesitation, when we say that the proceedings of these misguided young men deserve the heaviest punishment which the law can possibly afford, for however their intention may be explained, we say at least there is one peculiar trait in the evidence which stands out in bold and audacious relief and too plainly shows the base and prurient natures which these misguided youths (for they are but little more) must possess. We refer to the entrance of Park into the retiring room which is set apart for ladies in the Strand Theatre, who had the unblushing imprudence to apply to the female attendants to fasten up the gathers of his skirt, which he alleged had come unfastened.

This act, simple as it appears on paper, is sufficient in itself to arouse the just indignation of every true Englishman. We can now ask, and with just cause too, what protection have those who are dearest to our heart and hearth, those loved ones whom we recognize by the endearing titles of mother, sister, wife or daughter. Is it right, moral or just that their most sacred privacy should thus be ruthlessly violated?

Day after day, month after month and year after year we are startled out of our propriety by some fresh scandal, some fresh crime, the mere idea of which is more than sufficient to evoke the blush of shame upon the modest cheek. We are continually shocked and alarmed at the rapidly increasing follies and crimes of society, as they are laid before us in the columns of our newspapers.

And to those who are thinkers, it is, alas, too evident that the most revolting profligacies of the guilty cities of the plain, or the debauchery of Ancient Rome during the days of Messalina and Theodora, could not possibly outvie many of the atrocious phases of London life as they exist in the nineteenth century.

These young gentlemen (heaven save the mark!) rejoice in the respective cognomens of Ernest Boulton and Frederick William Park, their ages being twenty-two and twenty-three; the former describing himself as of no occupation, and the latter as that of a student of law. As we have no intention of endeavoring to screen these persons (for in our indignation we cannot apply a milder term) we copy from the newspaper reports the addresses which are, in all conscience, aristocratic enough; Boulton resided at Shirland Road, Westbourne Grove, and Park at Bruton Street, Berkeley Square—their present residency being at Her Majesty's House of Detention, and for the present they are guests of a paternal Government.

It appears that on Thursday night, the 28th April, that no little excitement was caused in the Strand Theatre by the entrance of two very handsome women, accompanied by a young gentleman, into one of the private boxes. In fact the personal charm of these ladies was so great that they attracted considerable attention, and we have it on good authority that more than one bet of no inconsiderable amount was placed between some of the regular habitués of this place of amusement, with the object of deciding to which nation they belonged. The general opinion throughout the house was that they were two stars about to shine in the firmament of the demimonde, and their beauty, their fascination and their paid-for smiles would, before the London season expired, cause many a poor dupe to curse the hour in which he had been born. These and numberless conjectures received their foundation from the nonchalant manner in which these ladies leaned over their box, twirled their handkerchiefs, and lasciviously ogled the male occupants of the stalls.

How few in that vast assemblage thought that these creatures were but men in masquerade. Lecherous leering and subtle fascinations, if displayed by women, are much to be condemned; but what words can paint the infamy of such hellish proceedings of men towards those of their own sex.

On Thursday night, 28 April 1870, Mr. Frederick William Park, a.k.a. Mrs. Fanny Winifred Park a.k.a. Mr. Vivien Gray, a.k.a. Miss Mabel Foster, a.k.a. Mrs. Jane or Fanny Graham, but known as Fanny to all her friends, was wearing a blue silk dress, and a wedding ring. With Fanny was Mr. Ernest Boulton, a.k.a. Lady Arthur Clinton, a.k.a. Stella, Star of the Strand. Stella was in low-cut, very low-cut scarlet satin with a white moiré antique trim and a white muslin shawl, a blonde chignon, bracelets, and a necklace and locket. White kid gloves, and a fan. Under the satin were white ladies boots, a very full padded bosom, stays, flannel and calico petticoats, but no drawers.

Fanny and Stella were being watched. They had been seen *giggling and chirruping* at each other. They had been observed touching each other under the chin and lighting their cigarettes with gestures of unnecessary flamboyance. It had been noted that *they did not swing their arms like men, but walked like women do.* As they left the theatre Fanny popped into the ladies' room to have her lace repinned.

"Was she dressed as a woman?"

"Dressed as a Lady. The Lady said, 'Have you a Ladies' Room,' and I said, 'Yes, madam, walk this way if you please.' I took them for gay Ladies."

Frocks adjusted, they stepped out onto the Strand, where the police were waiting for them. They were arrested on the charge of committing a "misdemeanor," of *being men and dressed in female attire,* and carried off to Bow Street.

Fanny and Stella's appearance in the dock there the following morning was by no means their first public appearance. The frocks they wore on that occasion, for instance, were merely the highlights of a much larger collection. The scale of their activities can be judged by the splendor of their wardrobe. A selection of their finery was later to be exhibited in court; a catalogue of confiscated items was solemnly recited: *One mauve satin trimmed with black lace. One corded white silk with white lace; one pink satin; one white glacé trimmed blue satin with lace. Stays, silk stockings, petticoats, twenty chignons and curls and plaits and all sorts of things. Curling irons, boxes of Violet Powder and Bloom of Roses. Colored kid boots, white boots and shoes.* Nor had the Strand Theatre been the only site of their infamy. Their behavior there was not exceptional, but typical. They had been seen in drag in Regent Street, Brunswick Square, the Holoborn Casino, the Haymarket, Highbury Barn (scene of a *Bal d'Opéra*), Portland Place, the Lyceum, the Alhambra (where, in March 1870, the ladies had once again been thrown out of the ladies' room), Evans Restaurant (where one Mr. Francis Cox, city businessman, had taken Stella and her lover to a champagne dinner. Mr. Cox's unsubtle advances to Stella had caused the lover to leave in a fit of jealousy, whereupon Mr. Cox took the opportunity to kiss *him, she or it, believing at the time that it was a woman.* When Stella revealed her true gender, he had her thrown out of the restaurant), the Burlington Arcade (their favorite trolling ground both in and out of drag, where they strolled *arm in arm with such an effeminate walk*. Stella was once seen to *wink at a gentleman and turn his head in a sly manner,* whereupon the Beadle asked them to leave. They refused. He attempted to eject them physically. Stella turned to him and she said, *I shall go where I like*), Cheltenham, the Boat Race, numerous minor country houses. This is not a random geography. Out of town, Fanny and Stella only appeared at the best places; they aspired to being treated not as women but as Ladies. In town their sense of place, like their sense of dress, was impeccable. They stuck to places of entertainment or crowded streets, or to private houses or fashionable districts where the appearance of wealth guaranteed their safety. They knew when to take cabs and when to walk. Moving carefully in and out of the West End, they seem to have known, like so many of us, just how far up, and just how far down, it is possible and advisable to go.

Although I'm sure that they looked less than dazzling after a night in the cells, during which they had been subjected to a forcible and illegal medical examination, Fanny and Stella attracted a large crowd to see them appear, exposed, in court.

It is important that we do not imagine Fanny and Stella as living only in public, indulging their taste for outrage in the peculiar anonymity of crowded streets or theatres until forced into visibility by the spotlight of police attention. They do not seem themselves to have conceived of their lives as "outrageous," necessarily public. They lived as queens off the street as well as on it. Stella lived with and was kept by none other than Lord Arthur Pelham Clinton, Member of Parliament. Though there is no record of Arthur taking Stella home to meet the family, Stella's mother was certainly delighted that her lower-middle-class son had a Lord and MP for a friend, especially when Arthur sent a case of champagne home for Ernest's twenty-first birthday party. The part of society mistress was played to the hilt. The housemaid at 36 Southampton Street, the Strand, who doubtless made the double bed in which the happy couple slept, and who heard Arthur calling Stella *darling* over breakfast, challenged her:

> I said to him, "I beg your pardon but I really think you are a man." He said he was Lady Arthur Clinton, he said, "I am Lady Clinton, Lord Arthur's wife."

And to prove her point Stella showed her the ring. She had monogrammed cards printed with the legend *Stella, Lady Clinton*. She had Arthur pay for a hairdresser who came to the apartment every day.

Worst of all, Fanny and Stella could not claim the alibi of originality. They could not appear in the dock as unique monsters, individual aberrations. They were not the only ones. The Public Record Office file from which these details are all taken contains the calling cards of several homosexual prostitutes; illustrated papers of the time carried pictures of a stereotyped, that is, widely recognizable, effeminate male homosexual; evidence at the trial described a circle of at least twenty young men who were in the habit of cruising the West End together, either in drag or at least in full slap. Some of the more effeminate witnesses even left the stand to the sound of appreciative laughter. In other words Fanny and Stella were recognized not as eccentrics, but as the visible representatives of another world. Mr. Thomas Gibbings, who had hosted drag balls at Haxell's Hotel, and whose voice and manner were decidedly effeminate, appeared to regard the modern pastime of *going in drag* as perfectly harmless; and was applauded for saying so.

It became clear in the course of their trial that they were not simply drag queens. They could not be dismissed as theatrical creations, men in private, women in public, alternately visible and invisible. At the time of their arrest they were engaged in what seems to have been their favorite joke: that of dressing and passing (with, apparently, complete success) as ladies. They had other habits, nastier, troubling—troubling because they involved not a concealment but a proclamation of the wicked ways (being a sodomite) which dressing in women's clothes only implied. When not in drag, they adopted a fearlessly effeminate style. Wearing tight trousers and low-necked shirts, opened very wide at the front, their necks powdered and their cheeks painted, they adopted the airs and gestures of prostitutes, looking over their shoulders and glancing at men. That is, they adopted a public style, a style which made public their sexual identity. Worse still, these queens made their style more than a hobby; they made it a career. They were actresses. In 1869 they had played polite melodrama and one-act operettas (making the most of Stella's wonderful soprano voice while it lasted) to full houses in Scarborough, Brentwood, Chelmsford, Southend, Maldon, Romford, Bishops Stortford, Gravesend, Billericay and Braintree. Their performances were by all accounts as outrageous as they were successful. When Stella took the part of Mrs. Chillinton, in a sentimental one-acter entitled *The Morning Call,* in which, according to the text, the said Mrs. Chillinton never leaves the stage, she nevertheless contrived to change her costume twice, appearing first in black corded silk embroidered with flowers; then in a mauve moiré antique with white lace; then taking the curtain in a pink number decorated with black stars. That night she received fourteen bouquets after the show, and photographs of her in costume sold as fast as they could be printed in the seafront shops of Scarborough. The *Essex Journal* reported:

> Looking at him with both one's eyes open, listening to his extraordinary voice and criticizing however narrowly his wonderful feminine appearance and charm, it is really difficult for a moment to believe that he is not a charming girl.

That is, the audience knew what they were seeing: a drag queen. One wonders what they made of a playbill published in 1868, advertising another show, entitled *Love and Rain,* announcing that the part of Lady Jane Desmond, a young widow, would be taken by Mr. Ernest Boulton Esq., while that of Captain Charles Lumley (the handsome soldier who wins the lady's hand) would be taken by Lord Arthur Clinton, MP. By what strategems, or was it just ignorance, did the audience contrive to enjoy the spectacle of a drag queen and her lover enacting a heterosexual seduction? Who saw, and how, that these were two sodomites?

This is the question which the trial set itself the task of dramatizing. It focused on a single question. Were Fanny and Stella visible? As their glamorous triple lives, as queens, prostitutes and actresses, were revealed and scrutinized in court, the confused fury of the law was expressed again and again in a single accusation: Boulton and Park, Fanny and Stella, had *exhibited* themselves.

The Attorney General opened the trial by declaring:

> Well, Gentlemen, the general nature of the charge is this: that the defendants . . . associated together, spoke and wrote to each other, in such a manner as to indicate that relations subsisted between them such as are only permitted between men and women; that by sometimes dressing in female costume, sometimes in male costume, with a studied air of effeminacy, powdering their necks, painting their faces, by amatory airs and gestures, they endeavored to excite each other's passions, and to make themselves objects of desire to persons of their own class.

He continued:

> Perhaps I am not going too far when I say that you and I and all of us will experience a sensation of relief if we could come to the conclusion that the popular apprehension was unfounded.

The actual charge was conspiracy to commit a felony. The Attorney General was arguing that the lives of Boulton and Park were to be read in their entirety as evidence of a single crime: that of sodomy, being a sodomite. At the same time he is announcing that he (the embodiment of the Law) wishes that such a thing as a sodomite did not exist. He suggests that the real purpose of the trial was to prove, somehow, that London was not the home of such a creature. The court is sitting not to punish, but to render the criminal nonexistent.

The trial scrutinized three main sets of details in its hunt for evidence. Even though all three were in fact very different, they were treated as if they were the same; scandalous, disgusting details which only the stern legal process had the manly stomach to itemize and interpret. All the gorgeous details of queenly life had to be reduced to one thing—evidence.

The extensive medical evidence given in court (given first, because then as now the body could not tell a lie) centred round a single question of interpretation: could dilation of the anus be considered proof of sodomy? Here, at once, the process of the trial began to falter. The shocked tones of Mr. James Paul, the police surgeon, "I have never seen anything like it before," failed to take effect. Precisely because he had never seen anything like it before, because he had no other cases with which to draw comparisons, his findings could not be interpreted. They were not "evidence" of any acknowledged or described phenomenon. They remained unsuggestive statements of fact.

Second, the court turned to the details of Fanny and Stella's external, public appearance. Their precious hoards of slap, frocks and jewels were displayed in court, as if they could give up the secret which the actual bodies had refused to betray. If it could be proven that the dresses had been worn to seduce men, if that was their meaning, then the defendants were definitely guilty. There was no question that they wore frocks; the question was, what did the frocks signify? The defence argued that they were merely signs of an adolescent sense of fun, of frivolity; the prosecution countered by observing, correctly, that "the adoption of these dresses was not an occasional frolic or escapade, but as far as we can make out it appears to have been made in a great degree the occupation and business of their lives."

The defence retaliated with the argument that their style of dress was indeed the sign of an occupation; it was the professional dress of actresses. Crucial evidence on this point was given by Miss Martha Stacey, who worked at 13 Wakefield Street, where Fanny and Stella kept their wardrobe and where they would drag up together. Martha was not sure if they shared a bed, but she was sure that they came dressed as men and left dressed as women. She knew that they took no trouble to conceal this from either her or their fellow lodgers, and she knew that their outfits were far from inconspicuous:

"I think it was very extreme."

"The dress was?"

"Yes."

Martha concluded that the dresses indicated that Fanny and Stella were regularly and frequently employed as theatricals. She could not let herself imagine that they meant anything else. I would read Martha's evidence differently. I would recognize that the frocks were the costumes of sodomites, and I would applaud the men who wore them in their determined efforts to use their frocks to create public space for themselves in London, in the separate but overlapping worlds of the actress, the prostitute and the demimondaine. Fanny and Stella themselves seem to have known exactly what they were doing. The nerve and precision of their performance is in marked contrast to the amateur criticism that the court subjected them to. They were well aware that they were playing precise games with their appearance, and that an exact understanding of the rules was a prerequisite of survival. They were always in danger, at the points where their codes of dress, which carried safe and assured meanings within their own culture, in their domestic lives and in their work as actresses, collided with the ignorance and potential violence of London at large. One solution was to make their drag so effective that they could pass safely as women, making themselves visible as sodomites only when and to whom they chose. Another was to adopt sufficient tokens of masculine appearance so as to confuse any suspicious members of the public, to bury one set of signs under another. This attempt was not always successful. One of Stella's admirers wrote:

> I have told mother that you are coming. I thought it well to tell her that you are very effeminate, but I hope you will do your best to appear as manly as you can, at any rate in face. I therefore beg of you to let your moustache grow at once.

A photograph of Fanny was produced in court.

> Is that a likeness of Mr. Park?
> Yes.
> Are you able to say whether this was a natural moustache?

I believe it was a natural moustache.

That is a male character in some performance?

That I am not able to say. I do not know if Mr. Park was in character at that time.

You never saw Park in a green satin dress with a moustache?

No.

Fanny did manage to grow both moustache and whiskers in time for the trial.

After ripping the costumes to shreds, the court scrutinized the script. The third area of evidence was the private letters of Fanny and Stella. The most "sensational" of these were read out in court by the prosecution in a final, convulsive fit of contorted, heterosexual logic. Explicit records of these men's lives were read out in public in an attempt to make them sound like cryptic messages of perversion, signs that could only reveal their meanings under cross-examination. The question was, who understood these letters; and how, and why, and on what terms.

> During the reading of the letters the audience in the body of the court appeared to be exceedingly amused, and the prisoners themselves smiled—the learned magistrates remarked that it certainly was no laughing matter.

Was the court laughing at or with the prisoners? Did it perceive as evident a set of meanings that the prosecution was attempting to depict as difficult, dangerous and dirty, even beyond belief?

Dec. 4 1868

I am just off to Chemlsford with Fanny where I shall stay till Monday. We are going to a party tomorrow. Send me some money, you wretch.

Stella Clinton

Undated

My dearest Arthur

You really must excuse me from interfering in matrimonial squabbles (for I am sure the present is no more than that) and though I am as you say Stella's confidante in most things, that which you wish to know she keeps locked up in her breast. My own opinion on the subject varies fifty times a day, when I see you together. Sometimes she may treat you brusquely, but on the other hand see how she stands up for your dignity and position. As to all the things she said to you the other night, she may have been tight, and did not know what she was saying, so that by the time you get my answer you will both be laughing over the whole affair, as Stella and I did when we fought down here—don't you remember, when I slapped her face. Do not think me unkind dear, as I have told you all I know and have not an opinion worth having to offer you. Goodbye dear,

Ever yours, Fan.

P.S. Is the handle of my umbrella mended yet? If so I wish you would kindly send it to me as the weather has turned so showery that I can't go out without a dread of my back hair coming out of curl.

To Stella, undated:
My darling Ernie,
I had another cry on the train after leaving you, then lay back and managed to get some sleep. After all as you say in a few weeks time we shall meet again. I am consoling myself in your absence by getting screwed.

I had a cry on the train, said the Attorney General. A man crying at being parted from another man for a few weeks? Gentlemen, what language is that? Is it the language of friends? Or the language of love? It seems to me strange, very strange, he being a grown-up man and not a mere boy, a man of at least twenty-six.

Indeed, what language is that? Who understands it? Who understands its slang? Who understands the significance of a Frederick signing a letter as Fan; who can judge whether the use of the phrase "matrimonial squabble" to describe a row between two men is literal, metaphorical or merely ironic; and on the basis of what experience do they make this judgment? The prosecution, without ever being able to bring itself to use the actual word sodomite, was quite clear in its understanding of whose language was being spoken here. It was not to be explained away as playful, metaphorical or theatrical. Its meaning was not to be blurred. Even though the letters contained no explicit admission of sexual relations, the Attorney General was quite right to say to the jury: *In such a case you do not expect mathematical proof, or proof at all approaching mathematical proof. You expect such proof as reasonable men ought to act on.* He continued: *Gentlemen, no stain is inflicted upon the honour of this country by such offences being committed by a comparatively few persons, for let us hope that they are few. But our national character might be stained if such offences, when detected and proved, were suffered to go unpunished.*

The fear of being stained, of being tainted, of being infected with a plague (all images that run through the prosection's case) was intimately related to the question of Fanny and Stella's visibility as sodomites. For the jury to accuse them, to announce that it saw them as sodomites, the jury would have to admit that they understood the letters, that they recognized the significance of the frocks. Such admission would suggest a dangerous proximity to the object of their scrutiny. It would involve an admission that they lived in the same city as Fanny and Stella. It would involve the admission of the existence of a world only two of whose representatives were in the dock. The Attorney General had asked the jury by their verdict to *stay the plague,* but the defence had asked them to *perform a nobler and better function,* and to declare by their verdict that no such plague existed; that *England was happily free from it, and was not yet tainted by its foul infection.* You cannot legislate against a language simply by imprisoning two people who speak that language. Better to deny the existence of the language altogether. Fanny and Stella's defence brought the case to its conclusion by doing just that:

> My friend used the expression that crimes of this kind are always committed with great precaution. True, gentlemen, from the very nature of the crime and its unnatural character of course it would be one which those who indulge in it, and who unsex themselves for the commission of such an outrage upon decency, Morality and upon Nature itself, would not be likely to bring public attention to their acts, but would try . . . to avoid exciting the suspicion of others. . . . But here the very course which my friend has taken, by producing evidence of visits to Theatres, visits to Casinos—visits to Arcades and other places of public resort and amusement and other acts—improper and unjustifiable acts if you please—acts of Extravagance and Folly on the part of those persons to whom I refer, yet those very acts themselves, in place of showing that they were contemplating something over which the pall of darkness was to be drawn—the indulgence of some such horrible crime that men should shrink from suggesting even a trace or suspicion to those who might be suspicious of their intentions—I would say that the mere fact of all this publicity is of itself a strong argument . . . in favor of my clients.

Mr. Digby Seymour, for the defence, is arguing that sodomy is shameful, furtive and ugly, and that therefore Fanny and Stella, whose public words and images were shameless, blatant and elegant, could not possibly be guilty of that crime. He is refusing the very possibility of a sodomite being visible on his own terms, of a sodomite speaking for himself.

After forty minutes of deliberation, the jury agreed with him.

Fanny and Stella were declared not guilty.

Fanny, bless her, fainted in the dock.

The verdict seems unbelievable. The evidence of Fanny and Stella's visibility was converted into proof that they didn't exist. The contortion of the law is testimony to how desperately it needed an appropriate verdict. Only by silencing, not punishing, the sodomites, could the court breathe a sigh of relief. When Boulton and Park were dismissed, declared improbable if not impossible, the existence of a homosexual culture in London was effectively denied. (I wonder what they did then? Did they leave the country, or just wait and then resume their metropolitan lives? Did Stella find a replacement for her lost Arthur—he killed himself when his name began to appear in the papers. Does anyone remember her? Perhaps someone kept her photograph.) The denial had to be actively maintained, however; it could not be a simple, single operation. The world of which Fanny and Stella were part was an extensive one. I was reading the *Illustrated London Police News* for 1889, and I turned to the wrong page as I was checking a detail of the Cleveland Street Scandal. And there I found a picture and a report of another queen, arrested on the street, arrested in a frock. The case of the Queen versus Boulton and Others was made sensational: we do not always make the front page of *The Times*. But it was not an isolated case.